aulkenie

THE CIRCLE GAME

SHADOWS AND SUBSTANCE IN THE INDIAN RESIDENTIAL SCHOOL EXPERIENCE IN CANADA

Roland D. Chrisjohn, Ph. D. and Sherri L. Young, M.A.
with Contributions by Michael Maraun, Ph. D.

Theytus Books Ltd.
Penticton, BC, Canada

Canadian Cataloguing in Publication Data

Chrisjohn, Roland David.
 The circle game

Includes bibliographical references and index.
ISBN 0-919441-85-8

 1. Native peoples--Canada--Residential schools. I. Young,
Sherri Lynn, 1967- II. Maraun, Michael. III. Title.
E96.5.C57 1997   371.829'97071   C97-910810-1

Editor: Greg Young-Ing
Editing Team: Marlena Dolan, Lil Sheps
Page Composition: Marlena Dolan
Cover Design: Marlena Dolan
Proofing: Regina Gabriel, Anna Kruger
Cover Photographs: Courtesy of Grace Greyeyes

Photographs:
Cogualeetza School
Sardis, BC

Girl in Photgraph:
Sally King

*The Publisher acknowledges the support of the Canada Council, the Department of
Canadian Heritage and the Cultural Services Branch of the Province of British Columbia in
the publication of this book.*

Printed in Canada

TABLE OF CONTENTS

PREFACE

DEDICATION

EXECUTIVE SUMMARY

CHAPTER 1: UNANSWERED QUESTIONS/UNQUESTIONED ANSWERS 1
    THE STANDARD ACCOUNT 1

CHAPTER 2: GROUND STERNLY DISPUTED 7
    INTRODUCTION 7
    MEN OF STRAW? 7
    BITS AND PIECES 9
        IMPUTING MOTIVES: SUPPOSING THE "WHY" OF RESIDENTIAL 10
            SCHOOL
        DISPUTING THE MOTIVES GAME 12
        RESEARCH, THERAPY, AND RECONCILIATION 13
        DISPUTING THE THERAPY MOVE 15
    DIZZYING LANGUAGE 16
        STRAIGHT FROM THE MINISTER'S MOUTH 17
        THE CHURCH SUBMISSIONS 19
        "LOSING" ONE'S WAY OF LIFE 19
        PARTNERS IN PROGRESS 20
        GROUNDS FOR ACTION 21
        MORE COSTS AND BENEFITS 22
        APPY-POLLY-LOGES 23
        CONCLUSIONS 24

CHAPTER 3: THE EVENTS 26
    INTRODUCTION 26
    THE NATURE OF THE INFORMATION 28
        TESTIMONY BEFORE ROYAL COMMISSIONS 28
        SOURCES OF INFORMATION 29
        ACTIONS 31
            PHYSICAL ABUSES 31
            PSYCHOLOGICAL/EMOTIONAL ABUSES 32
            ENFORCING UNSUITABLE LIVING CONDITIONS 33
        OMISSIONS OF ACTION 33
            CHURCH INACTION 33
            GOVERNMENTAL INACTION 33
        OVERVIEW 33
        QUESTIONS THAT ARISE FROM ACTIONS AND
        OMISSIONS OF ACTION 34

THE TESTIMONY BEFORE THE ROYAL   35
COMMISSION ON ABORIGINAL PEOPLES

CHAPTER 4: ... AND THEY CALL IT PEACE   40
  INTRODUCTION   40
  GENOCIDE   41
    INTRODUCTION   41
    GENOCIDE IN CANADA   41
      GENOCIDE DOES NOT REQUIRE KILLING   41
      PUNISHABLE ACTIONS   43
      ASSIMILATION IS GENOCIDE   43
      CANADA CANNOT EXEMPT ITSELF   45
      CONCLUSIONS   45
  WEDDING THE ZEITGEIST   48
  STOKING THE FEEBLE ENGINES   51
    THE "INDIAN PROBLEM"   51
    MEANS TO AND END   52
    ALL JOIN IN   53
  A TRIM RECKONING   55
  A DISTURBING NEW ANGLE   57
  SUMMATION   59
  CONCLUSIONS   60

CHAPTER 5: RESIDENTIAL SCHOOL SYNDROME   61
  INTRODUCTION   61
  EDUCATION AS A POLITICAL WEAPON   62
    THE INFANCY OF EDUCATIONAL IMPERIALISM   63
    FULL STRIDE   64
    MODERN PRACTICE   66
    CONCLUSIONS   67
  RESIDENTIAL SCHOOLS AS TOTAL INSTITUTIONS   68
    GOFFMAN'S TOTAL INSTITUTIONS   69
      INSTITUTIONAL TACTICS   70
      CONCLUSIONS   73
      INDIAN TOTAL INSTITUTIONS   73
      SUMMARY: 74
      DAY-TO-DAY LIFE IN A RESIDENTIAL SCHOOL
      CONCLUSIONS   76
    A STUMBLE   76
    OUTWARD AND VISIBLE SIGNS   77
    THE RHETORIC OF RESIDENTIAL SCHOOL SYNDROME   81
    WHAT PAINETH THEE IN OTHERS   83
      THE "REAL" SYNDROME   83
      CONCLUSIONS   87

CHAPTER 6: THE FOREST AND THE TREES   88
   INTRODUCTION   88
   METHODOLOGICAL INDIVIDUALISM   89
      METHODOLOGICAL INDIVIDUALISM IS CERTAINLY WRONG   91
      METHODOLOGICAL INDIVIDUALISM MISLEADS US   96
      IMPLICATIONS FOR UNDERSTANDING RESIDENTIAL SCHOOLING   99
   PEOPLE WITH GOOD INTENTIONS   99
      THE LOCATION OF THE PROBLEM   101
      AN ABSENCE OF EXPERTISE   102
      THE THERAPEUTIC STATE   104
   CONCLUSIONS   106

CHAPTER 7: RECOMMENDATIONS   108
   UNDOING WHAT HAS BEEN DONE   108
   RECOMMENDATIONS   109
   CONCLUSIONS   112

CHAPTER 8: The Circle Game   115
   FOOTNOTES   117

APPENDIX A. THE UNITED NATIONS GENOCIDE CONVENTION   149

APPENDIX B. RESEARCH AND RESIDENTIAL SCHOOLING: 155
IDEAS FOR FIRST NATIONS INDIVIDUALS AND COMMUNITIES
(CHRISJOHN & YOUNG)

APPENDIX C. PSYCHOLOGICAL ASSESSMENT AND FIRST NATIONS: 199
ETHICS, THEORY, AND PRACTICE
(CHRISJOHN, PACE, YOUNG, & MROCHUK)

APPENDIX D. COMMUNITY-BASED RESEARCH INTO RESIDENTIAL   221
SCHOOL EFFECTS: A SUMMARY OF THE CARIBOO
TRIBAL COUNCIL RESEARCH
(CHRISJOHN)

APPENDIX E. AMONG SCHOOL CHILDREN: PSYCHOLOGICAL   237
IMPERIALISM AND THE RESIDENTIAL SCHOOL EXPERIENCE IN CANADA
(CHRISJOHN & YOUNG).

APPENDIX F THE RED ROAD FROM ERROR TO TRUTH   251
AUTHENTIC RESISTANCE TO THE AFTERMATH OF INDIAN RESIDENTIAL
SCHOOLING
(CHRISJOHN & YOUNG)

APPENDIX G INTELLIGENCE RESEARCH AND THE   307
LEGACY OF CONFUSION
MARAUN & CHRISJOHN)

PREFACE

The Circle Game as presented here is derived from the report on Residential Schooling which we submitted to the Royal Commission on Aboriginal Peoples (RCAP) in October, 1994. As then, our book takes its title from our central essay, while supporting documents are given as appendices. In the time between our original submission and now little of substance has changed in Canadian attitudes towards this episode in their history or in church or governmental policy. Despite the hoopla surrounding the "Sacred Assembly" in Ottawa in December 1995, style took precedence over substance: we are informed that we of the First Nations people will now have our own official "day," and the churches, even the unapologetic ones, will consider helping with more "healing." It was all too depressingly familiar. With the status quo firmly entrenched in the minds of all Canadians and Aboriginal Peoples, little needed to be done to make our original report really offensive. Consequently, here we have limited ourselves to adding some references, eliminating typos, and elaborating some arguments that experience has shown were not understood as clearly or made as precisely as we would have liked. In addition, two wholly new appendices have been added; one on therapy and one on intelligence. The work on therapy was outlined during the time we worked on the Royal Commission report but for reasons elaborated upon below wasn't included in our final submission.

We have no idea how *The Circle Game* was received in Commission offices, apart from some initial expressions of enthusiasm. We do know that two months after we had submitted the *final* report the *Vancouver Sun* quoted unnamed Commission officials to the effect that "The royal commission on aboriginal peoples [sic] said in its *interim* report that many natives suffer from "residential school syndrome" — a result of the shock of family separation and the subsequent abuse (December 21, 1994; emphasis added)." This statement was not only factually inaccurate about the status of our report, as you will see it is diametrically opposed to the conclusions we actually reached. In any event, it became clear to us that if our struggle with understanding the Residential School Era was ever going to get circulation we would have to circulate it ourselves. To date, we have handed out (at our own expense) over 1000 copies of our manuscript in an effort to "jump start" an otherwise moribund discussion of real issues. Now, through the good offices of Theytus Books, we dare hope for an even broader distribution.

We've already received a great deal of feedback from friends and associates to whom we sent advanced copies. Frankly, having anticipated much of the criticism beforehand, the reception *The Circle Game* has received was dishearteningly predictable. Those in legal professions complained (1) that it "doesn't help us in the preparation of cases;" (2) that, as regards our use of United Nations conventions, there are no provisions within international law for enforcement or remedy; and (3) that, stylistically, we were entirely too "ideological." Our response to them was (1) "it wasn't *our* job (nor was it our intention) to make your jobs easier;" (2) who said we brought up international law as a means of pursuing enforcement or remedy?; and (3) that, unlike those making the charge (and their compatriots in other westernized disciplines), we chose not to hide our ideology, not to pretend we somehow didn't have our own beliefs. The "charge" of "being ideological" is a tiresome rhetorical manoeuvre intended to obscure what is, in fact, an *ad hominem* attack: one's opponents are "being ideological" while you, of course, are being objective, unemotional, and scientific. This was not the level of discussion of issues we had hoped to ignite, and, taken together, we encountered nothing in these objections that required more than the attention we're giving it here in this Preface.

Associates in the "helping" professions have complained that (1) our book is "too hard" on their disciplines; (2) *The Circle Game* is "judgmental;" and (3) don't we believe there is some place for a therapeutic reaction to Residential School experiences? We've responded that (1) on the contrary, we weren't nearly hard enough on their disciplines; (2) calling us judgmental is making a judgement... why is it you're allowed to be judgmental and we're not?; and (3) if taken seriously, our position requires a radical reformulation of what the "helping professions" think and do. In our opinion, this latter point did deserve some attention, particularly when, as stated above, we had outlined but not executed such a chapter for the original submission to RCAP. Consequently, we brushed off our notes and went back to writing, thankful for the two or three opportunities we've received to preview the chapter at First Nations conferences this past year.

Still, the reason we left this chapter out of our final report bears being made clear. We did not (and still do not) have any desire to see our proposals co-opted in the manner once described by Lawrence: "when we achieved and the new world had dawned, the old men came out again and took our victory to re-make in the likeness of the former world they knew." "Radical reformulation" means exactly that, but the helping professions, no less than political, religious, or judicial ones, maintain the *status quo* by eating *their* critics. It was a meal that, in October of 1994, we did not care to cater. And yet without being more explicit about the directions in which we believe reform should move we couldn't see that the meal would even be organized.

Our experience, as we distributed *The Circle Game* among helping professionals, was that none of them gave any more evidence of understanding the scope and implications of our work than had been shown by members of the legal professions. As a consequence, here we decided un-dis-include our work on therapy.

There have been two other interrelated criticisms (offered by people from all kinds of backgrounds): that we used "big words" and that the work is hard going. We grant the second point but dispute the first. With respect to the first comment we've replied by asking people to show us where we're using big words. They generally can't find any such instances, and when they can it's usually in places (like the technical chapter on psychoeducational measurement) where it can't easily be avoided.

We think that many people get the impression that we're using big words because of the fact (as we agree) that the work is hard going. We consciously avoided big words but incorporated big ideas, and the two are easily confused. Russell once wrote: "What *is* means is and therefore differs from *is*, for '*is*' would be nonsense." Here, by any technical "readability" calculation, is a readily understandable sentence, but it is one that, even in its original context, takes some work to become comfortable with. In *The Circle Game* we used language as direct as possible to get into the awfully elusive notion that the words written and spoken about Indian Residential Schooling uniformly avoided dealing with the topic. We consider this a big idea, and are not surprised that it is harder to become comfortable with than the notion that "Residential Schools were a mistake and were sometimes operated by bad people, but it's over now."

However, whether in word or in concept, the question then arises: why did we consciously make our book difficult? Here we have some real explaining to do.

First, as the book took shape, we began to see a need to do it in a single continuous narrative. So many different perspectives needed to be kept in mind that we felt that if *The Circle Game* went much beyond a single reading session, our audience would lose the thread of continuity we tried to infuse into our argument. Keeping it under a hundred pages thus became a consideration, and we adopted various tactics to ensure this: for one thing, as already mentioned we dropped the projected chapter on therapy (now installed as an appendix). For another, anything that detracted from the cumulative force of the narrative was relegated to endnotes (*not* footnotes; we didn't even want people looking at the bottom of the page the first time through the document). Thus, while we considered our endnotes one of the most import parts of our work (and please, do have a look at them: some of our best work was relegated to the endnote dungeon), they don't have to be read the first time through. The net effect of these devices was to make *The Circle Game* a punishing read, yet one that could be accomplished in a short time.

Second, we were influenced throughout by a sentiment once expressed by Thomas Paine: "We esteem too lightly that which we obtain too easily." Writing *The Circle Game* was a great deal of work and an emotional experience. We considered it selfish, in a sense, to deny the opportunity of similar experiences to future readers by levelling all the mountains or bridging all the rivers we encountered in our journey. Further, we never intended *The Circle Game* to be the "last word" on Indian Residential Schooling... rather, all along we've thought of it as the "first word." This is not to say that there isn't useful work out there (the works of Isabelle Knockwood, Linda Bull, Rosalyn Ing come to mind). But, by pretending to answer all the questions, and by arrogating to ourselves the road-map to the "one true understanding" of Indian Residential Schooling, we would be doing what we've criticized the churches and governments for doing: setting up artificial, damaging boundaries for a discussion that has a drastic need to be unbounded. We don't have many answers about Indian Residential Schooling (perhaps we don't have any). However, we do have the determination that unless the thinking, writing, and conversation about Residential Schooling changes dramatically, answers will never be sought, much less found.

It's conventional to thank people who have contributed to a work in the preface, but it is a convention difficult to adhere to in this case. So many have participated in one way or another that we will have to continue our policy of "straightness and narrowness" established in the text. From the offices of the Royal Commission we'd like to thank Dara Culhane, Louise Lahache, and Claudette Cote for their support, moral and otherwise. During the writing we inflicted large sections of this work on people in our vicinity, and for their patience and corrective feedback we'd like to thank Madeline McIvor, Sherilyn Calliou, Shelia TeHennepe, Paul Williams, and Diane Longboat. Special thanks are due to Mary Anne Chrisjohn and L. Shannon Chrisjohn for reading the completed manuscript through and providing commentary before anyone else. And, for intellectual support, and for providing us with an opportunity to talk about *The Circle Game* at a level that is often "uncomfortable" in polite society, we'd like to thank Vivian Ayoungman, Phil Beaumont, Wayne Sowan, Doris Greyeyes, Rosalyn Ing, Bernie Makokis, Linda Bull, Barbara Barnswell, Alison Macmillan, Thomas Szasz, Jeffrey Schaler, Bruce Alexander, Rebecca Tracy, Austin Tootoosis, Audrey Franklin, Cheryl Walker, Pamela Brett and Julia Brooke, and our editors, Greg Young-Ing and Marlena Dolan.

We also owe special thanks to Anita Konczi and John Cristescu; one, for being among the first to complete and comment usefully upon our manuscript; two, for providing technical assistance at various important points in our work; and three, for being there.

Finally, we'd like to thank the members of our immediate families. All of you helped more than you can know.

Whether or not you come to agree with what we've set out in *The Circle Game*, we ask that you please give some thought to our point of view. Thank you for your attention.

For Cindy

Executive Summary

What if the Holocaust had never stopped?

What if no liberating armies invaded the territory stormed over by the draconian State? No compassionate throng broke down the doors to dungeons to free those imprisoned within? No collective outcry of humanity arose as stories of the State's abuses were recounted? And no Court of World Opinion seized the State's leaders and held them in judgment as their misdeeds were chronicled? What if none of this happened?

What if, instead, with the passage of time the World came to accept the State's actions as the rightful and lawful policies of a sovereign nation having to deal with creatures that were less than fully human? And, what if, curbing some of the more glaring malignancies of its genocidal excesses, the State increasingly became prominent as both a resource for industrial powers and as an industrial power in its own right? What if the State could depend upon the discretion of other nations, engaged in their own local outrages, to wink at its past, so that the lie told to and accepted by other nations was one the State could tell itself and its "real" citizens without fear of contradiction? What if the men who conceived, fashioned, implemented, and operated the machinery of destruction grew old and venerable and acclaimed, hailed as "Fathers" of their country and men of insight and renown?

What if the Holocaust had never stopped, so that, for the State's victims, there was no vindication, no validation, no justice, but instead the dawning realization that this was how things were going to be? What if those who resisted were crushed, so that others, tired of resisting, simply prayed that the "next" adjustment to what remained of their ways of life would be the one that, somehow, they would be able to learn to live with? What if some learned to hate who they were, or to deny it out of fear, while others embraced the State's image of them, emulating as far as possible the State's principles and accepting its judgment about their own families, friends, and neighbors? And what if others could find no option other than to accept the slow, lingering death the State had mapped out for them, or even to speed themselves along to their State-desired end?

What if?

Then, you would have Canada's treatment of the North American Aboriginal population in general, and the Indian Residential School Experience in particular.

And here and now we are going to prove it to you.

CHAPTER 1

UNANSWERED QUESTIONS/UNQUESTIONED ANSWERS

> In the two decades of contemplating what happened to me, I have come to recognize that a forgiving and forgetting induced by social pressure is immoral...What happened, happened. But that it happened cannot be so easily accepted. I rebel against my past, against history and against a present that places the incomprehensible in the cold storage of history and thus falsifies it in a revolting way. Jean Amery, *At the Mind's Limit.*

THE STANDARD ACCOUNT

Initially there seemed to be little need for a study of the influence of Indian Residential Schooling upon Aboriginal Peoples. True, the decision by the Royal Commission on Aboriginal Peoples (RCAP) to include this particular topic in their survey was substantially conditioned by earnest submissions made by Aboriginal individuals and organisations at some of the earliest Commission hearings. However, everyone, Commissioners and presenters alike, already seemed to know all the answers. The tale, told in bits and pieces rather than in a single sustained narrative, went something like this:

> Residential Schools were created out of the largess of the federal government and the missionary imperatives of the major churches as a means of bringing the advantages of Christian civilisation to Aboriginal populations. With the benefit of late-20th century hindsight, some of the means with which this task was undertaken may be seen to have been unfortunate, but it is important to understand that this work was undertaken with the best of humanitarian intentions. Now, in any large organisation, isolated incidents of abuse may occur, and such abuses **may** have occurred in **some** Indian Residential Schools. In any event, individuals who attended Residential Schools now appear to be suffering low self-esteem, alcoholism, somatic disorders, violent tendencies, and other symptoms of psychological distress (called "Residential

School Syndrome"). While these symptoms seem endemic to Aboriginal Peoples in general (and not limited to those who attended Residential School), this is likely to have come about because successive generations of attendees passed along, as it were, their personal psychological problems to their home communities and, through factors such as inadequacy of parenting skills, perpetuated the symptomology, if not the syndrome. In order to heal the rift the Residential School experience may have created between Aboriginal Peoples and Canadian society at large, and in order to heal those individuals who still suffer the consequences of their school experiences, it is necessary and appropriate to establish formally the nature of Residential School Syndrome, causally link the condition to Residential School abuses (physical, sexual, or emotional), determine the extent of its influence in Aboriginal populations, and suggest appropriate individual and community interventions that will bring about psychological and social health.

This **Standard Account** (as we will call it) disposes neatly of all problems associated with Indian Residential Schooling. There is a statement of initial motive, a recognition of responsibility, an exoneration of victims (Aboriginal Peoples), and the expression of a determination to tackle present manifestations of existing, unintentional injuries with all the armamentaria of modern social science. In short, the Standard Account is an act of contrition.

When we began working on our Commission report, the regularity with which we encountered some version of this account was disturbing, more so when we considered that so little "systematic" ("social scientific") literature existed on the topic. Furthermore, with few exceptions,[1] we found that it rarely made a difference to whom we talked concerning the ongoing investigation of Residential Schools: governmental and organizational officials, priests, judges, lawyers, police officers, therapists, and many other professional and experienced individuals, of Aboriginal and non-Aboriginal descent, all repeated accounts recognizably contained within the sketch given above. But what was most interesting to us was that there seemed to be a significant ellipsis in the account: at the point when the possibility and extent of abuses at Residential Schools were raised, there should have been mention made of judicial process, criminal prosecution, and monetary compensation. **That the narrative took an extreme turn at that point in the direction of psychology, without delving very far into**

legalities, was difficult to miss. This was all the more obvious when we considered the sheer number of individuals with legal expertise present at any of the Commission proceedings. When it came to understanding Indian Residential School, everyone, it seemed, wanted to be a psychologist.

The more we encountered the bits and pieces of the Standard Account the more objectionable we found it. It seemed to us that, given the short supply of formal research on Indian Residential Schooling, the Standard Account was more myth than fact. This, of course, isn't necessarily a bad thing; myths are often a poetic and compelling means of expressing a complex truth in a form more readily grasped. But there are as well myths designed to distort and mislead, as in Plato's suggestion (in **Republic**) to create and maintain a rigid class society by setting forth a myth that the citizens of a city-state were fashioned in part with various metals, gold being mixed with the substance of the rulers (thereby justifying their privileges and superior status), baser metals being mixed with the substance of progressively inferior citizens. To our mind, then, clarifying what *kind* of myth was presented in the Standard Account would be an important task. Or, to put it another way, when a myth is given flesh and bones, is presented as revealed truth, and begins justifying our attitudes and behaviours, it doesn't do so of its own accord: myths, even when recognized as such, are deployed to some purpose.

In what follows, we will argue that the Standard Account, as popular and as widely accepted as it may be in the public at large and in Aboriginal circles, is a pernicious, misleading, and immoral myth (more correctly, an interconnected series of myths), whose important truths are buried under a singularly malevolent purpose. The "irregular" account we would like to substitute for the Standard one goes something like this:

Residential Schools were one of many attempts at the genocide of the Aboriginal Peoples inhabiting the area now commonly called Canada. Initially, the goal of obliterating these peoples was connected with stealing what they owned (the land, the sky, the waters, and their lives, and all that these encompassed); and although this connection persists, present-day acts and policies of genocide are also connected with the hypocritical, legal, and self-delusional need on the part of the perpetrators to conceal what they did and what they continue to do. A variety of rationalizations (social, legal, religious, political, and economic) arose to engage (in one way or another) all segments of Eurocanadian society in the task of genocide. For example, some were told (and told themselves) that their actions arose out of a Missionary Imperative to bring the benefits of the One True Belief to savage pagans; others considered themselves justified in land theft by declaring that the Aboriginal Peoples were not putting the land to "proper" use; and so on. The creation of Indian Residential Schools followed a time-tested method of obliterating indigenous cultures, and the psychosocial consequences these schools would have on Aboriginal Peoples were well understood at the time of their formation. Present-day symptomology found in Aboriginal Peoples and societies does not constitute a distinct psychological condition, but is the well known and long-studied response of human beings living under conditions of severe and prolonged oppression. Although there is no doubt that individuals who attended Residential Schools suffered, and continue to suffer, from the effects of their experiences, the tactic of pathologizing these individuals, studying their condition, and offering "therapy" to them and their communities must be seen as another rhetorical maneuver designed to obscure (to the world at large, to Aboriginal Peoples, and to Canadians themselves) the moral and financial accountability of Eurocanadian society in a continuing record of Crimes Against Humanity.

The problems so neatly disposed of by the Standard Account are thus brought back sharply into focus in our alternative; in our view, the Standard Account is no act of contrition, but another crime. In these pages we will, as far as possible, substantiate a case for our interpretation and cast doubt on what we take as the majority position. To do this, we will cite testimony from the four rounds of public and in-camera sessions of the Royal Commission on Aboriginal Peoples, review existing literature on Indian Residential Schools and related institutions, link the psychology and sociology of Residential Schools to historical, economic, and political factors rarely (if ever) connected with them, and, most crucially, develop an account of the world-view that has allowed so pitiless a machine as Indian Residential School to operate with scarcely a cloud on Canada's moral horizon. The choice between the Standard Account and **some** major alternative view (whether or not it is ours) means, we will argue, the choice between the *status quo* and the possibility of doing something useful.

There is much we cannot do, as well. Although many historical accounts of Indian Residential School are available,[2] the mix of churches involved in operating them, competing levels of government bureaucracy, regular changes in legislation, policy, and operating principles, and so on, make the development of a clear overview of the institution virtually impossible. Furthermore, entanglements of responsibility, culpability, compensation, and so on are so imbued with the nuances of Canadian law that only a lawyer might be capable of articulating and clarifying such issues. Consequently, issues related to the history, legality, and bureaucratic organization of Residential Schooling are dealt with in this book only at such points as we consider them important to our focus. Finally, much of the social, historical and political background of First Nations people which is needed to make our case is too extensive to review here; in order to keep the size manageable, we can only hope that our readers will either already have some of this background, or, if not, will be willing to do supplementary reading on their own.[3] We will cite directly as much as we can and hope that we will provide enough direction for anyone requiring greater detail to fill in our gaps.

Our focus will be entirely on the psychological and social consequences of Indian Residential Schooling. The prevailing opinion in "Aboriginal Country" is that these experiences have had a profound effect on the quality of life of Aboriginal Peoples, and this opinion is shared by many non-Aboriginals as well. **We see no grounds for questioning this opinion, and in fact share it**. However, what all of us **know** about the effects of Residential Schools and **what we think we know** about them is, for us, an important difference. **Why** we think we know the effects is the crucial nexus. The conceptual world-view that gave rise to the genocide of Aboriginal Peoples remains in place, unchallenged; its lineaments invade all aspects of present majority thinking about Indian Residential School. Unless this world-view is recognized, and the damage it has done and continues to do brought into focus, the long-term agenda of Indian Residential Schooling will succeed, even while we congratulate ourselves on having met it head-on and defeated it.

An acquaintance once told us that despite the intransigence of the Canadian government in dealing with Aboriginal Peoples, the majority of Canadians supported and had sympathy with our struggle. We didn't believe him then, and we don't believe him now. But if he was wise where we are foolish, no surprise would be more pleasant for us than for our analysis and non-standard account to be given a fair hearing. We have no doubts that there exist those (Aboriginal and non-Aboriginal alike) who have already made up their minds either to accept the Standard Account or some portion of it, and even some who hold their own non-standard version too extreme for us to bother with here (a simple but common example:

Aboriginal Peoples are whining sub-humans the world would be better off without). We don't think we have any chance with such individuals. If our acquaintance was right, however, there are many Canadians at least willing to entertain the idea that what looks like a generous and honest account may be grossly misguided; the road to Hell, after all, is paved with good intentions. It is for those individuals that we will present our case.

But more importantly, we hope to reach the many Aboriginal Peoples who have accepted the Standard Account as holding the promise that something will be done. Of the latter people we ask: hear us out. The urgency all of us feel to do **something** should not be allowed to dissipate into simply doing **anything**.

We begin.

CHAPTER 2

GROUND STERNLY DISPUTED

[P]erhaps I would do well to excuse myself at the start for the lack of tact that will unfortunately be displayed. Tact is something good and important—plain, acquired tact in everyday behavior, as well as tact of mind and heart. But no matter how important it may be, it is not suited for the radical analysis that together we are striving for here, and so I will have to disregard it—at the risk of cutting a poor figure. It may be that many of us victims have lost the feeling for tact altogether. Emigration, Resistance, prison, torture, concentration camp—all that is no excuse for rejecting tact and is not intended to be one. But it is a sufficient causal explanation. Jean Amery, *At the Mind's Limits*.

INTRODUCTION

The particular tack we are taking is likely to arouse strong reactions. We don't find this disagreeable in principle; however, we would prefer to have to deal with sensible and substantive objections, not absurd arguments focusing on minutiae. In an effort to head off debate of the latter form, we will throughout this report include as much detail as we think necessary to answer questions before they arise. Furthermore, because we believe a certain number of loose ends have already arisen in Chapter 1 we will use this chapter to answer them, and to establish the overall tone of what is to follow.

MEN OF STRAW?

To begin with, just how much merit is there at all in the agenda we've set out in Chapter 1? By our own admission, there is not a single, sustained version of the Standard Account anywhere to be found. Is it not the case, then, that it is a figment of our imagination? Or worse, does it not signal a tactless impertinence on our part, a dishonest attempt to make our own dubious account appear more satisfactory than it actually is by erecting a "straw man" competitor which we can publicly tear to shreds?

Of course these are possibilities. One of the persistent themes in our work will be identifying and revealing the word-games that have continually been used to pass off ideology as fact, to warp history as expediency has demanded, or to avoid or prevent any clear depiction of Aboriginal grievances. As disclosure of these rhetorical tricks will form such a central part of our exposition, it would be absurd to suggest we're not capable of doing much the same thing in our turn. Against this possibility we recommend vigilance; and we require in return that the same vigilance the critical reader brings to bear on our work be applied to all the future news from "Indian Country." As Winter[4] has pointed out, whether it is the truth about Oka, Meech Lake, the Gulf War, or any other modern issue, the Canadian public has been manipulated by the same techniques of public opinion management characteristic of despots operating in nominal democracies. If critical scrutiny of presentations of issues relevant to Aboriginal Peoples is to *begin* here, let it not *end* here.

Be all of this as it may, we still have the need to show that the so-called Standard Account is not pure fiction. To begin with, we remind everyone that the absence of a clear and unambiguous statement of a policy (or a tradition or a standard) does *not* mean that there isn't a policy. Great Britain has no constitution in the "American" sense; that is, you can't open a book and read it or visit a room and see it. It simply isn't codified.[5] This does not mean, however, that Great Britain is constitutionless. Another example is the argument, advanced by the United States and accepted by the other Allied powers after World War II, that although there were no specific international codes enjoining Germany from annihilating the Jews, those actions violated the pre-existing Common Law of Nations and, as such, constituted Crimes Against Humanity. Equating the basis of a practice with the existence of a physical representation of it is itself a rhetorical move. It has, among other misuses, permitted pseudo-historians to argue that, because no one has yet found a piece of paper reading: "Kill all the Jews; signed, A. Hitler," Hitler wasn't as bad as history makes him out to be.[6]

Furthermore, in many ways it is a convenience to be able to operate in the absence of explicit codification. In Kafka's novel *The Trial*,[7] Joseph K. was rendered impotent in a system that wouldn't tell him the charges against him, gave him no guidance on procedures, and otherwise operated by principles it was not obliged to share with him. Even more salient would be the recollections of almost any Aboriginal person one might care to ask of his or her Kafkaesque experiences with the Department of Indian Affairs; who doesn't have at least one tale to tell of arbitrary, high-handed, or dismissive treatment, all justified by the phrase: "That's the policy."

Or, consider that in 1919 an Indian Affairs employee, Duncan Scott, wrote:

I think it would be in the interest of good administration if the provisions with regard to enfranchisement were further extended as to enable the Department to enfranchise individual Indians or a band of Indians without the necessity of obtaining their consent thereto in cases where it was found upon investigation that the continuance of wardship was no longer in the interests of the public or the Indians.[8]

The existence of land mines like this can only be regarded as embarrassments by present-day bureaucrats. Scott would only have committed such a naked proposal to paper while labouring under a mistaken belief in the imminent success of his enterprise (which was the elimination of the "Indian problem" by the elimination of Indians). The modern bureaucrat would never make this mistake.

Our point, then, is that not only does there not have to be an explicit codification as the basis of actions and policies, often the existence of an explicit statement is a damned nuisance. Under such conditions, expecting to find a sustained narrative of the Standard Account seems (to us, anyway) comparatively fanciful.

BITS AND PIECES

Nevertheless, we think we can go a long way toward making the so-called Standard Account more concrete. Here we will cite odds and ends from various sources that support our claim that, although no one expresses the whole of the Standard Account in a single breath, many people say enough of it to demonstrate its currency as an "analysis" of Indian Residential Schooling. In no way do we do this to criticise or embarrass the people making the statements; it is important, however, to show clearly the extent to which we all subscribe to a position that, in our opinion, contributes to the systematic misrepresentation of Indian Residential Schooling.

The greatest strength of the Standard Account is that it is not a logically coherent set of beliefs. Thus, individuals from a variety of backgrounds or with diverse interests feel free to accept some portion of it while rejecting aspects of it they find objectionable (e.g., accepting that therapeutic intervention is the cure while rejecting the notion that the government acted out of generosity). But while *logically* incoherent, the Standard Account is *ideologically* consistent. That is, it embodies a world-view that, while certainly not true, is at present so widespread that it has ceased to be questioned or even noticed. By going along with a part of the Standard Account, individuals accept a world-view that can rhetorically be turned against them; acquiescence has committed them to share a particular overview of Indian Residential Schooling. The ideological coherence of the position will be the subject of Chapter 6. Here we will be content to show that people really do say the kind of things we attribute to them in the Standard Account.

Some aspects of the Standard Account are so pervasive they will require extended treatment as separate topics. For now we limit our attention to statements of the motivational presumptions of the Standard Account, as well as its therapeutic emphasis. In conjunction with the forthcoming extended treatments, this should be sufficient to establish the account's extension.

IMPUTING MOTIVES: SUPPOSING THE "WHY" OF RESIDENTIAL SCHOOLS

One feature of the Standard Account which we dispute is the presumed motivation behind their creation. Those holding the Standard Account attribute the "highest" or at least neutral, motives to the originators and operators of Residential Schools. Thus, from the executive summary of the submission by the Anglican Church:

> British/European missionaries were convinced that their unique culture and faith expression must represent the truest reflection of Christianity and, therefore, of God's will. The church felt it had a Christian responsibility to help the First Nations assimilate into the political, economic and social structures of the British Empire... Educating and converting children soon became a key component in meeting this responsibility.[9]

Or, here is another account, from the Permanent Council of the Canadian Conference of Catholic Bishops. This particular recasting of history runs together the Standard Account's expression of initial motive with "hindsight":

> Missionaries arrived with the armies and merchants of the fur trade. Most missionaries sincerely desired to share their most precious gift—their faith. They were generous, courageous, and often holy men and women. While some of their actions may be criticized today in light of new understandings, they tried to act

with love and compassion... Although not the sole instigators, missionary and educational activities contributed to the weakening of the spirit of the Aboriginal Peoples.[10]

The United Church of Canada's Brief to the Royal Commission is of the same tenor:

> The Residential School period coincides with the general partnership which existed between the established Christian churches and the Canadian Government in the process of nation-building, particularly the expansion of European-based settlement of the west and north. Church participation in Residential Schools **could be** [our emphasis] described as an inadvertent and unfortunate part of that shared nation-building project.[11]

On the governmental side, the Department of Indian Affairs has in recent years either refrained from historical revisionism, or limited itself to modes of expression less public than Scott's,[12] Chretian's,[13] or Nielsen's.[14] However, as a perusal of, say, Scott's writings would show, bureaucrats of earlier eras were children of their times, and perfectly at home repeating Canadian equivalents of the "White Man's Burden" as the philosophical and moral justification for their actions. Recent writers and commentators sometimes pick up and pass along this cant:

> Many came back [from Residential School] unable to speak the Cree language, in conflict with their parents, and with severe problems of identity... This kind of suffering was imposed **unwittingly** [our emphasis] in the nineteenth century, since education had not yet come to be seen as it is now...[15]

In the following excerpt, not only is the "unconsciousness" of the harm of Residential Schooling mentioned, education itself becomes a "right" granted Indians by the federal government:

> As we all know, education was granted as a fundamental right by the Canadian government during the early policy-making years. One thing the Canadian government **failed to recognize** [our emphasis] was the social implications of their policies and I am speaking in terms of the things [that] have happened to Native peoples as a result of the residential school era.[16]

At least some of the Royal Commissioners themselves seem ready and able to gaze into the minds of bureaucrats:

> We hope that this report will help government to **avoid bad policies** [our emphasis] that have been brought on too often in the past. I have in mind the Residential School policies.[17]

... as if Residential School policies should be attributed to inattention to detail. Examples could be manufactured endlessly, and they would not have to be limited to educational policy.[18]

DISPUTING THE MOTIVES GAME

This particular characterization ("mistakes") is of central importance to the Standard Account, first because it implies the churches and governments wouldn't have behaved as they did had they thought a bit or had better advisors, and second because the characterization mitigates blame. That is, if churches and governments "just didn't realise" what they were doing, what happened may be regrettable but is hardly damnable; we *all* make mistakes, after all, and nobody makes them *intentionally*. Of these two prongs, the first is more important. For some time the federal government's tactics in dealing with Aboriginal grievances has been to deny fiduciary responsibility for programs and services to Aboriginal Peoples;[19] that is, they hold that there is no *legal* reason for them to do what they do. This has been used to justify closing down or cutting back programs, ostensibly for economic reasons.[20] Why, then, do they carry out the programs they run at all (whether good or bad, useful or harmful, etc.)? As explanations, we are left with bureaucratic inertia (which, we think, is true to some extent, but still had to have *some* origin) and the goodness of the government's heart.

In disputing the characterisation, what is the point at which we are driving? It is **not** that we "really" know the motives of these people, and that the churches and government are lying. It is that motives, taken as "inner engines" driving the men who established and operated the Residential Schools, **don't explain anything.** We no more know what "really" went on in the heads of those early educators than the people producing today's revisionist accounts. If, as part of their mythology, the revisionists wish to tell stories about the motives of churchmen and bureaucrats, **we have no more grounds for disputing the stories they tell than they have for asserting them**.

What we **do** claim, however, is that regardless of the "truth" of the "saintly but misguided motives" model, there are obvious reasons (as will be developed in Chapter 4) for setting up and operating institutions like the Residential Schools which are completely ignored in the "motives" model. There is no need to posit and argue about the personal attitudes, values, morals, or "whatevers" of these men, when the political, economic, social, and legal inducements for them to act in a particular manner are so crystal clear. And finally, as we will show subsequently, if one still has an urge to translate these reasons into "inner engines," there is nothing saintly, generous, or even neutral about them.

RESEARCH, THERAPY, AND RECONCILIATION

We will examine research, therapy, and reconciliation **as** responses later in this book. Once again, here we limit ourselves to showing that many of the parties with an interest in Indian Residential Schooling do indeed consistently call for these responses. The body of the testimony given before the Royal Commission on Aboriginal Peoples is so replete with calls for "the healing process" and "reconciliation" (and less so for "research") that its replication here is unnecessary; a few moments with the record would be enough to convince even the most skeptical of its prominence. To be sure, some of this makes perfect sense: that researchers call for research and therapists call for therapy is as mysterious as farmers calling for seed or bakers calling for dough. What we do find noteworthy is when farmers call for dough and bakers call for seed.

Take, for example, the testimony of an RCMP officer who had spent considerable time documenting the sexual abuses perpetrated by a priest in a Residential School over an extended period of time. At the time he spoke, several charges successfully had been brought, but an even larger body of charges (against the same and additional priests) either remained to be laid or were still at the disposal of the court system:

> I think that the focus should be on healing and recovery. I know that Canim Lake has taken huge steps in that direction and I applaud them for that. I just hope that, in the end, the native Aboriginal people can overcome what happened to them at the residential school... It is still happening today, the ripple effect, and I'm sure that until the proper counselling is looked after and the people treated and a healing process started, it's just going to continue.[21]

From a race-relations program coordinator:

> Historically, Aboriginals who attended church-run schools have expressed horror and resentment about the treatment accorded them. Many years later, these mistrusts and injustices have surfaced and while some attempts are being made to correct these atrocities, there is still a lot of work to be done. The healing process will take a much longer time than expected and more so to rebuild the trust which has been broken.[22]

"Healing" and "therapy," as well as enough research to come to grips with the nature and extent of Residential School abuses, has been called for consistently by Aboriginal politicians, whether nationally, provincially, or locally situated. Ovide Mercredi, Ronald George, Philip Fontaine and others have included such calls as part of their presentations before the Royal Commission, although always a part of a longer list of recommendations; and in their lists they generally conjoin individual with community-level compensation.

Federal and provincial authorities have cast their lot for "healing" and "research," *de facto* if in no other way, first by funding (as part of the financially strapped health services[23]) "therapy" for "Residential School survivors," and then by making available through grant agencies (e.g., SSHRCC) monies for the scientific study of Residential School effects, family violence in Aboriginal communities, and similar initiatives.

Most emphatic in their call for "therapy," however, have been the churches:

> Several Church groups and religious congregations have made public statements acknowledging past sufferings. These have led to efforts to find avenues of healing and reconciliation.[24]

> In addition to the initiatives related to the Apology and social justice, the United Church has tried to hear the overwhelming cry of pain from Aboriginal peoples that has resulted directly from Residential Schools and is seeking appropriate ways to support healing.[25]

Sometimes, the churches aren't hesitant about telling the Royal Commission what it should be doing:

The results of the extensive project on Residential Schools which the RCAP is undertaking will play an important role in bringing the stories of survivors to public light. We look forward to the recommendations to the federal government and the churches by the Royal Commission with respect to the legacy of Residential Schools. The goal is to promote healing.[26]

And sometimes, the churches volunteer to just go ahead and do the therapy themselves:

The dioceses also committed themselves to establishing... local forums of dialogue and other avenues for listening that will bring together former students and their families and the religious, clergy and lay staff who were involved in the schools so that they may reflect on their experience and work towards healing and reconciliation.[27]

And on and on. The full tenor of the church submissions to the Royal Commission can only be obtained by reading them in their entirety, but while brief, we hold that these extracts are fair representations.

DISPUTING THE THERAPY MOVE

Indeed, acknowledged here and there within the submissions of the churches are the personal failures of school staff and church officials, and even many of the direct forms of abuse that will be catalogued in Chapter 3. But does it take Miss Marple to find it more than a little odd that those who admit responsibility (to a limited degree, to be sure) for a crime have assumed, prominently and without challenge, the role of defining it, judging it, and passing sentence upon it? And what a sentence it is to be! They will have to **listen** to the people they abused! Bishops of dioceses in which abuses took place will "encourage" other bishops to "make similar commitments to the healing process... and to support the participation of both Native and non-Native people in mutual healing exercises!" And we thought Devil's Island was "hard time!"

Lest it be thought we are being unduly harsh on the churches, let's return once again to Chapter 1. The conundrum that occurred to us there remains unanswered: lawyers, judges, officers of the law... does no one here recognize that crimes have been committed? We have searched in vain the testimony of those expert in criminal matters for any suggestion that the aggressive uncovering and prosecution of criminals should form any part of an appropriate response to issues of Indian Residential Schooling. Precisely how typical of the law enforcement and criminal justice systems is this attitude? Is "therapy for the victim" the bottom line in criminal law for, say, bank robbery, tax fraud, or insider trading?

Finally let's not overlook the calls for "therapy," "healing" and "reconciliation" that have predominated the testimony of Aboriginal Peoples ourselves. The churches, *quite accurately*, assert that the call for therapy, healing, and reconciliation (THR) consistently is heard in their consultations with Aboriginal groups, and portray (somewhat less accurately) their own THR calls as a consequence of those consultations. Is our own call for a "healing process" a studied, considered response based on a clear overview of the issues, or are we merely repeating what we have been told over and over again? Or, put another way, does the call for therapy have tangible grounds, or does it indicate the success of someone else's propaganda? Between the poles of these possibilities, we lean toward the second and away from the first. Apart from occasional compilations of testimonials, *there is no literature to suggest the efficacy of psychology in dealing with issues arising from Residential Schooling*; and were the occasional testimonial sufficient grounds for belief, we would have to believe that Elvis is still alive. Furthermore, while much insightful work on Residential Schooling has appeared (see Chapter 3, page 30 in this version), we hold, and hope to demonstrate, that only the surface of this issue has been scratched.

Here again we do not wish to indulge in the "motives" game we have already dismissed. We cannot see into the hearts and minds of those who have called so strongly for therapeutic or conciliatory responses to the Residential School, whether ecclesiasts, judges, or therapists of any stripe. Instead, we point out that unanimity has come about in the absence of any evidence to favor it. We ask if such unanimity really benefits Aboriginal Peoples. And we call attention (Chapter 4) to manifest economic, political and legal reasons such a smoke-screen would be created in the first place.

DIZZYING LANGUAGE

The differences between the Standard Account and our alternative is not a matter of sticks and stones, but of words. And, as Penelope[28] has pointed out, the nursery rhyme is a lie: words do hurt people, and so effectively that knowledge of how the word-magic works is a closely guarded secret. When the subject of Indian Residential Schools arises, the word-magic (better known as *rhetoric*) kicks into overdrive, but so smoothly and effortlessly that we scarcely notice that we're headed toward Never-Never

Land at warp speed.

Getting a grip on the rhetorical devices deployed against a clear understanding of Indian Residential School is therefore essential. This is why, for example, we took such pains to point out the use of "mistake" when Residential Schools were mentioned. **Crimes** are committed (that is, they are deliberate); **mistakes** just happen. **Crimes** are usually serious; **mistakes** are often trivial. **Criminals** commit crimes; **anyone** can make a mistake. **Crimes** may be confessed to; **mistakes** are admitted to. **Criminals** are apprehended, tried, sentenced, imprisoned, rehabilitated; **people who make mistakes** "try to do better next time." And so on.

As useful as such an exercise might be, we cannot turn this book into a primer of rhetoric. However, since word-games are so important to understanding and misunderstanding Indian Residential Schooling, in the remainder of this chapter we will spend some time pointing out some of the more blatant examples of word-gymnastics we have thus far encountered.

STRAIGHT FROM THE MINISTER'S MOUTH

When both the Royal Commission on Aboriginal Peoples and the Assembly of First Nations (AFN) were considering investigations into Residential Schooling, then-Minister of Indian Affairs Tom Siddon stated that he did not want inquiries into Residential Schooling to turn into a "Witch Hunt."[29] While neither ill-considered nor insignificant, these words *are* ambiguous. What *did* the then-Minister mean by his utterance?

Perhaps he meant to signal official disapproval of possible death sentences for those who would be found to have operated Residential Schools; after all, many of the women found guilty of being witches were hanged or burned alive at the stake.[30] Well, this seems unlikely; Canada doesn't have the death penalty on its books, and we are unaware of any mass movement to reinstate it specifically to punish Residential School bureaucrats.

Perhaps the then-Minister merely wished to forestall a rush by an enraged populace to visit retribution upon those responsible for Residential Schools. The Witch Hunts were, after all, a phenomenon of the masses, and the "good people" of various lands were not above taking the law into their own hands and saving officials the trouble of a formal examination of suspected witches. However, if this was Mr. Siddon's intent, he need not have worried; a country that can tolerate, among other things, the distorted media coverage of Oka, the equating of Reserves with paradises of the South-Sea Islands,[31] and abortions without anesthetic for Aboriginal Women as "lessons in self-restraint" can obviously put up with a lot when it concerns Aboriginal Peoples. There seems little danger that a mob would arise hell-bent for justice on them.

Did he perhaps mean that, like the crimes for which witches were executed (calling diseases down upon neighbours; making pacts with Satan; turning milk sour with evil eyes; etc.), Residential Schools and the abuses that have been associated with them are *fictions*, and, therefore, that investigating "pseudocrimes" and holding people accountable for them would itself be criminal? At first glance this, too, seems unlikely, for the "paper trail" of church and governmental operation of Residential Schools goes back well over a hundred years, and, with apologies (?) having been offered up by some of the churches, there seems to be general agreement that, given sufficient political/legal will, there *is* something for which a hunt could be organised. Still, we believe we perceive an element of the charge of "pseudocrimes" in the then-Minister's statement; but something more is needed to flesh out our suspicion.

"Witch Hunt" is evocative language. Properly speaking, it evokes the systematic torture and murder of women launched by men of rank (clerical and otherwise) during the European Dark Ages and due to end any day now. In the modern world it also evokes the political persecution of dissidents in the United States that began in the 1940's. We think the image then-Minister Siddon was trying to create, the parallel he was trying to draw, was this: **that an energetic and thoroughgoing investigation of Indian Residential Schooling would be an unjustifiable and immoral persecution of a helpless underclass by a draconian elite, intent upon establishing and/or maintaining its domination by any means at its disposal**. After all, this was the aim of the original Witch Hunts.[32]

The drawing of such a parallel, however, bespeaks either a complete ignorance of historical fact or an attempt at the Big Lie technique perfected earlier this century. For the implied parallel is no parallel at all: 1) Aboriginal Peoples and others concerned about Indian Residential Schooling are in no position of power remotely comparable to that of the Men of the Cloth who called forth the atrocities against women. There is no "draconian elite" behind the impetus to come to grips with Residential Schools, just people who want the truth; 2) the transgressors investigated in any inquiry regarding Residential Schooling would not be, like the women murdered during the Witch Hunts, a marginalised, oppressed underclass, but rather the opposite, members of a wealthy and/or powerful privileged class; and 3) as we shall show, it was the Indian Residential Schools that were an attempt to establish and maintain dominance, as is the struggle to **avoid** any kind of inquiry. The only domination the AFN or Royal Commission inquiries might be able to establish would be the domination of fact over fiction, truth over lies, or justice over oppression. The Witch Hunts, remote and modern, all opted for fiction, lies, and oppression.

Finally, we remain skeptical that anyone flew anywhere on a broomstick, that anyone soured anyone's milk with the Evil Eye, or that anyone turned anyone into a newt. However, Residential Schools, and the evils associated with them, are as sure as little green apples. And yet, this is another intimation behind the then-Minister's words. He cannot come right out and say abuses never happened, but he **can** subtly and circuitously attempt to trivialise them.[33]

We cannot speak to the then-Minister's possible ignorance, but we will speak to his rhetorical and obfuscatory choice of language. By the use of "Witch Hunt" to characterise inquiries into Indian Residential Schooling he ties his figurative and literal cronies to the stake with helpless, tortured women and shouts: Stop This Outrage! However, the only outrage is that the intellectual successors to this Medieval Crime Against Humanity would be arrogant enough to draw the distorted and dishonest parallel, and expect to get away with it.

THE CHURCH SUBMISSIONS

It might be thought that getting so worked up about by two off-handed words by a then-Minister is overkill. In our turn, we might agree it was indeed "two off-handed words" if we didn't see the same tactic cropping up everywhere we look. The finest examples of rhetorical obfuscation in the "analysis" of Indian Residential Schools that have come to our attention are the submissions to the Royal Commission by the Historic Mission Churches. Since they were issued in November of 1993 our students and associates have used them with profit in the study of Rhetorical Excess. Because the volume of work exceeds the then-Minister's two little words, we will offer here only a rogue's gallery of our favourites. And, in all truthfulness, we don't recall which rhetorical tricks were the ones we pointed out and which were the ones our students brought to our attention; once you get the hang of it, the tricks just seem to jump out at you from all over the page.

"Losing" One's Way of Life

Time and again the Church submissions speak of the "loss" of Indian land, language, identity, etc. For example, page 1 of the Anglican Church submission reads:

Aboriginal people today... speak repeatedly of their desire to recover the values and freedoms that have been **lost** [our emphasis] to them through the impact of the Europeans.

This is an odd choice of phrasing, because in fact we "lost" none of these things; they were stolen. Characterising, say, Aboriginal culture as having been "lost" makes it seem like absent-mindedness or carelessness by the Indians is at least partly to blame. To see this, suppose a thief "relieved" you of your car at gun point, and, relating this to an officer of the law the officer responded, "Oh, so you **lost** your car."

We note also that the word "recover" in this sentence is a trick, prefiguring the almost immediate conjunction of "recovery and healing" on the next page in a manner implying that Aboriginal Peoples' urge to "recover" our possessions is a plea for "recovery" in a therapeutic sense. Finally, notice what we are being told we want to "recover": our values and freedoms. There is no mention of land, trees, minerals, resources, and other things that in the Western World have a price tag associated with them.[34] Finally, "intangibles" the two of us would put on this list, like justice and honesty, are also conspicuously missing. Perhaps they're hoping we won't notice and accept *their* list.

Partners in Progress

Linking Aboriginal Peoples with the dominant European society as "partners" is also prominent in the Church submissions: partners in the Fur Trade in earlier times, partners in "healing" and "reconciliation" nowadays.[35] An interesting use of this notion is present in the submission from the Permanent Council of Catholic Bishops:

> Admittedly in the light of what we know today, these systems, services and institutions could have had much more positive results... had they aimed at making these peoples architects of their own development and partners in common projects.[36]

Putting aside until the end of Chapter 4 the question of what could possibly be meant by "positive results," the thrust of this and the other uses of the "partnership" metaphor is, once again, to implicate Aboriginal Peoples in how they were treated and how they will be treated. The extract quoted makes it seem as if Aboriginal Peoples **wanted** "development," and a development that was common with what was desired by the Europeans.

"Development" itself is a dishonest term: at best, a metaphor reified; and at worst, a polite term for exploitation.[37] In pushing the idea that Aboriginal Peoples should have had more input into their development, and should have such input in the future, Aboriginal grievances are again being undermined. Like the (only partially successful) attempts to recast the grievances of women and Blacks, the "partnership" metaphor assumes Aboriginal Peoples **desire to be like their oppressors** (that is, to get **their** chance to be rich and powerful exploiters). Well, we can't speak for all Aboriginal Peoples, but this doesn't seem to us to be the point at all. As we see it, on the "development" side, the struggle has always been how to accommodate some of the Europeans' obvious technical successes without buying into the warped world-view they try to sell along with it. On the "grievance" side, the struggle has been for justice.

Grounds for Action

Lurking in the Church responses, and explicit in some of their submissions, are the "economic realities" of our times. Thus, from the Brief of the Anglican Church of Canada:

> [T]he church's response should not be dominated by legal concerns, but should be quick and pastoral...[38]

Dominated is an interesting word here. What *should* the proportion be? 51% pastoral and 49% legal? 99% pastoral and 1% legal? If the churches are acknowledging their part in an immoral activity they now repudiate, why are legalities any part **at all** of their response? Shouldn't it be entirely on the morality (or immorality) of the activity? After all, they are supposed to be the moral leadership of Canada, and to suggest the pertinence of some basis for their action other than an ethical one means nothing less than forfeiting ethics. That is, they appear to be engaging in the same kind of "cost-benefit" analysis that gave North America the Pinto.

What we consider to be an **honest** appraisal of this kind of thinking appears in the submission of the Presbyterian Church:

> It was easy for the WMS [Women's Missionary Society] and the principals to lose sight of the fact that these institutions were, first and foremost, schools, and they became increasingly occupied with managing people and money... The government was unwilling to provide the schools with the financial resources necessary to do their job well. The Women's Missionary Society was unable to support the schools financially, choosing instead to manage the schools on behalf of the government. In the process of managing the schools, the WMS and the staffs of the schools sometimes

drifted away from the spiritual center that had created the schools in the first place.[39]

More Costs and Benefits

Cost and benefit considerations aren't limited merely to issues of what to do about the aftermath of Indian Residential Schools; they are also supposed to condition our evaluation of them. For example:

> Aboriginals have also benefited from educational and health care systems and from political, social and judicial institutions.[40]

> National Aboriginal organizations were beginning to find their own voice, and to bring into the larger public arena an eloquent, committed leadership, many of whom had learned in the residential schools how to deal with the mainstream society.[41]

Such sentiments, of course, are not limited to ecclesiasts but are prominent in North Americans of European descent at large.[42] Lodged within these sentiments is the idea that, while Residential Schools may have done harm, they also did some good, so we must mitigate our criticism of them with an analysis of this counterbalancing.

Apart from the obvious "ends justifying the means" sophistry, there is quite a lot of juggling specific and general issues here. In the first scenario meant to mitigate criticism there is an implicit **false dichotomy**: **either** the Indians had to receive Residential Schooling **or** no education at all. And yet, there were plenty of "educational models" about that did not require the extremes enshrined in the Residential School system (see Chapter 3). This line of reasoning is akin to another trick played today on Aboriginal Peoples: "You can have the provincial curriculum, or you can have a curriculum that inculcates Indian language and culture, but you can't have both." While the parents polarise around the choices, the fact that White Anglo-Saxon Protestant parents and children are not forced into making such a choice is conveniently ignored.

In the second scenario, there is a **false implied direction of causality**: it is **because** those leaders went to a Residential School that they are *leaders*. Harsh? Yes! Punishing? Yes! But it made **MEN** (sic) of them! This reasoning ignores the fact that those who attended Residential School also ate plenty of mush for breakfast, so maybe it was mush-eating that turned them into leaders; that there are plenty of "leaders" about who didn't attend Residential School; and that, as Miller[43] points out, this was far from the intent of Residential Schools, and thus taking credit for "creating leaders" (even were it defensibly related to Residential Schools) would be like defending the slaughtering of villagers by arguing you saved them from communism. Or, even more to the point, this reasoning isn't taken to its logical conclusion: why limit the benefits of this exercise in character-building to the Aboriginals (who, after all, have never properly offered their thanks)? Let's send **all** Canadian boys and girls at age 5 or 6 off somewhere far away (say, central Asia), and pay someone to beat and starve them into learning a new language, a new religion, and a new culture. Thirty or forty years from now, what a bumper crop of leaders this country will harvest!

What we feel is most important, however, is that both of these scenarios (and several others we could bring up) are attempts to alleviate criticism by bringing up "goods" that were associated with the "bads." There is some element of validity to the notion that, although there is no common currency to simplify calculation, good deeds make up for bad ones, but this is **not** the judgment that is asked for here. We are asked to believe that these schools **did good by doing bad**. We are asked to forget **why** they did what they did. We are asked to agree that the ends (even misrepresented ones) justify the means. And we are asked to put out of our minds the unnecessary and excessive harshness of how they accomplished what they accomplished, however intentional. These requests are not the pleas of the pious, but the pitch of someone selling snake oil.

Appy-Polly-Lodges

The final batch of rhetorical devices we shall look at here are the apologies that have been made for Residential Schools. It is often said and written, and it is widely believed, that the churches (and even the federal government) have apologised for the Residential Schools. But have they? It is quite possible for a statement to have the **form** of an apology without actually **being** one.[44]

Well, with regard to the Presbyterian Church in Canada and the Permanent Council of the Canadian Conference of Catholic Bishops there is no ambiguity; they haven't apologised.[45] In the brief of the Presbyterians there are actually some attempts to come to grips with issues; we can only wish they had been more successful at it. On those occasions when it is actually relevant to the issues of Indian Residential Schooling, the submission of the of Catholic Bishops consists largely of the kinds of evasions we have been looking at in this chapter. The Council does make mention of "apologies" that have been made by specific Catholic associations, but not only is care taken to emphasise the **local** and **unofficial** aspect of such statements, the nature of the statements themselves is strictly limited:

"Several Church groups and religious congregations have made **public statements arising from their examination of conscience** [our emphasis] (p. 6)." Not apologies. And even these statements take the form of the "apology" offered by the federal government at the First National Conference on Residential Schools in Vancouver in 1991: they apologise for the "mistakes" and the "pain and suffering" that occurred there, **not** for setting up and operating them. When we try to judge the sincerity of such apologies we would do well to consider that the Nazis **could** have carried out the Holocaust politely. Was their crime merely that they were excessively nasty and truculent in rounding up and transporting the Jews? By focusing upon only the occurrence of specific acts of inflicting pain and suffering, the Council ignores much more serious issues.

The apologies offered by the United Church of Canada in 1986 (as reproduced in their submission to the Royal Commission) and the Primate of the Anglican Church of Canada in 1993 (as reproduced in their submission) are complete and unalloyed, although unspecific. There is in our opinion a marked tendency in both toward verbosity (a charge they might well level against us), and present in their statements are more than a few of the flourishes we have identified in this chapter. However, this does not detract from the clear recognition of the wrongs, not only of the abuses that occurred in schools under their supervision, but **of having participated in such an institution at all**.

Nevertheless, to detect the distinction we are making the statements must be read in full. Summary accounts of the apologies (as in, e.g., newspapers) focus on the "pain and hurt" Residential Schools caused, and to us this lessens their impact and misleads the reader. In any event, their very existence and their reproduction in the briefs submitted by these churches attests to the importance of the distinction we are pointing out. The implications of all this must wait, however, until Chapter 4.

CONCLUSIONS

In a society that, nominally at least, rejects coercion as a means of control, persuasive argumentation (fair and unfair) takes precedence. As well in such a society, widespread understanding of the methods of control by persuasion is best avoided if 1) you are in control and 2) you don't want to be out of control.

The predominance of unfair persuasive language does not, of course, prove that we live in a society where those in control are working overtime to maintain it. The ease with which "slippery language" can be spotted in the literature on Residential Schools merely arouses our suspicion that either we are being led along the garden path, or that the kind of "radical"[46] analysis undertaken by Amery, *and called for by the churches*,[47] has yet to take place. It also should put all of us on guard that, if we merely accept uncritically what we are exposed to, we risk taking seriously a skewed picture of Residential Schooling. Unfortunately, it is the only warning we are likely to get.

Readers may be disappointed at the lack of progress made in the analysis of Indian Residential Schooling. However, we have, we believe, shown that there *is* some life in the monster we have called the Standard Account, as well as made an initial case for distinguishing specific abusive acts of commission and omission vs. the existence of the schools *per se*. A look at issues within each of these distinctions is taken up in the next two chapters.

CHAPTER 3

THE EVENTS

Witnesses in oral testimonies are not concerned with restoring the health of a people that has been impaired by history; instead, they recall the image of a self insulted not only by history, but also by particular men and women like themselves. No form of integration into an outer public world exists for the inner chaos that disrupts their memory. As audience, we long for such a correspondence to erase the barbaric opposition between what we hear and what we wish to know. But the more we listen, the more evidence we have that the question of inaccessibility may be our own invented defense against the invitation to imagine what is perfectly explicit in the remembered experience before our eyes and ears. Lawrence Langer, *Holocaust Testimonies*.

INTRODUCTION

To us it seems as if what we have to say could be expressed in three or four well-written paragraphs, but, try as we might, these have eluded us. Time and again we have vaulted over a discussion only to be draw back into it, for fear that readers won't make the connections and extrapolations that to us seem obvious. One such vault is the subject of the current chapter. It should be clear **what** the Standard and alternative accounts are **accounts of**, but is it? Many non-Aboriginals, it seems, have never heard of Indian Residential Schools, or if they have, what they **were** seems not to have penetrated. Wilcomb Washburn, noted scholar on North American Aboriginals, writes in a blurb for a study of an Oklahoma Residential School:

> Anyone who has attended a New England "prep" school or gone to Marine "boot camp" at Parris Island will feel a kinship to the students who attended Chilocco Indian School.[48]

These overdrawn comparisons are fairly common: apparently, many cannot tell the difference 1) between sending your own children off to exclusive boarding schools[49] (where "these young men govern the school for a time... as they expect to govern the country later") versus having your children removed under force of law to live under an alien system of language, religion, and culture, delivered by those with a stated and unremitting commitment to the genocide of their charges[50]; or 2) between young adults, irradiated with a jingoistic fervour, undergoing physical training to kill for the State while receiving three square meals a day versus children removed from their home to serve as inadequately nourished day labourers under the guise of education. At one time we hadn't thought such mistakes were this easy to make, but we now know better.

Lest the reader consider that our characterisation is too extreme (and we would agree that it doesn't describe all schools at all times), it isn't a matter of controversy: **the facts in the case of Indian Residential Schooling are not in dispute.**[51] In fact, nothing produced (for public examination, anyway) by the churches or federal/provincial governments impugns any of the above. Thus, to this extent, the facts about Indian Residential Schools have not yet reached the stage attained, say, in Holocaust Denial.[52]

When it comes to providing details of individuals' experiences in Residential Schools, or drawing generalisations about the form and function of the institution, there is also official silence. The churches and federal/ provincial governments have produced no histories, incident reports, legal opinions, psychologies, or sociologies of Indian Residential Schooling. There is a uniform inattention to these particular details. However, we don't consider this sloppiness or bad scholarship on the part of any of the parties involved. We can understand that it seems to be a reasonable "tactic" not to provide much detail about actions that are morally and legally indefensible anyway... why stir up an already hostile crowd?[53] To us, it is more important that this failure to contradict charges raised earlier and elsewhere is a further reflection that the facts about Indian Residential Schools are not in dispute.[54]

But although not in dispute, neither are the facts in public consciousness. Eurocanadians-in-general can only maintain the bogus image of Canada the Good World Citizen[55] by acquiring a studied ignorance of, for example, their role in East Timor,[56] their treatment of Japanese Canadians during WWII, "Home Children," and any number of issues arising out of their treatment of Aboriginal Peoples, including Residential Schools. The testimony we are about to examine here was compiled by the Royal Commission on Aboriginal Peoples for the edification of all Canadians. If the Commission is to have any chance of influencing Canadian public opinion, it is necessary to provide information on **the events no one wants to talk about**, and their psychosocial consequences for Aboriginal Peoples. We begin this task in this chapter.

Before beginning, however, there is an additional point to be mentioned. Implicit in much of the material of Chapter 2, but in need of further clarification here, is that because the conflict between the Standard Account and our alternative is **not** a matter of specific events (upon which, broadly, accounts agree), it is entirely a matter of **how events are to be understood**. At one time the churches and governments seemed determined to follow the customary damage control techniques of denying everything and smearing victims,[57] but this has become less central a strategy. What the Standard Account is designed to do is **manage how all of us are to interpret the abuse**. It aims to dictate such things as **who** we should hold responsible for **what**, **what** the consequences were, and **what** should be done about it. Indeed, its aim is no less than to frame for us precisely the nature of the abuses themselves. The rhetorical nature of this "spin control" as clarified in Chapter 2 will thus continue to be a matter of considerable importance.

THE NATURE OF THE INFORMATION

TESTIMONY BEFORE ROYAL COMMISSIONS

After many years of trying to gain public attention, concerned citizens finally succeeded in 1883 in pressuring the Crown of England into commissioning an inquiry into the aristocracy's use of burning, shooting, and starvation to drive Scottish peasants off their traditional lands in the 18th and 19th century, an episode now known as the Highland Clearances. When its final report was made public, the Napier Commission (as it was called) quite unexpectedly—for Napier was a member of the aristocracy—found that civil and military authorities had committed crimes and unconscionable acts of inhumanity against the peasantry. The Crown was immediately faced with the task of repudiating its own report. How was this done? In speeches and newspaper reports, members of parliament and other men of station denounced the Commission's findings as based on the testimony of ignorant peasants who didn't know right from wrong, who were recalling events that had happened years before, and who were willing (for a price, or even just for the chance to stir up trouble) to embellish their testimony or even manufacture it out of nothing. The testimony, they imperiously pointed out, wasn't *sworn* testimony, and as such couldn't be trusted.

We have brought up this matter because of parallels we see between Napier's Commission and the Royal Commission on Aboriginal Peoples. Calling crofters, clansmen, and their family members ignorant peasants and liars might have been an acceptable tactic in 1884 (it certainly forestalled doing anything about the crimes of the Clearances), but direct *ad hominem* attacks on Aboriginal People presenting to the Commission will, we hope, be less acceptable in 1997. (And, this is not to say that present-day authorities won't be pleased to let the modern undercurrents of racism do this work for them.) We **do** expect that some wag will ponderously point out that testimony before the Royal Commission on Aboriginal Peoples wasn't **sworn** testimony, implying that what has been presented concerning the abuses in Residential Schools wouldn't pass muster in the court system and therefore can't be trusted.[58]

It is against such a tactic that we have taken such pains to point out that, yes, indeed, there is (in Eurocanadian Law, anyway) a difference between Commission and courtroom testimony, but that our treatment of Commission testimony isn't **as if** it were courtroom testimony; neither, for that matter, is the treatment accorded it by the churches or governments. To protest that a presentation to the Royal Commission (in 1883 **or** 1997) isn't testimony before a court of law is like complaining that your car isn't a very good submarine.

What this means for us is that the legalities of actions or omissions of action on the part of church, civil, or governmental officials didn't consume our attention. If someone testified that he or she was beaten into unconsciousness in Residential School, we didn't look for scars, call for supporting witnesses, or demand to see a hospital intake report; to have done so would have been a further violation of those appearing before the Commission, and a fundamental abrogation of its mandate. The Royal Commission on Aboriginal Peoples was neither intended nor equipped to carry out the work the Canadian systems of law enforcement and criminal justice were supposed to have been doing all these years; nor does the validity of the Commission's record of abuses that occurred in Indian Residential Schools depend on the provability of individual charges according to rules of Canadian criminal law. We proceed accordingly.

SOURCES OF INFORMATION

While some of the abuses occurred some time ago, they exist in the living memories of people who testified before the Royal Commission. We now present an enumeration of specific abuses that took place in Indian Residential Schools, but the list is not complete: as shocking as it is, other charges are so horrifying that we question the Royal Commission as a forum adequate for verifying or refuting them. This is a matter we will return to in the chapter on recommendations. What we *do* present is attested to by multiple witnesses and information sources, existing court proceedings, and the victims themselves.

In compiling this list we have supplemented testimony before the Commission with a number of additional resources, primary among which have been:

Celia Haig-Brown, *Resistance and Renewal: Surviving the Indian Residential School.* Vancouver: Tillacum Library, 1988;

E. Brian Titley, *A Narrow Vision: Duncan Campbell Scott and the Administration of Indian Affairs in Canada.* Vancouver: University of British Columbia Press, 1988;

Roland Chrisjohn, Charlene Belleau and Others, "Faith Misplaced: Lasting Effects of Abuse in a First Nations Community." *Canadian Journal of Native Education,* Volume 18, Number 2, 1991, p. 161-197 (Also published as *Cariboo Tribal Council, The Effects of Residential Schooling.* Williams Lake: Cariboo Tribal Council, 1992);

Carl Urion, "Introduction: The Experience of Indian Residential Schooling." *Canadian Journal of Native Education,* Volume 18 Supplement, 1991;

Linda Bull, "Indian Residential Schooling: The Native Perspective." *Canadian Journal of Native Education,* Volume 18 Supplement, 1991, p. 3-63;

Rosalyn Ing, "The Effects of Residential Schooling on Native Child-Rearing Practices." *Canadian Journal of Native Education,* Volume 18, 1991, p. 65-118;

Sandi Montour, *Indian Residential Schools.* Six Nations: Author, 1991;

Kathleen Quigley, *Implications of Residential Schooling for a First Nations Community.* St. Catherines: Author, 1991;

Elizabeth Furniss, *Victims of Benevolence: Discipline and Death at the Williams Lake Indian Residential School, 1891-1920.* Williams Lake: Cariboo Tribal Council, 1992;

Isabelle Knockwood, *Out of the Depths: The Experiences of Mi'kmaw Children at the Indian Residential School at Shubenacadie, Nova Scotia.* Lockeport, Nova Scotia: Roseway Publishing, 1992;

Boyce Richardson, *People of Terra Nullius: Betrayal and Rebirth in Aboriginal Canada.* Vancouver: Douglas & McIntyre, 1993;

K. Tsianina Lomawaima, *They Called It Prairie Light: The Story of Chilocco Indian School.* Lincoln, Nebraska: University of Nebraska Press, 1994;

Assembly of First Nations, *Breaking the Silence: An Interpretive Study of Residential School Impact and Healing as Illustrated by the Stories of First Nations Individuals.* Ottawa: Assembly of First Nations, 1994.

These were examined along with more than 1,000 pages of Royal Commission testimony that was directly or indirectly concerned with Indian Residential Schooling. As well, we have read through the compilations of newspaper accounts of Indian Residential School experiences maintained by the Cariboo Tribal Council in Williams Lake, BC, and the Royal Commission in Ottawa. We have also viewed a dozen or so documentaries or videotapes of conference proceedings that were specifically concerned with Residential School abuses.

Finally, at the First National Conference on Residential Schools in Vancouver, June, 1991, at numerous conferences before and since, as health care service providers, and during an uncountable number of personal conversations with friends and acquaintances, the topic of personal experiences at Indian Residential Schools has come up. These less formal sources generated no novel forms of abuse, but rather served to confirm abuses attested to elsewhere.

ACTIONS

We have provided some artificial structure to the catalogue of abuses here; we say "artificial" because these violations of human beings did not, and in fact cannot, occur in isolation from one another. But in an effort to be as complete as possible, we have listed these crimes in something of limited, focused summaries.

Physical Abuses

- Sexual assault, including forced sexual intercourse between men or women in authority and girls and/or boys in their charge;
- Forced oral-genital or masturbatory contact between men or women in authority and girls and/or boys in their charge;
- Sexual touching by men or women in authority of girls and/or boys in their charge;

• Performing private pseudo-official inspections of genitalia of girls and boys;
• Arranging or inducing abortions in female children impregnated by men in authority;
• Sticking needles through the tongues of children, often leaving them in place for extended periods of time;
• Inserting needles into other regions of children's anatomy;
• Burning or scalding children;
• Beating children into unconsciousness;
• Beating children to the point of drawing blood;
• Beating children to the point of inflicting serious permanent or semi-permanent injuries, including broken arms, broken legs, broken ribs, fractured skulls, shattered eardrums, and the like;
• Using electrical shock devices on physically restrained children;
• Forcing sick children to eat their own vomit;
• Unprotected exposure (as punishment) to the natural elements (snow, rain, and darkness), occasionally prolonged to the point of inducing life-threatening conditions (e.g., frostbite, pneumonia);
• Withholding medical attention from individuals suffering the effects of physical abuse;
• Shaving children's heads (as punishment);

Psychological/Emotional Abuses
• Administration of beatings to naked or partially naked children before their fellow students and/or institutional officials;
• Public, individually directed verbal abuse, belittling, and threatening;
• Public, race-based vilification of all aspects of Aboriginal forms of life;
• Racism;
• Performing public strip searches and genital inspections of children;
• Removal of children from their homes, families, and people;
• Cutting children's hair or shaving their heads (as policy);
• Withholding presents, letters, and other personal property of children;
• Locking children in closets (as punishment);
• Segregation of the sexes;
• Proscription of the use of Aboriginal languages;
• Proscription of the following of Aboriginal religious or spiritual practices;
• Eliminating any avenue by which to bring grievances, inform parents, or notify external authorities of abuses;

• Forced labour;

Enforcing Unsuitable Living Conditions
• Starvation (as punishment);
• Inadequate nutrition (e.g., nutrition levels below that of needed for normal growth and subsistence);
• Providing food unfit for human consumption;
• Exploiting child labour;
• Forced labour under unsafe working conditions;
• Inadequate medical services, sometimes leading to children's deaths;

OMISSIONS OF ACTION

Church Inaction
• Failure to bring local incidents of abuse to the attention of higher church authorities;
• Failure to bring local incidents of abuse to the attention of federal and appropriate provincial governmental authorities;
• Failure to protect children under their care from the sexual predations of older children also attending Residential School;
• Failure to remove known sex offenders from positions of supervision and control of children;
• Acquiescence to federal funding levels below those the churches themselves believed necessary for operation;
• Starvation (as a cost-cutting measure);
• Neglect of their educational mandate;

Governmental Inaction
• Failure to adequately inspect or otherwise maintain effective supervision of institutions into which their legal wards had been placed;
• Failure to fund churches schools at levels sufficient for maintaining the physical health of their legal wards;
• Failure to live up to the spirit of treaties signed promising education for Aboriginal Peoples;
• Collaboration with church officials in covering up the criminal behaviour of officials, both governmental and ecclesiastical;
• Removal or relocation of internal personnel critical of Residential School conditions.

OVERVIEW
This, then, is an abbreviated and summarised list of abuses that occurred within Indian Residential Schools. Except for items under institu-

tional headings, it should be clear that church officials, bureaucrats, and school personnel were in principle equally well-placed (?) to carry out these abuses. That is, reports of beatings, racist outbursts, sexual abuse, and the like have been attached to members of all groups having contact with Aboriginal children. And, to repeat, with the exception of federal and provincial governments, these are abuses attested to by all parties involved, including the Historic Mission Churches. An excerpt from the brief of the Anglican Church of Canada should make this clear:

> Staff and members of the working group have heard a number of disclosures from people, both male and female, who were sexually abused while at residential school, either by staff or by older students. The experiences of abuse range from voyeurism to fondling, to oral sex, to forced vaginal or anal penetration, and from one-time experiences to multiple experiences repeated over long periods. Some survivors were abused by more than one person on different occasions. It is probable that many more people were abused than have come forward to date.

> Administrators sometimes covered-up occasions of abuse, transferring the perpetrators instead of providing help for the survivors and bringing the perpetrators to justice. In one instance, the parents of several young women who had been raped by a staff member were manipulated into signing statements saying the rapes had never taken place and their daughters had lied in reporting them. It was also common for the abusers, themselves, to use manipulation and threatened or actual physical violence to extract promises of secrecy from their victims.[59]

The bravery of this confession begins to approach (but only approach) that of the Aboriginal Peoples who have made public what they went through in Residential Schools; and its horror is only approached by those who now insinuate it wasn't at all as bad as Aboriginal Peoples have said.

QUESTIONS THAT ARISE FROM ACTIONS AND OMISSIONS OF ACTION

We believe that, after digesting this list, three questions naturally occur to the attentive reader: 1) how widespread were these abuses?; 2) why did the perpetrators of these abuses behave as they did?; and 3) what are the consequences of these abuses for the people who suffered them? Despite the urgency some may have to see these questions answered, we must postpone their consideration.[60] We have made no secret of the territory toward which we wish to move the understanding of Indian Residential Schooling. It follows that as it is **this list is incomplete**. None of the questions can be addressed until the full horror of what Indian Residential Schooling **was** has been made clear.

Nevertheless, it is at this point (enumeration of abuses) that many, if not most, submissions to the Royal Commission undertake to answer one or more of the three questions. The answers are, briefly: 1) it is impossible to tell how widespread abuses were. Obviously, the degree of abuse varied between schools and changed with the passage of time. A case-by-case analysis is the only way to determine whether a particular person was abused, or a specific person was an abuser; 2) the perpetrators behaved as they did because they were imperfect men and women. While they merit our universal condemnation, they also deserve our understanding as individuals suffering from their own forms of sickness, and, consequently, warrant whatever assistance and forgiveness we can muster; 3) the consequences are that many Aboriginal People now suffer from a psychological disorder known as Residential School Syndrome. In addition, the failure to accord psychological attention to this condition early on has led to its perpetuation (sometimes in mutated form) in Aboriginal communities, much as disease is spread in a susceptible, uninoculated population.

In short, answering the three questions at this point commits one to the Standard Account. The answers instantiate an attempt to manage how we are to interpret the abuses by responding on the basis of an incomplete picture of Indian Residential Schooling. If we are honestly committed to coming to grips with Residential Schooling, this intellectual encirclement must be resisted and the picture must be completed.

THE TESTIMONY BEFORE THE ROYAL COMMISSION ON ABORIGINAL PEOPLE

Before continuing on with our own attempt to complete the picture, we would like to tie up some loose ends in regard to the testimony delivered by Aboriginal Peoples and others to this Royal Commission. In reading through volumes of testimony we have reached certain conclusions about it, conclusions that will have some bearing on recommendations we will eventually make. Like any summary of such an immense and heterogeneous corpus of material, it is dangerous to treat our generalisations as unarguable, but we feel there is some utility to this exercise.

One thing that we noticed is that relatively few people came and spoke about things that happened to them personally. Rather, the experiences of a number of people were sometimes summarized by a single person who may or may not have undergone something similar. For example:

> I have heard people who have said, "I have left that Residential School, and I have been like a ship without a rudder." I have heard people say, "I have left that place, and I left there just like a robot, with no feelings, with no emotions."[61]

> But before I make my last point, one person was asking me to mention the atrocities at the Residential School that were put on the reserve for Aboriginal People; there was no mention of the sexual harassment that was given to Aboriginal People, just as was seen in the Mount Cashel orphanage. One person asked me to mention that and I didn't want to forget it.[62]

> X. X., from Lennox Island, ran away from the Indian Residential School in Shubenacadie. When he was caught, they shaved his head, then he was put in a closet for several days and given bread and water until they discovered that his feet were frostbitten. X's condition was neglected by the school, his toes had to be cut off. A former student of this school from Lennox Island fought for this country in World War II. This particular student was a prisoner of war. He said, "The prisoner of war experience was no worse than that of school in Shubenacadie." Y. Y. went to this school. They sent him to get coal when he was eight years old and a big lump of coal fell on his hand and cut his fingers...[63]

> I would like to share with you a comment made by one of the parents in the early 1980s when we were working with the centre and trying to make parents realise the importance of the language. She had attended Residential School and was punished for translating for one of her younger brothers who did not speak English. She states: "I will not speak or teach my children or grandchildren to speak Gwich'in as I was punished for translating for one of my younger brothers when he did not understand or speak the language."[64]

Several people talked about the electric chair that was used in the girl's playroom. It seems odd how an electric chair can find its way into a Residential School; however, it seems to have been brought to the school for fun. Nevertheless, all the people who remembered the electric chair do not remember it in fun, but with pain and horror.[65]

Some students were bribed to do what their keepers wanted of them. Others were encouraged to victimize their neighbours. We were beaten, starved and stripped of any human dignity or self-respect. There were deaths in some of the schools during the Residential School period, and after the Residential School period as a result of being in those schools.[66]

I was one of the fortunate ones in the residential school, but the boy who slept next to me wasn't very fortunate. I saw him being sexually abused. As a result, he died violently. He couldn't handle it when he became of age.[67]

When specific instances of personally-experienced abuses are mentioned, the descriptions are short and poignant:

I stayed in that Residential School for 10 years. I hurt there. There was no love there. There was no caring there, nobody to hug you when you cried; all they did was slap you over, don't you cry, you're not supposed to cry. Whip me when I talked to my younger brother. That's my brother, for God's sake. We were not supposed to talk to these people.[68]

I was even molested when I was in the Residential School and this was in my home town of Ile-a-la-Cross. I was sexually molested by a nun and I was abused.[69]

You know, I was seriously injured down there, I ended up in a hospital for I don't know how long, with my legs broken in three places. But today I am very fortunate to be walking.[70]

I am one of the victims as mentioned here forced to eat her own vomit. Today I am still suffering from that. You can't even make your own pet eat their own vomit. It has to be something very clean that I have to feed them. Every time that I try to feed my animals, it always comes back to me what I went through and I learned a lot from the suffering I had when I was at the residential school.[71]

It was obvious that speaking openly and publicly about these experiences was one of the most difficult things these people have ever done:

> In my case, I entered school when I was six. At 47, it took me some forty years before I could talk about my experience in Residential School, and that was just the first step. And I have a number of steps to take before I can consider myself a whole person. One that can walk and associate and relate to people as a... I don't know how to describe it... without shame, without any sense of embarrassment, because of what I experienced in Residential School.[72]

> It's really hard to live in this world pretending. It's really hard to be pretending all my life, smiling and happy, really happy. A lot of people say, "Oh, in residential school our kids always smile." I call that the smile of fear. You have to smile. That's the smile of fear. I became one of them. For the longest time I didn't have a real smile, I didn't.[73]

All in all, we found it difficult to avoid coming to some conclusions about the testimony about Residential School abuses to the Royal Commission: 1) the overall structure of sessions was incompatible with dealing with Residential School abuses in a completely satisfactory manner. The hearings were sometimes too public, the Commissioners sometimes too distant, the scheduling sometimes too tight for the people to say what they wanted to say, and be heard as they wanted to be heard. People, all too many people, had difficult things to say and not the best conditions under which to say them; 2) consequently, we suspect that more, and we do not know how much more, remains to be said:

> I was a member of a residential school for nine years. Throughout these years there have been experiences that I have had to deal with within the system. I think it is certainly good that we can have a forum like this, but, to be honest, I just wonder if one afternoon is going to do it. I don't think so...[74]

One other matter should be cleared up: what is the nature of the testimony before the Commission? We have already noted that it is not **legal testimony**, and that to pretend that is was was merely an old tactic, a rhetorical attempt to establish a base from which findings could be dismissed. However, we should be clear that it is not **data** either, in a "social scientific investigation" sense. To try to make the Commission hearings into data-gathering exercises would have been at least as serious a misuse of them (and those giving testimony) as turning them into criminal proceeding would have been, and has the same rhetorical purpose; dismissal of findings because there are no tables, numbers, correlations, etc. supporting them. **If** this kind of study is desirable and technically feasible, **then** other approaches will have to be taken. However, as we argue in Chapter 6, we consider the mentality that would demand such an accounting to be merely another facet of the world-view that gave rise to Residential Schooling in the first place. We consider such a study neither desirable, nor even **possible**.

However, the hearing did allow **information** to be presented, and understanding can arise from its examination. Lawrence Langer's work[75] gives an outstanding example of what can be done from people simply being given the opportunity to tell their stories.

Finally, we have thus far only surveyed a small proportion of all the presentations made to the Royal Commission. There were many that only indirectly addressed issues of specific abuses in Residential Schools (e.g., therapy), and, indeed, those greatly outnumbered those mentioning abuse. We also reached some conclusions about these presentations as well, but we will postpone their discussion until Chapter 6. We now move on to the task of trying to complete the picture thus far only sketched.

CHAPTER 4

... AND THEY CALL IT PEACE

> Most genocides in this century have been perpetuated by nation-states upon ethnic minorities living within the state's own borders; most of the victims have been children. The people responsible for mass murder have by and large gotten away with what they have done. Most have succeeded in keeping the wealth that they looted from their victims; most have never faced trial. Genocide is still difficult to eradicate because it is usually tolerated, at least by those who benefit from it. Christopher Simpson, *The Splendid Blond Beast.*

INTRODUCTION

In Chapter 2 we commented that "apologies" for Residential Schooling seemed to come in three varieties: 1) apologies for having participated in their operation and for abuses that took place within them; 2) apologies just for abuses associated with the schools; and 3) no apologies at all. We then spent Chapter 3 establishing groundwork for, and then elaborating, specific abuses that have been associated with Indian Residential Schools. We now turn our attention to apologies for the very operation of these schools. What is being apologized for? How important is the difference between a "type 1" and "type 2" apology? Does the movement from a "type 2" to a "type 1" apology affect at all the preliminary answers offered to the questions posed at the end of Chapter 3? What has any of this to do with the differences between the Standard Account and our alternative?

In our view, understanding the difference between a complete apology for Indian Residential Schooling and an apology for the "pain, mistakes, and suffering" associated with them means an understanding of the enormity of what Indian Residential Schools were. To understand the difference is to understand the political, legal, and economic grounds, which are **clear** and **public**, that stood behind the creation and maintenance of these schools, and to understand why there is such a rhetorical struggle today to see the schools in terms of the Standard Account. And, to understand the difference is to see what was once mundane and ordinary from a disturbing new angle.

We cannot appreciate the full horror of Indian Residential Schools until we understand that **their very existence**, in however benign a form, constituted an abomination.

GENOCIDE

INTRODUCTION

We are certainly far from the first to assert that Canada's treatment of Aboriginal Peoples in general, and its creation and operation of Residential Schools in particular, was and continues to be nothing short of genocide.[76] This charge has, as far as we can determine, elicited only three kinds of responses on the part of Canadians, whether private citizens or public officials. The first response is simply to ignore it; the second is to treat it as a rhetorical flourish on the part of the person making the charge; and the third is to react with the kind of rhetorical barrage we've been documenting as we've gone. The possibility that the statement is accurate is never seriously considered.

Here we confront the issue head-on. Included as our Appendix A is the complete text of the United Nations Genocide Convention. Canada signed the Convention on November 28, 1949 and adopted it by a unanimous vote in Parliament on May 21, 1952. Thus, depending upon the precise date at which you wish to date the closure of the last Residential School (late 70s to early 80s), **Residential Schools continued to operate for some 30 years after Canada had signed the Convention**. In what follows we will assume the reader is familiar with this document.

GENOCIDE IN CANADA

Although no one reading this report can now claim a lack of familiarity with the Genocide Convention, we feel compelled to call attention to certain of its sections, and supplement its relatively spare prose with information from additional sources.[77]

Genocide Does Not Require Killing

When we have spoken about genocide in Canada, we have almost universally been met with the contention that, although there was some pre-Confederation "trouble" on the East Coast, and although some Aboriginal children did die in Residential Schools, Canada never institutionalized the killing of Aboriginal Peoples, and that therefore Canada's policies cannot be considered genocidal.[78]

Whether or not the deaths of Aboriginal Peoples, in Indian Residential

Schools or elsewhere, were "institutionalized" is debatable,[79] but irrelevant. As even cursory inspection of Article II of the Convention will show, killing of members of a group (or groups) is only one of the acts that constitute genocide. We still think that, on the basis of the calculated underfunding of the Churches and the failure to provide health care as specified in the numbered treaties, a case could be made that Canada **did** bring about the deaths of Aboriginal Peoples, but this is unnecessary; actions as specified under sections (b), (c), and (e), and perhaps even under (d), undoubtedly **did** occur as part of Residential School operation, and they **also** constitute genocide.

That actions at Residential Schools fulfilled (b), causing serious bodily or mental harm to members of the group, and (c), deliberately inflicting on the group conditions of life calculated to bring about its physical destruction in whole or in part, is not in dispute. Not only does testimony before the Royal Commission substantiate the charges, in their submissions the Historic Mission Churches admit to them (*infra*). The intent of the government of Canada in these activities is clear from any number of public statements, such as the one below:

> I want to get rid of the Indian problem. I do not think as a matter of fact, that this country ought to continuously protect a class of people who are able to stand alone. That is my whole point. Our objective is to continue until there is not a single Indian in Canada that has not been absorbed into the body politic, and there is no Indian question, and no Indian department and that is the whole object of this Bill.[80]

The "Indian problem" referred to here was that there **were** any. In subsequent years, the phrase was projected back onto the Aboriginal Peoples themselves in a classic example of blaming the victim.[81]

Section (e), forcibly transferring children, has led to some interesting evasions. We have been told 1) that the Churches running Residential Schools were not "groups," and 2) that, generally after a dozen years or less, they gave the children back. As for the first evasion, the subtlety implied by the quotation marks around *groups* eludes us; perhaps someone can clarify to us why members sharing a common location, language, faith, and means of support isn't a group. As for the second, returning the children, after whatever time period, doesn't mitigate anything; the very fact of codifying the forcible transfer of children is enough to constitute an act of genocide. Finally, the fact that the federal government implemented in legislation the requirement to surrender children, and enforced it with its agents, makes the churches merely complicit with an act of genocide; **the federal government of Canada bears primary responsibility for adopting and implementing an explicitly genocidal policy.**[82]

Punishable Actions

Article III of the Convention specifies degrees of involvement in genocide ranging from committing acts set out in Article II to complicity. By convention, complicity includes abiding by and/or countenancing criminal acts.[83]

Along with the lack of awareness of what constitutes genocide, people in general also are ignorant of what their responsibilities are, as citizens of the world, in assuring that their governments do not commit genocide, cooperate in genocide, or otherwise operate in violation of the Common Law of Nations. Discussions of the range of these responsibilities are about,[84] but briefly, they include the responsibility to know what your government is up to, and "to vigorously—and, when necessary, **physically**—oppose the commission of a Crime Against Humanity by **any** party, official or otherwise."[85] From Article IV of the Convention, it does not matter whether you are an official or a private citizen; you are responsible for resisting genocide, conspiracy to commit genocide, attempts to commit genocide, and so on.

Assimilation is Genocide

About this point there has been and will continue to be controversy. The draft Genocide Convention proposals included an explicit statement proscribing cultural genocide (destruction of the specific characteristics of a group) as well as biological genocide (restricting births, sterilisation) and physical genocide (killing, whether quickly as by mass murder, or slowly as by economic strangulation). This proposal was immediately resisted by the United States (whose politicians were concerned that U.S. treatment of minorities would be in violation of such injunctions), and their efforts to derail those provisions were supported by Canada.[86] As a result, the present version of the Convention is often taken as not dealing with cultural genocide:

> The classification of genocide here includes physical and biological genocide; cultural genocide is not included **except partially in the case of forced transfer of children** [our emphasis]. "Existence" is a somewhat circumscribed notion in this context.

> It is not genocide if a culture is destroyed but the carriers of culture are spared. A forcible assimilation is therefore not proscribed by this Convention: there is no such offense in international criminal law...[87]

We find this interpretation of the Convention (which Thornberry does not endorse, but merely reports) objectionable. First, permitting **forcible** assimilation seems to us to bring this activity into conflict with Article II (b); how is forcible assimilation supposed to happen without causing serious bodily or mental harm? We consider forcing the members of a group to abandon their form of life to be, by definition, **inflicting serious mental harm on members of a group**; whether or not the "forcing" is accomplished by starvation, beatings, threats, or other physical or psychological means is completely irrelevant.

Second, the dualistic separation of a culture from its biological carriers is an implicit racialism of a kind the United Nations has itself rejected.[88] It takes culture as a kind of add-on to the "real" object of concern, the biological person. But how are we to conceive of a person without a culture, or a culture that is peopleless? It is philosophically incoherent to assert either; and codifying the "physical" person as primary over culture invites legal dodges like the creation of tissue sample archives (as "carriers of the culture") as a defense against the charge of biological or physical genocide.

Third, in any event, Residential Schools involved a forced transfer of children from their parents to the designates of the State, the explicit form of cultural genocide covered by the UN Convention. Documentation of the practice has already been given, and the rationality that gave rise to and executed it will be examined below.

From these (and other considerations raised by Thornberry, such as contradictions between the UN Covenant on Civil and Political Rights and the exclusion of cultural obliteration as genocide), we are unwilling to treat "cultural genocide" as a species of action divorced (or divorceable) from its universally recognized relatives. The machinations and intrigues that have surrounded the debate about the concept of cultural genocide have all the *savoir faire* of a schoolyard bully; powerful groups, in obvious double-faced violation of their own publicly stated human rights poses, have used their power to compel the rest of the world into going along with them. Consequently, we maintain, and will henceforth assume, that **assimilation is genocide**. Even the phrase "cultural genocide" is an unnecessary ellipsis: **cultural genocide is genocide**. Finally, in any intellectually honest appraisal, **Indian Residential Schools were genocide**. If there are any serious arguments against this position, we are ready to hear them.

Canada Cannot Exempt Itself

Raising the issue of the Genocide Convention with public officials usually brings assurance that Canada is well on top of everything, with specific injunctions implementing the Convention in Canada's Criminal Code. An examination of relevant sections of the Code, however, shows this not to be true.[89] Only Articles II (a) and (c), **killing** and **inflicting conditions of life calculated to bring about physical destruction**, are implemented. Of the sections ignored, two are directly relevant to Residential School practice and the other has yet to receive serious historical study with respect to Aboriginal Peoples.[90] To our minds, this is a hypocritical attempt to hold other countries accountable to the Genocide Convention while ignoring such injunctions at home.

The United States has attempted to do much the same thing in a slightly different way.[91] Ward Churchill's arguments against their manoeuvre also applies to Canada: a country cannot simply exempt itself from the Common Law of Nations (of which the Genocide Convention is a part), nor interpret the Law to its own advantage. Hitler's problem was **not** that he had failed to declare Germany outside international law; likewise, Canada cannot pretend the unimplemented sections of the Genocide Convention do not apply here. The fact that Canada has been, and may continue to be, successful in avoiding censure in regard to genocide doesn't alter the fact that genocide accurately describes their past and present policies concerning Aboriginal Peoples. As Roling has written, "The recognition of the crime against humanity as an international crime signifies that specific mass violations of human rights do not belong any longer to the sphere of domestic jurisdiction."[92]

CONCLUSIONS

In his examination of the moral implications of the Holocaust, Bauman writes:

> "Ordinary" genocide is rarely, if at all, aimed at the total annihilation of the group; the purpose of the violence (if the violence is purposeful and planned) is to destroy the marked category (a nation, a tribe, a religious sect) as a viable community capable of self-perpetuation and defense of its own self-identity. If this is the case, the objective of the genocide is met once (1) the volume of violence has been large enough to undermine the will and

resilience of the sufferers, and to terrorize them into surrender to the superior power and into acceptance of the order it imposed; and (2) the marked group has been deprived of resources necessary for the continuation of the struggle. With these two conditions fulfilled, the victims are at the mercy of their tormentors. They may be forced into protracted slavery, or offered a place in the new order on terms set by the victors—but which sequel is chosen depends fully on the conquerors' whim. Whichever option has been selected, the perpetrators of the genocide benefit. They extend and solidify their power, and eradicate the roots of the opposition.[93]

Canada never defeated an Aboriginal Nation. It took over a policy of dealing with Indigenous populations from the British, who had started in a position of needing Aboriginal help to hold whatever tenuous claim they had to North American territory, and ended by finding themselves legally and morally obligated to people they no longer wanted to deal with.[94] Burdened with responsibilities they never accepted, Canada adopted the tactics of "ordinary" genocide; one of their "shock treatments" was Indian Residential School; the place they made for Aboriginal Peoples could, only with generosity, be described as on the margin:

"Canada... must increasingly become... a country of white men rooted and grounded in those fundamental scriptural conceptions of the individual, of society, (and) of the state... as the same have been conceived and found expression through the struggles and conquests of the several peoples of British blood and traditions." The church felt it had a Christian responsibility to assist the Aboriginal people in this transition. Assimilation, like medicine, might be intrusive and unpleasant, might even hurt a great deal, but in the long run it was for the people's own good...[95]

The Canadian problem in Indian education is not primarily one of schooling Indian children the same way other Canadian children are schooled, but of changing the persevering Indian community into a Canadian community. When Indian children will not help but grow-up to be culturally Canadian, then the average Canadian school will meet their educational needs.[96]

Ever since the first permanent European settlement in Canada in

1604, efforts have been made to school the children of the Aborigines in the ways of the newcomers. Both Church and State felt it was their responsibility to christianize as well as civilize the poor ignorant dwellers of the North American forests... The **cultural transformation**, usually referred to as "education," is still lagging... Though the majority of native children now [1958] attend day schools on the "reserves" and an increasing number are assigned to provincial non-indian schools, the residential schools still play a major role in the field of native education... Hence the main objective of the workshop was to study together the basic problem of Indian acculturation, common to all indian and eskimo schools in Canada, and find out how the present structures and facilities of residential schools can be better used and improved towards a more efficient solution to this problem... Contrary to the layman's opinion, educating canadian indians means much more than simply teaching them the three r's or whatever is the basic curriculum in the schools of each province. Most of the indian pupils attending federal schools have started life in a cultural channel quite at variance with that of the majority of Canadians. In order to prepare them for integration, the school must literally switch them from the minority stream into that of the nation abroad. In technical terms, Indian Education is first and foremost an "acculturation" responsibility.[97]

Both [the Church and the State] wished to civilize and Christianize the Indians and to fit them into the lower echelons of the new economic order... Consequently, the schools were deliberately located away from reserves so that parental influence on the inmate would be reduced to a minimum.[98]

It amounted, as a candid missionary put it, to an effort to "educate and colonize a people against their will."[99]

The education of native children in day and residential schools was one of the key elements in Canada's Indian policy from its inception. The destruction of the children's link to their ancestral culture and their assimilation into the dominant society were its main objectives.[100]

Influenced by the conviction of many "experts" that Indians had

limited intellectual abilities, many Indian industrial schools intro-
duced vocational training to prepare their pupils to fill certain
limited occupations.[101]

We could continue indefinitely to multiply similar examples. As is, the
genocidal nature of Canada's policy toward Aboriginal Peoples is clear; the
direct, voluntary complicity of the churches in this genocide is established;
and the responsibility, both legal and moral, of average Canadians, who
countenanced these crimes against humanity, is evident. To the horrors,
then, of the abuses detailed in Chapter 3 we must now add an entirely new
set: the horrors associated with "ordinary" genocide.

WEDDING THE ZEITGEIST

We anticipated the protests from the apologists for genocide long
before we wrote the previous section. We predict that against us will be laid
the charge of contemporaneity or **presentism**: that we are applying modern
values and standards (which, we are sure, the apologists will identify as a
particularly virulent brand of radicalism) to actions and agendas that should
only be judged in light of the values and standards that existed **back then**.
We are, they will say, being **subjective** and not **objective** (like good social
scientists ought to be). To this we say: baloney.

Before beginning we note that a kind of "presentism" charge was laid
against the Allied powers conducting the Nuremberg Trials: Nazi Germany
was being tried by *ex post facto* laws. We repeat, the concept of the
Common Law of Nations, codified or not, was what Germany was held
accountable to. This is what we hold Canada accountable to **before** the
adoption of the Genocide Convention, while the code itself will do **after**
1952. That the Allies did not see fit to try themselves (for Dresden,
Hiroshima, or whatever) is a record we've already played: the powerful can
get away with things the weak cannot. That may make the world unfair, but
it does not exonerate the behaviour of the powerful.

With respect to the **now**, the first thing to recognize is that the charge
of presentism is rhetoric in the spirit of the Standard Account. The Standard
Account seeks to diminish the magnitude of the sins of the past for the
common person (whether descended from the perpetrators or the victims);
presentism is the parallel trick modified for use with social scientists. The
move does its work by suggesting (without evidence) that there has been a
"clean break" with past policy, by hinting at (but not embracing) a recognition of culpability, and by playing that Old Standby, "That's All Water
Under the Bridge." Let bygones be bygones, the refrain goes, and let's all

start over with a clean slate (in doing which, of course, we jump past all manner of unresolved issues, including outstanding grievances). This particular tune was a favourite of, for example, former President Ronald Reagan on the occasion of his dedicating a cemetery for former Nazi SS officers at Bitburg.[102] To illustrate the inanity of the charge of presentism, permit us a minor parody: what, exactly, is being said in making such a charge? "What you people don't realise is that it was **okay** to hate Indians back then... everybody did it! It's only in light of our newly-found touchy-feelyism that we now see it was perhaps less than completely nice. And, if you had had the decency to die off or assimilate when we had it all planned out, the rest of us, **right now**, could be beating our breasts and bewailing our past inhumanity; but **NOOO!**"

Charging "presentism" is intended to stifle an unfavourable line of inquiry by changing the subject. Present reaction of horror, anger, or disgust to actions that took place in the past are disqualified, unless it can be shown that the actions were horrific, infuriating, or disgusting **back then**. It reinterprets the reaction, "That was horrific!" as a statement of **objective fact**, and not as a spontaneous expression of empathy or emotion. The "objective" social scientist thus leaves two options to anyone reacting with horror; 1) spend all your time and effort *proving* that the event eliciting the reaction was *objectively* horrific (and waste your time and substance trying to prove an unprovable[103]), or 2) ignore their demands (and leave yourself open to summary dismissal). In either event, the "experts" retain control. The game of "burden of proof" is played fast and loose, and those who can be tricked into believing that their present expression of humanity is warranted **only if** it can be said to have been applied **objectively** can further be tricked into believing that the onus is upon **them** to demonstrate that, say, sticking needles through children's tongues, beating them into unconsciousness, or breaking their bones is "objectively" wrong. Where were these experts when Goering, Hess, and friends needed them?

Nor is this all. How is this "objective past" supposed to be admitted to dispassionate observation? Whose perspective is to be adopted?[104] Where is the "objective" data? As an illustration of the difficulties, Parenti,[105] in a parallel analysis, has remarked that in every slave society there was a large group of people opposed to slavery: they were known as "slaves." That they didn't have access to the forums of debate and policy-making back then doesn't mean they (and non-slaves sympathetic to them) accepted their lot; it simply means that their oppression precluded any effective means of protest. Historically, the tactic of stifling rather than encouraging debate (in whatever media available) has been around a very long time.

And if one inquires long enough and hard enough into that history, in general or with respect to Indian Residential Schooling specifically, one can time and again find those who protested what was happening, those who acted morally rather than expediently, those willing to stand and say **this is wrong**.[106] That these people are sometimes hard to find (usually because they were marginalised, removed, ignored, or ridiculed) does not mean they did not exist. Take one example: in the fight between the Roundheads and the Cavaliers, there was a group, the Levellers, that wanted the peace and freedom Cromwell was seeking for his faction for **all** peoples; one of their manifestoes, had it actually made an impression on the ruling classes at war, could have served as a model to restrain what was shortly to come in North America:

> Have we the right to deprive a people of the land God and nature has given them and impose laws without their consent?
>
> How can the conquered be accounted rebels, if at any time they seek to free themselves and recover their own?
>
> [Were not] Julius Caesar, Alexander the Great, William Duke of Normandy or any other great conqueror of the world [merely] great lawless thieves, and [is it not] as unjust to take laws and liberties from our neighbours as to take goods from another of the same nation?
>
> [Is it not the case that] those who pretend for freedom (as the English now) shall make themselves altogether inexcusable in entrenching upon others' freedoms, and [is it not the case that] the character of a true patriot [is] to endeavour the just freedom of all men as well as his own?[107]

In looking back at the dark pages of history, who are we supposed to be other than ourselves? For those who would charge presentism, the answer is simple: we are supposed to be **them**; the ones who apologize, explain away, "contextualize," and "frame" the horrors of the past; the "spin-doctors" of history. We are supposed to believe that expressions of race hatred, sexism, etc., are to be set aside because "it was natural for the time." We are supposed to believe the accounts of the Jesuits, the Conquistadors, the Puritans, the bureaucrats, etc., are the stuff of which an "objective" picture of Aboriginal American life may be built. To us, this would be like writing a history of the Jews from Nazi propaganda.

Thus, we do not see the charge of presentism as a sincere call for deeper, fuller understanding, but as an attempt at professional intellectual oppression. Were it sincere, we would see a lot more relevant research being done than is currently the case.[108] What work we do find relevant comes from people who own up to their biases, not from those who pretend not to have them. The two of us find the very establishment of Residential Schools, their continued operation well into contemporary Canada (under **whatever** set of circumstances), and the current attempts to smooth over their scandal to be **abominations**. Our "subjectivity" is thus open to inspection. But how dare anyone imply we are not entitled to it? And if any group holds they can put aside their own emotions, values, and prejudices, we reserve the right to disbelieve them, or hold them as being something other than human beings:

> If [human beings] are to be precluded from offering their senti-
> ments on a matter which may involve the most serious and alarm-
> ing consequences that can invite the consideration of mankind,
> reason is of no use to us; the freedom of speech may be taken
> away, and dumb and silent we may be led, like sheep to the
> slaughter.[109]

Stoking The Feeble Engines

We believe that most Canadians will feel remote from the characterisation drawn here of their political and social world. After all, **why** would the citizens (and the "best" citizens, at that: founding fathers, priests, social activists) of the "linchpin of democracy" engage in actions bearing comparison with the Nazi treatment of the Jews, the Turkish treatment of the Armenians, or the treatment of Aboriginal Peoples by the United States? The average Canadian has no ready answer to the question of why, and thus (we expect) finds the very idea of Residential Schools specifically (and Indian Policy generally) as **genocide** beyond contemplation; how much easier it is to chalk all this up to good intentions somehow gone awry and to get on with the here and now.

The "Indian Problem"

But there is an alternative easy answer to why: the "Indian problem" mentioned earlier in the quote from Duncan Scott (see note 80). Put bluntly, **the "problem" was (and is) that there were (and are) Aboriginal owners (and their legal descendants) inhabiting the land to which the Europeans wished to lay claim.** According to the Eurocanadian's own body of laws, traditions and practices, **our ownership of North America at time of contact (and now) was (and is) obvious and undeniable**. Also according to their laws, the only way to extinguish our title is by war, legal agreements (such as treaties), or termination of the legal line of descendants.[110]

In Canada to this day, there is not even a pretense that vast areas (such as most of British Columbia) have ever come under such legal agreements, nor has Canada ever fought (much less won) a war with an Aboriginal Nation. As well, many of the supposed "valid" surrenders of title would never withstand critical scrutiny by an impartial court.[111] If the time ever comes that Canadians are called to account for their uses, misuses, and outright thefts, many in higher political and legal circles know full well Canada does not have a leg to stand upon.

As we've already noted, Canada, as a political entity, came upon the scene late, after the British policy not to kill their allies had already been established and the treaty process begun. **First and foremost, the "ordinary" genocide of Aboriginal Peoples grew out of Canada's need to extinguish Aboriginal title to the land without violating the letter and spirit of established British policy.** How to do this was, and continues to be, the "Indian Problem."

Means to an End

Genocide by **cultural obliteration** met this need, and was the policy embarked upon; Residential Schools were a formidable part of that policy. As a program, the policy operated as follows:

(a) create means for systematically reducing the number of people who could "legally" claim status as a descendent of those holding Aboriginal title. Enfranchisement procedures and inducements, marriage statutes, and "status" disputes were and are aspects of this policy. As well, this tactic explains what Residential School attendance provisions were doing in a bill "legitimising" involuntary and unilateral termination of status: Residential School and enfranchisement had the shared purpose of obliterating Aboriginal Peoples.

(b) eliminate as far as possible any external sign of difference between Aboriginal title holders and Eurocanadian-Come-Lately's. For one thing, a people's form of life (as Bauman points out) is part and parcel of their ability to resist oppression and affirm their existence. For another, homogenisation strengthens the governmental fiction that Aboriginals are "another part of Canadian society," and that "It is ridiculous for one part of a society to have a treaty with another part." Residential Schools were, again, prominent in this particular ploy, as were tactics such as legislated prohibition of Aboriginal cultural and spiritual practices, destruction of their political, legal, and social institutions, and linguistic imperialism.

(c) make life as difficult as possible for those who still assert their Aboriginal identity. If everyone who stands up with pride as an Aboriginal person is cut off at the knees, the reasoning goes, people will eventually stop standing up. Then the government can claim that there is no one left with whom to negotiate Aboriginal title, and no one to pay off for what has already been stolen. Here, misdirection, such as racism (both institutional, as in the criminal "justice" system, and individual) and the public portrayal of Aboriginal Peoples (which encourages personal racism and permits other institutions to warp and misinterpret Aboriginal grievances), and physical ploys, such as the state of Aboriginal housing, health care, and employment, are called into action. The Residential School had the function of inculcating the self-hatred, feelings of inferiority, and **actual second- or third-rate education** needed to create the necessary atmosphere as early as possible in the lives of Aboriginal Peoples.[112]

(d) make a "safe" place for Aboriginal Peoples in majority society, a place where there is little chance of significant numbers of them becoming cognizant of what has been done and/or making common cause with other Aboriginal groups, or similarly aggrieved parties. Once again, the Residential School system plays an important role by preparing Aboriginal children to "accept their place," convincing them to wait for justice until the "next" world, and teaching them to be properly grateful for the crumbs thrown them.

ALL JOIN IN

It may seem as if we are charging that, at root, Canadian policy toward Aboriginal Peoples was (and is) a conspiracy of some sort. In individual cases, evil intent there might have been. However, as we will discuss in

Chapter 6 the engine of genocide by cultural obliteration does not require demons in human shape to make it work; adherence of Eurocanadians to a pervasive but unstated ideology is enough to assure their participation, at various levels and in various ways, in the entire program we have discussed:

> Who then, or what, is the splendid blond beast? It is the destruction inherent in any system of order, the institutionalized brutality whose existence is denied by cheerleaders of the status quo at the very moment they feed its appetite for blood.
>
> The present world order supplies stability and rationality of a sort for human society, while its day-to-day operations chew up the weak, the scapegoats, and almost anyone else in its way. This is not necessarily an evil conspiracy of insiders; it is a structural dilemma that generates itself more or less consistently from place to place and from generation to generation.[113]

The participation of Canadian citizens had to be framed within certain limits. Recall that Canada at confederation did assume **some** (but not all) of the British commitments to its former allies; gross violation (say, killing off inhabitants, as was being practiced by other "civilized" colonizers) of at least nominally legal title extinguishment procedures would probably have been too blatant a transgression of ethics even for those times. Thus, the engines of genocide were not feeble, but subtle: they had to do their jobs while concealing their purposes, not so much from their victims (who, after all, would have a ringside seat) as from their operators. Then as now, Canadians maintained a particular image of themselves to themselves, and it was not one of being thieves, liars, and oppressors.

The complicity of the "body politic" in genocide was assured by 1) providing some members of society with assignments they could interpret as benefiting their victims, such as missionary worker, educator, and bureaucrat;[114] 2) portraying to the larger Eurocanadian society a picture of a benevolent intervention with backward, ungrateful sub-humans, creatures who, as such, could no more own property than could squirrels or bears; 3) insulating the bulk of Eurocanadians from any thought of Aboriginal history, society, rights, or grievances; and 4) maintaining an ideologically consistent society in which controversy over what was being done to Aboriginal Peoples could never arise, much less be rethought, undone, or reformed in their favor.[115]

There are, of course, points of similarity between this list and the one we provided in our elaboration of genocide by cultural obliteration. It must be kept in mind that the former chronicled what Eurocanadian society did to Aboriginal Peoples; the latter chronicles what Eurocanadian society did to itself.[116]

A TRIM RECKONING

In Chapter 3 we spelled out specific abuses, documented from various sources, that had occurred in Indian Residential Schools. The abuses mentioned were, by and large, criminal actions (sexual acts, assaults, mistreatments, etc.) carried out by school or governmental personnel, or criminal omissions of action (failures to protect, failures to provide, etc.) on the part of those in authority. In a "just" society the transgressions would have been dealt with at the time of their commission; instead they were compounded, by hatching coverups, making threats, shifting personnel, and impugning the victims. **A single victim of Indian Residential School abuse thus gives rise to a host of perpetrators, only some of whom were involved in the original criminal act**. The factors impelling "keeping the lid" on the revelations from Residential Schools derive not merely from an in-group desire to protect its own, but also from a desire to avoid articulation of all the "links" of the chain of those responsible for compounding the original crime. The "needs" are not inaccessible urges, buried in individual psyches, but are obvious and unsurprising: the desire to avoid criminal prosecution and the desire to avoid legal, financial liability. Full disclosure of the abuses of Residential School would lead not only to at least some specific miscreants spending time in jail, but as well to the kind of scenario Berry sketches:

> A 92-page internal report to American bishops on pedophilia discussed financial ramifications... Mouton predicted that, absent a responsible policy, U.S. dioceses would lose $1 billion over the next decade. He based his projection on more than a dozen Louisiana cases and others around the country at the time. Although some 400 priests or brothers have been reported to the church or secular authorities in the last decade, the number of victims is much higher. The Orlando diocese paid $2.5 million to three [molested] youths;... [m]ore than 25 suits involving victims... in Lafayette, Louisiana, were settled or tried at a cost of $22 million to the diocese and its insurers. Two Minnesota dioceses settled seven lawsuits brought... on behalf of victims; ... An eighth case went to trial, with a $3.5 million jury verdict in

January 1991 that was lowered to $1 million by the judge and then appealed.[117]

This, from a **single** church, where the children were not legislated into church control. In Canada there were many more children, under church domination by force of law; many more churches involved; and many agents and bureaucrats in governmental posts, social service organisations, and police forces. All could be implicated directly or indirectly in criminal acts carrying legal liability.

As terrible as the crimes within Residential Schools were, however, we cautioned in Chapter 3 that the list was incomplete: **genocide** must be added to that list, and to genocide must be added the **whys**: to cover up the wholesale theft of North America from Aboriginal Peoples, to avoid having to compensate those whose property was stolen, to obviate the need to treat fairly with those owning property to be stolen in the future, and to obliterate the chain linking specific genocidal actions taken against Aboriginal Peoples (such as the actions that occurred in Residential Schools) to the legal, political, economic, and social elite that conceived and implemented genocide. Even Berry's "doomsday scenario" begins to pale in comparison with the economic and criminal implications of linking the governments of Canada and the Canadian public at large in wholesale theft of Aboriginal lands and resources and crimes against humanity.

Thus, there is an important point of contact between the need to suppress knowledge of abuses of Residential School and the need to eliminate Aboriginal Peoples: the costs of having to compensate victims. The churches undoubtedly bear financial responsibility for the abuse of Aboriginal children in Residential Schools, but they cannot bear **sole** responsibility even for this: they acted at the instigation of, in agreement with, and with financial support from, various Canadian governments, and thus with the Canadian people. With regard to genocide and theft, moreover, **Canada as a whole is implicated**, and the costs of compensating Aboriginal Peoples for these crimes may be, literally, incalculable. The desperate fight to avoid acknowledging the abuses of Residential Schools, as inflicted on Aboriginal Peoples as both individual objects of brutality and collective objects of genocide, is founded upon the worship of Mammon.

However, there is another battle going on as well: Canada's fight to maintain a particular self-image. A theme that unites 1) the covering up of specific abuses that occurred in Residential Schools, 2) the participation of church and state in genocide to conceal theft, 3) the legal and financial imperative driving what meagre responses that have been made thus far, and 4) similar activities is that all these actions are inimical to any pretense of morality or ethics on the part of their perpetrators. Canada cannot own up to genocide, because to do so would have legal and financial ramifications it does not care to address; however, **worrying about this** identifies the worrier as a greedy, grasping, homicidal thief, and not as a Prime Minister, a judge, or a priest. A nation that would do such a thing to other groups of people is not a nation of tolerant, industrious, god-fearing peacekeepers, but one of greedy, grasping, homicidal thieves.

Who has benefited from the theft of Aboriginal lands and the destruction of Aboriginal ways of life? That's easy: everyone but Aboriginal Peoples.[118] Individual Eurocanadians grew prosperous as "hewers of wood and drawers of water," but it was neither their wood nor their water. Who will benefit from keeping the facts of these crimes away from the Canadian public? Again, everyone but Aboriginal Peoples. But these benefits are purchased at the cost of Canadians abandoning any pretense of morality, any right to judge, or any claim to know right from wrong.

A DISTURBING NEW ANGLE

In his summation of his analyses of the genocides of the Armenians and the Jews, Simpson was less than sanguine about the effect international law would have on the behaviour of nations:

> For many senior policymakers in the U.S. and abroad, international law remains "a crock"... when it imposes any limit on one's own government... The logical question, then, is, What should reasonable people make of the defects in international law on issues of war, peace, and mass murder? For some, there will be a temptation to conclude that humanity might be better off discarding the present body of international law altogether and somehow start again with a fresh slate... But there is no such thing as a fresh slate, of course. The gutted and imperfect form of international law concerning war crimes and crimes against humanity that is presently embraced by the major powers is better than none at all, at least so long as those who seek the law's protection have no illusions about its scope. Compassion and good sense demand that the best features of international law be preserved and extended, even when existing treaties provide for little more than moral suasion in defense of human rights.[119]

Let's be frank: we can't imagine that, on the basis of arguments similar to the ones made here, the Canadian government is going to march itself off to a World Court and permit itself to be tried for crimes against humanity, or that churches and governments will plead *nolo contendere* in future litigations arising from theft, genocide, and the abuses of Residential School. Rather, we expect a continuation of the past record of obfuscation, temporization, and indifference. Why then bother even to bring this up?

Our primary reason is that this perspective clears up a great many loose ends. For one, the Standard Account stands revealed as an exercise in damage control, focusing attention away from clues to the nature and extent of Residential School horrors. For another, church and governmental reluctance to come right out and apologize is revealed as growing from the fear of having to accept a crushing financial and moral responsibility. And what is the difference between apologizing for participating **at all** in Indian Residential Schooling and for apologizing for "mistakes" that may have occurred in them? It is the difference between apologizing for **carrying out genocide** and apologizing for **acts of brutality and unnecessary abuse that occurred while carrying out genocide**. We repeat: the Nazis could have carried out the Holocaust politely; their crime wasn't simply that they implemented it in a cruel and disagreeable manner.

And what of the preliminary answers proffered to the questions arising from the abusive actions and omissions of action surveyed in Chapter 3? They are pitifully inadequate. The breadth of abuses is not difficult to calculate: they were universal. That some institutions managed to sugar-coat genocide while others didn't even try can hardly be considered a triumph; that some individuals may have no complaint concerning their treatment is neither here nor there. What was being done to them, and why, was systemically concealed from them, and their lack of a visible scar merely marks them as a different kind of success of the genocide machine than people who were raped, brutalized, or broken.

The answer to **why** is considerably broadened, as well. Yes, there were undoubtedly pathological individuals about, but they were not confined to the staff members in contact with Aboriginal children. They were in courtrooms, Houses of Parliament, board rooms, and other institutions and locales where theft, and genocide to conceal theft, was legitimized. We say again, in agreement with the analyses of Bauman and Simpson and others, that asserting this requires us **not at all** to make presumptions about the "inner engines" that drove people to behave as they did. If pushed on the matter, however, we cannot see anything moral or virtuous behind any of the actions or omissions of action surrounding Residential School, but only covetousness, lust, greed, pride, and all their relations.

With regard to the consequences, we must again beg off. While we have made our case for genocide, we have not as yet examined the aspects of incarceration in Residential Schools that are likely to be consequential, irrespective of the (also to be examined) effects of any mistreatment. We address these issues centrally in the next chapter, as well as completing our dismantling of the Standard Account by further disputing the "unintentionality" of Residential School harm.

Finally, we brought up genocide to alter the intellectual climate surrounding consideration of issues affecting Aboriginal Peoples. All too often the misrepresentation and/or misperception of the relation between Canada and Aboriginal Peoples has nurtured the utter waste of substance: attention has been diverted, and Aboriginal Peoples sucked into staid, demonstrably inadequate, and intentionally misleading channels of inquiry or response (as we will show with regard to "Residential School Syndrome"); moral posturing has taken the place of reasoned argument and counter-argument; and lies are left to abide all too easily with truths. Whether Aboriginal Peoples are dealing with an open and honest people, or with a bloodthirsty, unrepentant foe will clearly be revealed in how Canadian society responds to its recognition of its role in genocide.

SUMMATION

In designing, building, implementing, and operating the Indian Residential School system, the Canadian governments, major Canadian churches, and the Canadian people committed, or were complicit in the commission of, genocide against Aboriginal Peoples of North America. As this Crime Against Humanity was being carried out, and individual functionaries exploited their uncontestable positions of authority over their charges, its perpetrators concealed, from themselves and from the State's "real" citizens, the economic, legal, and political rationale behind the policy (the theft of every fragment of what belonged to Aboriginal Peoples) and put forth a "justification" based in Eurocentrism, racism, and self-serving rhetoric. As the tactic of Residential Schooling proved to be less than completely successful (in terms of cost effectiveness and the **positive result** of actually obliterating Aboriginal forms of life), and as the hypocrisy of the institutional anachronism became more and more apparent, Residential Schools were phased out. But the continued existence of Aboriginal Peoples, and their striving to reveal what happened to them in individual cases, added to the State's rhetorical burden of minimising financial liability and criminal culpability, and maintaining the national self-image.

We accuse Canada not only of the abuses suffered by Aboriginal children in Residential School, but of genocide in establishing the schools in the first place; and we reject the self-serving rhetoric that passes as a response to these issues. We challenge Canada to deal squarely and effectively with its past, and admit the utter immorality of what it has done and what it continues to do.

> It is individual human beings who make the day-to-day decisions that create genocide, reward mass murder, and ease the escape of the guilty. But social systems usually protect these individuals from responsibility for "authorized" acts, in part by providing rationalizations that present systemic brutality as a necessary evil. Some observers may claim that men... were gripped by an ideal of a higher good... But in the long run, their intentions have little to do with the real issue, which is the character of social systems that permit decisions institutionalizing murder to take on the appearance of wisdom, reason, or even justice among the men and women who lead society.
>
> Progress in the control of genocide depends in part on confronting those who would legitimize and legalize the act... It is essential to identify and condemn the deeds that contribute to genocide, particularly when such deeds have assumed a mantle of respectability, and to ensure just and evenhanded punishment for those responsible. But the temptation will be to accept the inducements and rationalizations society offers in exchange for keeping one's mouth shut. The choice is in our hands.[120]

CONCLUSIONS

Vespasian, later to become the Emperor of Rome, is said to have cured a blind man by spitting in his face. He was extremely reluctant to do this, because even an emperor must look bad behaving in such a way. But in the end he had to do it; you see, there was no other way to open the man's eyes.

CHAPTER 5

RESIDENTIAL SCHOOL SYNDROME

But am I attempting this rejoinder in full command of my mental powers? Mistrustingly, I examine myself. It could be that I am sick, for after observing us victims, objective scientific method, in its lovely detachment, has already come up with the concept of "concentration camp syndrome." I read in a recently published book... that all of us are not only physically but also mentally damaged. Nervous restlessness, hostile withdrawal into one's own self are the typical signs of our sickness. It is said that we are warped... [this] sets me the task of defining anew our warped state, namely as a form of the human condition that morally as well as historically is of a higher order than that of healthy straightness. Thus I must delimit our resentments on two sides and shield them against two explications: that of Nietzsche, who morally condemned resentment, and that of modern psychology, which is able to picture it only as a disturbing conflict. Jean Amery, *At the Mind's Limits*.

INTRODUCTION

Apart from those issues we have consistently postponed for discussion until Chapter 6, by our accounting we have left dangling only one big question and one rhetorical squabble (which, however, has two aspects). The big question is, what have been the consequences of the Residential School episode? We put off its consideration until we could see what Residential Schooling was in its entirety, and we could not draw a complete picture until we established its genocidal character. We now draw that picture and discuss those consequences.

In our initial presentation of the Standard Account, we asserted that its malevolent purpose buried its important truths. The truths of which we spoke are that Residential Schools have had a devastatingly negative impact on the lives of individual[121] Aboriginal People, and that that influence has not been confined purely to what it did to those individuals. In its haste to provide us with an answer to an incompletely posed question (i.e., "What has been the impact of the Residential School," without providing a complete picture of what Residential Schools **were**), the Standard Account has again revealed its malevolent purpose, **and** given us the wrong answer. Once again we find the conflict between the Standard Account and our alternative is not about particulars, upon which, broadly, accounts agree: it is instead a matter of how the particulars are to be understood. What the Standard Account leaves out, and how it moves us in a direction away from clarity and understanding toward deeper confusion and a continuation of our oppression, is the subject of this chapter.

Fortunately, in doing this we can also address the "squabble with two faces." At various places in Chapter 4 we had occasion to disparage the education that was delivered in Residential Schools, and it is likely that some (teachers and former students alike) will take umbrage at that description. An effective way to substantiate our charge is to show that the educational aims of Indian Residential Schools were strictly limited, and an effective way to show **that** is to link Indian Residential Schools with parallel ventures in education that also had limited academic goals. In drawing parallels between Indian Residential Schools and other Adventures in Bad Education, we can substantiate another charge we made against the Standard Account in Chapter 1 and have been picking at ever since: that the creators of Indian Residential Schools knew perfectly well what consequences this institution would have for Aboriginal Peoples. Thus, an analysis of this issue harmonizes well with the general purpose of this chapter, the examination of consequences.

EDUCATION AS A POLITICAL WEAPON

The malignancy that was Indian Residential Schooling neither emerged at the time the schools were created, nor was excised at the time they were decommissioned. "Limited" education had been a policy of European religious institutions long before Columbus, the tactic serving in earlier eras to establish and maintain the within-society colonisation known as **class** through obfuscations such as the "doctrines" of Innate Depravity, Original Sin, and the Divine Right of Kings, and the promise of "something better" in the "next" world.[122] This long history of the use of education as a weapon of oppression has largely been concealed, and though sometimes barbed with religion, sometimes predominantly secular, the weapon was, as was the case with Indian Residential Schooling, generally fashioned cooperatively by church and state. This "moralistic camouflage" has served both to isolate historically the aims and achievements of Indian Residential Schooling (thus contributing to its systematic misunderstanding), and to prevent the various victims of this strategy from comparing notes and making common cause. That Indian Residential Schooling was **historically** no unique phenomenon is what we will show in this section. The fact that this tactic had a long history of use before being applied to Aboriginal Peoples in Canada (and has found continuing utility afterwards) substantiates an important aspect of our alternative account: **the people who established Residential Schools knew exactly what they were up to**. Residential School-like institutions had already been tried and found to be successful in bringing about particular results. Thus, **accounts affirming the unintentionality of the consequences wrought by Indian Residential Schools reflect either naivete bordering on stupidity or blatant mendacity**.

In briefly reviewing some of the history of these efforts, we will concentrate somewhat on the English use of education as a tool of colonisation. This does **not** mean that the efforts of, e.g., Spain, France, Germany, etc. would bear scrutiny well, but that, as the "parent" of the group that eventually gained political control of most of North America, their educational practices have comparatively more relevance for present purposes.

THE INFANCY OF EDUCATIONAL IMPERIALISM

The slow movement in Western civilisation toward public education was inextricably bound to religion (so that common people could appreciate doctrinal disputes), political movements (so that the "common **man**" might be given the appearance of some small role in the body politic), and modernity (so that people might become useful, interchangeable components of an industrial order).[123] Apart from the within-society colonialism already noted, the first uses of education as an oppressive, colonizing force was seen (as is the case for so many forms of persecution) in its application to women,[124] where the aim of education was the creation of "fit consorts" to men of station. The earliest forms of Residential Schools, both of a religious (convent schools) and secular nature, targeted women, and it is important to note that even in the 15th century they were created to bring about a social and psychological result which resonates with the stated intent of Indian Residential Schools. The teaching was religious (so that women would learn not to question their "proper place" in god's universe), practical (so they could perform some limited services to their lords and masters), and circumscribed (so they could not present an intellectual challenge to their oppressors). In a familiar vicious circle, the inferior education of women became the "scientific" rationale behind denying them a reasonable education and political rights, since they hadn't "achieved" as much as men.[125] Of course, this circle of abuse has not yet been broken.[126]

The first people to suffer from the imperial aspirations of the English ruling classes were the descendants of the indigenous Celtic[127] tribes of the so-called British Isles: the Welsh, the Irish, and the Scots. Though Christians, they retained sufficient political autonomy, and enough of their own traditions (language, clan systems, dress, etc.), to provide an excuse for their systematic "pacification," the Welsh by the Normans, the Irish by the Tudors, and the Highland Scots by the Hanovers.[128] It is well established that the "proving grounds" for English North American colonialism was Ireland,[129] and many of the tactics subsequently applied to the Aboriginal Peoples of North America, including educational imperialism, were practiced first upon the indigenous British Islanders. In fact, the religious education imposed upon these peoples (and especially their children) focused upon the suppression of native languages and the denigration of traditional practices as "heathen."[130] The destruction of these tribal societies, using tactics later deployed against the Aboriginal Peoples of North America, is a history so successfully suppressed that, for example, many descendants of the dispossessed Scots who were shot, starved, and beaten out of their land during the Highland Clearances[131] have no idea why there are so many Scots living today in Canada.

Once again, when we ask why women and tribal societies were accorded this treatment, we hear the rationalizations that were to become familiar across North America: they were sinful, subhuman beasts, whose basic nature must be changed; and should they complain, it was necessary, even **merciful**, to deprive them of their every possession, including life itself.[132] We **see**, however, the same three factors we have already spelled out with regard to the genocide of the North American Aboriginal population: these people had the temerity to have moral and legal claim to some thing or things the oppressors desired; the oppressors had the might to take what they desired; and the oppressors were men immoral and ruthless enough to take what they wanted.

FULL STRIDE

Even as the British were sorting out their attitudes toward North American Aboriginal Peoples in the late 18th and early 19th century,[133] they were colliding with indigenous cultures around the world. In Tahiti, for example, within two generations of Wallis' and Cook's trips (1767-1777), the population had been reduced to 15% of what it had been at time of contact. The Tahitians had had their own system of formal education, with which early European sailors had little interest in interfering; however, Tahiti was a convenient source of food, water, and recreation, in unequal exchange for which the seafarers were more than willing to provide junk, alcohol, and manufactured goods that even Cook realized were destroying the Tahitian culture.[134]

It was left to English Protestant missionaries to administer the *coup de grace* to the Tahitians. They did this **first** by meddling with existing Tahitian institutions (including their educational system) or by establishing new ones, complete with practices that were to become familiar to the Aboriginal Peoples of Canada (education in European scriptures, creating local power struggles between converted and traditional Tahitians, cutting the "sinful and unsanitary" long hair of the youth, urging the Tahitians to the "productive labour" of growing products useful for European markets but impossible to maintain Tahitian self-sufficiency, etc.).[135] **Second**, the British missionaries provided the "justification" (by their high-handed treatment of French Catholic missionaries to Tahiti in 1835 and 1836) for the forceable annexation of Tahiti by France in 1843.

We pass over the long colonial history that followed, and merely comment on part of today's situation. With its "loss" of Algeria in 1962, the French "possessions" in the South Pacific have been the site of its nuclear testing program. France has suppressed medical information concerning cancer rates in Tahiti and surrounding islands since 1963.[136] Perhaps this is the "Island Paradise" MP Herb Grubel had in mind.[137]

The first English settlers arrived in Australia in 1788. By 1805 they were taking advantage of the legal directive to "'pursue and inflict [upon Aboriginal Peoples defending their lands and ways of life] such punishment as they may merit' without the formalities of a trial,"[138] and practising the "theory" of *terra nulluis* (which would be formalised in 1836) by appropriating Aboriginal land. By 1816 they had established their first Residential School for Aboriginal children (at Parramatta), and by 1818 Aboriginal Australians were retreating at the sight of approaching clergymen, in fear of having their children forcibly stolen from them.

The **stated** "goals" of this education resonate across time and distance to our experience: to save the children from the horrors of their own ways of life, to prepare them to take their "proper place" in White Australian society, and to bring them the benefits of Christianity and civilisation.[139] The day-to-day script of this drama resonates as well: children escaping whenever they could, practicing passive resistance (e.g., noncompliance) when they could not, and dying at unprecedented rates.[140] The **subtext** is just as familiar: the Aboriginal Peoples had to be made to accept the proposition that they really didn't "own" the land in the English sense;[141] that the place "made for them" in White society was that of labourers and domestics at best and "fertilizer" if necessary; that European **might** made **right**.[142] The history of this "experiment in social engineering"[143] matches or exceeds the inhumanity of the colonial enterprise of any European nation.

In 1992, the Australian High Court struck down the "doctrine" of *terra nulluis*, thus signalling Australian intentions to reverse or undo over 200 years of theft, murder, and hypocrisy. Whether this will actually come about in practice remains to be seen.[144]

MODERN PRACTICE

The survey of education of indigenous peoples throughout the world, both historically and in terms of its modern practice, reinforces our general point that education, when provided, is a weapon of the exploitation of indigenous peoples and their mental and physical enslavement.[145] The phasing out of Indian Residential Schools did not bring these tactics to an end[146] and we find it instructive to examine an instance outside North America where it has played a major role and continues to have impact. Particularly germane is the system established in the Soviet Union in Siberia after World War II.[147] Its aim was the "Russification" of Siberian ethnic minorities, and consisted of a program so parallel to that of Canada that one cannot tell who was looking over whose shoulder.[148]

The policy of "Russification," instituted after World War II, is described in detail by Vakhtin, but in brief it involved the economic exploitation of Siberian Native Peoples, combined with the destruction of the ethnic identities of Siberian Native Peoples by social/political restructuring, linguistic imperialism, and boarding schools. We quote Vakhtin at length:

> Originally, boarding schools were designed to give children of nomadic groups an opportunity to obtain a systematic education. In the larger villages, special buildings were erected, equipment was imported, teachers were trained and the children of reindeer breeders and hunters began staying there nine months a year, thus having an opportunity to reach a similar standard of education to that of the non-nomadic peoples.
>
> However, as part of the Russification policy, the system was later extended, firstly to cover the nomadic children of kindergarten and nursery age, and later to include children of the settled population. It soon became the only possible way to obtain school education and was made compulsory for all children. This

created an ugly situation whereby the parents had to "turn in" their children at the age of one year, first to the nursery, then to kindergarten, then to boarding school for six days a week 24 hours a day, while themselves living in the same village.

As a result of the boarding-school system, children became fully State-dependent in many places and deprived of a family upbringing. They also lost their native mother-tongues. At the age of 15 or 17, they returned to their families as complete strangers, with no knowledge of traditional native culture or of home life. Parents also suffered since, in many cases, they lost all their feeling of responsibility towards their children and delegated it all to the State.

Eventually, the boarding-school policy led to dramatic changes in traditional social and family structure and contributed to the formation of the above-mentioned "broken generation." It led (and in many areas still leads) to the situation where the majority of the Northern boarding-school graduates completely lacks the necessary living skills, and often emerges without initiative and energy. The dominant psychological characteristic for many of them is apathy combined with aggression; they experience enormous stress when they begin their adult life.[149]

Russians who "emigrated" to Siberia, and their descendants, form the ruling class of Russia's modern East. What is their opinion of the people whose land they inhabit with questionable legality?

The Chukchee and the Eskimos? They live in the stone age!... They are all idlers! All they can do is have children, but they can't even take care of them. The State has to do that... Nurseries, kindergartens, boarding-schools, even the University... Everything free, of course... Hunting? They don't need it: they can buy everything they need in the village... Money? So long as they have enough to buy alcohol they are happy...[150]

As Forsyth[151] observes concerning Farley Mowat's conviction that Russia has respected their Native Peoples' ways of life, "Sadly, this is untrue."

CONCLUSIONS

Whether at home or moving east, west, north, or south; whether their religions posed as spiritual or as worldly truths, or as some combination of the two; Europeans were singularly persistent in the educational work they undertook. From the earliest times of colonialism, certain attitudes have been an article of European faith; and the genocide that engulfed the Aboriginal Peoples of North American was nothing less and nothing more than a tune, with slightly different orchestration, that was being played throughout the world:

> That undeveloped races [sic] could not adapt themselves to "civilization," and were bound to die out, had come to be taken for granted by many pioneers. From believing this to expediting their departure to another world was no great step.[152]

The "education" delivered, time and again, did not have as its goal the broadening of intellectual horizons, but rather the inculcation of the images Europeans carried of themselves and of the oppressed **into** the oppressed.

RESIDENTIAL SCHOOLS AS TOTAL INSTITUTIONS

The revelations about Indian Residential School incline toward the dramatic, the shocking, and the corrupt. We consider this unsurprising in a world where popular interests seem invested in the kinds of events that sell newspapers in supermarkets. Talk of inaction on land claims, institutional racism, and the like has nowhere near the drawing power of even a minor accident on the Gardiner Expressway. Aboriginal Peoples become "news" to the rest of Canada when they are putting on a "good show," whether or not it is painful for the Aboriginal individuals involved.

The more shocking revelations are also more "graspable," for whatever reason, by the public at large. The formula of the television "miniseries" has been to reduce the complexities of human history (the North American Slave Trade; the American Civil War; World War II) to incidents in the lives of a small number of sympathetic characters who wander about through catastrophic world events. When Kunta Kinte was whipped, all North America could "understand" (if just for a moment) that slavery was bad. By extension, we think it plausible that, if the facts ever get into common circulation, it will be hard for the average Canadian to see any educational benefits to sticking needles through children's tongues, beating them into unconsciousness, or denying them treatment of their medical needs until their digits have to be amputated. They might even think such things wrong.

But for every horror story of abuse, we have heard a hundred stories of the less dramatic indignities and abasements that made up life at Indian Residential School: the constant stream of racist slurs that accompanied lessons; the regimented moment-to-moment attention to one's activities; the haircut and school uniform; the persistent undercurrent of hunger; the impenetrable loneliness; and so on. As well, we hear of good times, times that reveal the barrenness of the rest of the existence at Residential School: the delight of being allowed an hour's play with a Christmas or birthday present sent months earlier, but withheld; the relish in eating a good meal when an inspector or other dignitary was visiting; the swell of pride in an eleven year old child that has learned to handle the machinery or do the job of a full-grown adult; the explosion of joy at getting a visit from one's parents. Not *theatre*, perhaps, but human.

When we consider the impact of Residential Schools, then, not only must we look at the short and long term consequences of the more outrageous actions committed, we must come to terms with the whys and wherefores of the miseries of everyday existence. What are we to make of these "little atrocities?" Are they merely the day-to-day annoyances that are to be expected when lower-level functionaries (priests, nuns, agents, etc.), perhaps mentally and temperamentally unsuited to the tasks they have been assigned, rise to their particular levels of incompetence? While this might be the default explanation, once again it is an evasion of truth: the relentless burden of life in Indian Residential School was a deliberate, well thought out, long-practiced policy, undertaken to achieve particular results.

GOFFMAN'S TOTAL INSTITUTIONS

Bernanos once said, "One cannot understand the least thing about modern civilisation if one does not first realize that it is a universal conspiracy to destroy the inner life." Residential Schools, as part of its "civilising mandate," were designed to achieve this destruction in Aboriginal Peoples; the means whereby they carried out this assault were recounted by Goffman.[153] He described the sociology, psychology, and (less so) history of these tactics. However, it is important to see that he discovered nothing: rather, he merely reported upon and analysed institutional practices that had long been employed to bring about particular psychosocial effects in target groups. In doing this he cited research literature going back to the 1920s and church documents hundreds of years old.

Interestingly, Goffman, a Canadian, developed his account with no apparent knowledge of Residential Schools.[154] His examples and the principles of operation he abstracted were taken from homes for the aged, asylums, private boarding schools, monasteries, prisons, concentration camps, and the like. He called such places **total institutions**, defined (in "family resemblance" terms[155]) as social institutions which were "walled off" in some way from the world at large; which "broke down" the barriers that existed in greater society between places of work, sleep, and play; and which enforced and maintained an extreme power disparity between a large inmate population and a smaller supervisory staff (which continued to be integrated with the outside world). Goffman's interest in studying total institutions wasn't merely their non-conformity with the rest of society; it was in what these institutions were meant to accomplish, and their **means** of accomplishing it:

> The total institution is a social hybrid, part residential community, part formal organization; therein lies its special sociological interest. There are other reasons for being interested in these establishments, too. In our society, they are the forcing houses for changing persons; each is a natural experiment of what can be done to the self.[156]

Whether it was preparing prisoners for their eventual release into society, novitiates for service to a religious order, inductees to follow without question the orders of their superior officers, or victims of genocide to submit with minimal resistance to their destruction, the point of total institutions was the total war on the inner world Bernanos spoke of, and the reconstitution of what was left along lines desired, or at least tolerated, by those in power.

Institutional Tactics

The staff's almost complete control of the psychological and physical environments in total institutions made it possible to organise much more than mere occasional and circumscribed forays against the inmate's presenting self:

> The recruit [sic] comes into the establishment with a conception of himself [sic] made possible by certain stable social arrangements in his home world. Upon entrance, he is immediately stripped of the support provided by these arrangements. In the accurate language of some of our oldest total institutions, he begins a series of abasements, degradations, humiliations, and profanations of self. His self is systematically, if often unintentionally, mortified.[157]

The process of entrance typically brings other kinds of loss and mortification as well. We very generally find staff employing what are called admission procedures, such as taking a life history, photographing, weighing, fingerprinting, assigning numbers, searching, listing personal possessions for storage, undressing, bathing, disinfecting, haircutting, issuing institutional clothing, instructing as to rules, and assigning to quarters... Many of these procedures depend upon attributes such as weight or fingerprints that the individual possesses merely because he is a member of the largest and most abstract of social categories, that of human being. Action taken on the basis of such attributes necessarily ignores most of his previous bases of self-identification.[158]

...although sexual molestation certainly occurs in total institutions, there are many other less dramatic examples. Upon admission, one's on-person possessions are pawed and fingered by an official as he itemizes and prepares them for storage. The inmate himself may be frisked and searched to the extent—often reported in the literature—of a rectal examination. Later in his stay he may be required to undergo searchings of his person and of his sleeping quarters, either routinely or when trouble arises. In all these cases it is the searcher as well as the search that penetrates the private reserve of the individual and violates the territories of his self.[159]

Once the inmate is stripped of his possessions, at least some replacements must be made by the establishment, but these take the form of standard issue, uniform in character and uniformly distributed. These substitute possessions are clearly marked as really belonging to the institution and in some cases are recalled at regular intervals to be, as it were, disinfected of identifications... Failure to provide inmates with individual lockers and periodic searches and confiscations of accumulated personal property reinforce property dispossession. Religious orders have appreciated the implications for self of such separation from belongings.[160]

The barrier that total institutions place between the inmate and the wider world marks the first curtailment of self. In civil life, the sequential scheduling of the individual's roles, both in the life cycle and in the repeated daily round, ensures that no one role he plays will block his performance and ties in another. In total institutions, in contrast, membership automatically disrupts role scheduling, since the inmate's separation from the wider world lasts around the clock and may continue for years. Role dispossession therefore occurs. In many total institutions the privilege of having visitors or of visiting away from the establishment is completely withheld at first, ensuring a deep initial break with past roles and an appreciation of role dispossession... Although some roles can be re-established by the inmate if and when he returns to the world, it is plain that other losses are irrevocable and may be painfully experienced as such. It may not be possible to make up, at a later phase of the life cycle, the time not now spent in educational or job advancement, in courting, or in rearing one's children.[161]

In addition to personal defacement that comes from being stripped of one's identity kit, there is a personal disfigurement that comes from direct and permanent mutilations of the body such as brands or loss of limbs. Although this mortification of the self by way of the body is found in few total institutions, still, loss of a sense of personal safety is common and provides a basis for anxieties about disfigurement. Beatings, shock therapy... may lead many inmates to feel that they are in an environment that does not guarantee their physical integrity.[162]

But total institutions are not concerned merely with the **present** debasement of self; the management of inmates for its own efficient day-to-day operations is only a part of its aims. The war on the inner life continues, as has already been noted with respect to **role dispossession**, long after the inmate has been discharged:

There is an incompatibility, then, between total institutions and the basic work-payment structure of our society. Total institutions are also incompatible with another crucial element of our society, the family.[163]

Thus, if the inmate's stay is long, what has been called "disculturation" may occur—that is, an "untraining" which renders him temporarily incapable of managing certain features of daily life on the outside, if and when he gets back to it.[164]

Conclusions

In the name of efficiency, total institutions "unmake" the people over whom they gain control. It matters little how old an inmate is when he or she is placed under the institution's thumb; whoever that person **is**, and how he or she defends and asserts it, must be taken apart and reassembled enough to allow what remains to operate in accordance with the institutional requirements. By doing this, the total institution does not produce a **new** self, but **no self at all**:

> ... total institutions disrupt or defile precisely those actions that in civil society have the role of attesting to the actor and those in his presence that he has some command over his world—that he is a person with "adult" self-determination, autonomy, and freedom of action. A failure to retain this kind of adult executive competency, or at least the symbols of it, can produce in the inmate the terror of feeling radically demoted in the age-grading system.[165]

It should go without saying (but probably won't) that, if inmates become available at a young enough age, the tactics of total institutions won't merely "disrupt or defile" selves, but hinder their development in the first place. By **not allowing** the formation of "adult executive competency," the inmates are prevented from being or becoming persons **at all**. When used in this manner, total institutions are not, therefore, instruments of social engineering, intended to inculcate an alternative form of life: they are instruments of genocide, meant to produce things unrecognisable **at all** as human beings.

INDIAN TOTAL INSTITUTIONS

Well then, were Indian Residential Schools total institutions? Examination of virtually any source of information on life at Indian Residential School, such as the work of Celia Haig-Brown, Diane Persson, Linda Bull, Rosalyn Ing, the Cariboo Tribal Council, or Isabelle Knockwood, affirms that they were. Isabelle Knockwood's account flawlessly demonstrates this (we apologize for having to abstract from a superb narrative):

> Right off, Sister Mary Leonard began to explain that speaking Mi'kmaw was not permitted in the school (p. 26)... I found

myself serving Father Mackey a three-course meal... but I never did get to eat off the fancy dishes or taste the gourmet meals that the priest enjoyed (p.27)...Our home clothes were stripped off and we were put in the tub. When we got out we were given new clothes with wide black and white vertical stripes. Much later I discovered that this was almost identical to the prison garb of the time. We were also given numbers. I was 58 and Rosie was 57. Our clothes were all marked in black India ink—our blouses, skirts, socks, underwear, towels, face-cloths—everything except the bedding had our marks on it. Next came the hair cut (p. 28)... Sometimes the little girls would get thirsty during the night and go to the bathroom for a drink of water. If they were caught, they were dragged out of the room by the hair or ear and sent back to bed (p. 31)... Even those of us with families who lived nearby were sometimes not permitted to go home for Christmas. But it was the one day in the school year when we were allowed to be with our brothers and sisters (p.38)... We played with our toys all during vacation until Little Christmas, January 6th, when school resumed and the toys would be gathered up and packed in boxes under the tables or locked in the cloak room. Sometimes, we never saw the toys again but our dolls would be hung on nails on the walls of the recreation hall. One day, coming down from the class we found an empty space where the dolls had been... Nothing more was said about the dolls until next Christmas and the process was repeated again for another year and after that another year and on and on for forty years to hundreds of Indian children. On the boys' side the identical ritual was performed, only with gun holsters, cowboy hats, and hockey sticks.[166]

And on, and on. The particulars of Ms. Knockwood's experience were confirmed in testimony before the Royal Commission too many times to represent here. It made no difference where in Canada an Indian Residential School was located: the specific tactics enumerated by Goffman as "mortifications" of the self precisely describe the psychology of their operation.

SUMMARY: DAY-TO-DAY LIFE IN A RESIDENTIAL SCHOOL

What, then, was the atmosphere for a child in an "ordinary" Indian Residential School, one in which he or she wasn't subjected to the tortures, the rapes, the beatings, and other merciless, sadistic acts already catalogued in Chapter 3?

In terms of academic standards, the schools and its teachers were marginal. Where available, documentation consistently shows that, at best, only half the "school" day was spent in academic instruction. The rest of the time was spent in religious indoctrination (which was regarded as the primary "academic" task by school officials) and hard labour (which in various ways was used to offset the costs of school operation). The children's time was carefully monitored: recreational time, or time spent on one's own, was negligible.[167]

Even when it did not constitute torture, discipline (corporal punishment in particular) exceeded accepted "Canadian standards," as reflected in contemporaneous public school practice. Many of the infractions which "warranted" this treatment were not infractions for any children in Canada save Aboriginal ones, such as speaking in their own language, seeking contact with brothers and sisters, and being unable to do a fully grown person's work. Even if a given child was personally able to avoid severe treatment, she or he was likely to witness it being applied to other children. Not only did such demonstrations serve as warnings, they had the additional function of furthering the total institution's goals: "... there may be occasions when an individual witnesses a physical assault upon someone to whom [one] has ties and suffers the permanent mortification of having (and being known to have) taken no action."[168]

Considerations of discipline and punishment aside, Residential Schools tended to be harsh environments. Many have recalled how underheated the school buildings were, how cold the floors were in winter, how oppressive were the barracks-style living arrangements. Many former students report how they were chronically underfed, or provided with food unfit for consumption. Some were driven by hunger to obtain food by creative means (we refuse to use the word *steal* to describe a child's actions under such circumstances). This led to one kind of consequence if caught (harsh discipline), and another if not (guilt for "stealing," or for having more food than another child).

Often, the climate of Indian Residential Schools alternated between being emotionally overwhelming (on one extreme) and emotionally barren (on the other). Many have testified (to the Royal Commission and elsewhere) that they did not feel safe, or loved, or cared for; that they **were** or **felt they were** exposed to the predations of school staff or older, stronger students; that no one was there who was there for them. Children vied for the positive attentions of their custodians, who played favourites and set the children against one another with extra food, privileges and other inducements. The potential for emotional devastation was built into the

Residential Schools in terms of such regular features as: initial separation from parents and family; prolonged isolation from parents, family, and people; the period of adjustment to institutional rules; and the constant fault-finding and racial slurs addressed to them by staff.[169]

CONCLUSIONS

Even those who managed to escape the more sensational abuses of Residential Schools could not have emerged unscathed:

> All students recalled the homesickness, the loneliness, the aloneness, the lack of family contact, the unfamiliarity of the new environment, the lack of personal freedom, the "cold" atmosphere, or lack of feeling in the institution, the "distance" (social distance) placed between educators and Native children, and the fear—initially of the unknown, but later the fear that developed and that was instilled in their hearts and minds as little children.[170]

Residential Schools implemented a well-established technology that targeted the spirits, minds, feelings, and bodies of its wards. Its goal was not so much to create as to destroy; its product was designed, as far as possible, to be something not quite a person: something that would offer no intellectual or spiritual challenge to its oppressors, that might provide some limited service to its "masters" (should the "masters" desire it), and that would learn its place on the margins of Canadian society.

A STUMBLE

We have reached an important point in our presentation: to the best of our ability, we have set out those features and aspects of Residential Schooling that we feel should have consequences.[171] It seems natural now to provide some listing of what those consequences are, and perhaps close with a survey of what has been, and what should be, done about them. However, to do this without calling ourselves up short and interjecting a warning is premature. For the listing of symptoms and suggested remedies is what the Standard Account does (after, of course, providing an inadequate catalogue of features and aspects), and in joining in the game of symptom-naming or aftereffect-finding, we would find ourselves squarely on the track the Standard Account would have us.

From any point in time it is possible to look in two directions; the way one looks at the future is conditioned by the way one looks at the past, and *vice versa*. The Standard Account proclaims a bogus past, one in which genocide is ignored, racism and oppression are explained away, "motives" are elevated, and so on. The view forward from the Standard Account is founded upon those fictions. As attractive as someone might be able to make that view, it is at best only part of the picture, and at worst as bogus as the history it proclaims. Getting "on track" with the Standard Account because it suggests doing something you think should be done, **without explicitly challenging both that bogus past and the adequacy of the view forward**, is to stumble into accepting the Standard Account by default, **and the ideological limitations it invariably imposes**.

We call ourselves up short in an effort to prevent that stumble. A more concrete example of our concerns is immediately forthcoming. Before continuing, however, we felt we must restate a warning issued back in Chapter 2. Otherwise, the care we've taken to extend the list of consequences of Residential Schooling could easily be interpreted solely as a strategy to increase the number of consequences that should be anticipated. This would be a fundamental misunderstanding of what we are hoping to achieve. With this warning in mind, we now begin a look at the consequences of Residential Schooling.

OUTWARD AND VISIBLE SIGNS...

As might be expected by now, we do not intend to address this issue in a conventional manner. First of all, we think that this has already been quite competently done by the Assembly of First Nations in their report, **Breaking the Silence**. We can add nothing to it, and there seems to us nothing to gain from redoing something already done well.[172]

In practice, however, every time we started work in this area, we could turn out nothing that "rang true." Our largest problem was that we could not (and still cannot) convince ourselves that such a review is either necessary or appropriate. Who pretends to find it hard to believe that someone who was raped, beaten, and, in effect, imprisoned during his or her childhood, all because of the "unfortunate accident" of being an Aboriginal person, might grow up to have some personal problems? Who would be surprised that someone who had had this done to him or her might subsequently be less than enthusiastic about keeping company with the sons and daughters of those who did this? Or, perhaps most generally, once the Residential School era is recognized as unbridled genocide, is there some point or purpose in undertaking to show that at least some of the people who **went through** it **suffered from** it? In fact, we **were** able to answer those questions and similar ones, and we didn't like the answers.

Let's begin with the "general" question above. What would be the point in showing that people who attended Residential School suffered from it? First, why does anyone pretend there is an issue at all? Compare: after World War II there were, roughly, the same number of Jews who survived concentration camps as there were European Jews who had not been sent off to such camps before the war ended. Was there ever a suggestion that the world hold off judgment about what the Nazis had done to the Jews until there was some psychosocial accounting made? Compare: Apartheid is now officially over in South Africa. Did world economic sanctions and church condemnations of the policy arise from studies showing that Apartheid was "bad?" Compare: the Americans fought a Civil War, partly over slavery. Were the North and South fighting over the interpretation of research data? Once the immorality of crimes like Slavery, the Holocaust, Apartheid, or Residential School is made clear, no further accounting is necessary. The accounting that **does** happen is often undertaken by and for those **implicated** in the crimes, in an effort to prove to themselves that what they're doing is (or what they did was) justified. The Nazis and the Afrikaners had their "race specialists," the slaveholders had their psychiatrists expounding on *drapetomania*, and the majority citizens of Canada have... ?

We repeat, once the immorality of crimes like Residential Schooling is known, no further accounting is necessary. Suppose no negative consequences of Residential Schools could be found. Would it follow that the schools were okay? Certainly not. One possibility would be **that the schools were successful in obliterating Aboriginal forms of life**. But murdering a robbery victim doesn't make the robbery legal. A second possibility would be **that, under the maintenance of a plausible threat, subjects would repeat whatever would keep them out of trouble** (see Footnote 170). Even Home Children[173] caseworkers eventually learned to interview the children outside the hearing of the child's owner, but where do Aboriginal Peoples successfully evade the surveillance of Canadians? And a third possibility would be **that "social science" is unfit to render a judgment**.[174] A "Lucy Search" ("Charlie Brown's not here; Charlie Brown's not there; so he must not be anywhere!") isn't a search at all. (It should also be clear that these counter-examples are not mutually exclusive.) All this is to say, therefore, that even were there no demonstrations of negative effects of Residential Schools, **the schools still would be immoral**. To insist on "proof," or even to concede the desirability of the attempt, is to hold Aboriginal Peoples accountable to a standard applied nowhere else and to reduce morality to a show of hands. The former is racism; the latter is situational ethics.

Let's move on to considering personal problems. Why would anyone profess difficulty believing that some people suffered personal problems as a result of their treatment at Residential School? One kind of purported skeptic we've encountered pretends to mishear "some people suffer personal problems as a result of Residential Schooling" as instead "**all** people suffer personal problems as a result of Residential Schooling." It is this kind of reprobate who shows up to a meeting about Residential Schools with an Aboriginal Person in tow, who testifies "I went to Residential School, and nothing bad happened to me." The tactic is totally dishonest, and we wish Aboriginal People would stop allowing themselves to be used in this way; for such testimony, as we've pointed out earlier, is like people testifying at a murder trial that the accused didn't murder **them**. No one doubts that some people did not personally suffer, or may even have personally thrived, at Residential School, but such an experience says absolutely nothing about anyone else's experience: even if two people attend the same dance they don't have the same dance card, and Residential School simply wasn't the "same dance" for everyone.[175]

When pretending to wonder whether or not Residential School had a negative impact on at least some Aboriginal individuals, there are some notable blind-spots in evidence anecdotally called forth. Few people if any, for example, have noted the similarities between the informal symptomology literature that is developing with respect to former Indian Residential School attendees and the symptomology of Holocaust survivors, Japanese prison camp inmates, victims of torture and physical abuse, colonially oppressed peoples, and similarly aggrieved groups. But even a brief look at the literature on "concentration camp syndrome,"[176] the psychological consequences of torture,[177] or the psychology of colonial domination[178] establishes the correspondence: virtually nothing attributed to Aboriginal Peoples in the way of symptoms falls outside what has already been found for **any group of human beings subjected to severe and prolonged oppression and exploitation**. That includes elevated suicide rates, which historically were found, for example, in Jews who had received orders for transportation to concentration camps, Home Children, and the Aboriginals inhabiting the "Indies" when Columbus showed up.

Linking with this literature is beneficial beyond merely noting the similarities of psychological symptoms between these groups. For one thing, the "question" of whether severe mistreatment of Aboriginal Peoples can be "passed on" to generations or individuals who didn't attend Residential School has already been examined in some of these other groups,[179] and, we might add, no one thought the notion preposterous. For another, the extreme difficulty of conducting "after-effects research" and pulling "proof" out of it is clearly discussed.[180] For still another, contemplation of the **differences** between the experiences of Aboriginal Peoples and those of other oppressed peoples gives us an extremely important perspective on a number of issues. For example: 1) although Jews have long been marginalised, Jewish thought, religion, philosophy, etc., are foundational to the Western mind. Aboriginal forms of life have always been inconsequential to Europeans; hence, their willingness to slaughter us. This fundamental difference between the Holocaust and the treatment of North American Aboriginal Peoples puts the lie to all the nonsense about "reconciliation,"since there was never any "conciliation" to "re;" 2) however loudly nincompoops may shout, no thinking person believes the Holocaust never took place. The vast majority of "thinking" Canadians, however, do not even recognize the genocide that was Residential School. Consequently, Jean Amery, in an incredibly powerful essay,[181] can defend his emotional response to his Holocaust experiences against the bogus explications that they arise from his moral shortcomings or pathological condition ("concentration camp syndrome"). Aboriginal Peoples, with only "good intentioned mistakes" to "whine" about (and **not** a Holocaust), aren't even **entitled** to resentment. We must accept our moral inferiority and psychopathology, which, if we are nice, people with "good intentions" will help us overcome.

This strikes to the heart of our reluctance to go symptom-finding, regardless of how useful it might appear to be: **it requires Aboriginal Peoples to "demonstrate" and accept their pathology, and to parade it before the Powers That Be, before those Powers will condescend to undertake the merest of amends; and in doing this, Aboriginal Peoples must also accept the warped, pathological history those Powers would have in the place of truth.** Let's get this straight: a group of people invade our lands and steal our property. They take away our children, sending them off to be beaten and exploited as a labour force, "brainwashed" (to use an unfashionable term) into rejecting their rights and their ways of life, and, at least occasionally, forced to serve the sexual appetites of their warders. Now, in order to get some kind of action addressing all of this, we must stand up and prove how sick **we** are!

We have said before and we say again, if it is sickness you seek, don't look for it in the victims of genocide: in resides in the minds and hearts of the people who planned, designed, implemented, and operated the machinery of genocide, and who now seek to cover it up. The "meaning" of Indian

Residential Schooling is not the pathology it may have created in some Aboriginal Peoples; it is the pathology it **reveals** in the "system of order" giving rise to it.

Our reluctance to adduce "proof" of the damage caused by Residential Schools follows from a clear picture of the past, a rejection of the revisionism of the Standard Account, and the recognition of the **rhetorical**, not **scientific** nature of the demand for "proof." **And this is not to reject the work of, say, the Cariboo Tribal Council or the Assembly of First Nations!** No one believes the schools had no impact on the quality of lives of Aboriginal People who attended them, or on the lives of those only indirectly affected, and we dare say that includes the people who rush to explain away or deny. **No one** doubts the utility of Aboriginal helpers having some idea of what they will likely face, in the way of symptomology, in community-based intervention centres. The danger is in when the forces of "damage control" seize upon those results as an opportunity to insinuate their interpretation of events; they do this by projecting a picture of the future where Aboriginal individuals, seeking outside themselves for the means to come to grips with what happened to them, are "given" "professional help" in this quest. The desperateness of the plight of Aboriginal Peoples, the intense desire to do **something**, and the superficial resemblance between Standard Account "cures" and what many of us consider advisable, predisposes all of us to seize that future and ignore that past.

We will not call Aboriginal Peoples who suffered through the Residential School experience (whether they enjoyed it or not), nor those of us who have come to live in the toxic world it created, **sick**, any more than we would call the hungry Aboriginal children who crept into the larder at night for food **thieves**. We will **not** play this game.

The Rhetoric of Residential School Syndrome

In coming down to cases, much of our dissatisfaction as expressed above can be crystallised around the notion of a "Residential School Syndrome" (RSS). We've never found anything to recommend it, and have all kinds of reasons to condemn it. We'll be brief.

One: there is no reason to expect there to be a regular cluster of symptoms (a "syndrome") associated with having attended Residential School. The specifics of the experience certainly weren't uniform (see Footnote 175), and even if it was **physically** and **philosophically** coherent, there would be no reason to expect uniformity of response to it (compare any two works by Holocaust survivors). To believe there was such a thing as RSS, one would have to assert that people with **widely different experiences**, behaving in **widely differing ways**, were suffering from the same disorder.

Two: there is absolutely no evidence for RSS. Long gone are the days when a psychiatrist can write up some notes on a few of his patients and claim to make a "discovery" of a new "mental disorder." In fact, this was how the concept of "concentration camp syndrome" (subsequently shredded on methodological grounds by Solkoff and revealed as philosophically insipid by Amery) was inflicted on the world. Apparently, RSS came into use by a similar artifice, with the peculiar feature of a lack of any data supporting it. **Were there a literature** claiming to establish RSS, we would have a go at it; its non-existence limits our task to exposing its rhetorical nature.

Three: whatever else it might be, the experience of Residential Schooling is not a "disease," and yet RSS squarely places our efforts to understand the episode within the medical model. This is a **rhetorical** move and not a scientific one:

> RSS sidetracks all interested parties in a variety of confusing ways, disabling those who are supposed to be suffering from RSS, and exonerating those who are responsible for the mess... suppose you are helping people address personal problems in their lives, and you find out they attended residential school. If you subscribe to reification of RSS, their supposed possession of RSS "causes" them (in your view) to behave in the unproductive or destructive ways you are trying to remedy, much as the possession of a cold makes you sneeze, cough, and feel lousy. Just as you don't hold a person with a cold responsible for displaying cold symptoms, your tendency is to regard a "person with RSS" as not responsible for displaying any of the supposed RSS symptoms.
>
> This enterprise soon gathers momentum. The people who went to residential school are told that they suffer from RSS, and indeed that "their problems" arise from it. Not only does this release them from taking personal responsibility for their actions (e.g., "I beat my wife because I am suffering from RSS"), everyone, therapist and client included, collude in identifying the client as the source of the problem. True, the client is held to be somewhat blameless (curiously enough, even as he is being blamed), but interest has now been focused on **residential schooling as the problem of specific individuals** [emphasis added].

This move plays into the hands of the governmental and religious officials responsible for having devised, implemented, and maintained residential schooling. With everyone talking about people suffering from Residential School Syndrome, no one addresses the genocidal nature of residential schooling, the immorality of forced religious indoctrination, or the arrogance and paternalism that permeated the system. (Indeed, if these topics did come up, people might start considering the extent to which these features describe the systems in place today.) Such a diversion is so useful that, however intentionally, today's officials are willing to nourish this fiction to a considerable degree. Nominal funds are available for therapeutic rehabilitation of victims. Institutional perpetrators of offenses (be they priests, teachers, administrators, or what have you) are passed off as aberrant individuals who do not reflect the basic "good-heartedness" that motivated the organisation. And even more insidiously, since there are no residential schools in the old sense any more, abuses are "all in the past" and no present systemic changes are necessary.[182]

Breaking the Silence thoroughly examined, contextualised, and clarified the issues that sometimes arise with Aboriginal individuals who attended Residential School as children. In doing this, the authors had no need to call up a pseudo-scientific jargonish term which, in effect, slanders and misguides people who are seeking help and understanding. Residential School Syndrome is nothing more, and nothing less, than another attempt to place us on the rails of the Standard Account. But these rails are a siding; they do not lead to any place interesting or important. We can think of no reason to employ the notion of RSS unless we have no objection as Aboriginal Peoples to ending our days like the Donner Party.

WHAT PAINETH THEE IN OTHERS

THE "REAL" SYNDROME

On second thought, maybe we've been too hasty. There is a **lot** of pathology associated with Indian Residential School, and, unpleasant as we **personally** might find it, it is high time we acknowledged it. We only regret we didn't wise up in time to have our concerns included in the recently released Diagnostic and Statistical Manual of Mental Disorders-IV. Based on our extensive, first-hand clinical experiences, and with our apologies for our previous short-sightedness, what follows is our suggestion for inclusion in the next version, DSM-V.

301.82 Residential School Syndrome

Diagnostic Features

Residential School Syndrome is a personality disorder manifested in an individual's specific behavioral action of (1) obliterating another people's way of life by taking the children of the group away from their parents and having them raised in ignorance of, and/or with contempt for, their heritage; while (2) helping himself/ herself to the property of the target group. The behaviors are closely related, and indeed, some theorists have suggested that the "theft" of the target group's children should be seen as merely another manifestation of the overwhelming urge to steal everything belonging to the target group. People with this disorder have a grandiose sense of self-importance and unjustified feelings of moral superiority, and, while they seldom bother to actually respond to protests of the aggrieved group, they are sometimes heard repeatedly to mutter empty platitudes like "It's for your own good," or "I'm the expert, I know what I'm doing."

Further, those suffering from Residential School Syndrome demonstrate a complete lack of insight into their own motives. If asked about the morality of taking the property of the target group, they respond that it is "a small price to pay" for the blessings of the way of life being imposed on the target group, or aver that it is a "dirty job," but one they feel they have a "Christian responsibility" to perform.

At times they manifest a split with reality bordering upon that seen in certain forms of Schizophrenia. A sufferer of Residential School Syndrome may believe "Everybody wants to be like me," or "I know better than everybody else." These delusions are often buttressed by an elaborate hodge-podge of pseudoscientific jargon about the Innate Depravity of the target group, the racial superiority of his or her own group, and a bizarre, self-justificatory belief in a "Super Being" that wouldn't be letting him/her get away with what he/she is doing if it wasn't in harmony with the "Super Being's 'Divine Plan.'"

Individuals with Residential School Syndrome generally have a lack of empathy and have difficulty recognising the desires, subjective experiences, and feelings of their victims. Indeed, they sometimes act as if the targets of their behavior are incapable of feelings or anything more than simple animal desires. This attitude reflects the sometimes stated, sometimes implicit, notion that their targets are something less than human beings.

Associated Features
The relation between Residential School Syndrome and Schizophrenia has already been noted. Differential diagnosis is comparatively easy, however, because the more extreme sufferers of Residential School Syndrome are influential, and if you're powerful you're eccentric, not Schizophrenic. Sufferers of Residential School Syndrome often have the same fragile self-esteem of those with Narcissistic Personality Disorder, reacting to criticism sometimes with withdrawal or petulance, and sometimes with disdain, rage, or defiant counterattacks. They also often manifest the Narcissist's extreme need for admiration, insisting that members of the target group (adults and children alike) "thank" them for what has been and is being done to them.

Prevalence
At one time it was estimated that anywhere from 99 to 100 percent of the adult, non-Aboriginal population of Canada who were of European heritage suffered from Residential School Syndrome. Since the phasing out of Residential Schools, however, the sufferers have been forced to go "cold turkey," and, correspondingly, prevalence studies have become harder to undertake. There is widespread clinical suspicion that Residential School Syndrome is manifested in a variety of related behavioral disorders, including nostalgia for "the good old days" of Residential School operation; the aggressive (if not ferocious) denial that anything bad ever happened in Residential Schools; the unshakeable belief that members of the target group are whining ingrates; and borderline incontinence at the suggestion of criminal investigation of Residential School activities.

Diagnostic Criteria for 301.82 Residential School Syndrome

A pervasive pattern of attempted indoctrination of children of another group of people, combined with the theft of all manner of the group's property, beginning in the late 1800's and persisting through the 1970's. In addition to this characteristic behavior pattern, a diagnosis of Residential School Syndrome requires four (or more) of the following:

(1) a grandiose sense of self-importance and/or infallibility

(2) unjustified feelings of moral and/or intellectual superiority

(3) an intense desire to change the subject when the phrases "economic self-interest" or "crimes against humanity" arise, or the words "genocide," "racism," "colonialism," or "oppression" are heard

(4) lack of personal insight, or an absence of self-criticism

(5) unwillingness to accord human status or rights to creatures not passing arbitrary and inexpressible "standards"

(6) obsession with juggling history books and/or shredding documents

(7) marked fluency in rhetoric, including ability to sound like apologising without doing so, to call people "liars" without actually using the word, and to sound sympathetic while studiously avoiding accepting any criminal or financial liability

(8) tendency to repeat certain phrases, like "We don't need an inquiry," or "Let's let bygones be bygones"

Prognosis

Many of those suffering from Residential School Syndrome are doing very well indeed. However, the rest of us worry about the collective effect Residential School Syndrome sufferers have had, and will continue to have, on the minds and hearts of the Canadian population...

CONCLUSIONS

We really don't care whether or not anyone appreciates our attempt at humor. Like a lot of comedy, this parody has its roots in reality: that it is not the Aboriginal Peoples who are sick, but the society that, among other things, created the Residential Schools. The inability to face up to that fact, for whatever reasons, is a festering wound that bears dealing with.

We will not presume to lecture Eurocanadian society on curing its ills; however, the disease that had its particular manifestation in the creation of Indian Residential Schools is the same one Jean Amery and Zygmunt Bauman have already identified. They have much to tell the interested reader.

CHAPTER 6

THE FOREST AND THE TREES

I suppose if I were asked to pick out the point I most want to get across to the reader, it would be that the ideology of inequality is an enormously potent barrier to the achievement of equality. The concept of internal individual characteristics that differentiate the best of us from the worst of us both shapes our social institutions and warps our own consciousness so thoroughly that every move toward equality seems to swerve away from the goal or fizzle out into nothing. Even those of us who consciously set out toward the goal of equality must be expected to get mired down in the swamps of our own mistaken assumptions and to lose our way. William Ryan, *Equality*.

INTRODUCTION

In his review of Deborah Lipstadt's *Denying the Holocaust*, Siano[183] tried to draw distinctions between the Holocaust and other genocides in an effort to emphasize the Holocaust's uniqueness. Unlike the Jewish Holocaust, his argument went, the destruction of the Ukrainians under Stalin, the African Slave Trade, and the wars against Aboriginal North Americans were not driven by a pathological ideology, nor did the malefactors develop a cold-blooded technology similar to the gas-chambers to do their work. Finally, according to Siano, unlike these other historical events, the Jewish Holocaust exists in **living memory** among Americans. This makes it possible to use the Holocaust as a "standard for gauging oppression, horror, and evil."

Although there is much to recommend in Siano's review, we take exception to this particular argument. In Chapter 5 we showed that Indian Residential School was, indeed, a well established technology of genocide (warm blooded or cold, we can't decide), undertaken with the full anticipation of bringing about the effects it has had on Aboriginal Nations and individuals. Furthermore, the Residential Schools, and many other genocidal tactics undertaken by non-Aboriginal North American governments, do indeed reside in the **living memories** of many of us, whether we were touched directly or indirectly by them. That he and a lot of other people on this continent don't remember much if anything about our treatment speaks to the effectiveness of the propaganda machine in operation, of which he and the others are victims.

Our focus in this chapter, however, will be on the presumed absence of ideology in the attempts at our destruction. We will argue here, *contra* Siano, that Indian Residential Schooling **was**, and the Standard Account **is** driven by a pathological ideology; the difficulty, as is the case with those who uncritically accept the Standard Account (or part of it), is that like all good "believers," he takes it as revealed truth and not as an arguable position.

We take ideology, broadly, as an accumulation of doctrines, beliefs, or opinions that guide a group of people or constitutes the group's organising principles. An ideology is **arbitrary**, in that proofs of correctness of an ideology, however frequently attempted, are without force: an ideology is simply the way **this** group chooses to see things, do things, and talk about things. Ideology is a source of conflict, because groups often treat their beliefs as beyond question; to challenge another group's ideology is to challenge the group itself. However, ideology is not merely reactive. Masquerading as fact, it often provides the pretext for behaving in an oppressive or dismissive manner, particularly when there is a power disparity between groups holding different ideologies.[184]

In this chapter we will explicate the ideology behind the Standard Account of Indian Residential School. Our argument is that everything about the Standard Account is profoundly ideological. While some people might grant this without too much argument with respect to ecclesiastical, or even bureaucratic, domains, objections are likely to arise when we insist on including social scientific and therapeutic domains in the charge.[185] Hence, our explication of the ideological nature of the entire enterprise of the Standard Account will begin with these "dispassionate," "objective" disciplines. A grasp of why the work undertaken and the thinking dominating in these areas is shadow and not substance will make clear that our objection that the Standard Account is ideologically-driven is not some sophomoric plea to "tolerate multiple realities." We will show that the "need for a scientific understanding" of Residential Schools and the "demand for therapeutic counselling" for former residents, far from being divorced from the obvious biases of the purveyors of genocide, are slices of baloney from the same loaf.

METHODOLOCAL INDIVIDUALISM

The functional similarities between formal religions and social sciences have long been noted and commented upon.[186] Before there were psychiatrists and psychologists it was largely the task of the churches to convince the great mass of people they were unworthy sinners, doomed to their lot in this world, and doomed to suffer in the next should they get out of line. The "line" they shouldn't get out of, of course, was whatever was established by those invested with the Divine Right to rule, who were doomed (so to speak) to suffer riches and power in this world and torment in the next. As ridiculous as this may sound now, it was the primary means of justifying and maintaining the oppression of the masses of people for quite a long time, and still works in various parts of the world today. However, as people came to understand this particular game, variations had to be developed. The Medieval doctrines of Innate Depravity, Original Sin, and Divine Right of Kings have been transmuted into today's "skills deficits," "innate race differences in IQ," "learning styles," and "mental illnesses." Where the churches claimed the foundations of their doctrines to be in Divine Revelation (a notoriously difficult claim to substantiate, and fraught with emotion), psychiatry and psychology tied it to "mental science" (objective, dispassionate, and "replicable"). Where the churches determined your station by the way you dressed and who your parents were, social scientists conduct "assessments" to determine your place. The history of when, and how, and by whose hands these transmutations were made is well beyond our interests here. However, while the *abracadabra* has changed, the structure of the magic remains the same. For both the churches and social sciences, the "truth" is something deep and unobservable, accessible only to the initiated (raised up after a long period of indoctrination sometimes called higher education) after they've performed elaborate ceremonies (assessments). For their labours of keeping the herd out of the manor house, the functionaries are rewarded with a portion of riches of the material world and a degree of status which they can pretend approaches that of their masters.

Of course, this description will be remote to most social scientific functionaries. For the world in which they were raised, and now raise others, is steeped in the ideology of the internal determinants which "differentiate the best of us from the worst of us," in Ryan's trenchant phrase. In this they have gone beyond the churches, who at least had to deal with heretics, apostates, and devotees of different revealed truths. Like Mr. Jourdain, who spoke prose all his life without knowing it, most social scientists embrace the ideology called **Methodological Individualism** (MI) without having any idea what it is, or realising other opinions are possible. Ryan's fight to free himself of the fetters of the mind represented by Methodological Individualism is, in our experience, one attempted by precious few.

The fundamental notion of MI can be stated quite simply: it is "the view in social science according to which all phenomena must be accounted for in terms of what individuals think, choose, and do."[187] Bhargava's penetrating work lays out slight variations on this definition, but this simple version will do for our purposes. MI is a form of reductionism, one which says that complex, orderly phenomena (like economies, institutions, wars, etc.) are **built up** from orderly phenomena that involve individuals, and what individuals are capable of doing. Thus, there is an implicated **causal order**, in that the variability of the more complex phenomena (wars; depressions) are ultimately the result of what individual people think and do.[188]

Please take a moment to think about this. Does it sound reasonable? Is this a tautology of some sort, or does some kind of empirical demonstration of its soundness seem necessary? Actually, with a few moments reflection many people begin to find it dubious. Some can even come up with counter-examples. The problem is that **this way of thinking is so endemic to Western social sciences that even those who "intellectually" reject it embrace it in practice**.

We contend 1) Methodological Individualism is certainly wrong; 2) because it is demonstrably wrong, those who cleave to MI as a way of examining and understanding phenomena in the world are ideologues, not scientists; 3) even those who think they have a grip on the problems of MI slip into it all too easily. Our task in this section is to provide the proof of MI's incorrectness. We then examine, in terms of the way "social scientists" approach the problems of Indian Residential Schooling, how we are led to systematically misunderstand everything about it.

METHODOLOGICAL INDIVIDUALISM IS CERTAINLY WRONG

There are some disciplines, of course, that have a fairly good grip on MI, history being an example. A classic cartoon has a history professor in class on Day One saying "Well, what'll it be: kings and battles or the exploitation of the masses?" The choice being offered is an interpretation of history based on events moved and shaped by "great men" [*sic*] versus one based on economics, religious doctrines, or other factors that transcend any particular individual. Marxists tend to reject the former and embrace the latter, while everyone else goes the other way. Because of world animosities[189] the viewpoints have tended to polarize, which is unfortunate since it is not an either/or choice.

Most disciplines, however, do not have even this grip. As "sciences," they are less interested in philosophical disputes and more interested in gathering facts, establishing empirical relations, and developing theories to account for what they find. The "facts" gathered are what the science considers to be the building blocks of complex relations; making findings is accomplished through statistical analyses; and the theories developed are accounts of putative causal processes. For empirical sociologists, the building blocks of social relations and institutions are the actions of individuals within a particular society. Psychiatrists, psychologists, and therapists accept this and carry it one step further: the actions of individuals are themselves built up from the "mental contents" of individuals. The hope of psychological science is to provide a comprehensive picture of human behaviour; with this in hand the sociologist or social psychologist can provide their comprehensive picture of human social behaviour; and so on, like the Old Woman Who Swallowed A Fly.

The first question that arises is, why stop? Methodological Individualism legislates that the "right place" to stop in our investigation, our "explanatory bedrock," is when we run into "what individuals think, choose, and do," but why put the stop-sign there? Can we not, in principle, develop an account of "thinking" in terms of brain chemicals, blood flows, and the like? And is that account not itself reducible (again, "in principle") to the behaviour of atoms? Can we not break atoms themselves down further?[190]

We can go the other direction, too. We have a world with many societies, and our world is only one in this solar system, which is only one in this galaxy, and there are "billions and billions" of galaxies...

The stipulation of MI to stop at what individuals think, choose, and do is a **preference**, and not some kind of scientific principle. And the thing about preferences is that different people can have different preferences. If you think the hot dogs are best, but we want hamburgers, that's that. You can try to persuade us, but there is no **proof** that we should, instead, want a hot dog. Now, MI's can **prefer** that we stop the reduction of our investigation at choices made by individuals, but we can **prefer** otherwise.

If this seems like a quibble, we can do better. Believing that more complex phenomena are reducible to simpler phenomena is a good example of the Fallacy of Composition, which is taught in most elementary logic courses. Simply, it is a fallacy to believe that the characteristics of a composite (a higher-order phenomenon) are necessarily derivable from the characteristics of the constituents of the composite. A commonly heard cliche, "The whole is greater than the sum of its parts," expresses this, although a more accurate phrasing would be "The whole is something other than a function of its parts." It's easy to come up with examples: an **army** is something other than a bunch of individuals with weapons; a **fleet** is something other than a lot of boats; or, to use an example David Suzuki doesn't seem to be able to get Mac-Blo to understand, a **forest** is something other than a mass of trees.

Some philosophically-minded social scientists (B. F. Skinner comes to mind) recognized the reductionist nature of their enterprise and **rhetorically** (not logically or scientifically) headed off criticism by branding those raising these problems as subscribing to the "mysticism of emergent properties." There is nothing mystical about the criticism, however; rejection of the notion that an existing, observable orderliness is **necessarily** founded upon a lower orderliness is nothing more than **not** falling into the Fallacy of Composition.

Even more devastating to Methodological Individualism, there is a statistical analogue to the Fallacy of Composition: Simpson's Paradox. In 1951 Simpson stated a fundamental property of non-deterministic relations: it is possible, in principle, to break down any relation into subgroupings in which the original relation no longer holds, or is even reversed. He noticed this while looking at a type of data representation called *contingency tables*, but it was obvious (to statisticians) that this feature was demonstrable everywhere in statistics. The clearest picture of the difficulty can be obtained by looking at "correlation scatter-plots," such as are presented below.[191]

Scatter diagrams depict the form and strength of relations between variables. X and Y can be any two variables (say, IQ and Self Esteem), and the entries into a scatter diagram are "scores" or "assessments" obtained from individuals, plotted in Cartesian two-space. By convention, as one moves from right to left for variable X, one goes from low to high with respect to variable X; as one goes from bottom to top for variable Y, one goes from low to high with respect to variable Y. Thus, a person whose score is plotted into the upper right-hand corner of any of these diagrams is "high" with respect to both the variables; a point in the lower right corner is "high" with respect to X and "low" with respect to Y; and so on.

There are statistics calculated from the entries into scatter diagrams to quantify the degree of association between variables. We won't go into details here,[192] but the closer the entries cluster about any single non-horizontal or non-vertical straight line drawn through them, the stronger the degree of association.

Some of the possible forms of Simpson's Paradox are illustrated in the four diagrams below. In **A**, taking all the points together, there is only a minimal relation between X and Y (that is, any single straight line drawn as close as possible to all the points just isn't very close to them all); however, within each of the three subgroups outlined, there is a strong direct relations between X and Y. In **B**, X and Y overall have a strong positive relation; within each of three subgroups, however, X and Y are unrelated. In **C**, overall X and Y are unrelated, but within one subgroup there is a strong positive relation and within the other a strong negative relation. Finally, in **D**, the overall relation is fairly strong and negative, while within each of the subgroups, the relation is fairly strong and positive.

In these diagrams, and countless others we could generate, the Fallacy of Composition grows fangs and takes a bite out of the fundamental assumption of Methodological Individualism, that the "bedrock" of understanding complex, multi-individual phenomena is what individuals think, choose, and do; for **there is no necessary correspondence between the**

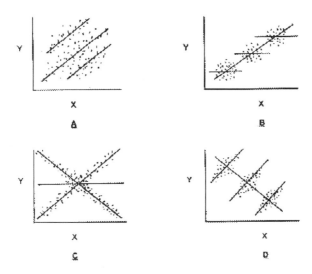

form, structure, or magnitude of relations at differing levels of complexity. Organization found at one level doesn't necessarily carry forward to higher levels, nor does it itself necessarily follow from organisation found at simpler levels. The fact that, in principle, we will be able to generate subgroups in which higher-order relations will either cease to exist, or even reverse themselves, gives us an additional problem: **which picture is right**? Favouring one over another is, again, a **preference**. There can be no proof that the form and magnitude of any result we obtain is more "correct" than a higher- or lower-order result, **from the same data**, that contradicts it. Let's make this absolutely clear: in, for example, diagram **C** below, assume that the points running from the lower left to the upper right corner all represent men and that the points running from the upper left to the lower right corner all represent women.

The statement: "the relation between X and Y is positive, or it's negative, or it's zero, depending on whether you're a man, or a woman, or either or neither a man or a woman," is perfectly descriptive (in a mathematical sense) of what's going on, regardless of whether it makes any common sense. Ignoring, say, the women and only speaking about the men may allow us to **pretend** we've solved the problem, since the "data" would then "say" that the relation between X and Y is positive. But of course, nothing has been cleared up, since we've manage to produce the result only by ignoring half of humanity, and because, as Simpson assures us, even within the "strongly positive linear relation for men" we will be able to find sub-groupings of men that overturn **that** generalization.

If we wished to get fancy, we could throw in modern chaos theory, which in part is based on the fact that **completely unpredictable sub-processes** underlie regular and predictable higher-order processes. However, all this was anticipated long ago:

> No supposition seems to me more natural than that there is no process in the brain correlated with associating or with thinking; so that it would be impossible to read off thought-processes from brain-processes. I mean this: if I talk or write there is, I assume, a system of impulses going out from my brain and correlated with my spoken and written thoughts. But why should the system continue further in the direction of the centre? Why should this order not proceed, so to speak, out of chaos? The case would be like the following—certain kinds of plants multiply by seed, so that a seed always produces a plant of the same kind as that from which it was produced—but nothing in the seed corresponds to the plant which comes from it; so that it is impossible to infer the properties or structure of the plant from those of the seed that it comes out of—this can only be done from the history of the seed. So an organism might come into being even out of something quite amorphous, as it were causelessly; and there is no reason why this should not really hold for our thoughts, and hence for our talking and writing. It is thus perfectly possible that certain psychological phenomena cannot be investigated physiologically, because physiologically nothing corresponds to them.[193]

Throughout this work we have tried to keep this insight firmly in mind.

We have refrained (as far as possible) from temptations to cast aspersion on the motives of perpetrators and "spin doctors," to impute diseases and disorders to victims, or to permit mitigation of crimes by an appeal to "good intentions" or other inner engines. We do not mean that there weren't people with intentions good or bad, or individuals with injuries or without. Again, it is not that either a macro-level or a micro-level analysis is right. What the refutation of Methodological Individualism helps us understand is that the immorality of Residential Schools is not founded on the ability to demonstrate a collective injury. The pain and suffering inflicted upon one individual does not require the demonstration of similar patterns of injury for other individuals. The "whole" of Indian Residential Schooling is something other than a function of its parts; to understand it does not require its reduction to something deeper, hidden, or more basic, but rather its examination in terms of its various issues at their different levels of complexity.

METHODOLOGICAL INDIVIDUALISM MISLEADS US

We can show more than merely the philosophical and analytical ineptness of the ideology of Methodological Individualism; we can demonstrate that it misrepresents that which it tries to understand. To do this we borrow and elaborate upon the **hypothetical** story of Mr. Su, which first we told in our work on community-based research (Appendix B).

SOME HYPOTHETICAL DATA

SUBJECT #	A1	A2	A3	F1	F2	F3	o1	o2	o3	v1	v2	v3	Y
1.	12	4	99	119	24	3	-4	19	1	298	32	1.5	0
2.	8	6	87	122	18	3	0	18	1	311	54	1.1	0
3.	11	9	98	104	19	3	-6	21	1	301	52	1.9	1
Mr. Su 4.	13	7	72	109	25	4	-3	22	1	291	45	1.2	1
5.	9	8	101	118	24	2	-2	20	1	292	47	1.6	0
6.	11	5	74	101	23	3	-3	19	1	312	49	1.3	1
7.	14	7	92	125	22	1	0	17	1	303	50	1.5	0

Mr Su is a farmer with a small parcel of land somewhere in the interior of China during the late 19th century. Unfortunately, Mr. Su and many of his neighbors are addicted to opium, but a group of time-travelling

Methodological Individualists have transported back to his village in an effort to help. They are armed with advanced computers, statistical programs, and assessment devices, and neither sleep nor eat until they finish gathering the data that will allow them to pinpoint the causes for this dread disease. Their data are symbolically represented above. As you can see, Mr. Su was given (arbitrarily) Subject Number 4. There are many more people in the research project than shown, and many more variables, but you get the picture. The variables are grouped in rough categories (the a's are personality test scores, the f's are body measurements, the o's (except for o3, which is a "special" variable as discussed below) are school records, the v's are vegetable consumption statistics), and literally **any** variable the MI's from the future can imagine[194] was targeted, assessed, and entered into the data base. The outcome variable, Y, whether or not the subject is an opium addict, is for convenience represented here as 0 (no) or 1 (yes), but of course it could easily be made more complicated than this. The problem facing the MI team is how to use the data to come up with the reasons the people of Mr. Su's village are opium addicts (or not). From this, perhaps they will get an idea how to overcome this plague.

Well, how do they proceed? Let's assume for convenience sake that the MI's have some 26th century analogue to our correlation/regression model. They relate the variables, singly or in groups, simultaneously or successively, etc., to the outcome variable of interest, and develop a statistically sound "model" relating the predictors to the outcome (let's even assume they've developed a math that avoids Simpson's Paradox). What can we say about the model they triumphantly present to Mr. Su and his fellow villagers?

We can say it is wrong. For there is not (nor can there be) a variable in their analysis representing a major causal force in Chinese opium addiction: the British in the 19th century had an unfavourable balance of trade with India.

The story in brief was this: Indian cotton products were beating, in price and quality, competing British goods. To help their textiles industry, England invaded India, destroyed Indian factories, and wiped out Indian cotton production, "encouraging" the Indian spinners and weavers (by systematically breaking their thumbs) to grow poppies instead. England also had an unfavourable balance of trade with China. Chinese policy was to accept only precious metals in trade for tea, silk, porcelain, and spices, all of which were in great demand in Europe, and all of which China had in abundance. The English (and other European powers) had no manufactured goods the Chinese wanted, and hence the metal drain in Europe became serious. The English hatched a plan: take the opium being manufactured in India (which they didn't want in Europe anyway), addict the Chinese population to create a demand, then trade opium for tea, silk, porcelain, and spices. England and the European powers fought two wars in China for the "right" to export opium there.[195] Mr. Su was not singled out for addiction; he just had the bad luck to be **where** he was **when** he was. It did not take long, however, to turn a Machiavellian English economic policy into a Chinese racial defect.[196]

Why can't the MI's put this variable in their analysis? Because **it's not a variable: it's a constant**. Have a look at variable O3: we use this variable to code, somewhat verbosely, values for "living in a world in which the British government has embarked on a policy of promoting opiate addiction in China as a means for alleviating some of its economic difficulties." All the people in Mr. Su's village receives (as, indeed, everybody in the whole world at that time would receive) a "1," meaning "yes, this subject lives in such a world." On purely technical grounds, the scatter plot between any other variable and this constant would yield (as indeed it would for **any** constant) a horizontal line, meaning "association not defined." Mathemathically, it's "contribution to accounting for the variance in Y" is nil.[197] Since there is no variability in "living in a world..." there is statistically no information in that column, and consequently it **cannot be analysed**.

Even more importantly, this factor (not variable) **isn't a characteristic, or feature, or descriptor, or whatever, of Mr. Su**. Mr. Su need never have heard of England, or India, or international economics, or anything along the chain of events leading up to his addiction; **there is no necessity for any internal, personal, individual representation of English economic policy anywhere inside Mr. Su, or any of his fellow villagers**. And yet, this is the manner in which a Methodological Individualist investigation must proceed, because "all phenomena (including drug addiction) must be accounted for in terms of what individuals think, choose, and do." When we limit what we are pleased to call "scientific investigation" in such a manner, we are ideologically bound to develop at best an incomplete, inaccurate understanding of what is going on. Finally, if we let Simpson back in, the findings produced by any analysis will, in principle, be disputable as well.

IMPLICATIONS FOR UNDERSTANDING RESIDENTIAL SCHOOLING

Methodological Individualism is a demonstrably limited and inaccurate way of viewing the world and the forces that move and shape it. The Standard Account, as a product of that warped ideology, produces a limited and inaccurate picture of Indian Residential Schooling, and a limited and inaccurate way of making sense of that picture. Residential School problems were the **individual and personal** shortcomings of particular school or governmental functionaries; the harms these people inflicted had to be seen in the **personal, internal** problems of **individual** former students; the proper way to establish blame and pursue compensation is to prove **personal, individual** injuries, to justify charges being brought by **individuals** against **individuals**; the way to undo the damage is to send **individuals** off to jail (or better still, cure or remediate their **personal, internal** dysfunctions), and provide **individual** victims with therapy focused on healing the **personal, internal** injuries they have.

Though monotonous, this is accurate, **as far as it goes**. But like Mr. Su's opium addiction, this scenario is a systematically limited picture. How are "genocide," "economic oppression," "institutional racism," etc., turned into personal, internal, individual characteristics? What if someone doesn't **want** to stand up in a room full of strangers and recall, and talk about, and **dispute** the most horrible moments of her or his life, but still wants **justice**? And how can anyone believe this picture accurate, even for a moment, when it provides not even the tiniest glimpse of the Splendid Blond Beast?

As an ideology, the philosophy behind the Standard Account doesn't admit such questions into consciousness. Not merely vigilant, it snuffs out trouble before things get too far; some examples: 1) **Breaking the Silence** isn't "scientific;" 2) testimony before the Royal Commission wasn't sworn in a legal proceeding; and, one we expect to hear, 3) the RCAP report thinks there was a big "conspiracy" against Aboriginal Peoples. We've already commented on the inanity of 1) and 2), and our response to 3) is explicit in this chapter. Of course there doesn't have to have been a conspiracy: as we've just showed everyone who can read, there need be no connection between systemic features and the characteristics of individuals operating within that system. Whoever said "The road to Hell is paved with good intentions" understood this very well.

PEOPLE WITH GOOD INTENTIONS

As we've mentioned earlier, the submissions to the Royal Commission from Aboriginal individuals were overwhelmingly concerned with therapy, healing, and reconciliation. These presentations, as we've also noted, were less concerned with relating personal experiences in Residential School than with documenting the therapeutic needs of Aboriginal communities and, occasionally, summarising the experiences of acquaintances who had attended Residential Schools, and who were unwilling or unable to testify before the Commission themselves.

We expressed initial doubts about the universal emphasis on therapy way back in Chapter 2 and have largely ignored it since then. We found it odd that the call by the churches for therapy went unchallenged; disturbing that presenters from non-therapeutic specializations struck a uniformly therapeutic line; and, frankly, frightening that Aboriginal presenters joined in the chorus with little indication of critical evaluation of that emphasis.

We think that by now our readers will have a reasonable idea of our objections to therapy, healing, and reconciliation as effective responses to Indian Residential Schooling. Once again, we have no doubt that many people's experiences in Residential Schools have caused them physical and emotional pain, pain which **to this day** continues to affect the quality of their lives. Further, we have no doubt that speaking about these experiences and these pains to someone who is non-dismissive and empathic may provide these individuals some degree of benefit or relief, however permanent.

Having said this, however, our analysis is that the push to therapy and healing (we've already dismissed reconciliation as bogus) is primarily another manifestation of the Standard Account. Its philosophical foundation is the ideology of Methodological Individualism; its function is to maintain the intellectual and emotional oppression of Aboriginal Peoples; its purpose is to do the least while appearing to do something. Fortunately for us, the work of demonstrating the basis of the therapeutic state in Methodological Individualism was recently undertaken by Celia Kitzinger and Rachel Perkins:

> Psychology is rooted in modern liberal individualism and places the individual at the center of the moral and political universe. Contemporary psychology manifests an intense concern with the individual self in pursuit of private goals of freedom of choice and liberation. "Empowerment" is offered as a substitute for "power," "oppression" is reduced to the individual pathology of the oppressors, and liberation becomes a psychic rather than a political phenomenon... Psychology has invaded our speech partly by coopting existing political words, reinterpreting them with-

in its own individualized and privatized frame of reference; partly by infiltrating new terms of its own that replace political
words; and partly by demanding that we expunge certain words
from our vocabulary. The result is psychology's colonization of
our political terrain.[198]

We recommend their work highly, particularly for frontline workers who
may be beginning to see some point to our presentation.

Relieved of the necessity of developing a general argument, we will be
able to focus on these issues as they apply to Residential Schooling. As
before, the difficulties arise from an unquestioned, even unexamined, alle-
giance to a "system of order" underlying therapeutic thought and technique. Consequently, we do not question the motives of those people,
Aboriginal and otherwise, who undertake to do this work; we are sure they
all have good intentions.

THE LOCATION OF THE PROBLEM

Therapeutic approaches are Methodologically Individualistic in locating the "problems" of Residential Schooling squarely within individual former attendees. "Assessment" of the "problem" proceeds by testing, interviewing, and measuring the erstwhile student, and any program of intervention begins and ends there as well. "Progress" in treatment, too, is
assessed by monitoring the individual, and the "cure"[199] achieved either
when the patient displays the proper profile of behavioural and psychic
characteristics, or when his or her Medical Services Branch (MSB) funding has run out. The "system of order" that has grown up around these
shared assumptions is termed the Therapeutic State by Szasz[200] and
Polsky.[201]

Again, personal problems in living may be part of the picture, but it is
only a part. Completely unmentioned, unanalysed, and unmonitored are the
workings of the system of order which gave rise to Residential Schooling.
How does this omission "play out" in the thinking of the client? To the
extent this ideologically-limited version of history is successful in focusing
attention away from the non-personal, non-internal causes of their present
states, the clients must consider their experiences extremely bad luck on
their part (i.e., they were overtaken by some "natural disaster") or righteous
retribution for some personal failing.

But Residential School was an Unnatural Disaster, not a natural one,
and it was a bureaucracy, not a conspiracy to single out victims for
abuse.[202] In "Olden Days" the churches treated the excesses of class

oppression the same way they did the whims of Mother Nature: 1) your personal unworthiness is responsible for what happened to you (Innate Depravity, Original Sin, and so forth); and 2) keep your head down and ride out the storm. Nowadays, therapy advises 1) what happened to you is reflected in your personal unworthiness (your signs and symptoms, which are the motivations for, and targets of, intervention); and 2) keep your head down and ride out the storm (learn to "adjust"). No one, it seems, has been interested in storming the manor house. Not much has changed, except that Innate Depravity has become an Acquired Depravity (Residential School Syndrome).

Would there be any therapeutic point in looking outside the individual, personal, and internal? **Therapy** would be the wrong word for it, but Kitzinger and Perkins for two think the critical examination of legal, political, social, and economic forces dominating women a damn sight more useful than the mawkish navel-gazing of the Revolution from Within;[203] Malcolm X thought untangling the roles of alcohol and drugs in Black oppression would overthrow the grip they had on Black People; and William Ryan argued that the quest for justice and equality begins with looking outside the confines imposed by a philosophy of internal, individual gifts or shortcomings. We couldn't agree more with these folks.[204] We can even see such an exercise turning out to be "personally" therapeutic as well, since the ideologically endless loop of "bad things happened to me because I'm bad"and "I'm not responsible for what I do because bad things happened to me" (see Footnote 202) is shattered.

AN ABSENCE OF EXPERTISE

Well, couldn't therapists just broaden their pitch a little to include coverage of these broader, non-personal issues? Considering the *panache* with which they carry out what they're supposed to be doing, we have our doubts.

First, the Therapeutic State has a long history of misunderstanding or reinterpreting non-personal issues as personal. With specific reference to Residential Schooling, we have yet to see the merest glimmer from the quarter that genocide, economics, revisionist history, etc., have any important role in its understanding. That is, the Therapeutic State has entirely gone along with efforts of the churches and governments to limit concerns to specific sick people, deflecting scrutiny away from inquiries into systemics. It is an old song:

The political challenge to the casework approach has been neutralized through a deft rhetorical strategy. Social personnel begin by acknowledging their role as instruments of the elite domination and the limitations of their method. Then, having admitted the truth of much of the criticism, they proceed largely as though they never heard it at all. The refrain runs something like this: Yes, casework only tries to fit people to an oppressive order without changing conditions. Yes, for people without money or medical care or decent housing, social justice is a more urgent concern than individual counseling. Yes, neighborhood residents must be given a say in agency operations. But we have tilted the balance too far away from individual intervention under professional direction. We can see the importance of personal counseling when we consider, for example, the disorganized lives and the chaotic family relationships of the underclass. And so we cannot be content with promoting access to hard services. The lives of marginal citizens can be made more decent and worthwhile if we guide them to the personal social services they really need and provide those to which they are entitled. By the same token, though we want our agencies to be responsive to local wishes, we cannot "sacrifice the capacity for expertise and standards."

Having glossed over the charges against them, social personnel go on to contend that their accusers are callous about the fate of the very people they claim they want to protect...[205]

Their tendency to conflate "the personal is political" with "the political is personal," and then to concentrate on the latter, is understandable, since this is the locus of their purported expertise. This is to say no more, however, than that **they are intellectually committed to making this mistake**.

Second, just as there is no evidence for Residential School Syndrome, there is no evidence that the therapy lavished (the government "throws nickels around like they were manhole covers") upon Aboriginal Populations is actually curing anyone of anything. Programs are recommended, established, and fought for in the belief that they're working, but apart from occasional testimonials there is no "therapeutic outcome" literature to evaluate. We suspect (but, of course, with no evidence) existing testimonials owe more to "hype" than any real progress on issues, personal or otherwise. Now, *we* don't think this necessarily problematic, but then we have a very different view of things; therapists, in their role as dispassionate, objective scientists, are **professionally committed to producing such evidence**. That they do not produce it, and that consequently they are so eager to endorse and institute supposedly different therapeutic interventions without a shred of evidence for them, bespeaks religious fervour, not reasoned judgment; indolence, not discipline; opportunism, not commitment.

Third, "healing" and cognate terms are tossed about so furiously that we can barely get the question, "Healing what?" in sideways. It is an important question, though, in that members of the therapeutic state have given every indication that they do not understand what they're dealing with. Do they wish to imply that they just "heal," whatever the problem might be, so that understanding the problem is beside the point? If so, we ask: why then all the talk of syndromes, special techniques, assessment devices, and so on? In a one-size-fits-all world, measuring tapes and related paraphernalia are unnecessary. If not, we ask: how do you presume to treat an injury you haven't diagnosed?

Finally, Aboriginal communities have produced a "feeding frenzy" of lunatic fringe pop-psychologists, who swoop in like buzzards and out again once the funds have dried up. We've heard appalling tales of incompetence about supposed "helping professionals" (if you are uncomfortable disrobing in a public locker room, you were sexually abused as a child; distortion in your visual periphery are memories trying to get out; sickness comes from a misuse of human free will as expressed in sin; step on a crack and you'll break your mother's back); no "legitimate helping professional" steps forward to call humbug **humbug**. We do not hold Aboriginal communities responsible; the buzzards **sound** like the "real thing," and they have big degrees, too. How are community-level people supposed to tell the sizzle from the steak? Maybe, just maybe, no one can tell.

THE THERAPEUTIC STATE

But this is all shadow-boxing. **Whatever the personal motives of individual therapists**, the Therapeutic State is a part of the Splendid Blond Beast. It is a small, badly-funded, marginalized part, but it is a part.

Social services and intervention programs in Canada receive a pittance, but it is sufficient to keep agencies running as long as they perform as required. The Therapeutic State thus has a vested interest in playing along with the "help the diseased" emphasis of the Standard Account, which, of course, was constructed to **limit** things to "help the diseased" and not let it become "and pay for rebuilding Aboriginal Nations and pay for all the resources stolen and give back the land stolen and put everyone responsible up for trial," and so on.

In doing its part, the Therapeutic State sets up its version of the Land

Claims Commission. "Come in one at a time and show us your scar; if you can prove how you got it, we'll cover it up with makeup for you. Remember, **you** don't tell **us** what it is you want, **we'll** tell **you** what you're going to get."

And what exactly is the makeup that's being applied? Polsky calls it **normalisation**:

> Lower-class clients do not seem to require merely a bit of support, like their middle-class counterparts, but instead wholesale personal and family reconstruction. Intervention sets out to foster new behaviors, instill another set of mores, and cultivate a different outlook toward self and family. By bringing about profound changes at the most intimate levels of human experience, the state aims to integrate marginal citizens into the social mainstream. Further, resistance on their part will not be tolerated...[206]

When carried out by an oppressive society upon the members of another society (or societies), there is another word for normalization: **genocide**.

What money there is flows from government to therapist or agency, with Aboriginal groups getting to "authorize" the transfer (that is, wave at it as it goes by). If the therapist or agency is Aboriginal, it is funded because it has demonstrated its willingness and ability to abide by the ideology of the Splendid Blond Beast.[207] And the government and churches get to gush over "all that money" being spent in helping their Poor Red Relations.

And what is "success?" Success can be 1) when the client comes to accept himself or herself as the problem, works to change, and "accepts a place in the new order on the terms set by the victors." (If this be success, maybe it's good that therapy is as bad as it is. As Polsky writes: "The enduring inefficiency of the therapeutic sector remains, from the standpoint of personal liberty, one of its few saving graces (p. 210).") And success can also be 2) keeping things more or less as they are. No harm there.

But success **cannot** be the clarification of the political, economic, legal, social, and psychological bondage in which Aboriginal Peoples are held. Not for the Splendid Blond Beast. Who wants a crowd of secure, focused, determined, and knowledgeable Aboriginals looking at treaties, land claims, damage suits, and the like?

And there's the rub. The ceremony made of **individual** and **personal** attention and **individual** and personal **fulfilment** is hypocrisy, a ritual passing off as a rebirth (entry into useful society) what is, in fact, a funeral (the successful destruction of an "inner life"):

> Whoever submerges his individuality in society and is able to comprehend himself only as a function of the social, that is, the insensitive and indifferent person, really does forgive. He calmly allows what happened to remain what it was. As the popular saying goes, he lets time heal his wounds... As a deindividualized, interchangeable part of the social mechanism, he lives with it consentingly...[208]

The function of therapy is to talk us out of our justifiable anger; to put some time between the "wounding" and the present; to trick us into accepting our psychic murder as restitution.

It is relevant to point out that after World War II, the German government set up a board to adjudicate and award compensation to Jews who had suffered during the Nazi era. It has always been relatively easy (compared to some things Holocaust survivors have had to put up with) to obtain awards to pay to psychiatrists or psychologists treating individuals for "concentration camp syndrome,"[209] but claims regarding real estate and material wealth that was stolen spawned an entire legal sub-discipline, and litigation of cases continues to this day.[210] Again, we don't know who is looking over whose shoulder, but in another fifty years, perhaps neither Canada nor Germany will have anything to worry about.

CONCLUSIONS

Methodological Individualism and related concepts (Peter Kulchyski's **totalization** and William Ryan's **blaming the victim** come to mind) are not the enigmatic creeds of some obscure cult; they are the means whereby the Splendid Blond Beast can say one thing and do the opposite. In the legal system, in schoolrooms for students of all ages,[211] in social welfare policies and the agencies that implement them, in international politics, and in every other corner of a Westernized world, one can find the **ideology** of individualism.

One is also confronted with the failures of the ideology of methodological individualism, intellectual and otherwise. Lifton and Staub try to understand the "inner dynamics" that allowed people to become Nazi butchers, but are reduced to listing internal, individual paraphrases of "they were bad." The insights of Amery and Bauman are remote from Lifton and Staub's Methodologically Individualistic world, from their very way of thinking. For Bauman sees that modernity **constructs** a distinction between "the rationality of the actor and the rationality of the act," that "reason is a good guide for individual behaviour only on such occasions as the two rationalities resonate and overlap," and that:

> The coincidence of the two rationalities—of the actor and of the action—does not depend on the actor. It depends on the setting of the action, which in turn depends on stakes and resources, none of them controlled by the actor. Stakes and resources are manipulated by those who truly control the situation: who are able to make some choices too costly to be frequently selected by those whom they rule, while securing frequent and massive selection of choices which bring closer their aims and reinforce their control. This capacity does not change, whether the aims of rulers are beneficial or detrimental to the interests of the ruled.[212]

And Bauman sees: "**In a system where rationality and ethics point in opposite directions, humanity is the main loser**. Evil can do its dirty work, hoping that most people most of the time will refrain from doing rash, reckless things—and resisting evil is rash and reckless (p. 206)." Methodological Individualism is not merely the misunderstanding of the Holocaust or Indian Residential Schooling: for the members of the societies that constitute the Splendid Blond Beast, it is a legislated misunderstanding of themselves.

And that part of the Beast that is caring and therapeutic casts a glance around, **and quite properly** sees the pain and suffering it has brought about. But it does not see **that** it has brought it about, nor in a world in which all the mirrors have been covered up can the Beast turn its gaze upon itself. It does not see and does not care to understand its own pathology. Well, in this chapter, we have tried to be its glass.

The idea that we can, should, or will understand the Persian Gulf War by examining the personalities of Bush and Hussein; that racism in our society will be eradicated by "unmaking" racists one by one; that by planting a lot of trees we will build a forest; or that by examining the "mental contents" of the people who ran and the people who attended Residential Schools we will understand what Residential Schools were all about; all these and much more are revealed as being the misdirected presumptions of ideologues, who do not understand (or perhaps ignore) the fact that their tactics and aims follow from an elementary error in undergraduate logic, and are a **studied** ignorance.

CHAPTER 7

RECOMMENDATIONS

When SS-man Wajs stood before the firing squad, he experienced the moral truth of his crimes. At that moment, he was with **me**— and I was no longer alone with the shovel handle. I would like to believe that at the instant of his execution he wanted exactly as much as I to turn back time, to undo what had been done. When they led him to the place of execution, the antiman had once again become a fellow man. If everything had taken place only between SS-man Wajs and me, and if an entire inverted pyramid of SS men, SS helpers, officials, Kapos, and medal-bedecked generals had not weighed on me, I would have died calmly and appeased along with my fellow man with the Death's Head insignia. At least that is the way it seems to me now. Jean Amery, *At the Mind's Limits.*

UNDOING WHAT HAS BEEN DONE

As we read, watched, and listened, what became clear to us was how easy it has been throughout the history of Indian Residential Schooling to absorb and assimilate concerns, criticisms, or pleas into the status quo. When Aboriginal Peoples, concerned bureaucrats, or critical clergy undertook to right obvious wrongs, what got returned to them, when the bureaucracy took any trouble at all respond, was their petition interpreted back to them as something the system of order was already doing, or mangled into something the system was willing to do in its own limited way. The arrogance implicit in **clarifying**, **doing for**, **strongly suggesting**, and similar euphemisms for ignoring, dominating and imposing became a recurrent theme.

We had no interest in being on either side of this rhetorical barrier, neither the petitioners ignored nor the "interpreters" telling people what they "really" said. Consequently, assembling a list of recommendations has been our most difficult task. We felt uncomfortable repeating recommendations made at Royal Commission hearings, in that, as must be apparent from this report, we suspect the sincerity of a good many of them. However, we felt just as ill at ease dismissing or reinterpreting them, for this was what the Beast has done all along to its critics.

What we have tried to do, then, is walk a middle ground and present recommendations based on what we've reviewed and the issues we've raised. Some are indistinguishable from recommendations presented to the RCAP, and some may strike presenters as distorted versions of what they've advised. So be it; we will admit only that this is the best we could do. Our recommendations have been influenced by the philosophical precedent established by Jean Amery's work: that the only moral response to a crime of this magnitude is that it be undone. As impossible as that is, to undertake or demand less is to assure that the injuries done will endure indefinitely. We present our recommendations in no particular order of importance.

RECOMMENDATIONS

One: we recommend a special inquiry be commissioned to investigate all aspects of Indian Residential Schooling, with legislated powers to examine any relevant documents, hear testimony, subpoena witnesses and lay charges.

The call for an inquiry focused on Residential Schools was, apart from therapeutic concerns, the one most frequently raised at the Royal Commission hearings. We admit that early in our work we had doubts about the advisability of such a move; the expense involved, and the time and effort it would take away from developing new initiatives, made it comparatively unattractive to us. However, we were operating under the assumption that the churches and governments would, as the Royal Commission progressed in its work, "come clean" with respect to events and accept their responsibilities. This has not been the case. There does not seem to us to be any way to make progress on the full disclosure of the abuses associated with Indian Residential Schooling without creating a special body with the power to investigate at the limit of what is compatible with the operation of a democratic state.

Two: we recommend comprehensive apologies and recognition of wrongs be offered by all the civil and ecclesiastical organisations that participated in Indian Residential Schooling. The apologies must provide the clear recognition that there can be no mitigation of their responsibility for what happened to, and no question of the nature of the abuses suffered by, Aboriginal Peoples, individually and collectively. The apologies must form part of a campaign to educate Canadian citizens at large of their role, however indirect, in these unconscionable acts.

A major requirement for **Undoing What Has Been Done** is full recognition of What Has Been Done. Any commitment to "undo" which leaves the "what" unspecified is an empty gesture, and as such is not commitment at all. As well, the Canadian public has continued to express skepticism concerning grievances of Aboriginal Peoples with respect to their treatment in Residential Schools; it is time they became educated.

Three: we recommend the establishment of a resource archive on Indian Residential Schooling, modelled upon the Fortunoff Video Archive for Holocaust Testimonies at Yale University.

The Fortunoff Archive was created as a permanent resource against those who deny the reality of the Holocaust. While Indian Residential School revisionism has not yet reached similar abysmal levels, there is no reason to suppose one day they won't; thus, we recommend taking proactive measures. In addition, it is obvious from the Royal Commission transcripts that their hearings were no place for Aboriginal individuals to tell their stories. We also find it unlikely that a special inquiry (even if created) will provide an appropriate atmosphere. In our opinion, that the advisability of providing Aboriginal individuals with the opportunity to recount their experiences in Residential Schools is beyond dispute; consequently, we suggest the creation of this archive to do just that.

The archive should be fully under the control of Aboriginal Peoples, and not necessarily affiliated with any academic setting. We think it should be located in Western Canada, where Residential Schools had their greatest impact, but this of course is only a suggestion. The facility should have the capacity for both fieldwork and transporting contributors to the site, and be capable of working in whatever medium contributors might desire.

Four: we recommend the fair, just, and immediate settlement of land and resource claims.

The politics and legalities of this recommendation are well beyond us, and we hope reports released by the Royal Commission will provide details we cannot. However, in our opinion these are the issues that lie at the heart of the efforts at our destruction. Leaving them unresolved merely invites continued attempts.

Five: we recommend the fair, just, and immediate settlement of
Residential School abuse claims.

If the churches cannot find some way to react to the revelations of the
abuses perpetrated by their designates upon Aboriginal children other than
by temporising, covering up, and offering self-serving tokens, they have
forfeited any claim of morality, warranting the nullification of the privileged status accorded them and exposure of their pretensions of righteous-
ness. If the governments similarly cannot find some other way to react to
the revelations made concerning their designates, they relinquish by a conflict of interest any right to sit in judgment of abuse proceedings, and any
legitimate claim to being anything but despotism.

Six: we recommend the governments and churches establish an
open-ended fund to be used by Aboriginal Nations to undertake
works to reconstitute their societies.

We recommend this in recognition of the fact that the influence of
Indian Residential Schooling carried well beyond solely those injuries,
physical and emotional, that were inflicted upon Aboriginal children incar-
cerated. It further acknowledges that Residential Schools were only one of
the tactics deployed to bring about the "normalization" of Aboriginal
Peoples. We suggest the fund be open-ended simply because there are no
guidelines extant concerning how long such reconstitutions will take and
the costs of the means by which they might be achieved.

How the governments and churches maintain funding levels is none of
the Aboriginal Peoples' business; how the Aboriginal People use it is none
of theirs. In justice, the culprit may sometimes influence the magnitude of
his or her penalty, but has no right to specify how the victim will spend the
award.

Seven: we recommend the dismantling of that part of the
Therapeutic State that impacts upon Aboriginal Peoples, and its
replacement by institutions reflecting Aboriginal philosophies
and under Aboriginal controls.

For far too long the pacific aspect of the Splendid Blond Beast has hidden what it was: the velvet glove covering the mailed fist. While possibly
capable of performing a useful function in Aboriginal communities if suitably modified, its uncritical acceptance is an invitation to the Beast to do as

it pleases. As Sally Kempton warns us, it's hard to fight an enemy with outposts in your own head.

> Eight: we recommend that those suffering the effects of physical,
> sexual, and emotional abuse experienced in Residential School
> be given unrestrained access to the treatment of their choice.

Despite our misgivings about the intent and effectiveness of much of the therapeutic work being done with Aboriginal individuals who were abused in Residential School, we are in no position to prejudge the manner in which an individual has learned to cope. Nor, for that matter, are we or anyone else in a position to decide "how much of what" it will take before he or she feels well enough to continue without such support.

However, we **do** ask those involved in this work: please consider your own standing as an agent of damage-control; **real** therapy has the liberation of your client as its purpose, not the camouflaging of chains, psychic or otherwise.

> Nine: if nothing is to be done in the way of bringing about these
> or similar recommendations, we ask that an open and honest dec-
> laration be made that our destruction, as Aboriginal Peoples, is
> official governmental policy.

Hypocrisy is very thin soup; it nourisheth not, and is also monotonous. We, for two, would rather live out our days on a "level killing field" than to die, in pieces, from a disease we're all too polite to name.

CONCLUSIONS

While working on these recommendations we received any number of warnings, all from Aboriginal sources, to mitigate our analyses. "Be practical," we were told, "recommend something doable, and there's a chance it may happen." Or, "If you come across as too extreme, you'll be dismissed without a hearing; the good will be thrown out with the bad." We recognized the voice of experience talking, but in the end we had to ignore it. There were four reasons.

First, we could find no point in recommending anything less than what we thought would work. We're getting rather tired of the attitude, "Well, we have to do **something**!," and we think we recognized it here. And it matters not at all whether we hear it from an Aboriginal person or someone else. If anything, we're troubled to be hearing it more and more from our own quarter: it smacks of the "willingness and ability to abide by the ideology of the Splendid Blond Beast" we wrote of earlier. Doing something we know is wrong just to do something isn't compromise: it is capitulation. And recommending it isn't being realistic: it is committing suicide.

Second, the "threat" of being marginalized is no threat at all. We all should be used to it by now. Creating a bandwagon in the hopes others will leap onto it might give us the comfortable feeling of being in "the majority," but as Dr. Stockman reminds us, "It takes fifty years for the majority to be right; and then the majority is **never** right, until it **does** right." If people object to our recommendations on conceptual or analytic grounds, and wish to argue about them, or even ignore them, that is one thing. It is quite another to object they are initially unappealing.

Third, why prefigure what Canadians as a whole will be willing to do? Their international reputation, their National self-image, and their Immortal Souls may be as important to them as they say they are. If we are less than honest in what we think it will take to undo what has been done, what right of complaint do we have if they fail to undertake effective measures?

Fourth, by laying out our recommendations, extreme or not, at least they are there, and tied to our understanding of the habits of the Splendid Blond Beast. The Beast that has sought our destruction, and which we have tried to characterize here, is the same Beast leaving its claw marks on Canadian health care, social program, education, and countless areas more remote. Canadians in general thus have more common cause with the whining, complaining Aboriginals than they realize, and someday will have to make the same journey.

Jean Amery never saw even the first step on what he considered the only honest path toward resolution of the Holocaust:

> ... the problem could be settled by permitting resentment to remain alive in the one camp and, aroused by it, self-mistrust in the other. Goaded solely by the spurs of our resentment—and not in the least by a conciliatoriness that, subjectively, is almost always dubious and, objectively, hostile to history—the German people would remain sensitive to the fact that they cannot allow a piece of their national history to be neutralized by time, but must integrate it... It would then, as I sometimes hope, learn to comprehend its past acquiescence in the Third Reich as the total negation not only of the world that it plagued with war and death but also of its own better origins; it would no longer repress or

hush up the twelve years that for us others really were a thousand, but claim them as its realized negation of the world and its self, as its own negative possession. On the field of history there would occur what I hypothetically described earlier for the limited, individual circle: two groups of people, the overpowered and those who overpowered them, would be joined in the desire that time be turned back and, with it, that history become moral. If this demand were raised by the German people, who as a matter of fact have been victorious and already rehabilitated by time, it would have tremendous weight, enough so that by this alone it would already be fulfilled. The German revolution would be made good, Hitler disowned. And in the end Germans would really achieve what the people once did not have the might or the will to do, and what later, in the political power game, no longer appeared to be a vital necessity: the eradication of the ignominy.[213]

Should he have expected less? Should we?

CHAPTER 8

THE CIRCLE GAME

And the seasons, they go 'round and 'round,
And the painted ponies go up and down;
We're captive on a carousel of Time;
We can't return, we can only look
Behind, from where we came;
And go 'round and 'round and 'round
In the Circle Game. *Joni Mitchell*

The circle is a metaphor much used by various North American Aboriginal Nations. The sun; unity; wholeness; the change of seasons; all this and more has, at some time and at some place, been captured by Aboriginal Peoples in the simplicity of a circle. And for the non-Indian inhabitants of North America, the circle, too, is a symbol: the empty nonexistence of zero; the vacuity of circular definitions or circular arguments; the endless loop of the carousel. This contrast was implied in Joni Mitchell's song, although she was not specifically concerned with the cultural dissonance that has been our focus here. Rather, she created an image of a headlong rush to nowhere in particular, where, through the transit of one circle (whether it be that of a carousel or the daily or yearly revolutions of the Earth) we become carried away, imperceptibly, from our starting point.

Like myths, much of the strength of metaphors comes from their ability to assist communication, to simplify the complex, and to clarify the murky or muddled. When questions arise about one people's understanding of another, what better way to show understanding than to use the other's poetic language, to adopt their forms of expression? Yet such uses must be examined thoroughly, for the strength of metaphors immediately identifies them as the tools of rhetoric. When we read and heard circle symbolism being used in a familiar and reassuring manner, but coming from unexpected directions, we looked long and hard. What we saw was an attempt to lull our critical sensibilities. Like those who have told Aboriginal Peoples, "Oh, I understand about Residential School... my parents sent me to boarding school, too!," or "Yes, I know how you feel... I remember being spanked in class for goofing off," the people who spoke of circles in an Aboriginal sense were using them as carousels, to carry their listeners away, imperceptibly, from where the conversation had started.

We wanted off that merry-go-round; it was making us dizzy. The only people who seemed unaffected were those who hadn't been invited on the ride in the first place. At a small presentation of some of the Cariboo Tribal Council work a few years back we had a piece of the research explained to us by a Woman Elder. We had found that "anger" was the primary emotion associated with thinking about Residential School days, but, as we explained, the questionnaire we had used hadn't made provision for determining "anger about what?" "That's easy," she jumped in (and we are paraphrasing her; our apologies), "I'm angry that nothing has ever been done about it. I've been angry for fifty years, and all anybody does is try to talk me out of it! And that makes me angry, too!" In ten seconds or so she had articulated the Standard Account and provided its sincerest refutation.

There was some thought, and perhaps there still is some expectation, that the testimony before the Royal Commission on Aboriginal Peoples would provide the "data" to demonstrate the horrors of Indian Residential School. But it is no more "data" than it is "sworn testimony," and trying to make it something it is not invites its dismissal. Further, once we accept the specious premise that it is up to us to prove what they did was harmful to us, we find ourselves jumping through their hoops. And they have an endless supply of hoops.

But the Commission testimony is information, and what can be extracted from it is more of what that Woman Elder had provided to us many years ago. With the proper delineation of whose responsibility it is to prove what, with a clear notion of what personal narratives can demonstrate and what they cannot, and with awareness of how rhetoric can make shadows appear substantial, careful consideration of Commission testimony carries us toward understanding, not away from it.

ENDNOTES

1. The exceptions will be dealt with in greater detail later in this report.

2. For example: Elizabeth Furniss, *Victims of Benevolence: Discipline and Death at the Williams Lake Indian Residential School, 1891-1920*. Williams Lake, BC: Cariboo Tribal Council, 1992. Isabelle Knockwood, *Out of the Depths: The Experiences of Mi'kmaw Children at the Indian Residential School at Shubenacadie, Nova Scotia*. Lockeport, Nova Scotia: Roseway Publishing, 1992. Celia Haig-Brown, *Resistance and Renewal: Surviving the Indian Residential School*. Vancouver: Tillacum Library, 1988. Wendy Grant, B.C. *Residential Schools: An Historical Overview*. Ottawa: Assembly of First Nations, 1993. E. Brian Titley, "Red Deer Indian Industrial School: A Case Study in the History of Native Education." In Nick Kach and Kas Mazurek (Eds.), *Exploring our Educational Past: Schooling in the Northwest Territories and Alberta*. Calgary: Detselig Enterprises, 1992. E. Brian Titley, *A Narrow Vision: Duncan Campbell Scott and the Administration of Indian Affairs in Canada*. Vancouver: University of British Columbia Press, 1986. K. Tsianina Lomawaima, *They Called it Prairie Light: The Story of Chilocco Indian School*. Lincoln: University of Nebraska Press, 1994.

3. Some reasonable starting points include: Olive Dickason, *Canada's First Nations: A History of Founding Peoples from Earliest Times*, Toronto: McClelland & Stewart, 1992; James Frideres, *Native Peoples in Canada: Contemporary Conflicts*, 4th ed., Scarborough: Prentice Hall, 1993; Richard Gosse, James Henderson, & Roger Carter (Eds.), *Continuing Poundmaker & Riel's Quest: Presentations Made at a Conference on Aboriginal Peoples and Justice*, Saskatoon: Purich Publishing, 1994; Peter Kulchyski (Ed.), *Unjust Relations: Aboriginal Rights in Canadian Courts*, Toronto: Oxford University Press, 1994; and Boyce Richardson, *People of Terra Nullius: Betrayal and Rebirth in Aboriginal Canada*, Vancouver: Douglas & McIntyre, 1993.

4. James Winter, *Common Cents*. Montreal: Black Rose Books, 1992.

5. S. E. Finer, *Five Constitutions: Contrasts and Comparisons*. Markham, Ontario: Penguin Books, 1979, on the British Constitution: "In the first place, there is no authoritative selection of statutes, conventions, common-law rules and the like which together comprise 'the Constitution'; every author is free to make his own selection and to affirm that this is the one, even the only one, that embraces all the most important rules and excludes all the unimportant ones—though nobody has ever been so foolish as to assert this. What is or is not 'the Constitution' is a matter for the scholars' individual judgements." P. 34.

6. See Pierre Vidal-Naquet, *Assassins of Memory*, Columbia University Press, 1992, for a survey of such moral gymnastics.

7. F. Kafka, *The Trial*. New York: Vintage Books, 1964.

8. As cited in E.B. Titley, *A Narrow Vision: Duncan Campbell Scott and the Administration of Indian Affairs in Canada*. Vancouver: UBC Press, 1986. P. 48.

9. From the Royal Commission on Aboriginal Peoples, Special Consultation with the Historic Mission Churches, November 8-9, 1993, p. i-iii of the submission by the Anglican Church of Canada.

10. From the Permanent Council of the Canadian Conference of Catholic Bishops, Let Justice Flow Like a Mighty River. Submission to the Royal Commission on Aboriginal Peoples, November 8-9, 1993, p. i.

11. The United Church of Canada, Brief to the Royal Commission on Aboriginal Peoples, November 8-9, 1993, p. 8.

12. See E. Brian Titley's excellent *A Narrow Vision: Duncan Campbell Scott and the Administration of Indian Affairs in Canada*. Vancouver: University of British Columbia Press, 1986.

13. Jean Chretian, Statement of the Government of Canada on Indian Policy, 1969. Ottawa: Queen's Printer, 1969.

14. Eric Nielsen, Indian and Native Programs, A Study Team Report to the Task Force on Program Review. Ottawa: Minister of Supply and Services, 1985.

15. Helen Buckley, *From Wooden Ploughs to Welfare: Why Indian Policy Failed in the Prairie Provinces*. Montreal: McGill-Queen's University Press, 1992. P. 48.

16. Presentation to the Royal Commission by Ron Eldridge on May 28, 1992.

17. Commissioner Rene Dussault, Royal Commission Proceeding of October 29, 1992.

18. For example, Frank James Tester & Peter Kulchyski, *Tammarniit (Mistakes): Inuit Relocation in the Eastern Arctic, 1939-1963*. Vancouver: UBC Press, 1994.

19. Murray Angus, *"And the Last Shall Be First:" Native Policy in an Era of Cutbacks*. Toronto: NC Press Limited, 1991. Boyce Richardson, *"Concealed Contempt."* In O. McKague (Ed.), Racism in Canada. Saskatoon: Fifth House Publishers, 1991.

20. For an explication of this strategy with regard to Aboriginal Peoples, see Murray Angus, *"And the Last Shall Be First:" Native Policy in an Era of Cutbacks.* Toronto: NC Press Limited, 1991. For accounts dealing with the public at large, see Linda McQuaig, *The Quick and the Dead: Brian Mulroney, Big Business and the Seduction of Canada.* Toronto: Viking Press, 1991; and Sidney Plotkin & William Scheuerman, *Private Interest, Public Spending: Balanced-Budget Conservatism and the Financial Crisis.* Boston: South End Press, 1994.

21. Presentation to the Royal Commission by Robert Grinstead on March 8, 1993.

22. Presentation to the Royal Commission by Harold Rampersad on June 3, 1993.

23. Ron Blinn colourfully likens treatment funding levels to "throwing 3 pork-chops to 14 dogs" in his testimony on May 28, 1992.

24. Permanent Council of the Canadian Conference of Catholic Bishops, Let Justice Flow Like A Mighty River; submission to the Royal Commission on Aboriginal Peoples, November 8-9, 1993, p. ii.

25. United Church of Canada, Brief to the Royal Commission on Aboriginal Peoples; November 8-9, 1993, p. 14.

26. United Church of Canada, Brief to the Royal Commission on Aboriginal Peoples, p. 16.

27. Permanent Council of the Canadian Conference of Catholic Bishops, Let Justice Flow Like A Mighty River, p. 6.

28. Julia Penelope, *Speaking Freely: Unlearning the Lies of Our Father's Tongues.* New York: Pergammon, 1990.

29. As was recalled, for example, by Philip Fontaine in his testimony before the Royal Commission on April 22, 1992.

30. Anne Barstow, *Witchcraze: A New History of the European Witch Hunts*, San Francisco: Pandora Books, 1994, characterises the Witch Hunts as "the greatest [European] mass killing of people by people not caused by war."

31. As intoned by MP Herb Grubel; see the *Vancouver Sun*, June 10, 1994.

32. Anne Llewellyn Barstow, *Witchcraze: A New History of the European Witch Hunts,* San Francisco: Pandora, 1994; Marianne Hester, *Lewd Women and Wicked Witches: A Study of the Dynamics of Male Domination*, London: Routledge, 1992; Thomas Szasz, *The Manufacture of Madness: A Comparative Study of the*

Inquisition and the Mental Health Movement, New York: Harper & Row, 1970; David Oshinsky, *A Conspiracy So Immense: The World of Joe McCarthy*, New York, The Free Press, 1983; Victor Navsky, Naming Names. New York: Penguin Books, 1981.

33. As this report was in review, William Johnson, Ottawa columnist for the *Montreal Gazette*, published a column (which ran August 18, 1994 in the *Vancouver Sun*) critical of the study of Residential Schooling sponsored by the Assembly of First Nations. Part of his critique was based on a blatant misrepresentation of the results of a study the two of us had participated in, but the newspaper has refused to correct the erroneous impression Mr. Johnson has left with his readers that a "controlled study" found "very few differences" between Residential and non-Residential attendees. The Fourth Estate thus seems eager to create and maintain the "pseudocrime" image Mr. Siddon called forth.

34. Just to show this isn't an "Anglican" thing, from page 10 of the Brief by the Permanent Council of the Canadian Conference of Catholic Bishops [all emphases ours]: "What was lost, or nearly so, was the free expression and celebration of the spirituality of the First Peoples of this land. This weakening of the spirit of the Native Peoples was the most profound loss at the heart of the more obvious losses of Native culture and land. This has been a loss for the Native Peoples, but it has also been a lost opportunity of enrichment for this country and our Church. As our North American culture becomes ever more consumed by materialism, we are profoundly in need of learning the values from the wise spirituality of the original Peoples." We might be more inclined to credit sincerity to this expression if it was accurate concerning how things got the way they did. As it is it makes it seem like we should all feel sorry for ourselves, and that it is up to the Aboriginal Peoples to lead the way to a brighter future by rejecting materialism... an evasion identified by Bertrand Russel as "the Superior Virtue of the Oppressed" (*Unpopular Essays,* London, Unwin Books, 1968).

35. "Also, Aboriginal groups are turning their mind towards the future. There is a lot of healing that has to take place following various policies, one of them being of course the residential school policies, but again the message I think is that everybody should, as soon as possible, be able to turn their mind to the building of a new [emphasis added] partnership." R. Dussault, remarks to the Royal Commission, November 3, 1992. Omitted here is any mention of what the "old" partnership was.

36. The Permanent Council of the Canadian Conference of Catholic Bishops, *Let Justice Flow Like A Mighty River*, submission to the Royal Commission on November 8-9, 1993, p. 5.

37. Wolfgang Sachs (Ed.), *The Development Dictionary: A Guide to Knowledge as Power*, London, Zed Books, 1992; Wolfgang Sachs (Special Editor),

"Development: A Guide to the Ruins," *The New Internationalist*, No. 232, June, 1992; Richard Norgaard, Development Betrayed: The End of Progress and a Coevolutionary Revisioning of the Future, London, Routledge, 1994.

38. Page 23, A Brief Prepared by the Anglican Church of Canada, November 8-9, 1993.

39. Presbyterian Church of Canada, Reweaving the Relationship with Aboriginal Peoples, brief submitted to the Royal Commission, November 8-9, 1993, p. 10. We do not, of course, agree with the missionary sentiment expressed, but are merely pointing out that even the churches now realise they moved from spiritual grounds to economic ones.

40. Permanent Council of the Canadian Conference of Catholic Bishops, Let Justice Flow Like A Mighty River, p. 5.

41. Brief to the Royal Commission on Aboriginal Peoples by the Anglican Church of Canada, November 8-9, 1993, p. 7.

42. J. R. Miller, in "The Irony of Residential Schooling," *Canadian Journal of Native Education,* Volume 14, 1987, writes: "Now Indians are organized, politicized and led by people who understand the relationship between the native population and the government. These leaders appreciate the need of the aboriginal peoples to acquire the means to control their own lives. Ironically, it was the residential school, which was designed to be the benign exterminator of Indian identity, that indirectly played a role in its perpetuation and revitalization." We don't really see the irony of this, but rather a certain inevitability. In an era where approximately 50% of all Indian children attended Residential School, and where, of those who didn't, many failed to receive any formal education at all, it isn't hard to expect "the leadership" to have, at some point in learning to read and write, spent time in a Residential School. We don't mean to suggest Dr. Miller shares the agenda of the church officials we cite in this section, but only point out that, once again, people with an axe to grind have appropriated, abstracted, and bent a possibly interesting topic for conversation to their own purposes.
Less in danger of misinterpretation is Chief Justice Marshall of the United States Supreme Court, writing in 1823 and cited in Daniel M. Friedberg, *Life, Liberty, and the Pursuit of Land*, Buffalo, Prometheus Press, 1992: "[T]he bestowing of civilization and Christianity upon the inhabitants of the New World itself [our emphasis] constituted ample compensation for the denial of sovereignty to its original inhabitants." Not a man to haggle with, no doubt.

43. J. R. Miller, "The Irony of Residential Schooling," *Canadian Journal of Native Education*, Volume 14, 1987.

44. Take the following exchange:

Joe: "You're a smelly ignorant fool."
Bob: "What a hurtful and unkind thing to say!"
Joe: "I'm sorry you feel that way."

Joe hasn't retracted anything, but he has, after a fashion, said that he's sorry. The art of apologising without apologising is a growing field of study in rhetoric. Witness a recent effort of the Jesuits trying to "heal" the damage done by one of their number (Mr. Epoch) to victims of sexual abuse in southern Ontario: "Though not accepting liability for the aberrant acts of one of our members, the Jesuits express sorrow, regret and humility for the Epoch acts... (Kitchener-Waterloo Record, November 30, 1994)." While perhaps confusing humility (a feature attributed to someone, not self-ascribed) with humiliation, the structure of the "apology" must have warmed the hearts of lawyers everywhere.

45. Pace the thin coverage (electronic and otherwise) of the "Sacred Assembly" in Ottawa (December, 1995), major churches continue to avoid apologising while acknowledging specific abuses.

46. Another "scare word." To brand someone a radical is like branding them a Witch 300 years ago; it is an attempt to try and convict them, and dismiss their message, without the tedium of having to listen to what they say. In fact, radical means "root" or "fundamental," as in deep rather than superficial or original rather than derivative. If in the "dichotomous logic" forced upon us we have to choose between "radical" analysis and the succession of band-aids passed off on Aboriginal Peoples today, then we choose radical.

47. Page 23-24 of *Let Justice Flow Like A Mighty River:* "Within the Catholic community, we are committed to educating our people at the most foundational [radical] level. In their hearts and minds there must be a profound [radical] and vital sense of the dignity of each person and of the value of diverse cultures. We are committed to creating the possibilities for non-Native Christians to understand the wisdom, the strength and the contribution of the Aboriginal Peoples of this land. We are committed to education that will also make our people more conscious of the ways in which the image of God has been defaced through the injustices done to the Aboriginal Peoples. We will increase awareness of the rights of Aboriginal Peoples, the history of cultural oppression, and the dangers of cultural arrogance." Nice words... they should be followed by nice deeds.

48. From the jacket of K. Tsianina Lomawaima, *They Called It Prairie Light: The Story of Chilocco Indian School.* Lincoln: University of Nebraska Press, 1994.

49. ... as disagreeable as these might be: George Orwell, "Such, Such Were the

Joys," in Volume 4, *The Collected Essays, Journalism and Letters*; London: Penguin Books, 1958.

50. See below, Chapter 4, for substantiation of the charge of genocide.

51. See Chrisjohn and Young, *Among School Children: Psychological Imperialism and the Residential School Experience in Canada*, 1993, included in this report as Appendix E. Also, within each of the presentations made by the Historic Mission Churches to the Royal Commission on Aboriginal Peoples, November 8-9, 1993, are explicit recognitions that sexual, physical, and emotional abuses took place at Indian Residential Schools. Even the pseudo-apology issued by the Indian Affairs Branch in 1991 recognizes that such abuse took place.

52. While not as yet into the wholesale historical revisionism characterising the Holocaust denials, this indeed is a direction in which some hope to move everyone. The leading edge is the attempt to paint Residential Schools as "not as bad" as some former victims have made them out to be. For example, at meetings addressing Residential Schooling a common tactic adopted by church officials has been to bring along former residential school inmates who testify to what a swell time they had there. Of course no one can deny that this was indeed the experience of some individuals, but we merely point out that it is irrelevant: such testimony is the logical equivalent of the defense having people testify at a murder trial that the accused didn't murder them. Also, Footnote 33 brings us some recent brushes we've had with an historical revisionist of the press.

53. Not talking about specifics also has a legal basis (why admit to something that any potential litigant will have to prove in court?) and an aspect of "manufacturing consent," in that, were Canadians at large to know the facts of the matter, they might expect their political and ecclesiastical leaders to do the right thing. All three tactics (don't stir up trouble, admit nothing, keep everyone misinformed) will resurface in what follows.

54. This is not to say that the legal representatives of churches and governments have acquiesced when charges have been brought against their members; the law is about what can or cannot be proved according to its rules of evidence, not what did or did not happen. Thus, for example, it is no contradiction in the European tradition for the churches to admit (as some have in their "apologies") that abuses took place in Residential Schools even as they dispute whether a particular incident of abuse took place or was carried out by a particular official.

55. Stephen Dale, "Guns n' Poses: The Myths of Canadian Peace-keeping," *This Magazine*, Volume 26, Number 7, 1993, p. 12-16.

56. Sharon Scharfe, *Complicity: Human Rights and Canadian Foreign Policy, The*

Case of East Timor. Montreal: Black Rose Books, 1996.

57. See, for example, the collection of news clippings concerning the Williams Lake Residential School revelations, available at the central office of the Cariboo Tribal Council in Williams Lake, BC. Read sequentially, there is at first no credence given the "wild" claims made by victims while official denials are given prominence and respect. Then, as accusations increase and charges are laid, and as similar charges by non-Indians are made against Catholic orders elsewhere in Canada, the lineaments of the Standard Account begin to appear: some abuses probably occurred, but what is needed most is understanding, forgiveness, and healing.

58. As of mid-1996, members of the Reform Party seemed most intent on auditioning for the role of "wag" in this comedy.

59. Brief, submitted by The Anglican Church of Canada to the Royal Commission on Aboriginal Peoples, November 8-9, 1993, p. 19.

60. See, especially, page 76 of this document.

61. Presentation to the Royal Commission by Elmer Courchene on October 29, 1992.

62. Presentation to the Royal Commission by Charles Joseph Bernard, Jr. on May 6, 1992.

63. Presentation to the Royal Commission by John Joe Sark on May 5, 1992.

64. Presentation to the Royal Commission by Sara Jerome on May 7, 1992.

65. Presentation to the Royal Commission by Edmond Metatawabin on November 5, 1992.

66. Presentation to the Royal Commission by Charlie Cootes, May 20, 1992.

67. Wilson Okemaw, testimony before the Royal Commission, June 10, 1992.

68. Presentation to the Royal Commission by Jeannie Dick on March 8, 1993.

69. Presentation to the Royal Commission by Arthur Darren Durocher on May 27, 1992.

70. Presentation to the Royal Commission by Stephen Sunnipas on May 6, 1992.

71. Angela Sheeshish, testimony before the Royal Commission, November 5, 1992.

72. Presentation to the Royal Commission by Philip Fontaine on April 22, 1992.

73. Dave Belleau, testimony before the Royal Commission, March 8, 1993.

74. Patrick Bruyere, testimony before the Royal Commission, October 29, 1992.

75. Lawrence L. Langer, *Holocaust Testimonies: The Ruins of Memory*. New Haven: Yale University Press, 1991.

76. See, for example, Eric Robinson and Henry Bird Quinney, T*he Infested Blanket: Canada's Constitution—Genocide of Indian Nations*. Winnipeg: Queenston House Publishing, 1985; Robert Davis and Mark Zannis, *The Genocide Machine in Canada: The Pacification of the North*. Montreal: Black Rose Books, 1973; Maggie Hodgson, *"Spirituality vs. Religion"* and First Nation's Response to Healing of A Government's Decision to Set Social Policy to Dictate Christianity as the Solution to Assimilate Our People. Edmonton: Nechi Institute, 1991; Wendy Grant, B.C. Residential Schools: An Historical Overview. Ottawa: Assembly of First Nations, 1993.
The term "genocide" came up briefly a number of times at Royal Commission hearings concerned with Indian Residential Schools (for example, Will Basque's presentation on June 5, 1992; Charles Cootes' presentation on June 20, 1992). However, none of the Commissioners probed the assertions in their responses, in essence reacting politely to what was treated as a rhetorical flourish.

77. Primary among these sources have been Ward Churchill, *"Bringing the Law Home: Application of the Genocide Convention in the United States,"* in W. Churchill (Ed.) *Indians Are Us Culture and Genocide in Native North America*. Toronto: Between the Lines, 1994; Robert Davis and Mark Zannis, *The Genocide Machine in Canada: The Pacification of the North*. Montreal: Black Rose Books, 1973; Leo Kuper, International Action Against Genocide. London: Minority Rights Group, 1982; B. V. A. Roling and Antonio Cassese, *The Tokyo Trial and Beyond: Reflections of a Peacemonger*. Cambridge: Polity Press, 1993; Christopher Simpson, *The Splendid Blond Beast: Money, Law, and Genocide in the Twentieth Century*. New York: Grove Press, 1993; Zygmunt Bauman, *Modernity and the Holocaust*. Ithaca, New York: Cornell University Press, 1989.

78. There are some interesting variations on this. Some have argued that since all the Indians weren't killed, it couldn't have been genocide. We simply ask, did the Nazis succeed in killing all the Jews? That intellectual of the Right, Rush Limbaugh, has written "There are more American Indians alive today than there were when Columbus arrived or at any other time in history. Does this sound like

a record of genocide?" No, it reads like a record of stupidity. Not only is his assertion based on a known underestimate of pre-Columbian North American Indian populations, (see Al Franken's *Rush Limbaugh Is A Big Fat Idiot* and Other Observations. New York: Delacorte Press, 1996, p. 52-53) The Worldwide Jewish population has now climbed past pre-Nazi levels. Does he mean to suggest the Holocaust never took place?

79. In The Story of a *National Crime: An Appeal for Justice to the Indians of Canada*, Ottawa: Hope & Sons, 1922, Peter Bryce (Chief Medical Officer of the Indian Department from 1904 to 1921) documented a pattern of Canadian government neglect of First Nations health that he would have called "genocide" had the word existed in 1922. First Nations peoples were dying from tuberculosis at unprecedented rates (higher, it was later noted, than the death rates at some Nazi concentration camps) while perfectly operational programs of treatment were successfully being implemented for non-Indian Canadians. A connection between Residential Schools and the spread of TB was obvious to Bryce, although the precise relation was never investigated.

Bryce was hardly the "bleeding heart" he might be portrayed as today: he didn't have any problem with the "civilizing" mandate of the Indian Department, and assisted in the program of demonizing the developmentally challenged of Canada in the early years of this century (see P. Rooke and R. Schnell, *Discarding the Asylum: From Child Rescue to the Welfare State in English-Canada 1800-1950*, New York: University Press of America, 1983. For the pattern Canadian organisations were following, see J. Trent, Inventing the Feeble Mind: A History of Mental Retardation in the United States, Los Angeles: University of California Press, 1994). Even a conventional hard-liner like Bryce, however, could not keep silent about the government's unconscionable treatment of human being to whom it owed an obvious debt.

80. Duncan Scott, cited in E. Brian Titley, *A Narrow Vision*, p. 50. The Bill referred to here is the controversial Bill 14, an amendment to the Indian Act which permitted the federal government unilaterally to enfranchise (annul the Indian status of) anyone they chose. It also restated the government's "right" to compel attendance at Indian Residential Schools. Why school attendance should be twinned with unilateral powers of arbitrary cultural genocide is an issue to which we shall return.

81. William Ryan, *Blaming the Victim*. New York: Random House, 1971.

82. E. Brian Titley, *A Narrow Vision*.

83. W. Michael Reisman and Chris T. Antoniou, *The Laws of War: A Comprehensive Collection of Primary Documents of International Laws Governing Armed Conflict*. New York: Vintage Books, 1994.

84. Ramsey Clark, *The Fire This Time: U.S. War Crimes in the Gulf*. New York: Thunder's Mouth Press, 1992; Michael Walzer, *Just and Unjust Wars: A Moral Argument with Historical Illustrations*. New York: Basic Books, 1992; Burleigh Taylor Wilkins, Terrorism and Collective Responsibility. London: Routledge, 1992.

85. Ward Churchill, *Indians Are Us* Toronto: Between the Lines Press, 1994, p. 45.

86. An episode described in Davis and Zannis, *The Genocide Machine in Canada*. They also speculate on Canada's own self-interest in avoiding scrutiny on cultural genocide charges.

87. Patrick Thornberry, *Minorities and Human Rights Law*. London: The Minority Rights Group, 1991, p. 13-14.

88. The United Nations position is presented in *UNESCO, Race and Science*. New York: Columbia University Press, 1961. Pat Shipman, *The Evolution of Racism: Human Differences and the Use and Abuse of Science*. New York: Simon & Schuster, 1994, sketches an interesting history of the controversies surrounding the United Nations statement on race.

89. Frank Chalk and Kurt Jonassohn, *The History and Sociology of Genocide*. New Haven, Connecticut: Yale University Press, 1990, p. 50.

90. Angus McLaren, *Our Own Master Race: Eugenics in Canada, 1885-1945*. Toronto: McClelland & Stewart, 1990.

91. See Ward Churchill, *Indians Are Us?*, p. 16-23.

92. B. V. A. Roling and Antonio Cassese, *The Tokyo Trial and Beyond: Reflections of a Peacemonger*. Cambridge: Polity Press, 1993, p. 56.

93. Zygmunt Bauman, *Modernity and the Holocaust*, p. 119.

94. Robert S. Allen, *His Majesty's Indian Allies: British Indian Policy in the Defense of Canada*, 1774-1815. Toronto: Dundurn Press, 1993. Paul Williams, The Chain. Toronto, Author, 1978.

95. Brief to the Royal Commission by the Anglican Church of Canada, p. 4. Note another rhetorical trick here: the genocide of Aboriginal Peoples is presented as assisting the Aboriginal People, and not the government. Just whose work does the church pretend it was doing?

96. P. A. Renaud, *"Education for Acculturation." In Residential Education for*

Indian Acculturation. Ottawa: Indian and Eskimo Welfare Commission, Oblate Father in Canada, 1958, p. 36.

97. Oblate Fathers in Canada, "Background and Objectives," Residential Education for Indian Acculturation. Ottawa: Indian and Eskimo Welfare Commission, 1958. Spellings and inconsistencies are as given in the original.

98. E. Brian Titley, *"Red Deer Indian Industrial School,"* 1992, p. 55.

99. J. R. Miller, *"Owen Glendower, Hotspur, and Canadian Indian Policy,"* Ethnohistory, Volume 37, 1990, p. 396.

100. E. Brian Titley, *A Narrow Vision*, p. 75.

101. Hana Samek, *The Blackfoot Confederacy 1880-1920: A Comparative Study of Canadian and U.S. Indian Policy*. Albuquerque: University of New Mexico Press, 1991, p. 140.

102. Alexander Cockburn, *Corruptions of Empire: Life Studies and the Reagan Era*. London: Verso, 1987. We have encountered an interesting variation of this theme in our work on Residential Schooling: "Why do Indian harp about the past? What good will it do to harass some old priests and bureaucrats? Do they think criminal prosecutions will give them back their childhoods or make them mentally and spiritually healthy today?"
Notice once again the decided turn into the Standard Account, that the point of prosecution is individual, personal therapy. In response, we've asked: Which criminal prosecution procedure is it that undoes the crime? If someone were to say "Well, we know so-and-so murdered your son, but prosecuting him isn't going to bring your boy back to life," or "We understand you suffered a lot of stress when so-and-so burgled your house and terrorized you, but we got your stuff back and throwing him in jail isn't going to undo the mental torment you underwent so we're not going to charge him," would anyone think this makes sense?

103. As we have held elsewhere (Chrisjohn & Young, Research and Residential Schooling: Ideas for First Nations Individuals and Communities, 1993, included in this report as Appendix B), matters of morality are conceptual issues, not empirical ones, and thus "data" (findings, results of experiments, etc.) do not bear on moral issues. The philosophical arguments behind this deserve attention, but here we must suggest additional reading rather than treat it directly in the text. We recommend Paul Johnston, *Wittgenstein and Moral Philosophy*. London, Routledge, 1989; Zygmunt Bauman, *Modernity and the Holocaust*. Ithaca, New York: Cornell University Press, 1989; and Zygmunt Bauman, *Postmodern Ethics*, Oxford: Blackwell, 1993. *Modernity and the Holocaust*, in particular, would repay close study many times over.

104. Useful recent summaries of views on objectivity are Louise M. Anthony & Charlotte Witt (Eds.), *A Mind of One's Own: Feminist Essays on Reason & Objectivity*. San Francisco: Westview Press, 1993; and Allan Megill (Ed.), *Rethinking Objectivity*. Durham, North Carolina: Duke University Press, 1994.

105. Michael Parenti, Human Nature and Politics. Videotape of a speech given in 1990, available from People's Video, P.O. Box 99514, Seattle, Washington, 98199.

106. See, for example, Elizabeth Furniss, *Victims of Benevolence*, or Peter Bryce, *The Story of a National Crime*.

107. From Information on Ireland, *Nothing But the Same Old Story: The Roots of Anti-Irish Racism*. Nottingham, The Russell Press, 1984, p. 27.

108. Some examples of sound, involved social scientists are E. Brian Titley, Howard Zinn, Stephanie Coontz, John Shotter, and Julia Penelope.

109. Attributed to George Washington, 1783.

110. Of course, this discussion should not be taken as endorsing the self-serving legalistic double-talk that has been created to "explain" and legitimise the European countries' acquisition of land in the Americas. For example, the acquisition of land by conquest, recognized in international law, is nothing more than "Might Makes Right" dressed up in sheep's clothing. The concept of the "Just War" is thinly-veiled fraud, as reflected in Sepulveda's position (as cited in Tzvetan Todorov's *The Conquest of America,* New York, Harper & Row, 1984, p. 154) that a legitimate war was:
1. To subject by force of arms men whose natural condition is such that they should obey others, if they refuse such obedience and no other recourse remains.

2. To banish the portentous crime of eating human flesh, which is a special offense to nature, and to stop the worship of demons instead of God, which above all else provokes His wrath, together with the monstrous rite of sacrificing men.

3. To save from grave perils the numerous innocent mortals whom these barbarians immolate every year placating their gods with human hearts.

4. War on the infidels is justified because it opens the way to propagation of Christian religion and eases the task of the missionaries.

Reason 1 is racism, hatched by Columbus to justify his genocide of "New World" inhabitants and his creation of the African slave trade; Reason 2 is an old canard, exposed by Arens in *The Man Eating Myth*, where he shows that the "cannibals" were always "the people who live somewhere over that way," and that the only self-confessed practicing cannibals in existence are Catholics; Reason 3 is mouthed by a man of a faith responsible for the Inquisitions; and Reason 4 lip-service used ever-afterwards to justify human slaughter. Richard Hakluyt, in trying to persuade Elizabeth I to Colonise the Americas, gave Sepulveda's Reason 4 as his Reason 1. "Amusingly," writes Daniel Friedenberg (in Life, Liberty, and the Pursuit of Land), "Hakluyt concludes with a list of men useful in colonizing, and though it is long—including fisherman, husbandmen, construction men, and soldiers—somehow he forgets to include Anglican ministers."

Another long-time favourite, that the land was "uninhabited" (the doctrine of *terra nulluis*), is now recognized as a fabrication even by Australia. The early settlers there set about trying to turn their "discovery" into *terra nulluis* with gunfire, starvation, and the like, but Australian courts have recently rejected the "doctrine" (see Footnote 144).

Finally, the Eurocentric notion (prominent in McEachern's racist judgment against the Gitksan-Wet-suwet-en land claim; see Frank Cassidy [Ed.], *Aboriginal Title in British Columbia*: Delgamuukw v. the Queen, Lantzville, BC: Oolichan Books, 1992) that the Aboriginal Peoples were not putting the land to its "proper" use, thus justifying its seizure by people who would, was not only articulated on the basis of a systematic evasion of fact about Aboriginal lifestyles (see, for example, Chapter 5 of Francis Jennings *The Invasion of America: Indians, Colonialism, and the Cant of Conquest*. New York: Norton, 1975), it hasn't been taken to its logical consequence: is cutting down all the trees and polluting the water "proper" use "Loading the ground with PCB's or Agent Orange" Or, even more simply, isn't someone not presently driving her car in effect putting it up for grabs (after all, it's not being employed in its "proper" use)?

All these "principles" smack of invention to justify what had already been done. In fact, the process of land acquisition in the Americas comes down to three points: (1) people owned and possessed that which other people (European men) coveted; (2) the European men had the technological might to take what they coveted; and (3) the European men were bloodthirsty and unprincipled enough to take what they coveted.

111. See, for example, Bradford W. Morse, *Aboriginal Peoples and the Law: Indian, Metis and Inuit Rights in Canada*, Revised 1st Edition. Ottawa: Carleton University Press, 1991; Peter Kulchyski (Ed.), *Unjust Relations: Aboriginal Rights in Canadian Courts*. Toronto: Oxford University Press, 1994; L. C. Green and Olive P. Dickason, *The Law of Nations and the New World*. Edmonton: University of Alberta Press, 1993. By "impartial" we of course do not mean the Canadian court system; it is part and parcel of the Euro-Canadian system responsible for the thefts. The point, with respect to Aboriginal rights, is made most clearly by Kulchyski: "There can be no answer to the question 'what are Aboriginal rights?' that is not in the terms of the dominant, non-Native society, a society that strives

for fixity, for the definite and for definitions. Or, any answer to the question 'what are Aboriginal rights?' is already an attempt to confine, constrain, demarcate, and delimit those rights and consequently part of the process of confining, constraining, demarcating, and delimiting Aboriginal peoples" (p. 4).

112. See Chapter 5, below.

113. Christopher Simpson, *The Splendid Blond Beast*, p. 286.

114. In Hitler's Germany, for example, at least some diplomats were convinced of the necessity (even morality) of killing Jews by being able to frame the issue to themselves as a ploy in international negotiations; some doctors were co-opted by seeing the Final Solution as an issue of public health or medical research; at least some functionaries were brought on board by being able to treat it wholly as a problem in bureaucratic organization; and so on. See Christopher R. Browning, *The Path to Genocide: Essays on Launching the Final Solution*. Cambridge: Cambridge University Press, 1992; Christopher R. Browning, *Ordinary Men: Reserve Police Battalion 101 and the Final Solution in Poland*. New York: HarperCollins Books, 1993; Paul Weindling, *Health, Race and German Politics between National Unification and Nazism*, 1870-1945. Cambridge: Cambridge University Press, 1989; Zygmunt Bauman, *Modernity and the Holocaust*. Ithaca, New York: Cornell University Press, 1989.

115. Peter Kulchyski's (*Unjust Relations*, p. 1) has aptly described this attitude as "Totalization: the process by which objects, people, spaces, times, ways of thinking, and ways of seeing are ordered in accordance with a set of principles conducive to the accumulation of capital and the logic of the commodity form."

116. Some have argued that Aboriginal Peoples themselves embraced and fought for the creation of Residential Schools, one implication being that they thereby become complicit in abuses associated with them. In rebuttal, only two points need be made: first, Indian Residential Schools were at the time the only schools the government of Canada offered Aboriginal Peoples, so the "choice" being presented was between bad education and no education at all. Had the government presented a third option, say, Aboriginally controlled on-site day schools, we question whether even a single Residential School would ever have been built.
Second, as the targets of genocide, we find it impossible to believe the word "choice" applies in any way to their actions. In this regard, it should be recalled that some Jewish groups set up police forces ("Judenrat") to assist in the implementation of Nazi policy in the Ghettos and concentration camps. Furthermore, in some cases, Jews paid for their own transportation to the death camps. Does anyone seriously maintain such actions were "choices" signalling their desire for or acquiescence to or complicity in genocide? By extension we reject any notion that First Nations parents or organisations are responsible in any way for Residential

Schools: as oppressed, marginalised populations, First Nations were offered an immoral pseudo-choice by the government, a pseudo-choice designed to implicate them unfairly in their own destruction. For a parallel analysis see Bauman's *Modernity and the Holocaust.*

117. Jason Berry, *Lead Us Not Into Temptation: Catholic Priests and the Sexual Abuse of Children.* New York: Doubleday, 1992, p. 371.

118. To the retrograde mentality that here objects "Wait a minute, I know quite a few Indians that have done pretty good!" we limit ourselves here to pointing out that a People isn't a collection of individuals. If this isn't enough to quell the "objection," the reader will have to await Chapter 6.

119. Christopher Simpson, *The Splendid Blond Beast: Money, Law, and Genocide in the Twentieth Century.* New York: Grove Press, 1993, p. 285.

120. Christopher Simpson, *The Splendid Blond Beast*, p. 287.

121. We do not say "all."

122. Michael Parenti, *Land of Idols: Political Mythology in America.* New York: St Martin's Press, 1994, Chapter 5.

123. With the demise of the first two factors, of course, the third factor assumes priority as the rationale behind public education: "'Parent choice' proceeds from the belief that the purpose of education is to provide individual students with an education. In fact, educating the individual is but a means to the true end of education, which is to create a viable social order to which individuals contribute and by which they are sustained. 'Family choice' is, therefore, basically selfish and anti-social in that it focuses on the 'wants' of a single family rather than the 'needs' of society." Quoted (and effectively disputed) in Richard Mitchell, *The Leaning Tower of Babel.* New York: Simon and Schuster, 1984, P. 241. For a look at what corporate society has lined up for Canadians specifically, see John Calvert & Larry Kuehn, *Pandora's Box: Corporate Power, Free Trade and Canadian Education.* Toronto: Our Schools/Our Selves Education Foundation, 1994.

124. See Martine Sonnet, "A Daughter to Educate." In Natalie Zemon Davis & Arlette Farge, (Eds.), *A History of Women in the West: Volume III, Renaissance and Enlightenment Paradoxes.* Cambridge, Massachusetts: Belknap Press, 1993.

125. See Nancy Tuana, *The Less Noble Sex: Scientific, Religious, and Philosophical Conceptions of Women's Nature.* Bloomington, Indiana: Indiana University Press, 1993.

126. See Dena Attar, *Wasting Girls' Time: The History and Politics of Home Economics*. London: Virago Press, 1990; Carol Jones & Pat Mahony (Eds.), *Learning Our Lines: Sexuality and Social Control in Education*. London: The Women's Press, 1989; Dale Spender, *Invisible Women: The Schooling Scandal*. London: The Women's Press, 1982.

127. It is doubtless the case that many groups preexisted the various Celtic nations that were encountered in the British Isles at the beginning of historical times. By the time of the nation-building of the Medieval period, however, Celtic and pre-historic forms had blended.

128. A. L. Morton, *A People's History of England*. London: Lawrence & Wishart, 1938.

129. Nicholas P. Canny, "The Ideology of English Colonization: From Ireland to America." William and Mary Quarterly, Vol. 30, 1973, p. 575-598; Information on Ireland, *Nothing But the Same Old Story: The Roots of Anti-Irish Racism.* Nottingham: The Russell Press, 1984. Milan Rai, *"Columbus in Ireland." Race and Class, Vol. 34*, 1993, p. 25-34; Bill Rolston, "The Training Ground: Ireland, Conquest and Decolonisation." *Race and Class, Vol. 34*, 1993, p. 13-24.

130. From Nancy C. Dorian, *Language Death: The Life Cycle of a Scottish Gaelic Dialect,* Philadelphia: University of Pennsylvania Press, 1981, p. 21: "From the society's founding in 1709 up until 1766, the use of Gaelic was forbidden in S.S.P.C.K. schools, despite the fact that most of those schools were in monolingual Gaelic-speaking areas. The goals of the society appear clearly set forth in its 1716 Memorial to the Court of Police: 'Nothing can be more efectuall for reducing these countries [that is, the Highlands and Islands] to order and making them usefull to the Commonwealth than teaching them their duty to God, their King and Country, and rooting out their Irish language.'" See also Oliver Macdonagh, *States of Mind: Two Centuries of Anglo-Irish Conflict*, 1770-1980. London: Pimlico, 1983; Information on Ireland, *Nothing But the Same Old Story: The Roots of Anti-Irish Racism*. Nottingham, The Russell Press, 1984; Ray Hindley, *The Death of the Irish Language: A Qualified Obituary*. London: Routledge, 1990; Charles W. J. Withers, Gaelic in Scotland, 1698-1981: *The Geographical History of a Language*. Edinburgh: John Donald Publishers, 1984, esp. Chapter 7. Welsh may be something of an exception to this form of imperial domination, at least early in English history. It remained so strong a language that church officials chose to operate within it instead of forcing the courtly language down everyone's throat. Its decline was more a result of discriminatory language and economic policies against Irish and Scottish Gaelic during the 1800s. See Roland Mathias, *"The Welsh Language and the English Language,"* in Meic Stephens (Ed.), *The Welsh Language Today*. Llandysul: Gomer Press, 1973.

131. John Prebble, *The Highland Clearances*. London: Penguin Books, 1969; Marianne McLean, *The People of Glengarry: Highlanders in Transition, 1745-1820*. Montreal and Kingston: McGill-Queen's University Press, 1991.

132. Anne Llewellyn Barstow, Witchcraze: *A New History of the European Witch Hunts*. London: Pandora, 1994; Bill Rolston, "The Training Ground: Ireland, conquest and decolonisation." *Race and Class, Vol. 34*, 1993, p. 13-24; Reginald Horsman, *Race and Manifest Destiny: The Origins of American Racial Anglo-Saxonism*. Cambridge, Massachusetts: Harvard University Press, 1981; Information on Ireland, *Nothing But the Same Old Story: The Roots of Anti-Irish Racism*. Nottingham: The Russell Press, 1984.

133. Robert S. Allen, *His Majesty's Indian Allies: British Indian Policy in the Defense of Canada, 1774-1815*. Toronto: Dundurn Press, 1993.

134. See Alan Moorehead, *The Fatal Impact: An Account of the Invasion of the South Pacific, 1767-1840*. Harmondsworth, England: Penguin Books, 1966, p. 96.

135. About the missionaries Alan Moorehead (*The Fatal Impact: An Account of the Invasion of the South Pacific, 1767-1840*. Harmondsworth, England: Penguin Books, 1966) writes: "They had little interest in anthropology or in Tahitian rites and customs—indeed, they were out to suppress them. They were not collectors, nor were they concerned with scientific discoveries, nor had they any of Cook's tolerance and gift for compromise. They were practical workers in the cause of the Lord, and they were determined to recreate the island in the image of lower-middle-class Protestant England (p. 107-108)." See also Charlotte Haldane (*Tempest Over Tahiti*, London: Constable & Co., 1963) and David Howarth (*Tahiti: Paradise Lost*, London: Harvill Press, 1983) for additional, but somewhat more Eurocentric, accounts of Tahiti's destruction.

136. Erich Weingartner, *The Pacific: Nuclear Testing and Minorities*. London: The Minority Rights Group, 1991.

137. Or maybe it's Kwajalein; see Alexander Cockburn, *"The Truth about the Blue Lagoon,"* in A. Cockburn (Ed.), *Corruptions of Empire*. New York: Verso, 1987, p. 173-177; and Jane Dibblin, *Day of Two Suns: US Nuclear Testing and the Pacific Islanders*. London: Virago Press, 1988.

138. Robert Hughes, *The Fatal Shore: The Epic of Australia's Founding*. New York: Random House, 1988, p. 275.

139. J. Brook and J. L. Kohen, *The Parramatta Native Institution and the Black Town: A History. Kensington, Australia:* New South Wales University Press, 1991; Julian Burger, *Aborigines Today: Land and Justice*. London: Anti-Slavery Society, 1988.

140. See J. Brook & J. L. Kohen, *The Parramatta Native Institution and the Black Town: A History. Kensington, Australia*: New South Wales University Press, 1991.

141. The point, once again, is not whether Australian Aboriginal Peoples "had" a concept of land ownership identical to that of the Europeans; trials about car theft don't begin with establishing that all interested parties have the "same" conception of theft, ownership, private property, etc., nor would demonstrating any conceptual difference warrant the theft. It is that in the European concept of land ownership, and therefore according to the European's own rules, the Australian Aboriginal Peoples were the owners. New rules therefore had to be concocted on the spot and the Aboriginal Peoples beaten into accepting them, or the Aboriginal Peoples had to be eliminated (physically or culturally).

142. Henry Reynolds, *The Other Side of the Frontier: Aboriginal Resistance to the European Invasion of Australia*. Markham, Ontario: Penguin Books, 1982; David Pollard, *Give and Take: The Losing Partnership in Aboriginal Poverty*. Marrickwille, NSW: Hale & Iremonger Pty Limited, 1988.

143. Although we found Brook and Kohen's account of Parramatta interesting, they have a pronounced tendency to portray the education of Aboriginal children as a "noble attempt that failed," which of course is the same rhetorical blindness we dispute with respect to Indian education in Canada.

144. For an up-to-date and multifaceted account of the decision and its ramifications, see *Race and Class, Vol. 35*, No. 4, April-June 1994, for a special issue compiled by Peter Poynton, *"Aboriginal Australia: Land, Law and Culture."*

145. See Philip G. Altbach & Gail P. Kelly (Eds.), *Education and the Colonial Experience*. New Brunswick, New Jersey: Transaction Books, 1984; Johannes Fabian, *Language and Colonial Power: The Appropriation of Swahili in the Former Belgian Congo* 1880-1938. Berkeley: University of California Press, 1986; Timothy J. Scrase, *Image, Ideology and Inequality: Cultural Domination, Hegemony and Schooling in India*. London: Sage Publications, 1993; V. G. Kiernan, *The Lords of Human Kind: European Attitudes to the Outside World in the Imperial Age*. Harmondsworth, England: Penguin Books, 1972; Basil Davidson, *The Black Man's Burden: Africa and the Curse of the Nation-State*. New York: Random House, 1992; Basil Davidson, *Africa in History*. New York: Collier Books, 1991; Nat Colletta, *American Schools for the Natives of Ponape: A Study of Education and Cultural Change in Micronesia*. Honolulu: University Press of Hawaii, 1980; Alan Ward, *A Show of Justice: Racial "Amalgamation" in Nineteenth Century New Zealand*. Toronto: University of Toronto Press, 1973.

146. See Randy Fred's Preface to C. Browns's *Resistance and Renewal*, 1988.

147. Nikolai Vakhtin, *Native Peoples of the Russian Far North*. London: The Minority Rights Group, 1992. This monograph is also reprinted in the MRG book, *Polar Peoples: Self-Determination and Development*. London, Minority Rights Group, 1994. Also relevant is James Forsyth's *A History of the Peoples of Siberia: Russia's North Asian Colony 1581-1990*. Cambridge: Cambridge University Press, 1992.

148. Again, the example of the Russian treatment of its Siberian minorities should in no way be taken as the only example of how the modern State (of whatever political persuasion) deals with educating an underclass: for examples, Bulgaria operated and continues to operate Residential Schools for the Rom minority (Isabel Fonseca, *Bury Me Standing: The Gypsies and their Journey*, New York: Knopf, 1995), while India's educational system for the Adivasi (i.e., Indigenous Peoples) is shrouded in enough secrecy as to permit only the knowledge that it is oppressive, perfunctory, and residential (Roger Moreau, The Rom, Toronto: Key Porter Books, 1994, and Randy Fred, Preface to *Resistance and Renewal*, Tillacum Library, 1988). Even with these additions, our list is far from complete.

149. N. Vakhtin, *Native Peoples of the Russian Far North*, p. 22.

150. Quoted in Vakhtin, *Native Peoples of the Russian Far North*, p. 17.

151. James Forsyth, *A History of the Peoples of Siberia*, p. 397.

152. V. G. Kiernan, *The Lords of Human Kind: European Attitudes to the Outside World in the Imperial Age*. Harmondsworth, England: Penguin Books, 1972, p. 276.

153. Erving Goffman, *Asylums: Essays on the Social Situation of Mental Patients and Other Inmates*. Garden City, New York: Anchor Books, 1961.

154. However, the relevance of his analysis to Indian Residential Schools has not been overlooked; see, for example, Diane Persson, *"The Changing Experience of Indian Residential Schooling: Blue Quills, 1931-1970."* In J. Barman, Y. Hebert, and D. McCaskill (Eds.), *Indian Education in Canada, Volume 1: The Legacy*. Vancouver, UBC Press, 1986; Sandi Montour, *Indian Residential Schools*. Six Nations: Author, 1991; Assembly of First Nations, Breaking the Silence. Ottawa: Assembly of First Nations, 1994.

155. Family resemblances, as discussed by L. Wittgenstein, are concepts without necessary and sufficient membership conditions. For example, there is no characteristic shared by all things we call games; rather, there are overlapping features

that are present or absent in any particular game. We get a sense of what game means not by specifying what quality something must have in order to be a game, but by putting forth examples of games and saying... and activities like that.? Wittgenstein showed that a demand for clear and unambiguous definitions was fundamentally misguided, since, apart from mathematical concepts (which have no necessary relation to the external world), such definitions have nothing to do with how most of our language works; family resemblances (and other variations he analysed) were far better depictions. Goffman provided what in fact was a family resemblance description of total institutions: "Before I attempt to extract a general profile from this list of establishments, I would like to mention one conceptual problem [sic]: none of the elements I will describe seems peculiar to total institutions, and none seems to be shared by every one of them; what is distinctive about total institutions is that each exhibits to an intense degree many items in the family of attributes. In speaking of 'common characteristics,' I will be using this phrase in a way that is restricted but I think logically defensible (*Asylums*, p. 5)."

156. Goffman, *Asylums*, p. 12.

157. Goffman, *Asylums*, p. 14.

158. Goffman, *Asylums*, p. 16.

159. Goffman, *Asylums*, p. 28-29.

160. Goffman, *Asylums*, p. 19.

161. Goffman, *Asylums*, p. 14-15.

162. Goffman, *Asylums*, p. 21.

163. Goffman, *Asylums*, p. 11.

164. Goffman, *Asylums*, p. 13.

165. Goffman, *Asylums*, p. 43.

166. Isabelle Knockwood, *Out of the Depths*. Much more could be cited from this extraordinary work, but please read the book for yourself.

167. For example, Nellie Carlson, testimony before the Royal Commission, June 11, 1992; Linda Bull, *"Indian Residential Schooling,"* p. 39; Isabelle Knockwood, *Out of the Depths*, Chapter 3; Roland Chrisjohn et al., "Faith Misplaced," Table 1. Generalisations drawn in this section derive from the sources listed in Chapter 3.

168. Goffman, *Asylums,* p. 33. Zygmunt Bauman (*Modernity and the Holocaust.* Ithaca, New York: Cornell University Press, 1989) mentions a related phenomenon: couples who are victims of the same hostage-taking incidents often split up shortly after the incident becomes resolved. He speculates (as do others) that observing your "significant other" grovel in the face of terrorism destroys the trust relationship between couples. The Residential School's disciplinary structure, via the Goffmanesque "permanent mortification," thus may have created permanent distance in the Aboriginal World between family, friends, and future spouses.

169. The Assembly of First Nations report, Breaking the Silence, does a thorough job of enumerating this toxic atmosphere.

170. Linda Bull, *"Indian Residential School,"* p. 41.

171. In case a review is needed, they are: (1) incidents of sexual, physical, and/or emotional abuses experienced by students; and (2) the students' placement in an organization which conducted a methodical attack on their selfhood and humanity. To these we can add as necessarily following: (3) the unlikelihood that Residential Schools would have arisen in a society that valued and respected Aboriginal Peoples, and thus all Aboriginal individuals would be forced to exist in the racist world created, exposed to the further machinations of people ill-disposed toward them; and (4) students and other Aboriginal individuals were existing in a society that had successfully insulated itself from its genocidal intentions. At the very least, such a society would be unlikely to treat grievances of the oppressed group with any degree of seriousness or sensitivity. The Toxic Planet thus created for Aboriginal Peoples is why (see Appendix B and Appendix D) we consider the "medical" or "disease" metaphor completely inappropriate for understanding Indian Residential School. An accurate metaphor is that Residential Schools were like atomic blasts, obliterating or severely injuring those closest to "ground zero," but polluting the air, land, and water, bringing about a nuclear winter, and creating long-term malignancies for anyone more distant.

172. We'd like to take a moment to clarify a widespread misunderstanding of the Cariboo Tribal Council study, a misunderstanding that unfortunately was passed along in *Breaking the Silence.* The "very few differences" found "between former residential and non-residential school students in the day-to-day particulars" of their adult lives were, in the context of the report, strictly limited to what were called "life-outcome variables." All kinds of differences were found (see, for example, Tables 1 to 5). However, we put together a number of variables with the following scenario in mind: suppose education is as important in Canadian society as Canadians claim, and given (from the results of earlier analysis) that Residential Schools differed from public schools in any number of academically-relevant ways (more time on spent on academics; better materials; more highly-qualified staff; better emotional environment; etc.,), then we would expect to see some material

differences (which we dubbed "life-outcome variables"), on average, between those who attended public school and those who attended Residential School. It was with respect to these variables, as we carefully noted in the report, that "very few differences" were found. To us, this must call into question the supposition that education is as important as Canadians claim. The economic suppression of Aboriginal Peoples, their marginalisation as a work force, their underrepresentation in higher education, etc., suggested to us, then and now, that other factors (institutional racism; discrimination; scapegoating; etc.,) were better explanations for our relative position than simply the "quality" of our education.

This is also not to say we dispute what the writers of *Breaking the Silence* concluded from their reading. We have grave doubts concerning the advisability of pursuing Western-style research (we include our own suggestions for local research into Residential Schooling in Appendix B, and a comprehensive argument against employment of pyschoeducational measures in Appendix C), and consider their approach preferable to 99% of the psychological literature we see published concerning Aboriginal Peoples today.

173. As this manuscript has circulated, it has become increasingly apparent to us that most Canadians have never heard of the "Home Child" episode in their history. Briefly, British "colonies" (Canada, Australia, Rhodesia, New Zealand, and South Africa) participated in a white child slavery operation with England for well over a century, Canada's complicity ending officially in 1925 and unofficially in 1948 (what an interesting date; see page 28 infra). English orphans or children seized from their parents by "benevolent" organisations were shipped to Canada (at a cost of $2.00 each for the Canadian government) and assigned as farm labourers, domestics, or whatevers to the Canadian public at large. The children were, among other outrages, exploited as labourers, occasionally bought and sold with the farms upon which they resided, often denied an education, and more than infrequently abused (sexually, physically, and emotionally) by their owners. For more detail, see Kenneth Bagnell, *The Little Immigrants: The Orphans Who Came to Canada.* Toronto: Macmillan, 1980; Phyllis Harrison (Ed.), *The Home Children.* Winnipeg: Watson & Dwyer, 1979; Phillip Bean & Joy Melville, *Lost Children of the Empire: The Untold Story of Britain's Child Migrants.* London: Unwin Hyman, 1989; and Margaret Humphreys, *Empty Cradles: One Woman's Fight to Uncover Britain's Most Shameful Secret.* Toronto: Doubleday, 1994. The American government had a similar program, scooping up their own inner city children as well as buying some of the English "overflow" (Marilyn Holt, *The Orphan Trains: Placing Out in America.* Lincoln: University of Nebraska Press, 1992). Perhaps non-Indians who are sceptical about the horrors of Residential Schooling would find them more believable were they aware of what their government was willing to perpetrate upon defenseless non-Indians...

174. For example, there are no psychosocial instruments that have met the fundamental ethical requirements for use with Aboriginal Peoples. Hence, there are no

"objective" measures of any outcome variables of interest. See Appendix C.

175. There is a disturbing tendency on the part of those trying to "explain away" Residential School issues to treat "Residential Schooling" as a uniform experience. However, to be familiar at all with the history of Residential Schooling is to be aware of the heterogeneity of the institution. The schools were run by very different denominations; the character and style of any school changed along with changes in personnel; in any one school, the children encountered personnel with very different dispositions toward them in particular, and Aboriginal Peoples in general; the policy, curriculum, and philosophy of Residential Schools changed over time; the qualifications of the teaching staff changed over time; some children attended Residential School on their home reserves, while others were sent hundreds (thousands?) of miles away; some attended Residential Schools with more or less culturally-consonant and homogeneous children, while other attended Schools with a culturally heterogeneous group; some attended a year or even less, while other attended for over a decade; and on and on. Anyone who believes Residential Schools were more or less the same could also believe that Aboriginal Nations were more or less the same.

176. Leo Eitinger, "The Concentration Camp Syndrome and Its Late Sequelae," in Joel Dimsdale (Ed.), *Survivors, Victims, and Perpetrators: Essays on the Nazi Holocaust*. New York: Hemisphere Publishing, 1980.

177. Metin Basoglu and Susan Mineka, *"The Role of Uncontrollable and Unpredictable Stress in Post-Traumatic Stress Responses in Torture Survivors."* In M. Basoglu (Ed.), *Torture and Its Consequences: Current Treatment Approaches.* Cambridge: Cambridge University Press, 1992.

178. Albert Memmi, *The Colonizer and the Colonized*. Boston: Beacon Press, 1965; Frantz Fanon, *Black Skins, White Masks*. New York: Grove Press, 1967; T. Gladwin and A. Saidin, *Slaves of the White Myth: The Psychology of Neocolonialism*. Atlantic Highlands, New Jersey: Humanities Press, 1980; Ashis Nandy, *The Intimate Enemy: Loss and Recovery of Self Under Colonialism*. Delhi: Oxford University Press, 1983.

179. Axel Russel, "Late Effects—Influence on the Children of the Concentration Camp Survivor." In Joel Dimsdale (Ed.), *Survivors, Victims, and Perpetrators: Essays on the Nazi Holocaust*. New York: Hemisphere Publishing, 1980. William Niederland, "The Clinical Aftereffects of the Holocaust in Survivors and Their Offspring." In Randolph Braham (Ed.), *The Psychological Perspectives of the Holocaust and of Its Aftermath*. New York: Columbia University Press, 1988. Janice Bistritz, "Transgenerational Pathology in Families of Holocaust Survivors." In R. Braham (Ed.), *The Psychological Perspectives of the Holocaust and Its Aftermath*. New York: Columbia University Press, 1988. Helen Epstein, *Children*

of the Holocaust: Conversations with Sons and Daughters of Survivors. New York: Bantam Books, 1979.

180. Paul Marcus and Alan Rosenberg, "A Philosophical Critique of the 'Survivor Syndrome' and Some Implications for Treatment." In Randolph Braham (Ed.), *The Psychological Perspectives of the Holocaust and of Its Aftermath.* New York: Columbia University Press, 1988. Falk Pingel, "The Destruction of Human Identity in Concentration Camps: The Contribution of the Social Sciences to an Analysis of Behavior Under Extreme Conditions." *Holocaust and Genocide Studies, Vol. 6,* 1991, p. 167-184. Norman Solkoff, "The Holocaust: Survivors and Their Children." In Metin Basoglu (Ed.), *Torture and Its Consequences.* Cambridge: Cambridge University Press, 1992. See Appendix B for our thoughts on the difficulty in conducting "scientific" research on the topic.

181. Jean Amery, *"Resentments."* Chapter 4 in his book, *At the Mind's Limits: Contemplations by a Survivor on Auschwitz and Its Realities.* New York: Schocken Books, 1986.

182. *Faith Misplaced*, p. 183.

183. Brian Siano, "Watching on the Rhine: A Review of Denying the Holocaust by Deborah Lipstadt." *Skeptic, Vol. 2, # 4,* 1994, p. 72-75.

184. For a readable summary (and a great more detail), see Terry Eagleton, *Ideology: An Introduction,* New York: Verso, 1991.

185. The charge can be made to stick with respect to the "hard" sciences, as well. See, for example Richard Lewontin, *Biology as Ideology,* Concord, Ontario: Anansi Press, 1991; Robert Proctor, *Value-Free Science: Purity and Power in Modern Knowledge,* Cambridge: Harvard University Press, 1991; Mary Midgley, *Science as Salvation: A Modern Myth and Its Meaning,* New York: Routledge, 1992; Andrew Pickering (Ed.), *Science As Practice and Culture,* Chicago: University of Chicago Press, 1992; Ruth Hubbard, *The Politics of Women's Biology,* London: Rutgers University Press, 1990. These examples could be multiplied indefinitely.

186. Thomas Szasz, *The Manufacture of Madness: A Comparative Study of the Inquisition and the Mental Health Movement.* New York: Harper Torchbooks, 1970. T. Szasz, *Insanity: The Idea and Its Consequences.* New York: Wiley, 1987.

187. Rajeev Bhargava, *Individualism in Social Science: Forms and Limits of a Methodology.* Oxford: Clarendon Press, 1992. p. 1.

188. We try to keep things manageable here, but there are profound philosophical

muddles underlying Western ways of thinking about things, and these are manifested in the mundane ideology of Methodological Individualism. For an analysis of three such muddles, see Chrisjohn and Maraun's, Intelligence Research, Discourse Analysis, and the Legacy of Confusion, Maraun's Causality, and Young and Chrisjohn's Here Be Dragons: The Myth of Psychological Empowerment. All are in manuscript form, but we will circulate them to interested parties.

189. There is good reason to believe that the articulation of methodological individualism was driven by American-Soviet animosities. F. A. Hayek, individualist economist, gave one of the earliest accounts, and it was given philosophical form during the early Cold War partly by anti-communist philosophers like Karl Popper. To hold that "the thoughts and behaviours of individual actors" weren't irreducible building blocks of society obviously looked to some like the Creeping Red Menace.

190. Of course, there are some "schools of thought" that do indeed try to get us to place the stop sign somewhere else. The sociobiologists, for example, labour mightily to convince us that our genes do everything while the rest of our body is just kind of along for the ride. How this stop sign has been developed into scientific racism is well documented in Ruth Hubbard & Elijah Wald, *Exploding the Gene Myth: How Genetic Information is Produced and Manipulated by Scientists, Physicians, Employers, Insurance Companies, Educators, and Law Enforcers.* Boston: Beacon Press, 1993; Richard Lewontin, Biology as Ideology: The Doctrine of DNA. Concord, Ontario: Anansi Press, 1991; and Dorothy Nelkin & M. Susan Lindee, *The DNA Mystique: The Gene as Cultural Icon.* New York: W. H. Freeman, 1995. A guide to un-confusing this gobbledygook (as well as the other kinds of gobbledygook we've been dealing with here), and one that is in keeping with the philosophical perspective under which we work, is Peter Hacker's *"Language, Minds and Brains,"* in C. Blakemore & S. Greenfield, Mindwaves: *Thoughts on Intelligence, Identity and Consciousness.* Oxford: Basil Blackwell, 1987.

191. These are adapted from Allen L. Edwards, *An Introduction to Linear Regression and Correlation, 2nd Ed.* New York: W. H. Freeman & Company, 1984, p. 41. A problem with Edwards' diagrams is that many psychologists, in looking at them, expect to see things this clear and obvious "if" Simpson's Paradox is lurking in their data. Examining their own scatterplots and not seeing any Edwardian Extremes, they proceed as if there's nothing to worry about. This commits an empirical error and a philosophical error. For the former, there is no reason to expect the subgroup relations to differentiate themselves so nicely, to form such decidedly obvious alternate forms of relations: they will be "squnched" together, overlap, take all forms of gyrating relations, and so on. Edwards draws them as he does so the problem may be conceptually appreciated: he is not giving us previews of what to look for. Concerning the latter, once again psychologists treat a philo-

sophical problem as if it is an empirical one, and go off on another "Lucy Search." If they can't find a subgrouping that destroys the form of the general relation, they presume there isn't one. But Simpson's point isn't that these can be ruled out by such searches, regardless of how comprehensive they might be. It is that such subgroupings are a feature of the mathematics of non-deterministic systems; they're there whether you can find them or not. Thus, one doesn't "refute" Simpson's algebra by elaborating counterexamples. In a very real sense, the "Paradox" is no paradox at all, but merely a demonstration of the analytic and philosophical shortcomings/confusions of the great mass of social scientists.

192. The chapter "Understanding Correlations" from the forthcoming *Handbook of Research and Evaluation for First Nations Communities*, is available from the authors (Chrisjohn, Maraun, Harrison, and McDonald) upon request. Of course, Edwards' book (see previous Footnote) is also recommended, although a bit heavy on algebra for most people.

193. *L. Wittgenstein, Zettel. 2nd Ed.* Oxford: Basil Blackwell, 1981, p. 105.

194. This includes qualitative and quantitative variables. The current fashion of believing qualitative data analysis superior (at least for some things) to quantitative data analysis is founded on ignorance: there is no substantial difference between analyses of these different kinds of variables, as was well known as early as 1936. That qualitative analyses have become all the rage, and portrayed as something intrinsically different from quantitative analyses, is just another indictment of modern higher education.

195. The Compilation Group, Futan University and Shanghai Teachers University, The Opium War, Peking: Foreign Languages Press, 1976; J. Scott, *The White Poppy: The History of Opium*, London: Heinemann, 1969; Hsin-pao Chang, Commissioner Lin and the Opium War, New York: W. W. Norton, 1964.

196. "A century ago, a voice of British liberalism described the 'Chinaman' as 'an inferior race of malleable orientals.'" Noam Chomsky, *For Reason of State*, New York: Vintage Books, 1973, citing Frederick F. Clairmonte, Economist, October 31, 1862.

197. But of course, conceptually it's something much greater than nil. Another shortcoming of "standard" approaches is that they have a very insecure grasp of how to deal with such findings.

198. Celia Kitzinger and Rachel Perkins, *Changing Our Minds: Lesbian Feminism and Psychology*. New York: New York University Press, 1993, p. 72.

199. We use the term guardedly; nowadays therapy teaches its patients that they are

never "cured," but at best in remission.

200. Thomas Szasz, *The Therapeutic State: Psychiatry in the Mirror of Current Events*. Buffalo: Prometheus Books, 1984.

201. Andrew Polsky, *The Rise of the Therapeutic State*. Princeton: Princeton University Press, 1991.

202. From Appendix B, *Research and Residential Schooling:*
Decisions made at an institutional level eventually come down to cases: in residential schools, actions motivated or legitimated by policy were carried out by individuals upon individuals. And, since we experience life as individuals, it was personal pain, humiliation, anger, etc. that was experienced, not the "clash of cultures," the "exploitation of resources," the "industrial revolution," or what-have-you.
But even though we experience the world this way, it does not follow that the way the world works must be understood in terms of individual forces. All too often we focus on the individual forces and, inappropriately, ignore influences that are not immediately apparent. For example, children of divorced parents often believe themselves responsible for the breakup; women who were sexually assaulted are often accused of having "brought it on themselves" by dressing or acting "provocatively;" or, unemployed people are frequently described as "just not wanting to work." Similarly, people who attended residential school sometimes attribute their negative experiences to their own actions, something about them that accounted for their treatment. These internal explanations can last a long time, and resurface when trying to understand events far removed from residential schools. Well, speaking your Native language may have led to a specific beating, but factors like the "why's" and "wherefore's" of the school's language policy, the disciplinary guidelines, and the very mentality that conceived of residential schooling in the first place (all non-personal factors) contributed as much as anything to the specific act. Failure to see the broader context is like dousing a pile of dry leaves with gasoline, handing someone a sparkler, shoving him/her into the pile, and saying "You started a fire!"

203. Celia Kitzinger and Rachel Perkins, *Changing Our Minds*, Chapter 6.

204. We hesitate to present our own suggestions for "therapy" here, for three reasons: first, this was the territory to be covered by *Breaking the Silence*, and we didn't wish to poach; second, while strongly related to our critique of Western approaches to understanding Residential Schooling, it would carry us quite a distance off covering a host of related topics that would have greatly increased the size of the present report; third, we didn't want to encourage any action toward "skipping" the "dull stuff" and jumping right to the "therapy stuff." However, some of our ideas in brief include the following:

(1) We reject the medical model, as well as "psychologism" and "sociologism," finding all three to be but slightly different versions of the same philosophical errors.

(2) Conceptual analysis of the issues the client wishes to deal with is not only useful, but is a necessary first step. Not only should self-descriptors be subjected to this analysis, but the operation of the Therapeutic State, as well.

(3) Concentrating on "symptoms" simply vacillates between blaming and ignoring the victim. Understanding the "symptoms" (at least partly) as the outcomes of colonialisation and oppression is absolutely necessary to working out issues of responsibility.

(4) Spirituality (not religion) is essential; however, if approached in the Pan-Indian fashion we have seen all too often, it becomes merely dogmatic following of empty ritual (an Invented Tradition, in Hobsbawm's phrase), and is of no benefit to anyone.

(5) We reject Western approaches which in essence mechanise both the "client" and the "therapist." To believe that useful work with a client can be reduced to technique is like believing that if you removed the paint from the Mona Lisa you'd find a "paint-by-numbers" canvas underneath.

Work by David Smail, Bell Hooks, Thomas Szasz, Seymour Sarason, and Celia Kitzinger & Rachel Perkins would be useful references for those wanting to follow up on these notions.

205. Andrew Polsky, *The Rise of the Therapeutic State*, p. 208.

206. Andrew Polsky, *The Rise of the Therapeutic State*, p. 4.

207. They pursue the same degrees and training, accept credentialling and certification, demand it of their employees, follow established non-Aboriginal agency procedures, conduct or commission assessments, and so on. Polsky speaks to the co-opting of community initiatives via "professionalism" at various points of his work.

Parallels with the undermining of Aboriginal educational initiatives abound (see, for example, Dianne Longboat, "First Nations Control of Education: The Path to our Survival as Nations," in J. Barman, Y. Hebert, and D. McCaskill, *Indian Education in Canada, Volume 2: The Challenge.* Vancouver: UBC Press, 1987). Educational "control" is "doled out" to Aboriginal Peoples as they "prove" themselves "worthy" by performing in a manner indistinguishable from what non-Aboriginals have been doing all along. Of course, when we are indistinguishable from our oppressors, we are our oppressors.

208. Jean Amery, *At the Mind's Limits*, p. 71.

209. Aaron Hass' *The Aftermath: Living with the Holocaust.* New York: Cambridge University Press, 1995, clearly documents the post-war German government's

unwillingness to concede without putting up severe resistance the point that the concentration camp experience might have induced psychological trauma in some of the survivors. The notion that "you're not so badly off from your experiences" is the Nazi equivalent of the Canadian notions that Aboriginal Peoples are exaggerating the negativity of Residential Schools, and that all the "psychic baggage" can be off-loaded in 12 to 20 "sessions" with a "therapist." These attitudes, of course, only add to the baggage.

210. See, for example, Cindy Shiner, "Ghosts from the Holocaust Haunt Switzerland's Banks," *Calgary Herald,* July 6, 1995.

211. Maude Barlow, "Class Warfare: The Assault on Canada's Schools." *Our Schools; Our Selves, Volume 5*, 1994.

212. Zygmunt Bauman, *Modernity and the Holocaust,* p. 149.

213. Jean Amery, *At the Mind's Limits*, p. 77-78.

APPENDICES

Appendix A

The United Nations Genocide Convention

The Contracting Parties having considered the declaration made by the General Assembly of the United Nations in its resolution 96 (1) dated 11 December 1946 that genocide is a crime under international law, contrary to the spirit and aims of the United Nations and condemned by the civilized world; recognizing that at all periods of history genocide has inflicted great losses on humanity; and being convinced that, in order to liberate mankind from such an odious scourge, international cooperation is required; hereby agree as hereinafter provided:

ARTICLE I: The Contracting Parties confirm that genocide whether committed in time of peace or in time of war, is a crime under international law which they undertake to prevent and to punish.

ARTICLE II: In the present Convention, genocide means any of the following acts committed with intent to destroy, in whole or in part, a national, ethical, racial or religious group, as such:
(a) Killing members of the group;
(b) Causing serious bodily or mental harm to members of the group;
(c) Deliberately inflicting on the group conditions of life calculated to bring about its physical destruction in whole or in part;
(d) Imposing measures intended to prevent births within the group;
(e) Forcibly transferring children of the group to another group.

ARTICLE III: The following acts shall be punishable:
(a) Genocide;
(b) Conspiracy to commit genocide;
(c) Direct and public incitement to commit genocide;
(d) Attempt to commit genocide;
(e) Complicity in genocide.

ARTICLE IV: Persons committing genocide or any of the other acts enumerated in article III shall be punished, whether they are constitutionally responsible rulers, public officials or private individuals.

ARTICLE V: The Contracting Parties undertake to enact, in accordance with their respective Constitutions, the necessary legislation to give effect to the provisions of the present Convention and, in particular, to provide effective penalties for person guilty of genocide or any of the other acts enumerated in article III.

ARTICLE VI: Persons charged with genocide or any of the other acts enumerated in article III shall be tried by a competent tribunal of the State in the territory of which the act was committed, or by such international penal tribunal as may have jurisdiction with respect to those Contracting Parties which shall have accepted the jurisdiction.

ARTICLE VII: Genocide and other acts enumerated in article III shall not be considered as political crimes for the purpose of extradition. The Contracting Parties pledge themselves in such cases to grant extradition in accordance with their laws and treaties in force.

ARTICLE VIII: Any Contracting Party may call upon the competent organs of the United Nations to take such action under the Charter of the United Nations as they consider appropriate for the prevention and suppression of acts of genocide or any of the other acts enumerated in article III.

ARTICLE IX: Disputes between the Contracting Parties relating to the inter-predation, application or fulfillment of the present Convention, including those relating to the responsibility of a State for genocide or any of the other acts enumerated in article III, shall be submitted to the International Court of Justice at the request of any of the parties to the dispute.

ARTICLE X: The present Convention, of which the Chinese, English, French, Russian and Spanish texts are equally authentic, shall bear the date of 9 December 1948.

ARTICLE XI: The present Convention shall be open until 31 December 1949 for signature on behalf of any Member of the United Nations and of any non-member State to which an invitation to sign has been addressed by the General Assembly. The present Convention shall be ratified, and the instruments of ratification shall be deposited with the Secretary-General of the

United Nations. After January 1950, the present Convention may be acceded to on behalf of any Member of the United Nations and of any non-member State which has received an invitation as aforesaid. Instruments of accession shall be deposited with the Secretary-General of the United Nations.

ARTICLE XII: Any Contracting Party may at any time by notification addressed to the Secretary-General of the United Nations, extend the application of the present Convention to all or any of the territory for the conduct of whose foreign relations that Contracting Party is responsible.

ARTICLE XIII: On the day when the first twenty instruments of ratification or accession have been deposited, the Secretary-General shall draw up a process-verbal and transmit a copy of it to each Member of the United Nations and to each of the non-member States contemplated in article XI. The present Convention shall come into force on the ninetieth day following the date of deposit of the twentieth instrument of ratification or accession. Any ratification or accession effected subsequent to the latter date shall become effective on the ninetieth day following the deposit of the instrument of ratification or accession.

ARTICLE XIV: The present Convention shall remain in effect for a period of ten years as from the date of its coming into force. It shall thereafter remain in force for successive periods of five years for such Contracting Parties as have not denounced it at least six months before the expiration of the current period. Denunciation shall be effected by a written notification addressed to the Secretary-General of the United Nations.

ARTICLE XV: If, as a result of denunciations, the number of Parties to the present Convention should become less than sixteen, the Convention shall cease to be in force as from the date on which the last of these denunciations shall become effective.

ARTICLE XVI: A request for the revision of the present Convention may be made at any time by any Contracting Party by means of a notification in writing addressed to the Secretary-General. The General Assembly shall decide upon the steps, if any, to be taken in respect of such request.

ARTICLE XVII: The Secretary-General of the United Nations shall notify all Members of the United Nations and the non-member States contemplated in article XI of the following:

(a) Signatures, ratifications and accessions received in accordance with article XI;

(b) Notifications received in accordance with article XII;

(c) The date upon which the present Convention comes into force in accordance with article XIII;

(d) Denunciations received in accordance with article XIV;

(e) The abrogation of the Convention in accordance with article XV;

(f) Notifications received in accordance with article XVI.

ARTICLE XVIII: The original of the present Convention shall be deposited in the archives of the United Nations. A certified copy of the Convention shall be transmitted to all Members of the United Nations and to the non-member States contemplated in article XI.

ARTICLE XIX: The present Convention shall be registered by the Secretary-General of the United Nations on the date of its coming into force.

Appendix B

Research and Residential Schooling:

Ideas for First Nations Individuals and Communities

Roland Chrisjohn and Sherri Young

CHAPTER 1:

INTRODUCTION

Time and again, First Nations peoples have spoken of how their worlds were altered (sometimes for the better, sometimes for the worse, but always irretrievably) by residential schooling. Even a mediocre understanding of modern day relations between the First Nations and the rest of Canadian society requires some knowledge of residential school, its history, its purposes, and its effects. Thus, when the Royal Commission on Aboriginal Peoples (RCAP) began its hearings on April 21, 1992, First Nations immediately and persistently urged that an inquiry into residential schooling form a part of RCAP's investigation. Consequently, from its earliest days of operation the Royal Commission has resolved to examine this topic as comprehensively as possible given its terms of reference.

This appendix formed part (an insignificant one) of the Royal Commission's residential school investigation strategy. From the outset, we must emphasize that the needs and requirements of the Royal Commission constitute the least of the reasons for the production and distribution of this booklet. Far more important is the hope that it will assist individuals and First Nations communities to develop their own appraisal and their own understanding of how residential school has helped create their world today. If, after taking their own work as far as they desire, First Nations individuals and communities wish to share their insights, we would be very grateful. But research that speaks centrally to the issues of *local* First Nations is of overriding importance to us.

The reason for our emphasis is easy to find: how many of you have been approached by government workers or academics who have promised that much will come from some proposed research, only to find the process rude, invasive, costly, or irrelevant, and the results wishy-washy, incomprehensible, useless, or even nonexistent? Is there any reason this pattern of interaction should continue? Is there any reason First Nations individuals and communities should **not** take the lead in conducting their own community-based research? Is there any reason such an important topic as residential schooling should not be under direct control of First Nations peoples and communities? Our answers are: too many of our communities have been disappointed with the formal studies conducted by academics or government functionaries; we can see no reason that this situation should continue; there is no reason we should not conduct our own investigations; and, the residential school experience is too important a topic to trust to those who already have demonstrated their insensitivities.

The only obstacle we can see to First Nations communities undertaking First Nations research is the lack of information on how to go about it. True, there are thousands of books on research design, statistics, survey implementation, data analysis, and so on, but there is so much information of this type that it threatens to overwhelm (rather than assist) enthusiastic communities. In addition, however, it is our opinion that this "embarrassment of riches" is more apparent than real. Research is, as are countless other things, an institution of Western culture, and as much a reflection of the ideology of the West as government, religion, or anything else that might be named. Ignore this, and your research (regardless of who conducts it) will carry out the ideological program for which it was designed: there is a real risk that research carried out following the established canons of academia will have the same kind of outcomes as the research we criticized earlier, and rather than providing a voice to First Nations individuals and communities, once again we will be silenced.

With this appendix, therefore, we aim to provide an accessible account of research practices and procedures that avoid the ideological tentacles of Western academic research while bringing to centre the life experiences of First Nations peoples. In this we aim to achieve a "practical" revolution, one that will allow First Nations to conduct their own inquiries into residential schooling while maintaining exacting standards of investigation. We would be wrong to imply that the weakness of "traditional academic" research is not an issue in modern social science, or that what we propose here is entirely our own creation. Rather, what is wrong with social science research has been known for quite some time, and what we propose here is (we feel) a judicious selection of what has been offered as improvements. What we hope to do then, is to make practical suggestions about conducting personal and/or community research into residential schooling; using methods that go well beyond what standard psycho-social-anthropological investigators would propose, we hope to fashion a truly innovative, community-based approach.

One word of caution: because residential schooling has meant very different things to different people at different times and places, there is no one methodology that can possibly satisfy everyone's needs. Therefore, we offer a range of suggestions which may be more or less useful depending on your own particular purposes. Furthermore, we do not claim to have a comprehensive range of suggestions, and, should this booklet help you to develop something unique (or even if you come up with new methods entirely on your own), we urge you to make your innovations known. This first attempt at an alternative methodology for First Nations community-based research can get better only if you and your Nation are willing to help.

CHAPTER 2:

ETHICAL CONSIDERATIONS

Before beginning, there are issues related to research that must be mentioned. Foremost among them are ethical considerations, or the **standards of conduct** for those who will carry out research on residential schools. For a significant number of people who would be interested in participating (either as informants or as researchers), going over this past will form one of the most intellectually and emotionally demanding tasks they have ever undertaken. It would be callous to ignore or belittle this truth, and irresponsible to proceed without taking every precaution imaginable. Ethical considerations, then, help us anticipate the problems that may arise, and plan for dealing with them in caring, sensitive ways.

Ethical concerns are nothing new, and there already exist many texts that would be useful in resolving ethical problems. The Royal Commission has produced *Ethical Guidelines for Research*, and numerous other ethical guidelines are available from libraries and bookstores (for example: *Planning Ethically Responsible Research: A Guide for Students and Internal Review Boards*, Joan Sieber, Sage Publications, 1992; and *Standards for Educational and Psychological Testing,* American Educational Research Association, 1985). Because those materials cover ethical concerns in a broader way, and because we would rather not repeat information that is available elsewhere, here we will highlight those ethical concerns which, in our opinion, naturally arise as a part of investigating residential schooling. However, what we present here should be combined with other ethical guidelines when planning your research.

We will break our presentation down into four areas, each area covering a few related ethical considerations. These areas are not more or less important than one another: an ethical study is one that adequately addresses the points raised in each of these areas.

THE RIGHT OF PRIVACY

People have the right to be left alone, regardless of how much of a contribution someone else believes they can make. Thus, **non-participation** is a right, as is **freedom from coercion** (the attempt to induce a person to change her or his mind). A researcher may ethically request participation, but once refused the matter is closed. Further, no stigma should be attached to this person's decision: speculation about the "why's and wherefore's" of a person's refusal participate is malicious, and the decision is the person's business, not the researcher's.

Related to non-participation is the right to **withdraw from participation**. A person may start out taking part in the research and then, for his or her own reasons, decide to discontinue. This decision must not be questioned, and withdrawal must not provoke any kind of retaliation on the part of the researcher. For instance, should counselling services be part of the investigation, withdrawal from participation would not mean the person withdrawing must lose access to the counsellor. In this case, it is possible that the early stages of the investigation has dredged up issues the person no longer wants to discuss, but continues to need to work through.

The reverse side of these first two rights is **the right to be included**. Whether we are talking about the national, community, or personal levels, First Nations peoples have something to say about residential schooling and have a right to be heard. As far as humanly possible, then, provision should be made to include all interested parties. Financial and logistical limitations may make this impossible in practice, and in these instances the researchers should be open and above-board about such difficulties. But while it may be impossible to involve **all** First Nations peoples in all research activities, it is more likely that **most** of those desiring to participate can be included in **some** activity.

Even if people choose to be a part of research, they are entitled to certain forms of protection. If desired, **anonymity** (where information is given or written without reference to who provided it) is one of these rights. By this we do not mean that, for instance, unsigned submissions making wild allegations that are unsupported by any other evidence must be given credence; however, someone providing credible evidence supported by other sources of information has the right to request his or her name not be used in reconstructing an account of events. There are no general rules for deciding whether a specific instance is closer to the first scenario or the second; the important point is that sources of information have a right to request and expect that, if they so desire it, their names will not be used.

Participants also have a right to **confidentiality**, that their personal accounts or private lives will not become public knowledge. Some of the events that took place at residential school are painful beyond imagination to those who suffered through them. Should these individuals agree to disclose these events for research purposes, what they tell the researchers has no business becoming "nosed-about" in public. **What is presented in private must remain private**. There is no ethical offense worse than breech of confidentiality.

Rights of privacy also include the right to **information security**. It is likely that, in some manner, information obtained as part of researching residential school will have to be compiled and stored for periods of time. Whether the information is retained as transcripts, interview notes, audio or videotapes, computer files, or whatever, participants have a right to expect that, as a matter of privacy, such information is inaccessible to people not specifically concerned with its research uses. Thus, the physical records of research (like notes or tapes) must be kept in secure areas (such as locked filing cabinets in supervised storage areas). Where possible, identities of informants should not appear on physical records; private coding systems can be worked out if for some reason specific individual records have to be accessed as part of the research. When information is stored in computers, both direct and remote access to the computer must be limited. In addition, there are a number of easily used "encryption" procedures available with commonly available computer utilities programs like *PC-TOOLS* and *NORTON UTILITIES*. These utilities operate so that, should someone who does not know the "password" attempt to access the file, all they will see is gobbledygook. Encryption programs can be of particular use in small First Nations communities, where an interloper might, even without a list of names, be able to figure out "who said what" from access to an unscrambled data file.

Individuals providing information for research purposes are doing researchers a favor that cannot be repaid. Researchers have no "right" to information, and individual people have every right to keep private information **private**, without consequences to them. For those who do choose to share portions of their private lives with a researcher, a reasonable expectation for such an indispensable act of generosity is that their privacy will be protected at all costs. To do less is to elevate "research" and the researcher above simple human decency.

THE RIGHT OF INFORMED CONSENT

The decision to take part in research, once made, constitutes a large commitment on the part of the individual participants. In simple terms, the right of informed consent is that **the prospective participant must, beforehand, have as complete an understanding as possible concerning what their participation will involve.** The "beforehand" is particularly important, since it has been found (in general) that once people have started to agree to some action, they tend to continue to comply well past a point they would have refused had the request for compliance started there. Ask any encyclopedia salesman.

While in "simple terms" informed consent does not seem too difficult, there are several thorny issues to be addressed here. First, whether or not a prospective participant is **competent** to give informed consent is an issue. By law, people under the legal age of adulthood or people who are under some form of guardianship (for example, individuals involuntarily committed to a mental institution) **cannot** give consent because they are deemed incompetent to do so. If research has to be conducted with such individuals, legal release forms signed by the guardians of the individuals **must** be obtained. In **addition** to the consent of any legal guardian, it is important to explain the research to the person whose participation is sought. Ensuring that he or she is willing to participate is not just ethical, it is common courtesy.

Depending on the specific direction of an inquiry, residential school researchers will, in some cases, want to avoid involving participants from certain age groups. For instance, if a report of sexual abuse about someone not legally an adult is obtained, the researcher is **legally required** to report it to the appropriate provincial child welfare agency. By working with adults, researchers are not required to report anything, since competent adults are deemed capable of deciding whether or not to bring a charge against an abuser.

Assuming, then, that researchers are dealing with people (or their guardians) competent to evaluate what participation would involve, what kinds of information should be presented to them? In general, researchers must explain as best they know the **risks and benefits** associated with participation, with both **personal and societal** risks and benefits being addressed. Examination of similar cases in the literature, talking with people who have already participated in or undertaken similar research, and simple common sense are tactics whereby researchers can obtain some idea of the personal and societal risks and benefits, but it must be admitted that unanticipated outcomes almost always crop up. The general rule, then, is for researchers to do their level best in developing a clear and comprehensive overview of risks and benefits, and to expect the unexpected. Furthermore, it is not the researcher's place to try to balance or weigh the benefits of a particular research study against its possible risks: that is the **sole right and privilege** of the prospective participant.

In research on residential schools, the risk of foremost concern is that recollection of traumatic past experiences will emotionally overwhelm participants. Even individuals who have expressed no particular complaints about their residential school experiences have, as interviews progressed, recalled incidents long forgotten or trauma they believed they had come to terms with, only to be overpowered by their old memories. The real possibility that this might happen must be prominent in all discussions of risk and benefits.

Discussion of risks and benefits should also include **how the researcher intends to minimize the risks and maximize the benefits**. With respect to the risk just discussed, for example, an ethical research program would include safety mechanisms like interviewers trained in recognizing and dealing with emotional trauma, and on-call professional backup and support facilities for occasions where interviewers were unable to provide sufficient assistance. Thus, participants have a right to expect that **reasonable access to remedies** will be afforded to them for any personal risks, and **reasonable safety procedures** (like computer encryption) will be followed throughout. Ethically, the researcher is responsible for the safety and well-being of participants.

Although it is a little out of place, we would like to mention here that discussion of residential school experiences is an emotionally-charged situation for both speaker **and** listener. Ethical research will recognize the strain involved in eliciting accounts from participants, and remedy the possible impact these accounts may have on interviewers.

It is simply unfair (and ethically irresponsible) to subject people to circumstances you knew about but hid from them. If research has a bad reputation with First Nations peoples, lack of informed consent may well be a large part of the difficulty. It should also be mentioned that, often, when people withdraw from a study (as mentioned above), it is because they encountered something they did not anticipate. The requirement of informed consent is aimed at avoiding such a situation: to the extent there are any surprises for participants, researchers are ethically bound to make them as small as possible.

THE RIGHT OF INFORMATION ACCESS

So far we have covered the right of individuals to participate (or not) in research, and their right to understand what their participation might require of them. We now "skip ahead" to the time when their involvement has come to an end, when their **right of access to information from the research** is at issue. This involves a number of interrelated issues. Primarily, participants have a right to understand as fully as possible the complete context of the research. That is, they have a right to know how the researcher is conducting the program of research **and** why. While much of this information might be raised earlier (in the consideration of risks and benefits), participants have a right to understand the "nuts and bolts" of the study as they came to know them by participating. "Why did you ask all those questions about my sleeping habits? Why did you want to know my income? What conclusions are you likely to draw from the fact I've been married twice?"... and so on, are questions that might reasonably occur to someone after answering a survey. The researcher must answer the questions as fully as possible, even if the answers are as unsatisfactory as "I don't know yet whether I'll make anything out of your being married twice." "I don't know" is an acceptable answer here, because the termination of an interview is not usually the same as the termination of a research study.

Consequently, because there is more work to be done after any specific interview is completed (e.g., the research team must analyze data, write reports, etc.), after answering whatever question he or she can (often called in social sciences literature, rather pompously, **debriefing**) the researcher **must** undertake to make the final, general findings available at some time in the future to all participants who request it. While this condition is often taken as satisfied when interested participants are sent a copy of any research publication, a more strict condition (and one we recommend) is that any such summary be in language and format that is clear to the participants. If a written account is suitable, preliminary versions of the report could easily be evaluated by community representatives and modified until a suitable version is produced. Wittgenstein once said that anything that can be said can be said clearly and simply, and all too often, researchers, in an apparent effort to display their "vast learning," have chosen to clothe their findings in incomprehensible jargon. It is time we all learned the real wisdom behind Wittgenstein's words.

The right of access to the results obtained from a research project is thus an essential part of true community-based research. Participants should not be regarded (as they commonly are in the social sciences) as "subjects," but must rightly be seen as **full collaborators** in a research enterprise. This collaboration, by the way, entails a responsibility on the part of the participant **not to disclose** what they have learned to anyone until after the study has been completed; it is possible that information "leaks" could bias the final results should some of the specific features of the research become generally known.

We think "leaks" are less likely to happen when participants and researcher can assume they will be treated with equal respect. An appreciation of the importance of the research **includes** the knowledge of how it can adversely be affected by premature disclosures. And, if you can't trust your colleague in research, who can you trust?

THE RIGHT TO VALID RESEARCH

One ethical concern recently gaining more prominence is the right to **valid** research. Participation is often annoying, time consuming, and emotionally draining, and little (if anything) can be expected by way of personal compensation. Participants, then, should at least have the right to believe that their hard work and patience contributed to results and conclusions that actually have meaning, and that they haven't been wasting their time.

Let's presume that we are concerned here only with First Nations researchers working with First Nations participants: by doing so, we won't have to consider in detail the problems of how western researchers obscure what they're doing and evade, rather than answer, hard questions about why they're doing what they're doing. Of course, a First Nations researcher who adopts a westernized research perspective is, for the purpose of this distinction, more appropriately lumped together with the western tradition than included as a practitioner of community-based research.

There are only two ways to make concrete the right to valid research. One is for participants and those giving local approval to a research project to **insist that they understand the technical and philosophical basis for conducting an inquiry in a particular way**. This presumes, of course, that researchers and participants are different groups of people.

The second way to solidify the right to valid research is to **do it yourself**. If First Nations want community-based, relevant, non-intrusive, clear, valid research, none will be as motivated to provide it as we ourselves. As long as it is profitable, there will be plenty of "outsiders" (whatever their complexion) **claiming** they are providing all of this; but without knowledge of research matters being resident in our own communities, we will never be able to tell for sure whether they are misleading us. In the long run, then, developing local capacity to conduct research is the only solution, and "a job well begun is halfway done." We strongly urge that it can begin here, in the community-based study of residential schooling.

CHAPTER 3:

RESEARCH PRELIMINARIES

WHAT IS RESEARCH?

In any dictionary you can read that research is a "systematic inquiry into a subject in order to find out or check facts." This seems simple enough, but "systematic" doesn't really set any boundaries; it merely means that facts aren't collected aimlessly. The "aim," of course, is no part of research; like interests or preferences, you may have a particular aim for any reason or for no reason. Thus, research doesn't specify the "aim," merely that you have one (and there are no contradiction inherent in having more than one reason to do research). "Facts" is also a slippery term, in that, for one thing, many things we **know** aren't subject to doubt: for instance, we know that "a bearded man" is a man without having to check. A fact can thus only refer to what may or may not be true about the world, and some effort may be required to sort out, 1) what we take to be beyond dispute, from 2) what we are uncertain about. Finally, "subject" narrows down nothing, either, as topics of possible interest do not exist in isolation from one another. An example of this is the Royal Commission's study of residential schools; while initially not designated as part of the inquiry, residential schooling connected up with so many other topics (social policy; education; public forums; etc.) that it had to be included. Thus the "subject" of the status of First Nations in Canada had to be broadened to include a topic not given prominence from the outset of the Commission's work.

"Research," then, is a broad term that must make room for any number of specific activities, undertaken for any number of reasons. Checking public records, going through government archives, talking to witnesses, giving out and analyzing questionnaires, consulting history books, and similar activities must all be taken as research activities. Because you're curious, because you feel it has current, practical importance, because you want to write a book, or "just because" must all be taken as valid aims of an inquiry. As long as you are occupied in "non-random finding out or checking facts," you are doing research. It should also be clear that no one has to do **all** of these activities to be engaged in researching: some forms of inquiry will necessarily serve some purposes better than others. Thus, in doing research on a 200 year old Royal Proclamation it is unlikely you will find it necessary or useful to design and administer a questionnaire.

"Non-random finding out or checking facts" can be carried out by any individual or any group. Consequently, research about First Nations persons or communities is not something that has to be turned over to outsiders, and keeping it "at home" may make clear what its aims are, or at least eliminate agendas that are hidden from or conflict with local concerns. In addition, because there is no absolute form that research must take, First Nations individuals and communities need not have access to extensive resources or previous experience to conduct research. The only necessary ingredient is the determination to do it. In what follows, we will take the **fundamental resource base** of research to be the interest, motivation, and time of those who wish to engage in an inquiry. Concern and the personal commitment of individuals are the prerequisites; expensive consultants, elaborate computer programs, boundless libraries, and other such things, although desirable in some circumstances, are not essential features of research. We also take the aim of community-based First Nations research to be to produce results of interest and use to First Nations persons or local communities. Whether someone outside the community will find the results useful or interesting is beside the point.

WHY RESIDENTIAL SCHOOL RESEARCH?

As stated at the beginning of Chapter 1, of this appendix, residential schooling is connected up, in an uncountable number of ways both subtle and obvious, with the past and present (and therefore future) lives of First Nations peoples across Canada. This single fact is reason enough for all of us to want to know as much as possible about residential schooling. But even such a central and overwhelming rationale for conducting research must acknowledge a variety of reasons that will be associated with any particular study. In other words, apart from the general purpose of coming to understand residential schooling, there are countless specific reasons for undertaking residential school research. The relative strengths of these reasons will vary depending on the purpose of the researcher. For instance, someone documenting their own personal treatment at a specific residential school may be trying to work out how they[1] were affected by their experiences, how they in turn influenced others, or even how they became who they are. Someone looking at residential schooling as a part of worldwide colonialism may try to look at the similarity of rules in Canadian and Russian residential schools, examine church documents in Tasmania and Canada for statements of missionary zeal, or, in general, focus less upon the personal experiences of specific individuals. Regardless of emphasis, how-ever, we believe the overall aims of First Nations researchers (whatever the "level" of their investigations) do not contradict one another, and they all share a unity of purpose: to develop as clear and as comprehensive an account of residential schooling as possible, including its past, present, and future relation to our lives.

Of course, there are others looking at residential schooling who do not share this general purpose (can you guess who these might be?). For our purposes in this booklet we will be less interested in the personal and insti-tutional motives of those "others" and concentrate on the motives of those sharing the aim stated above. We do this for two reasons: first, examining the purposes of research often gives hints concerning **what information to look for**, and knowing what you're looking for is often a good indication of **how** to look for it. As we move along through this handbook we'll give more than a few examples of how this works.

Second, the unity of purpose we referred to earlier will be seen most clearly when the motives, information sources, and methods of different researchers are made as explicit as possible. Take for example two researchers, one investigating residential school for personal reasons and one for international reasons. Without understanding one another's agenda it is likely each will think the other "off on the wrong track," using "improper methods," and finding out things "of no value to me." The way to avoid the dissension being brewed by such thinking is to be clear from the outset that different purposes **require** different tracks, different meth-ods, and different **specific** conclusions. But if everyone is moving in the same direction, we can do things according to our own requirements that will help one another get to where each of us wants to go.

Therefore, in what follows we will distinguish **personal, community,** and **provincial-national** interests in the study of residential schooling. These interests are not divorced from one another, any more than **distin-guishing** wives and husbands **divorces** wives from husbands. Good research reflects a community of purpose and a union of minds, and is "a great grief to foes and a great joy to friends."

WHAT RESIDENTIAL SCHOOL RESEARCH CAN AND CANNOT DO

Research is so often promoted as being the solution (or at least a nec-essary first step) to any problem that it is important to keep in mind what its limitations are. This precaution is necessary if creating false expectations about the benefits of research is to be avoided. We therefore include here an overview of what an inquiry into residential schooling can and cannot achieve, as well as what it may help achieve.

Research will not demonstrate the immorality of residential schools. First of all, there is no need for such a demonstration: several of the organizations that participated in residential schooling have already admitted the immorality of the program, and anyone with a conscience realizes it was a blatant attempt at the cultural genocide of First Nations peoples. But more importantly, in general, empirical evidence does not bear on moral issues. For example, was research necessary to **prove** the immorality of the Nazi attempt at the extermination of the Jews? Is world opinion about South African Apartheid **founded** on research that demonstrates the ill effects of that system? To believe that a moral judgment about the "goodness" or "badness" of residential school must be based on an **empirical** evaluation of effects is to hold First Nations peoples accountable to a standard of evidence not applied elsewhere.

The irrelevance of research to morality judgments can be shown more easily. Suppose the goals of the federal government had been completely achieved by residential schools. Would the fact that there would no longer be any self-identified First Nations peoples (or that any still left would say publicly that they thought the destruction of their cultures, their religions, their languages, and their forms of life was a **good** idea) make the cultural genocide morally acceptable? No more so than the genocide of the Tasmanians has made their extermination justifiable.[2]

Studies of the effects of residential schooling are studies of the effects of residential schooling, nothing less and nothing more. The confusion of research issues with moral ones arises, perhaps, from western legal systems where compensation is often tied to the amount of damage demonstrated. For example, a judge in England recently sentenced a rapist to paying for a vacation for his victim, on the grounds that it "wasn't much of a rape." To hold, however, that demonstrations of harmful effects are needed for (or even contribute to) the evaluation of the moral foundations of residential schooling is to confuse separate issues, and (as the English judge so nicely confirms) to invite the wholesale dismissal of First Nations grievance when and if such demonstrations cannot be made.

Research will not establish "the" effects of residential schooling. The belief that research will uncover a set of psychological "irregularities" characterising individuals who attended boarding school ("Residential School Syndrome;" RSS) not only has no evidence whatsoever to support it, it is an inaccurate, misleading, and ultimately demeaning interpretation of First Nations peoples and communities. We consider it important that people who are about to undertake local research at least be aware of our concerns, even if in the final analysis they do not share them. Consequently, it seems we must belabour this point a bit.

There are good reasons not to expect any degree of uniformity of psychological features of attendees of residential schools. Residential schools differed, in both style and in substance, from place to place, and within place across time. Not only that, but two people at the same school during the same time could easily have markedly different experiences. Just because person "X" enjoyed his time at residential school it does not follow that person "Y" must have enjoyed hers; **both** experiences are equally valid and possible.

Even characteristics like the isolation and strangeness of residential schools cannot be considered constants. Some children went to school on or very near their home reserves, and enjoyed frequent contact with their families and other members of their Nation. Others were removed incredible distances and housed with First Nations children with whom they shared neither language nor culture, and were provided with no opportunity for family or cultural contact.

To these difficulties we must add another, that even today what is not considered "residential schooling" sometimes has a great deal in common with the older system. Some students still must travel incredible distances and live under conditions which **practically**, but not legally, limit their access to their families and their First Nations. It is true that such students aren't under the "lock and key" restraints often characteristics of residential schools, but the relative importance such similarities and differences have for personal growth and health is entirely unknown.

"The Residential Schooling Experience" sounds as if it refers to something uniform, but from these considerations we argue that it does not. Indeed, unscrupulous bureaucrats have moved to exploit this diversity by bringing along individuals who favorably recall their residential school experiences to meetings where such issues will come up. Their hope, often achieved in practice, is that this will start an argument between First Nations peoples (those supporting vs. those denouncing residential schooling). The easiest way to avoid falling for this "divide and conquer" strategy is for **both** sides to realise their experiences don't necessarily apply to everyone. This will allow those with honest grievances to get on with the work of dealing with them.

And, as long as we are talking about "dividing and conquering" First Nations, we should mention another division that has no business taking up our attention: First Nations peoples who attended residential school vs. those who did not. The idea that there must be large differences between these two groups, again while popular, merely reflects the thinking behind the belief in RSS. To see the problem with this notion, remember that residential schooling was only a part of a pervasive economic, religious, social, cultural, and political attack on First Nations. Those who somehow avoided residential school did not, somehow, also avoid day-to-day discrimination, racism, prejudice, or other poisonous experiences. The difference between attendees and non-attendees is thus roughly analogous to differences between Jews imprisoned in Nazi death camps vs. those who took refuge in hiding places: the imprisoned Jews had much the worse time of it, but no one in either group had any reason to be cheerful.

Finally, we must bear one more point in mind: if residential schools were not completely successful in **destroying** First Nations, they did succeed in **disrupting** them. With varying degrees of success, the schools attacked our languages, our religions, our family structures, and our very sense of who we are, even as other attacks (as mentioned above) were aimed at our economic, political, and cultural integrity. How much sense does it make to say that someone, raised by parents who got their lessons about love and discipline from priests, nuns, and bureaucrats, is not affected by residential schools? How much sense does it make to say that someone, not taught to speak their own language by parents beaten for having spoken it in school, is **not**, in some form, one of its products?

The most suitable metaphor for residential schooling is **not** that it is a disease, located in those who experienced it. That metaphor, as we have argued, artificially divides First Nations peoples, denying the experiences of some (those who do not feel harmed by their schooling) and minimizing the experiences of others (those less directly affected). Rather, residential schooling is better thought of as a nuclear explosion, a blast which does immediate damage to those closest to it, but which lingers on, poisoning the surrounding air, land, and water indefinitely. As such, it is inaccurate, misleading, and demeaning to First Nations as a whole to try to draw hard and fast distinctions between those who attended and those who did not. From a purely scientific point of view, the considerable similarity between supposedly different groups of people must lead at **least** to inconsistent findings. Much worse, it is very likely to lead to non-significant results, which, as we argued earlier, invites wholesale dismissal of our complaints.

Residential schooling, whether directly or indirectly experienced, is many things to many people. The fiction that there will be some cross-individual regularity in the impact of that experience, **and** that research will reveal that regularity, **and** that demonstrating that regularity is necessary to making judgments about the morality of residential schooling (see the previous section) must be revealed for what it is: an attempt to sidestep our justifiable outrage at residential schooling and the mentality that gave rise to it.

Research will not "relieve" the effects of residential schooling. Research, as noted earlier, is about gathering and checking facts. There is nothing inherent in this activity that must make the "gatherers and checkers" feel better. In fact, our own experience and the experience of others we have talked with has been that research has, at times, made us feel frustration, anger, depression, and a host of other emotions, both negative and positive. Nor it is the case, should the "gatherers and checkers" be distinguishable from their "subjects," that subjects must feel better as a result of their participation. It is true that, sometimes, talking about the past may make one feel better about it. However, this ventilation (regardless of how good it may feel) must not be confused with **resolving**, or even addressing, personal or social issues associated with residential schooling. Research may have a contribution to make when it comes time to deal directly with societal and/or personal issues, but **research** and **action to take as might be recommended by research** are distinct enterprises. Perhaps it is useful to keep in mind, as emphasised earlier, that talking about the past may just as easily make one feel worse about it as better. To mistake a research interview for therapy or compensation is to believe that something is being done when it is not.

Research will not determine what to do about residential schooling. This is a subtle point, one that sometimes seems to be universally misunderstood, and therefore it needs a lot of careful thought: knowing all about a problem **doesn't** include knowing what to do about it. It may make certain reactions more plausible than others, or it may suggest where and how to begin, but working out what to do is going to involve trying things and watching what happens. To illustrate this, let's look at an old story...

Probably all of us have heard of the little Dutch boy who, noticing a hole in the dike, stuck his finger in it and thus saved his entire town from death and destruction. The fact that this is singled out as an example of quick thinking and bravery shows that, presented with "the problem," there were all kinds of ways of responding to it: running for help, putting a bucket under the leak, standing there and watching it, ignoring it, and so on and so forth. Thus, **the clear perception of a problem** (a leak) **does not dictate a particular response to it**. Notice also that the reaction chosen was, at best, temporary: just how long would you stand there, even with a crowd of people praising you, before the realities of life would begin to intrude? You have to eat, sleep, go to the bathroom, do your homework, and your finger is turning into a long prune! What, then, is the right thing to do about this leak in the future? Line up a bunch of substitute Dutch boys? Stick a wad of gum in the hole? Leave town (and say goodbye to the unfortunate "last" Dutch boy)? Research no more provides a long-term answer than it does a short term one, **and having a suitable stopgap measure for a problem does not dictate the optimal long-term response to it.**

If we can think like structural engineers for a moment, we should also notice that the Dutch boy's action certainly did not have to be the right thing to do. Plugging that particular hole totally changed (however minutely) the interplay of stress and strain between the water and the dike, and his action could have brought about all manners of dire consequences, like creating innumerable holes along the entire length of the barrier. **In principle,** the little Dutch boy could not have known beforehand that plugging the hole would not lead to disaster: research is about the dynamic system **you have,** not some hypothetical dynamic system that might exist if you made some adjustment. (And, however complex a wall might be, human beings are much more so.) Research **at best** provides us with a snapshot, a picture of what went on within certain limits; no part of that picture is what **will** happen if adjustments are made to the interplay of forces outside those limits.

Research, then, doesn't answer questions, but instead poses more of them. That is, a clear view of problems in a dynamic system **can** provide a background against which interventions can be judged; however, any understanding about what a change has brought about will require more work to get a clear view of the revised system. As to coming up with interventions, research enforces no conditions. Your own creativity is important, and looking up (researching) what others have done about similar problems can sometimes help as well. But there is no research that can be done that proves someone else's answer must work for you.

Research is less an **activity** than it is an **attitude,** a frame of mind adopted by the people doing research that shows they're serious and (as mentioned earlier) that they're willing to try things out and see what happens. With regard to residential schooling, knowing all about what happened **then** will not tell us what to do about it **now,** and while the work of others may suggest possibilities, there will be no substitute for trying various things and seeing the response.

Research will help determine what happened in residential school. As odd as it may seem, the vast majority of people know next to nothing about residential schooling in Canada. We have heard it likened, by sympathetic people who should know better, to boarding school for children of the well-to-do, and even to summer "camp." Others have told us that it was (or must have been) largely indistinguishable from provincial schooling, with similar administrative structures, curricula, goals, and so forth; these people find it difficult to believe the experiences of some of the former students. Others have simply never heard of residential schooling at all.

Even those closer to it do not have a complete view of it, whether formerly they were administrators, staff, or students. Governmental or church officials, in the act of developing policy, had no sadistic vision of specific things happening to specific children; local staff or administration, even when operating within guidelines, didn't have the "rulebook" in one hand as they punished with the other; and students, on the receiving end of the Great Social Experiment, knew only that they were hungry, afraid, or in pain, **not** that their treatment flowed essentially from the legal need to eliminate them. Knowledge of residential schooling is thus likely to be limited to the frame of reference one adopted (or had to adopt) as being part of the "system."

Consequently, the puzzles of residential schooling have many pieces, fitting together in various levels. No level is more complex than another (a tree isn't less complicated than a forest, it is merely a different kind of complexity), and each deserves serious attention. One of the goals of research is to put together each of these puzzles, and to identify the connections linking one level to another. Understanding "what happened" at residential schools will not be exclusively a matter of compiling personal incidents, cabinet meetings, teacher's manuals, or secret agreements, but rather, such tasks each will have its role in comprehending the whole.

Research may help individuals understand their experiences more broadly. As mentioned above, even those who underwent residential schooling cannot know all about it, for no one does. Of course, former attendees of residential schools have a unique perspective on it, as the "targets" or "end products" of the many competing agendas, ideas, initiatives, and motives of a great many western institutions. Decisions made at an institutional level eventually come down to cases: in residential schools, actions motivated or legitimated by policy were carried out **by** individuals **upon** individuals. And, since we experience life as individuals, it was **personal** pain, humiliation, anger, etc. that was experienced, not the "clash of cultures," the "exploitation of resources," the "industrial revolution," or what-have-you.

But even though we experience the world this way, it does not follow that the way the world works must be understood in terms of individual forces. All too often we focus on the individual forces and, inappropriately, ignore influences that are not immediately apparent. For example, children of divorced parents often believe themselves responsible for the breakup; women who were sexually assaulted are often accused as having "brought in on themselves" by dressing or acting "provocatively;" or, unemployed people are frequently described as "just not wanting to work." Similarly, people who attended residential school sometimes attribute their negative experiences to their own actions, something about **them** that accounted for their treatment. These internal explanations can last a long time, and resurface when trying to understand events far removed from residential schools. Well, speaking your Native language may have led to a **specific** beating, but factors like the "why's" and "wherefore's" of the school's language policy, the disciplinary guidelines, and the very mentality that conceived of residential schooling in the first place (all non-personal factors) contributed as much as anything to the specific act. Failure to see the broader context is like dousing a pile of dry leaves with gasoline, handing someone a sparkler, shoving him/her into the pile, and saying "You started a fire!"

One thing research can do is help everyone see the big picture, regardless of where each was (or is) located within it. This is particularly important for First Nations peoples, since we are continually being fed only the localized, individualized picture as "Truth." As long as that is the only picture we see, we will be limited in how we think about residential schooling and what we do about it, as individuals **and** as Nations. For instance, as argued above, trying to maintain a hard-and-fast distinction between attendees and non-attendees is a fiction created by failing to see that schooling was intended to destroy our societies for all time (not just for attendees), and was part of a general, more comprehensive assault on First Nations.

It is important for non-Aboriginals as well. They, too, are being fed the localized, individualized picture, partly, once again, because it will effectively limit their understanding of the scope of residential schooling (and consequently what they will consider to be a reasonable response to it), and partly because it allows those with little or no interest in Aboriginal issues to dismiss it as not concerning them. (This is, of course, not a comprehensive list of the motives behind maintaining this distortion of reality.) However, the broader picture we hope research will help draw will make it more difficult, morally and scientifically, to ignore the obvious.

Research may assist in laying charges. Bringing criminal charges against priests, nuns, bureaucrats, or whomever for actions or omissions of actions that took place in residential school will be a personal decision, and as such is no one else's business. However, properly done research may make it easier for some wishing to do this to develop information that will contribute to their cases. For instance, part of the Royal Commission work will include "guidebooks" to some of the material available in official archives. Research locally done may help identify witnesses, either to specific instances of abuse or to the physical and emotional climate that existed in a particular school.

One other way in which research may help bring charges is in letting people who suffered abuses know their experiences were not isolated incidents, carried out by some aberrant individual within the system and stimulated by some unique flaw within them, the victim (see the previous section). The institutional move to internalize and individualize abusive incidents **separates** people with common cause (see, for example, Chrisjohn & Young, 1993), and fosters the tendency toward self-blame discussed earlier. Research can help overcome the isolation enforced by this institutional pose.

Research may make thoughtful individuals, previously unaware of the role of their society in cultural genocide of First Nations, create the political will for the Canadian governments and churches to deal honorably and fairly with issues arising from residential schooling. In our opinion, there is little or no need to elaborate upon this comment. Suffice it to say that the "sinkhole of memory" is no place for the history of residential schooling to reside.

CONCLUSIONS

By itself, research rights no wrongs, salves no wounds, nor even signals a determination or willingness on the part of **anyone** to address such issues. At best, research merely supports an argument that there is an issue to address; the fact that research is taking place does not mean that anything is going to be done about any condition or problem research may identify. Whatever **response** there may be will arise from moral, political, economic, or social forces, not from the "empirical force" of research (whatever that might be).

Having said that, we still believe research has its place. As difficult as it may seem, if it is well done it will help create the conditions necessary for the response we hope will arise. And remember one of the lessons of the little Dutch boy: doing nothing **is** doing something.

CHAPTER 4:

RESIDENTIAL SCHOOL RESEARCH: PERSONAL

PERSONAL NARRATIVES

> [I]t is not true that the past is dead. It determines our present lives, not absolutely... but certainly more strongly than any power of reason, or any alleged law of politics or sociology or economics. Changing the past therefore means also changing the present, whether by direct example, or by liberating us from our historically determined prejudices... (Murray, preface to Venye's *Bread and Circuses,* 1990).

There are undoubtedly many specific reasons to undertake the personal study of residential schooling, but one reason seems to us to be foremost: the passion to understand one's residential school past, and the past of those who went before, is the desire to see the present in ways other than as it would be depicted by those responsible for it. It is a desire to **make sense** of one's own experiences, as they relate to residential schooling, to sort out one's **current** life dynamics in terms (to some degree) of what has happened before. Indeed, the past is not dead, and, for those for whom residential school is a continuing reality, undoing the myths and half-truths of their experiences is a step toward personal and social freedom.

Well, how does one go about doing this? It's pretty obvious that most of the standard "techniques" of research that have been applied to First Nations peoples are useless here: what are you going to do, give yourself questionnaires? Interview yourself a hundred times and see if you form a consensus? No, this line of thinking leads very quickly to nonsense.

Instead, we consider **personal narratives** the most suitable way to proceed here. Briefly, a narrative is "a way of linguistically representing past experience, whether real or imagined;" if you're concerned with your past, it is a personal narrative. The "linguistically representing" part is a little grandiose, since, to our way of thinking, it only rules out representational forms like mental telepathy, divine inspiration, and racial memory, and these, even if they exist, are notoriously undependable.

WHAT DOES A NARRATIVE LOOK LIKE?

A narrative doesn't look like anything in particular; any way in which a person can express what he or she wishes to express will constitute a narrative. Of course, some "modes of expression" will be more accessible to people in general than others (in expressive movement, for instance, "jumping for joy," could be confused with "sitting on a tack"). If part of your reason for generating a narrative is to make it possible for others to examine it, the more direct and physical the narrative is, the better. Rather than attempt a single, overall definition of narrative forms, we will give some examples.

Autobiographies and Biographies. There are a number of books, some biographical and some autobiographical, about the residential school experiences of individual people. These are not merely records of events, they are also courageous and moving personal histories. Isabella Knockwood's *Out of the Depths* is an excellent example, one we recommend for anyone considering this kind of work. In relating her own experiences, she also tells us of the experiences of other children, her family, the teachers, and others; in giving us her personal history, she documents the history of the school, the problems of recovering the history of the school, and the dynamics of what it was like to live and work there; in the honest portrayal of her own struggle with the task of writing, she lays bare the personal and social difficulties in recounting a hidden past.

As difficult an undertaking as biography or autobiography is, Ms. Knockwood gives a lucid account of the positive and negative aspects of such work. We owe her, and others like her, a great deal: her work has benefitted us all.

Fiction. As Hollywood has been showing us for some time, the line between fact and fiction is a blurry one. Simply because elements of a story are untrue, or are re-ordered for dramatic effect, or are depicted from particular points of view does not make them useless for the purposes of understanding the world. For example, Edward Said's *Culture and Imperialism* undertakes to show how what the novels of imperialist countries take for granted reflects their attitudes toward the rest of the world. Ward Churchill's *Fantasies of the Master Race* examines novels, films, and essays as to how they portray Aboriginal North Americans and what those portrayals mean.

Thus, fiction generated by First Nations peoples, whether it is in the form of novels, plays, short stories, or what-have-you, may also say something useful and important aside from the artistic merit of the work. A good example of a fictional narrative with information value is Shirley Sterling's *My Name is Seepeetza,* an account of her childhood contrasting life inside and outside a residential school. The CBC teleplay about residential school, *Where the Spirit Lives,* is useful in spite of (and because of) some of its limitations.

We must realize that, sometimes, adopting a fictional form of expression allows one to keep a distance from emotionally charged events not easily maintained when treating it as personal history. As long as fiction is **identified as such**, there is little danger of over interpretation and every chance it will say something important.

Declarations. The Royal Commission has already received a considerable number of narratives on residential schooling, in the form of submissions presented at the community sessions that have thus far taken place. In these sessions, some of which have been held in public and some **in camera**, people have simply gotten up and spoken about their experiences. Videotapes/audiotapes of some of these sessions have been made, and comments relevant to the residential school experience transcribed. Other submissions to the Commission have consisted of written accounts, generated by community members, describing their experiences in residential school. All of these are perfectly legitimate sources of information from which the Royal Commission evolved their findings. This kind of material could as well serve informational needs of First Nations communities.

However, personal declarations do not have to be restricted by, for instance, time limits at Commission hearings, willingness of someone to transcribe a narrative, or the accessibility of Commission sessions. Any record such as mentioned above that can be looked at by interested parties would be of use to the community and national work of understanding residential schooling. And, although one person's experience might not bear much specifically on someone else's, the cumulative effect of such declarations could do much to educate ourselves, our children, and the Eurocanadian public about what happened.[3]

Summary. Whether narratives report personal musings, small-group conversations, personal recollections, stories told by one's parents or grandparents, or what-have-you, they can contain material that will help us (individually or collectively) develop the comprehensive understanding of residential schooling described earlier. The format of these narratives is unimportant, except that it provide something that can be used by other, **if such use is to be allowed by the person generating the narrative**. Even if the task is solely to come to grips with one's personal experiences, the act of recording one's experiences may itself be useful. Further, being able to draw upon someone else's journey (which depends on the experiences of these others being available) may help us clarify our experiences to ourselves.

THE GROUND THAT PERSONAL NARRATIVES MIGHT COVER

While the **form** of what's in a narrative can be practically anything, people may still have questions about the narrative's **content**. Again, there are almost no limits; within the ethical boundaries we discussed earlier, people should put anything they consider important into their narratives. However, because some people may feel uncomfortable with so much latitude, we offer here some suggestions concerning what might go into these works. We wish to stress that these are only suggestions, of potentially the same value of any free advice (and that is **nothing**!). Also, this "list" is in no way complete; as you will soon see, when any question is considered for a moment or two, crowds of additional questions (which we don't list) arise pretty much by themselves. We offer these suggestions in the form of a string of potential questions one may pose to oneself:

How do I look back on my time in residential school? What was good about it, and what was bad about it? What happens to me when I think of those times? Do I get angry, sad, nostalgic, etc., or some combinations of these emotions? Do I associate different emotions with certain people, events, or locations?

What do I remember specifically about my time? Where and when did I go to residential school, and who else was there? Who were my friends, and who were not? What did I do? How much did I learn, and **what** did I learn? What things other than learning did I do, and under what conditions (voluntarily or involuntarily) did I do them? Which activities did I enjoy, and which not?

What do I remember about my experiences? What were the significant events, or at least the things that I remember best? What happened, who took part, and what were the circumstances?

What do I remember about other people's experiences? What significant or memorable events did I witness? What happened and what were the circumstances?

How did my life in residential school contrast with my life outside the school? What were the physical, psychological, or emotional differences and similarities between my time in these different surroundings? How did I react to those differences; how did the transition from one place to the other make me feel?

What did residential school teach me about First Nations in general and my Nation in particular? What were the explicit **and** implicit messages about First Nations that were sent to me during my schooling? Were they positive or negative, or a bit of both? How did these messages affect me personally? Did they try to make me feel proud or ashamed, grateful or ungrateful, good or bad, or what? Did I take these messages seriously?

What did my schooling teach me about the world, and the place of First Nations peoples within it? Was it any part of my learning, and why was it or wasn't it? Did I accept the message then, and do I accept it now? Did it seem to me like I was being treated as I was because of **me, personally**, or because of some other reason?

How have I dealt with my residential schooling? Have I perhaps forgotten certain things, or maybe blown other things up to much greater significance than they deserve? Do I consciously avoid thinking about my experiences, and if so, why? Do I feel the past as an influence here in the present, and is it a good presence or a bad one? More broadly, how has my schooling affected my current life? Did if affect things like my spirituality, my feelings toward my people, my connection to my language and culture, my feelings toward non-Indian people, and my feelings about myself? If so, how? If not, why not?

How am I, today, to talk and think about my past? Are there people I wish to thank, or perhaps blame? If I had the chance, what would I say today to the people who ran the residential school while I was there? What would I say to the bureaucrats, politicians, and other officials who conceived and designed the system?

What can I do that I have not done about my past schooling? What should I tell my friends, my family, and my children? What do I have to say that I would like them to hear?

There is no "proper order" in which to address these suggestions, or any questions that might arise from thinking about them, any more than there is a "right way" to express yourself on these topics. Saying what you feel is necessary, in the way you wish to say it, **for the reasons you wish to do it**, is what is important.

THINGS WE RECOMMEND TO KEEP IN MIND

Don't Do This Alone. Even when a personal narrative is to be used exclusively for your own purposes, or even if it is fictional, or whatever the particulars of your case, this is not a journey to undertake by yourself. Secure the help of a friend who will at the very least lend you a sympathetic ear from time to time. Although not a co-author, this friend should be aware of what you're doing and why, and be given a copy of ethical guidelines and other materials that will let them[4] know something about what they've agreed to do.

One reason we recommend this is of course practical: even an audience of one will help you organize your thoughts and keep at the work, especially when the audience shows a genuine interest in what it is you're doing. Even more significant, however, is the real possibility (which we mentioned earlier) that going over such emotionally-charged material will impact on your present life. A friend who knows what you are doing, and who is somewhat more removed from your experiences than you are, can act as an early warning system and notice hazards overlooked by someone too close to the path to see the stones.

Explanation versus Description. We think that it is important to keep in mind the relevance of a personal narrative. What is it for? What does it tell me that I (or others) don't already know? These are serious questions, for how they are answered may steer narrative-based conclusions into dangerous areas. One way to look at a personal narrative is as an analysis of causes: "I'm the way I am **because** such-and-such happened to me; our community is in such-and-such a way **because** this happened to our members." Such readings of narratives we will call **causal**, because they imply action-reaction linkages between events and interpret narratives as reports concerning those linkages.

As we will argue more thoroughly elsewhere, we do not favour a causal interpretation of narratives. Philosophically, these kinds of explanations commit those holding them to the mechanistic, victim-blaming positions (a la Residential School Syndrome) we have already rejected. Furthermore, from a technical viewpoint, it once again invites the wholesale dismissal of First Nations grievances if and when such linkages fail to be demonstrated.

Rather than looking at narratives as reports about the action of causes in a person's life, we think it more reasonable to think of them as **descriptions**, as ways of elaborating other circumstances of a person's life that make other actions by that person more intelligible. Thus, some people may credit their "business success" and others attribute "difficulty in sharing emotion" to their respective experiences in residential school. There is no contradiction between these accounts, nor is there anything objectionable about the assertions, unless one presumes a uniformity of residential school experience and a mechanistic view of human behaviour. Rather than conflicting accounts of cause-effect connections, these attributions are part of descriptions of the lives of these people, descriptions that may make their present circumstances more understandable.

Instead of falling into the habit of making or assuming our personal narratives are some kind of causal explanation for our actions, then, we recommend thinking of them as descriptions that make us more intelligible to one another.

Don't Overgeneralize. We mentioned earlier that there is no inconsistency between some people saying they liked residential school while others say they hated it. However, controversy arises quickly when those statements are extended past their limits, as for example, when "Residential school was good for me" becomes "Residential school was good for me, and therefore it was good for all Indians." The "therefore" part doesn't make sense at all.

Such "extensions" are so common that people on different sides of an argument often make them without even realizing it. Often, the extensions are not even stated, but merely taken for granted. We call this **overgeneralizing,** and consider it dangerous because 1) it goes beyond the available evidence (knowing one bad teacher doesn't mean all teachers are bad), and 2) it emotionally polarizes the issues under discussion (no one enjoys being prejudged or preclassified on the basis of information about someone else).

In developing your personal narrative, our suggestion is to avoid as far as possible the tendency to draw general conclusions from your personal experience. Perhaps a better way of thinking about this is, as mentioned earlier, not to confuse **what you know** with **what you think you know**. There is absolutely no harm in having an opinion and expressing it; however, opinion disguised as fact misleads some people, angers others, and invites nit-picking by critics.

If combined, overgeneralization and unsupportable causal explanation leads to the kind of nonsense that passes as, for example, psychological "science." In working out and sharing your personal narrative, telling **your** story will be an unique contribution that will last for all time. Even if it is not something you wish to share, it will become neither more useful to you nor a deeper, more penetrating analysis if dressed up in the pomp and circumstance of empty pseudoscientific jargon.

Don't feel obligated. We have stated earlier, and repeat here, that no one should feel coerced into participating in research. Since, with personal narratives the "researcher" and the "researched" is one in the same, this amounts to warning people thinking about constructing a personal narrative **not to let your desire to tell your story override your wish to keep private matters private**. Your decision to develop a narrative or not must be based on a consideration of your ethical responsibility to yourself.

Furthermore, even if you decided to develop a "tangible" narrative for strictly your own purposes (that is, it isn't to be shared with your community, the Royal Commission, or others), you should be aware that, once having written it (or otherwise made it concrete), there will be a lingering danger that it will fall outside your control. Ultimately, the safest place for your private matters to reside is in your own head.

How do You Start, And When Are You Finished?

We honestly don't know how to start. Our experience has been that personal narratives, like good conversations, seem to have started by themselves sometime before anyone noticed that there was one going on. Our suggestion, then, is merely to make it possible for it to happen... think about some of the questions we posed, talk to a friend here or there about it, and so on... and it will come. In truth, many people who attended residential school have long ago begun working on their "personal narratives," but merely haven't committed their work to a form more solid than their memories.

Unfortunately, we are even less helpful when it comes to stopping. Research, in the form of a personal narrative or otherwise, is **never** finished. At some point, you must make an arbitrary decision to cut back or even stop one activity in order to pursue others, and this will happen for your work on your narrative. If your narrative is something to be shared, whatever part of it that is available, in whatever stage of completion, will be a contribution.

We are "Works In Progress," and our willingness and ability to share ourselves with one another are two of the more important parts of being human.

CHAPTER 5:

RESIDENTIAL SCHOOL RESEARCH: COMMUNITY

INTRODUCTION: THE ROLE OF COMMUNITY RESEARCH

In many ways our recommendations concerning community-level research are just extensions of what we have already written about in earlier sections. The limitations as discussed in Chapter 3, of this appendix, apply as much to community as they do to personal research, and the ground to be covered and the things to be kept in mind are of similar relevance whether one's approach is aimed at either the community or the personal level. Here we cover a few more information sources pertinent to a community approach, and bring up community-level issues that don't arise when your focus is on your personal residential school experiences.

The work of a community-based researcher is with a different **form** of complexity than that confronting someone working on a personal narrative. Where individually-based researchers are concerned with making their current lives intelligible in light of their pasts, community-based researchers aim at making a local populace intelligible to itself, **as** a populace, in light of the history of the community (which includes the history of its individual members). This isn't a matter of somehow adding up a number of "individual pasts" and averaging. While individual, personal dynamics have some degree of relevance to the dynamics of a group, they are not functions of one another. How a social **group** might (in a metaphorical sense) collectively deal with the worries, fantasies, strengths, weaknesses, abilities, deficits, trials, and tribulations of its **membership** will be an end result of **a local, entirely unpremeditated sequence of events**. (We say "metaphorical" because social groups are not human beings, and it is stretching language to talk as if they were. For example, the dike in the story of the little Dutch boy didn't decide to behave the way that it did; it just turned out that way). A **description** of how a group of people coexist, which is one of the aims of community research, will have no generalizations to make, and will include relatively few **conscious** decisions to behave one way as opposed to another.[5] Community-based researchers thus have the enormous job of saying **how** without falling too far into saying why.

Furthermore, **social** forces, which intrude upon us constantly but which we seldom consider when trying to understand **individual** behaviour, are more obviously pertinent to an understanding pegged at a community level. For example, it sounds terribly odd to say Mr. Su (a hypothetical 19th century citizen of China) was addicted to opium in part because of England's unfavourable balance of trade with India, but less odd to say that opium addiction in 19th century China was due in part to the same economic influence. Nevertheless, both assertions are quite defendable. Identifying and incorporating such social factors into a community description is thus a major part (perhaps the most important part) of the task of community-based researchers. Because our life experiences are **necessarily** personal and individual, and because western ideology works (through education, media, political debate, "professional standards," and other forms of indoctrination) to limit our understanding to personal and individual influences, individuals developing personal narratives will generally (though not always) **see the unfolding of their residential school experiences in personal and individual terms!**[6] As we will show in more detail elsewhere, this leads both to self-blame ("bad things happened to me because I'm bad") and denial of responsibility ("bad things happened because of bad circumstances outside my control").

Community-level research, by reaching outside the boundaries set by a philosophical viewpoint limited to internal, individual influences, thus establishes a broader framework for understanding local and personal events. In this space, individual people will be able to work out more clearly what aspects of their lives they are and are not responsible for.

Community-based researchers thus have a **different** puzzle than that confronting their individually-focused compatriots. The fact that some pieces work for both puzzles sometimes confuses us into believing there is only one puzzle, or that one of them is only a part of the "bigger" puzzle, or that one puzzle is "truer" than the other. Each puzzle, however, presents its own problems and deserves consideration upon its own merits. Thus, the role of community-based researchers is to work on **their** puzzles, sharing as requested pieces of their work that will assist people in their individual projects, and, ultimately, trying to make clear whatever portion of their puzzle they are eventually able to assemble.

SOURCES OF COMMUNITY-BASED INFORMATION

Personal Narratives. In general, a major source of community-level information will be narratives generated by members of that community. Rather than being involved with working out their own narratives (which they may or may not do as a **personal** decision), in our opinion a central concern of community-based researchers is creating the conditions that will help community members develop their own narratives. This may involve acting, as mentioned earlier, as the "sympathetic ear" to people working on their narratives, or connecting up different community members when the pairing is useful and agreed upon by the members, or having knowledge of and contact with community services that may be required by people working on their narratives, and so on.

Should individual researchers receive access to individual narratives of community members, these will assist in developing an understanding of the community as a whole, though not, as we have argued, by some kind of averaging. Specific narratives may be used to **illustrate** part of the description being developed. Or they may help make an historical description more vivid through eyewitness accounts of what happened.[7]

Meetings, Conferences, and Workshops. Another way in which a community-based researcher may act to create the conditions for people to develop their own narratives is by organizing local events with residential schooling as theme. These do not have to be large, formal gatherings, nor need residential schooling be the only topic under discussion. Indeed, meetings held locally, in informal circumstances, will help individuals working on personal narratives find a supportive atmosphere for sharing experiences and information, and lessen the isolation often experienced during narrative development.

Of course, such get-togethers carry the ethical constraints of any research activity. Meeting organizers, being aware of the personal psychological impact the discussion of residential schooling might raise, should either be prepared to address those needs themselves, or make provisions for others to provide assistance as needed.

Not only do community-based researchers benefit from whatever assistance such meetings lend to work on personal narratives, the proceedings, minutes, notes, or other records of the meetings (if transcribing is permitted) themselves become additional sources of information. Furthermore, because these records will usually be interpersonal rather than personal, they may assist researchers at something closer to the form of complexity they operate at.

Interviews. Another form of active (rather than reactive) development of information is for community-based researchers to conduct interviews with consenting parties. This approach more obviously falls within the purview of western research, with its attendant statistical/ideological presumptions. However, simply because it was built that way doesn't mean it has to be **used** that way. In this vein, mention should be made of the exemplary work of Linda Bull *(Indian Residential Schooling: The Native Perspective)* and N. Rosalyn Ing *(The Effects of Residential Schools on Native Child-Rearing Practices)* who conducted their work, in part, via interviews. Their writing would repay close study by anyone thinking about undertaking community-based research.

One advantage of an interview approach is that community-based researchers are not constrained by the willingness of individuals to develop and share their personal narratives. Also, as long as a community researcher doesn't take on too many associations at one time, individuals may take their interviews as being narrative work, with the researcher acting as the "interested listener" as described in Chapter 4 of this appendix.

The disadvantages of interviewing stem from its ideological heritage. Most obviously, there is a built-in disparity between the interviewer (the "objective scientist") and the interviewee (the "object of study"). Even the slightest inclination along this line of thinking leads to the kinds of problems First Nations peoples have always had with outside researchers. At the very least it is a surreptitious reformulation of the "narrator-interested listener" relationship we have argued for thus far. And not too far down the road, it leads to all the misplaced precision and imperiousness of western research: "standard" questions are recorded verbatim, transcribed, and analyzed privately later to reveal the "underlying truth" (of which, of course, the informant is ignorant), which is then published (with suitable accolades) in a "scientific" journal. Well, la-de-da!

To our minds, the way to avoid this scenario is to use an interview in the way you wish instead of in the way someone else says you must. Make explicit and take seriously any relationship you work out with a community member; **what** is to be used by **whom**, and in what format, are matters to settle before any conversation takes place; don't put words in their mouths, and remember **they** are the ones to say whether or not you have; have some general idea about the ground to be covered, but don't reduce it to a checklist which has to be completed; let the interview unfold in its own way, like a good conversation.

In terms of community researchers drawing their conclusions from interviews, we think it important to keep in mind (here as elsewhere) the technical points we have been raising all along: describe, rather than explain; avoid overgeneralization; broaden and supplement the individual perspectives you obtain with social, political, economic, and historical information as appropriate. And finally, don't let anyone make you think that any modifications you found you had to devise to a "standard" approach has rendered the interviews intrinsically worthless; nobody owns the concept of "an interview."

Archival Information. A fourth contribution that can be made by community-level researchers is through accessing archival data, information such as might be found in public records, governmental or school document centers and repositories, libraries, museums, collections, and so forth. If a number of individuals are working on personal narratives, information from these sources can help them fill in details of their specific experiences. (In *Out of the Depths*, for example, Isabella Knockwood reproduced the form her parents were required to sign to "transfer" her to the control of Indian Affairs.) To the extent that, in a particular community, a number of people will be looking for similar old records, each will be reproducing the other's work in finding it. Community-based researchers can make this task easier for everyone by letting people know what kind of information is available, and where to find it.

For the community-based researcher personally, this kind of material is useful as well in their task of describing the community as a community. Archives may provide the historical background of a local First Nation, helping show a continuity between past and present circumstances. Details of local First Nations (numbers, ages, language groups, etc.,), both for the present and for times past, may be available, and existing reports may contain specific information of interest (numbers of students at a local residential school in a particular year; names of students and staff; amounts of money spent on clothes or food for resident students; etc.,). All this and more could contribute to describing as comprehensively as possible the local community and how residential schooling functioned with respect to it.

Of course, archival information might "speak" quite eloquently all by itself. Although not directly concerned with residential schooling, a superb example of how this can be achieved is Andre Lopez's *Pagans in our Midst*. With little commentary and only the broadest organization, Lopez simply reproduces the news items and advertisements that had First Nations content for a dozen or so local newspapers between 1885 and 1910. The ideological biases of non-Indian society, prejudice, racism, and so on become clear as you work your way through the material, with a cumulative intellectual and emotional impact that is convincing and overpowering. This kind of "personal project," which could be developed from various archives of materials dealing with residential schooling, does not depend on infringing upon anyone's narrative. And yet, as a "biography" of a community, it could be as useful and as important as **any** piece of work.

Summary. These do not in any way exhaust the informational resources of community-based researchers. As we noted earlier, once research has begun it is likely that refinements, extensions, and completely new ideas will occur to any researcher. In judging your own particular approach to generating information, you must first be convinced that the ethical criteria discussed at length in Chapter 2, of this appendix, are satisfied. In deciding what an information source can and cannot tell you, our recommendation is to make your best case, as explicitly as possible, about the scope and quality of your data. If others disagree with your assessment, at least they will be dealing with **your** position and not with what **they say** your position is.

Finally, we hope it goes without saying that these approaches do not exclude one another. Certain kinds of information might come by different approaches in different places, and whatever it takes to tell the story of a community is fair game.

Toward a Community-Level Understanding of Residential Schooling

Assembling the Puzzle. We hope we have given community-based researchers a sense of how their work differs from that of individual community members, even as it depends upon it. We also hope that we have been able to provide a general idea of what sources of information are available for this work. Figuratively speaking, information is all around us, and as community-based researchers get into their work, we think they will be able to supplement greatly the sketch we have offered here. The last technical matter we will consider is what to do with all this information.

Competitive plausibility. Narratives, publications, archives, and other locally developed sources of information are somehow to be combined in as comprehensive a description as possible of a First Nations community. When residential schooling is the topic, the point of the work is to try to understand what residential schooling has meant to the community; metaphorically, from what parts of the world, and into what parts of the community, has residential schooling reached? How has it operated inside and outside the First Nations community? How does it continue to operate?

There is an almost overwhelming tendency to think there must be a "right way" to put all this information together. However, this is just another form of the western bias to view personal and interpersonal activity in terms of internal, individual, causal forces. There is no right way; one account may have longer words than another, or be better organized, or emphasize different points, or make more use of personal narratives, and so on. But once we see that differing accounts aren't approximations to a "real" or "true" account (that lists the "true" variables and that specifies the "right" causal forces), we will be able to judge community descriptions according to how well they do the possible, rather than in terms of how well they do the impossible.

To talk about what's possible we've borrowed (and modified) Martin Bernal's (*Black Athena*) concept of competitive plausibility. Assume that there are at least two ways of accounting for a body of information. Information from multiple sources, that has "gaps" in it, and that doesn't (and can't) identify its connections with other pieces of information, simply will not help us to decide definitively between the two accounts. Rather than abandon both as undecidable, he suggests we view the adequacy of each account in light of its plausibility given the alternative(s). The notions of "proof" and "truth" are, he argues, inappropriate under these conditions, while a judgment of "account A seems more plausible than account B" may well apply.

In Bernal's approach, there is still the latent notion of "truth" (an unknowable one) lurking about, and we would prefer to avoid accepting even this much; one could with little difficulty find oneself speculating on all manners of unknowable inner causal mechanisms. In addition, plausible alternative syntheses (what big words!) seem easier to come by in Academia than elsewhere; locally derived accounts of local circumstances are unlikely to have given rise to systematic alternative accounts. Thus, community-based researchers, having the additional task of suggesting other ways of viewing the information at their disposal, may become open to the charge of demolishing "straw men" when the researchers themselves have to propose alternatives to their favored accounts.

We suggest community researchers go ahead anyway, developing as plausible an account as they can and bringing up alternatives (straw ones or not) as their explications require. Let's be serious: what are alternative accounts for the residential school experience, at a personal or a community level? Indians and their children are innately depraved and the schools were an attempt to save their souls? The governments designed, approved, and operated the systems out of the goodness of their hearts? Children who had a bad time of it were stupid, unruly savages who might have benefitted from having their spirits broken? Childhood sexual experiences are a way of developing healthy adult sexuality? When unstated counterarguments are made explicit, they are as ugly, racist, and paternalistic as anything local researchers are likely to come up with. The fact that they all have the logical and moral force of "straw men" reveals the depth of the injustice done.

Consequently, we can't understand why **we** should have to apologize for the vacuity of **their** arguments.

So, community researchers, go ahead as needed and build your men of straw: if nonIndians get upset enough, they may be moved to a serious examination of the histories and motives of their own societies.

Stepping Outside Your Community: Throwing Away Band-Aids. We have been quite specific that even successful research concerned with residential schooling leads to no particular program of what to do about it. More specifically, if, say, one wishes to make therapeutic recommendations, additional therapeutic research will have to be carried out; legal recommendations will require legal research; and so on. And yet, research on different specific topics can make contributions to inquiries in other areas. Just as individual dynamics and social dynamics are not functions of one another but can be mutually relevant, research on one topic often has something to tell another topic, and vice versa. We predict, then, that during the time allocated for putting the information together, concerns will arise about how the research on residential schooling may contribute to doing something about it.

We see both an indirect and a direct way a contribution can be made. Indirectly, once a community has successfully carried out its own research it becomes easier to do it again. Experience really is the best teacher, and after your first go, research into other topics (community reclamation, therapy, law, etc.,) may follow easily. At the very least, even if your First Nation decides to seek specialized assistance in future research, you become a critical consumer and less susceptible to the elliptical blather of a smooth-talking consultant.

However useful this might be, it does seem somewhat pie-in-the-sky and unsatisfactory. Isn't there some use to be made that is more practical and direct? Yes. We said earlier that perhaps the most important task of community-based researchers was to identify and incorporate broad social forces into their accounts of communities. Well, an inquiry into the local community dynamics can easily include an examination of how local social forces are controlled by forces more remote. Let's be blunt: we often complain that the programs we develop or administer are merely "band-aids" that really don't make any long-term changes. This is true, but the complaint doesn't generally lead to a critical examination of questions like where we're getting the band-aids and why we keep applying them. We think this is something that needs to be hit very hard at the local level, for all too often the reliance on those outside our communities, Aboriginals or not, has merely meant bringing in various kinds of band-aid salespersons.

If we want to change the system, our first task is to understand how it works, not just at one level but at all levels. Once this is more completely understood, any change that is made can be examined in terms of how the system has reacted as a whole. Research may not be able to tell us precisely what to do about residential schooling, for individuals or for communities, but if we want eventually to do something useful, an understanding of the forces that brought about and maintain its influence, and an examination of our own role in this dynamic, is of primary importance.

CHAPTER 6:

THE FUTURE ROLE OF THE ROYAL COMMISSION

We began this appendix by stating that our interest was in making what contribution we could to community-based research (that is, research that was initiated, developed, implemented, analyzed, and controlled by First Nations communities). The Commission is, of course, engaged in its own research on the topic, **and any and all materials bearing on residential schooling submitted to the Commission will gratefully be accepted.** However, our need was never our motive, and we would be more troubled by receiving information released reluctantly than by receiving no information at all.

Nevertheless, it is only fair that those contemplating this possibility be aware of how their submissions will be handled.[8] First, all submissions will be treated with strict adherence to the ethical protocols as laid out in Chapter 2 of this appendix. All submissions will be under lock and key when not under physical supervision, and access will be limited to individuals with a direct professional interest in the material. As well, these individuals have agreed to abide by the Commissions ethical guidelines. Second, to the extent permitted by our ethical requirements, the Commission will in the final report acknowledge the contributions made by all submitters. We will not be able to be too specific directly in the text, but we will give full and public credit for contributions.

Finally, we should try to address just what we will do with the information submitted. Unfortunately, the best we can do is to say it will encompass all the suggestions in Chapters 4 and 5, of this appendix, made for both individual and community researchers, and more. We are in the position of the community researcher seeking the assistance of someone writing a personal narrative: we have the aim of what we hope to achieve set out in broad stroke, but we can't say at this time just what use we will be able to make of any particular piece of information. Broadly, we intend to produce a history of Indian Residential Schooling (and produce a guidebook for finding material available in government and church archives), an overview of the existing social and psychological work that has been done in residential schooling and related areas, and survey the legal issues (national and international) that arise out of Canada's residential school past. Further, we hope to put all of this together in a way that leaps past whatever individual limitations we who are working on this issue may have. But in the final analysis, we can only promise what community researchers promise the members of their local groups: you will have our absolute best effort.

FOOTNOTES

1. Following Penelope (1990), we will on occasion employ the plural pronoun "they" (and its cognates) rather than clumsier constructions like "he or she." The former is the way we really speak, and the latter is a reflection of a linguistic snobbery up with which we should not put.

2. Of course, the genocide of the Tasmanians was a bureaucractic and scientific achievement... there are still plenty of "genetically" indigenous Tasmanians around, it's just that the government of the oppressive Tasmanians of European descent has defined them out of existence. With this act the government defined their obligations to the indigenous peoples out of existence, as well. See Cove, 1995.

3. By the way of analogy, the Fortunoff Video Archive for Holocaust Testimonies in New Haven, Connecticut, has collected over 1,500 videotapes of accounts of those who suffered during the Nazi Holocaust. this archive is not only a record to be used by future historians, it is a powerful refutation to those who pretend today that the Holocaust never took place.

4. We told you!

5. Some may argue that social groups make conscious decisions all the time, e.g., elections, adopting a constitution, passing laws. We would argue that much of this is purely imaginary (did Canadians consciously adopt the convolutions of Free Trade? How many actually contributed to the agreement?) or part of the social mythology used to maintain group cohesion and intergenerational continuity. The myths and illusions of a culture are certainly interesting, but it is stretching them to treat such accounts as statements of fact. These issues aside, we intend our assertion to be more modest; simply, that most of the day-to-day activities of a social group weren't **adopted**. That is, they didn't come about as a result of a conscious decision to do things "that way," or, if they did, we have little or no need to know about them now. Why are books the size they are? Why does school end at 3:30? Why do we drive on the right side of the road? These are not mysteries, but practices that have grown up for reasons now remote to most of us.

6. This isn't intended as a slight to anyone: as Chomsky has pointed out numerous times, any successful system of indirect control (like advertising) must **seem** to be ineffective, or we would get upset at blatant attempts to manipulate us. Thus **all of us**, regardless of how vigilant we are, will from time to time fall victim to the habit of focussing on personal, internal influences while overlooking nonpersonal, external influences. We all just have to keep trying.

7. This can be taken too far, as in the ludicrous television "miniseries" format which purports to help us understand some incredibly catastrophic occurence (like World War II or the American Slave Trade) in terms of how it affected three or four central characters.

8. All materials submitted thus far to the Royal Commission on Aboriginal Peoples have been treated in accordance with the ethical protocols described in this appendix.

Work Cited in The Text And Useful Supplementary Materials

Anderson, K. (1991). *Chain Her by One Foot: The Subjugation of Women in Seventeenth-Century New France*. New York: Routledge. How European economic, political, and ecclesiastical imperialism subverted Huron and Montagnais societies. Important for its ability to show the "big picture," and its comparison of gender relations in the two worlds.

Bernal, M. (1987). *Black Athena: The Afroasiatic Roots of Classical Civilization*. Vol. 1. Rutgers, New Jersey: University Press. An incredibly engaging account of African and Levantine influences on classical civilization. Of methodological interest here 1) in his development of the argument for competitive plausibility, and 2) in his examination of the role of academic racism in the development of historical philology.

Bull, L. (1991). Indian Residential Schooling: The Native Perspective. *Canadian Journal of Native Education*, 18, 3-63. As stated in the text, a model of what can be accomplished by a community-based research approach incorporating multiple sources of information.

Chrisjohn, R., Belleau, C., & Others. (1991). Faith Misplaced: Lasting Effects of Abuse in a First Nations Community. *Canadian Journal of Native Education*, 18, 161-197. A report of the Cariboo Tribal Council's comprehensive attempt to examine the impact of residential schooling, and what might be done about it. It shows what's possible, and impossible, via standard methodological approaches.

Chrisjohn, R., Pace, D., Young, S., & Mrochuk, M. (1997). *Psychological assessment and First Nations: Ethics, Theory, and Practice.* Appendis C of this volume. A look at problems with presuming psychological tests apply to First Nations people. Emphasis is on showing the technical basis for particular ethical standards, though philosophical limitations are noted as well.

Chrisjohn, R., & Young, S. (1997). *Among School Children: Psychological Imperialism and the Residential School Experience in Canada.* Appendix E of this volume. An examination of how the worldview of psychology and other social sciences undermine an effective understanding of, and response to, residential schooling.

Churchill, W. (1992). *Fantasies of the Master Race: Literature, Cinema, and the Colonization of American Indians.* Edited by M. Annette Jaimes. Monroe, Maine: Common Courage Press. Churchill shows how western oppression of First Nations is reflected, both subtly and blatantly, within a range of media (films; detective novels; etc.). Extremely entertaining scholarship.

Churchill, W. (1994). *Indians Are Us?: Cultural Genocide in Native North America*, Monroe, Maine: Common Courage Press. More pertinent essays and analyses by Churchill. The introductory chapter is an important and readable exposition of genocide in international law and how it applies to the lives of the Indians of North America today.

Cove, J. (1995). *What the Bones Say: Tasmanian Aborigines, Science and Domination.* Ottawa: Carleton University Press. Genocide the easy way...

Devens, C. (1992). *Countering Colonization: Native American Women and Great Lakes Missions*, 1630-1900. Los Angeles: University of California Press. Another useful examination of the breadth of the attack on First Nations forms of life.

Furniss, E. (1992). *Victims of Benevolence: Discipline and Death at the Williams Lake Indian Residential School.* Williams Lake, British Columbia: Cariboo Tribal Council. A look at the institutional history of the St. Joseph's school, and how it was experienced by the First Nations in and around Williams Lake. Well carried out, and a model for this kind of investigation.

Freedman, D., Pisani, R., Purves, R., & Adhikari, A. (1991). *Statistics.* 2nd Ed. New York: Norton. The discipline of Statistics is useless for most of the methods discussed in this booklet, but if you must, then learn from the best. This is an introductory level text, but reflects more understanding of statistics than any other book we're familiar with.

Haig-Brown, C. (1988). *Resistance and Renewal: Surviving the Indian Residential School.* Vancouver: Tillacum Library. An interview-based examination of the institution of residential schooling and its impact on the lives of individuals. A classic account.

Ing, N. R. (1991). The Effects of Residential Schooling on Native Child-rearing Practices. *Canadian Journal of Native Education*, 18, 65-118. Community-based research, primarily using interviews, looking at lingering consequences of residential schooling. A solid and important contribution.

Jaimes, M. A. (Ed.). (1992). *The State of Native America: Genocide, Colonization, and Resistance*. Boston: South End Press. A collection of thoughtful essays covering a range of topics particularly useful to the task of developing the "big picture." Essential.

Knockwood, I. (1992). *Out of the Depths: The Experiences of Mi'kmaw Children at the Indian Residential School at Shubenacadie, Nova Scotia*. Lockeport, Nova Scotia: Roseway Publishing. A moving autobiographical account of Ms. Knockwood's schooling. She also provides insight into the personal struggles involved with working out one's personal history. Highly recommended.

Lopez, A. (Undated). *Pagans in Our Midst*. Rooseveltown, New York: Akwesasne Notes. An unsurpassed, eloquent book on race relations, demonstrating the power of simply letting the facts speak for themselves.

Penelope, J. (1990). *Speaking freely: Unlearning the Lies of our Father's Tongues*. Toronto: Pergammon. A penetrating account of the subtle ways that racist, sexist, paternalistic frames of reference are presumed. Be sure to read the introduction (she really isn't as anti-male as many seem to take her). An absolute must.

Said, E. (1993). *Culture and Imperialism*. New York: Alfred A. Knopf. A brilliant account of how the west's perspective is mirrored in their literature, poetry, and other narrative forms. Difficult going, but indispensable.

Sieber, J. (1992). *Planning Ethically Responsible Research: A Guide for Students and Internal Review Boards*. Beverly Hills, California: Sage. Thorough overview and discussion of ethical issues associated with research. Strongly recommended.

Sterling, S. (1992). *My Name is Seepeetza*. Vancouver: Groundwood Books. A prize-winning fictionalized account of Ms. Sterling's childhood, in and out of residential school. Very well done.

Standards for Educational and Psychological Testing. (1985). Washington, D.C.: American Psychological Association. The ethical guidelines that educators, psychologists, and other test administrators are *supposed* to be following. The shortfalls between ethics and practice are commented on in Chrisjohn, Pace, Young, and Mrochuk (infra).

APPENDIX C

PSYCHOLOGICAL ASSESSMENT AND FIRST NATIONS:

ETHICS, THEORY, AND PRACTICE

Roland Chrisjohn, Deborah Pace, Sherri Young, & Marcia Mrochuk

Versions of this paper previously have been presented at the MOKAKIT Conference, Ottawa, 1990, the Canadian Psychological Association Conference, Calgary, 1991, and the Treaty 7 Education Conference, Calgary, 1993.

INTRODUCTION

Many years ago a psychologist who tested a number of school children on one of our reserves (RDC) with the Wechsler scale concluded that somewhere between 50% and 75% of us were mentally subnormal. Some thirty years later another psychologist came out, armed with the revised version of Wechsler's scale, for another session. His conclusion, at times fairly percolating with optimism (for he had read the first study), was that nowadays "only" 25% to 50% of us were mentally subnormal.

Were we inclined to be generous, we suppose that this could be regarded as progress of a sort; but to us these incidents reflect more an astonishing lack of progress in appreciating the problems that arise when using tests with people for whom they were not developed. This particular misapplication points, however, to an even bigger problem in test usage, ignorance of psychometrics. The knot of illogic and bad psychometric practice standing behind the conclusions drawn by brother educational psychologists separated by 30 years is tangled beyond anything Alexander the Great ever had to deal with. And yet, in our experience, their behaviour is the norm rather than exceptional.

In considering what leads psychologists and psychometrists to pronounce such absurdities with a straight face, try as we might we can only come up with three explanations. For the purposes of this paper we concentrate on the first: psychologists, educators, and other test users who do such things just don't understand the connections between psychometric theory and their own ethical guidelines for testing. Our other explanations (two, that they don't know their ethical guidelines for testing, or three, they don't care that they're violating them) would obviate the pedagogical strategy we will pursue here and make litigation preferable. Indeed, to the extent that at least some test users are describable in terms of our second and third explanations, litigation will be necessary. However, we would like to think (and we may be deluding ourselves) that once the theoretical basis of ethical practice is made clear, most of the problem will disappear.

There are, of course, psychometrists who know full well why the guidelines are the way they are. We ask their indulgence if we try their patience, but must point out that their efforts to reign in their colleagues seem to have gotten nowhere. Maybe we will have more success.

Our self-appointed task, then, is to play the part of Alexander with the "knot" mentioned above. Like Alexander we will let our urgency show, and, after some preliminary fiddling hack our way through it. Unlike Alex, however, our urgency does not arise from impatience as much as from our perception of the seriousness and depth of the problems to be discussed. Even a little spade work in the psychological and educational literatures on First Nations peoples will reveal absurdities that match or exceed the story we began with: e.g., as a population, Indians are "right-brained," have aberrant "learning styles," suffer from an abundance of fetal alcohol "effects," are variously "learning disabled," and, in general, are just less intelligent than (almost) everyone else. Most of these conclusions have been reached through the misuse of "cognitive" tests like the Wechsler series, but orectic obloquy ain't far behind: e.g., elsewhere it has been declared, on the basis of work using the Minnesota Multiphasic Personality Inventory (MMPI), that Lakota children (and, it is implied, all First Nations children) are successful students to the extent that they are not Paranoid, Depressed, Schizophrenic, Hypochondriacal, etc., etc. In all these cases and more, the treatment of psychological test results as absolute measures, in violation of ethical standards, is foundational.

All these concerns are magnified in a society that, nominally at least, prides itself on not being a "melting pot," but instead celebrates the diversity of its population. If the commitment of psychologists and educators to multiculturalism is to be other than an ill wind, they must understand clearly what they can or cannot achieve in assessing people who do not share a Eurocentric "form of life." While we focus on problems of cross-cultural assessment of First Nations Peoples, we hope you will agree the issues raised are more fundamental.

EXISTING ETHICAL STANDARDS AND TESTING

The present ethics code, **Standards for Educational and Psychological Testing** (American Educational Research Association, American Psychological Association, and National Council on Measurement in Education, 1985), superseded the 1974 version and was adopted by the parallel Canadian associations shortly after it was accepted in the United States. The late Melvin Novick, who chaired the committee which did the rewrite, certainly knew the dangers of pushing the results of an assessment further than psychometric theory allowed (many of his papers were concerned one way or another with the topic), and the **Standards** are suffused with warnings to that effect.

The basic thrust of these warnings can be summarized in three statements: (1) the psychometric properties of any standardized test are a function of the group upon whom it is developed; (2) in giving a standardized test to a new group, the psychometric properties of the test change, perhaps slightly, perhaps greatly, but there is no way to tell without looking; and (3) therefore, before drawing the same conclusions from the test results in a new group as you would for the norming group, the psychometric properties of the standardized test must be reestablished in the new group. It should go without saying that it is not tests that are biased, but rather people's interpretations of them: people have prejudices, are racist, are sexist, etc., and standardized tests are merely some handy tools that can be and are employed for ideological ends. It is to the credit of Novick and his colleagues that, in the **Standards**, they make a concerted effort to mitigate the usefulness of these tools toward those ends, and they do this by pointing out, simply, that educational and psychological measures are not absolutes. Whether or not this was done with humanitarian or egalitarian motives is, for our purposes, irrelevant, as Novick himself would agree: warnings against using or interpreting tests outside test development groups are based on the mathematics and statistics of applicable test theory, not on Novick's politics, whatever they were.

Broadly, then, we are in agreement with the thrust of the **Standards**. Having said this we still have some bones to pick with them. For one thing, much of the wording is, in our opinion, overly qualified; for example, what is the precise moral force of "should" (rather than "must") in a statement of ethics? The Ten Commandments would have lost a lot of bite had they passed through this particular committee. For another, the discussion of the issue we're writing about here is considerably spread around in the text of the **Standards**, making it somewhat difficult to see as a coherent issue, and, occasionally, making it seem as if misuse of tests is not an issue in some domains of application, because it isn't explicitly raised. Finally, although the warnings are clear enough once ferreted out, explaining the connection between a guideline and its psychometric rationale is not one of the strong points of the manual. Since we believe that commentary about this connection is important to getting the "average" test user to alter his or her practice, this is what we will undertake here, avoiding as much as possible commentary that already appears in the manual.

PSYCHOMETRIC NUMEROLOGY: TECHNICAL STUFF

Before having a look at some of the **Standards** we think it appropriate to introduce some psychometrics, just to make sure we are on common ground. Let's begin with some terminology. **Test construction** is an earlier stage of test development, where items are written, edited, pretested, selected, and so on, by means of a variety of conceptual and analytic procedures, until the specific item content of a test is determined. In **test norming,** one takes the test created in the construction phase as fixed, administers it to specific groups of people, and calculates **norms,** or characteristic standards of performance. Future test-takers will then be evaluated against those standards. **Test validation** is an ongoing conceptual and analytic process of justifying inferences drawn on the basis of test performance. These are related but conceptually distinguishable activities, and there are well-established reasons for keeping them practically distinct as well (Cureton, 1967). While the **Standards** follows this prescription (indeed, earlier versions of the Standards helped established it), in practice these activities are often run together (e.g., in orectic testing). We will try to keep the following discussion consistent with these distinctions, but because the confusion of these activities is rife in the thinking we will examine, a certain amount of jumping around will be necessary.

We will also need some mathematics before reviewing the **Standards.** It is said that most "soft" scientists are afraid of math. If that's true, then their shying away from psychometrics becomes understandable (though not forgivable). But for all the complex number-crunching-data-gathering-model-testing done by pure psychometrists, test theory isn't particularly mathematical, and what's wrong with using a test with a group of individuals for whom it was not developed is relatively easy to show. In Figure 1 we present a scatterplot of the relation between responses to a single item (along the vertical) and status on a latent dimension (the horizontal). The single item is represented as binary (it could have any number of response options, but it's easier to see the point with just two), and it makes no practical difference whether the dichotomy is thought of as right/wrong, true/false, keyed/non-keyed, or what-have-you. The form of the plot is easily described: the higher you go along the "capacity" dimension (that is, move from left to right horizontally), the easier it is to find people answering in the keyed direction (that is, that are along the top rather than along the bottom of the figure). If, for example, this was a spelling question, the more "verbal ability" (latent capacity) a person had, the more likely he or she would get this spelling item right (be plotted at the top, rather than the bottom, of the figure). In classical test theory the slope of the line that predicts a person's response to an item from their status on the latent capacity would be termed the "item-total r" (really a regression), and is the foundation for test development (item selection, internal consistency, factor structure, etc.,). Modern test theory differs from classical theory in the presumed form of this relation (non-linear vs. classical test theory's linear form) and in its correction for some obvious mathematical absurdities of the simple additive linear model (e.g., error distributions).

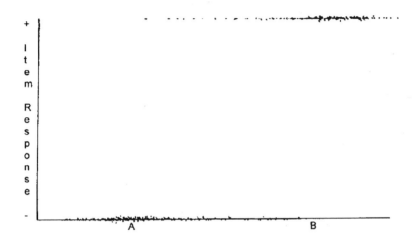

Latent Dimension Representing Variations in "Capacity" Needed to Answer Item

Figure 1.
Scatterplot of + vs. - responses to a single item against underlying "capacity."

    Also, before going further, we would like to emphasize that the problem we are showing at the item-test level could as easily be shown as problematic at item-item or test-test levels. Since we will be redundant elsewhere, here we will show the effects of sampling on association once and trust you will make the proper extrapolation.

    Take a long hard look at Figure 1. Imagine yourself drawing various samples and plotting the corresponding regression lines. It should be easy to see that depending on your sample you can get anything from a nearly straight up-and-down line to a horizontal one. For example, to get a horizontal line, just take a sample of four people, one each who got the item wrong and right from the region of capacity around "A," and one each who got the item wrong and right from the region of capacity around "B." A horizontal line would represent no relation between item and latent capacity, because people grouped at different levels of capacity would be performing identically to one another (and hence, you couldn't tell "low capacity" people from "high" ones). Conversely, a vertical line represents a perfect relation between item and latent capacity, as a "+" or "-" answer will identify respondents as belonging to one of two non-overlapping groups. Depending on the quirkiness of your sample, however, the vertical line could be interpreted as either positive or negative association between item and latent capacity; to make r negative, just select cases low on the dimension who got it right and those high on the dimension who got it wrong. Technically speaking, then, the item-total association can range anywhere between +1.0 and -1.0, depending on your sample. Or, finally, assume that you sample only people lower than point "A" (or, equivalently, people higher than point "B"): here the regression isn't even defined, since performance within such samples is constant, not variable.

The reason technical psychometrists are obsessed with sample size (N) is precisely because they know about the dangers lurking in Figure 1. By now, you should be able to see that the smaller the sample, the easier it is to get a weird regression line. With large enough samples, psychometrists feel confident they are dealing with the "real" picture and not some N-induced data spasm. How large is large enough? Edwards (1970) considers 400 the minimum for orectic tests, and for cognitive tests, depending on the theory of measurement presumed (classical or modern) we have seen suggestions ranging anywhere from 200 to 10,000. Further, for tests designed to measure performance that varies over time (e.g., cognitive tests), the minimum N must be gathered at each performance point of interest. Thus, the Wechsler's children's scales sample 100 boys and 100 girls at each half-year step along the range of ages the particular scale will be applied to. Under the assumption that our "personalities" are fairly constant at maturity, most orectic tests are not sampled with anywhere near this degree of comprehensiveness (many popular tests don't even reach Edward's N = 400). However, some researchers are starting to appreciate that using one test for children, teens, adults, and the elderly is not without its problems.

Regardless of sample size, however, the point should now be clear: statistical indices of classical test theory are sample specific, and once a psychometric device is used in another sample the values of those indices will change. Since the values of these indices provide the empirical justification for conclusions drawn about individual test takers, the psychometric coherence of the indices in a new sample is a logical prerequisite for putting forth any interpretation. If one wishes to draw the same conclusions in a new sample as one would in the old, the same pattern of relations between psychometrically interesting events is required.

At this point, modern test theorists might wish to jump in to say their approach avoids these problems by generating sample-invariant test indices. We have several responses. First of all, the tests we're complaining about here (those used for personality or psychiatric diagnoses, education-al prescriptions, employment decisions, and so on) were developed using classical theory; modern theory is not only more mathematically scary than its older sib, it's harder to do because of the enormous sample sizes required. Hence, virtually none of the battery of tests used to pound First Nations Peoples (or anyone else, for that matter) have modern test theory as their mathematical basis. Second, in the most fundamental way, modern test theory does not differ from classical theory. Though we haven't com-mented upon it until now, the "latent dimension representing capacity" is crucial to determining the item-total relation, and yet there is no possible solution to the problem of locating people along this dimension. The dimension is simply a fiction, a fundamental indeterminacy in latent vari-able models of all sizes and shapes (Maraun, 1993), whether classical or modern. Third, the sample invariance of modern test theory is theoretical; if we are willing to accept their assumptions (described in Hambleton & Swaminathan, 1985, or Hambleton, Swaminathan & Rogers, 1991), then maybe they can achieve sample invariance. However, the assumptions are arguable (even dubious; Goldstein & Wood, 1989), and there are no practi-cal demonstrations of the invariance they claim. Finally, like classical the-ory, modern theory derives from a long tradition of bad philosophical psy-chology, where empirical means are thought to clarify conceptual prob-lems. However, there are unanswerable philosophical objections to this position, and one or two simple demonstrations that psychological empiri-cism must fail in its enterprise (Chrisjohn & Maraun, 1994). In sum, mod-ern test theory is no panacea (Goldstein & Wood, 1989).

At the risk of boring everyone, then, we restate the lesson of Figure 1: item-total associations (and, indeed, the associations between all events of psychometric interest) are a function of the samples from which they are calculated. The only protection against perverse samples is to make N large, but even this can only make perverse samples less probable; nothing can eliminate them. Thus, the only justification possible for using a test with a group of people for whom it was not normed is the empirical demon-stration of the equivalence of the test's psychometric properties in the new and old samples.

This provides, we think, more than adequate grounds for our discus-sion. Let's now have a look at how the **Standards** express and codify these purely psychometric considerations.

A Survey of Testing Standards

Standard 3.10: When previous research indicates the need for studies of item or test performance differences for a particular kind of test for members of age, ethnic, cultural, and gender groups in the population of test takers, such studies should be conducted as soon as feasible.

Reflected in this particular standard is recognition of the dependence of test parameters on the characteristics of the group being tested. This recognition is half-hearted, however, for as worded 3:10 makes it seem that the "default" belief should be that test characteristics are sample-invariant unless someone produces data to suggest otherwise. This is bad science, in theory and in practice. If anyone, in any branch of science, were to claim to have an invariant measuring instrument for anything, his or her claim would be greeted with skepticism. One thing Einstein taught the world was that a foot is not a foot, nor an hour an hour; rather, the "absolutes" of space and time were a function of the speed at which an observer making measurements was travelling, the location of the observer in a field of gravity, and so on. Any real scientist realizes the conditionality of measurement, and yet many psychologists seem to think of their measures as absolutes. And in real science, the "burden of proof" is on the party making the extraordinary claim (Strahler, 1992). We think it safe to say that, *prima facie*, psychoeducationally-invariant measurement is the extraordinary claim here.

We don't have to keep this strictly theoretical, either. We have been unable to locate any instances where proper psychometric technology has identified an invariant test for any group. A good example is Hanna's (1984) study, where administrations of the same achievement test to the same students two years apart failed by and large to demonstrate invariance of test structure. That curious branch of psychometric fantasy, validity generalization, has made claims of universal applicability for "ability" tests, but from a technical point of view their attempt to find sample specificity is equivalent to Lucy's search for Charlie Brown: "He's not here; he's not there; so he must not be anywhere." In practice, then, test invariance just hasn't happened. And, perhaps even more to the point, where anyone has taken the trouble to look at data for First Nations groups (e.g., Seyfort, Spreen & Lahmer, 1980; Mueller, Mulcahy, Wilgosh, Watters, & Mancini, 1986), the "previous research" documenting performances differences (needed to instigate the search for performance differences alluded to in Standard 3.10) is already available.

Note finally the qualifications "should" (not "must") and "as soon as feasible." With respect to the first, if psychoeducators "don't" even when they "should," what are the consequences to them? Whatever they might be, they are nowhere near as severe as those experienced by people to whom the tests, in clear violation of this standard, have been applied. With regard to the second, for the First Nations of North America, "feasible" continues to be a long way off.

> Standard 4.3: Norms that are presented should refer to clearly described groups. These groups should be the ones with whom users of the test will ordinarily wish to compare the people who are tested.

One logical consequence of the sample specificity of tests developed by classical methods is that the more discrepant an individual (or a group of individuals) is from the population in which a test was developed, the less likely the test will be an appropriate standard by which to judge the individual (or group). Despite another double weasel-wording ("should" and "ordinarily") in the second sentence, the instruction is clear: in order to justify applying a test to a subject, the subject must be drawn manifestly from the norming population within which the test was developed. As regards First Nations, then, the application and interpretation of any of the widely used psychoeducational devices whatsoever is in clear violation of the **Standards**, since none of them has had First Nations peoples as its normative group.

Some dim awareness of this state of affairs is reflected in a number of attempts to compensate for this obvious breech of ethics. One reaction has been to develop test-specific supplemental norms for First Nations people. Test users would then go on as before in applying the test, but reference a different set of performance standards when interpreting results obtained from First Nations respondents. A second reaction has been to include First Nations peoples (and other minority group respondents) in test construction samples. It is thought that the norms eventually obtained as one of the final stages of a program of test development would then apply to First Nations respondents by virtue of their group's having been included earlier. Let's take each reaction in turn.

To date, none of the attempts to develop norms for First Nations peoples have demonstrated any grasp of the psychometric demands for norming or renorming a test. Recall that somewhere between 200 and 10,000 respondents are recommended as a sample size, depending on what kind of test is being normed and which test theory is being presumed. What can actually be found in practice? A "norming" of the Kaufmann Assessment

Battery for Children on a total of 20 First Nations students ranging in age from 6 to 19; a "renorming" of the Wechsler Intelligence Scale for Children (with a "proof" of "right-brainedness") on 15 First Nations children from an unspecified range of ages; a "restandardization" of the MMPI on 30 First Nations young adults; and on and on. We won't name names, but both the formal and the informal literatures that claim to provide norms for standardized tests for First Nations peoples are simply pathetic. There is no indication of an understanding of the "quirkiness" of small samples, of how unlikely it is that such a small number of individuals could possibly furnish a standard against which to judge everyone else.

Apart from the sizes of "samples" for renorming, we must also object that the development of supplementary norms uncritically accepts far too much about the appropriateness of the test under consideration. Norms are developed once there is evidence that a test is indeed measuring something of psychoeducational interest, but giving a standard psychometric instrument (even to a large number of First Nations respondents) and calculating "standards" of performance presumes the invariance of the test. This invariance, of course, is the same one we have already identified as dubious in our discussion of Standard 3.10. Practically and conceptually, then, development of supplemental norms for First Nations groups is a misguided effort.

If the effort at "norming and renorming" is pathetic, the idea of including members of minorities in test development sounds much better: at least it addresses the "applicability" issues raised in the previous paragraph. However better it sounds, this procedure, while not pathetic, is downright pernicious. Let us first inquire (considerations of overall N aside), what constitutes an appropriate sample for a new test? The answer is far from clear (see Kruskal & Mosteller, 1979), but to much of the public, and to too many researchers, an appropriate norm is one that is a miniature of the population to which the test will eventually be applied; so that if a sample of 200 had, say, 10-20 First Nations people in it, the test would be "okay" for use with them. While this sounds fair and democratic (it is neither), it ignores the relation between the sampling and the psychometric issues.

What is the point of this kind of test development program? In effect, it combines the requirements of Standards 3.10 and 4.3 by trying to construct a test with invariant test parameters while calculating norms which can be applied to all constituent groups. The point of including First Nations Peoples (or women, or other minorities) in such a program is to show that the test statistics replicate (to a reasonable degree) across all constituent groups, thus demonstrating the universality of the psychometric reasoning linking testing results and inferences drawn from testing results. Or, a better way to put this would be that working with such a sample gives the test developer a chance to examine, through standard significance test procedures, whether or not the characteristics of a test (and hence, the inferences drawn from test results) in fact replicate across constituent groups.

Putting one's measurement device to such a stringent test would indeed be admirable practice. However, if there are large differences in the numbers of individuals from different groups in the test development sample (as the "population-in-miniature" model suggests), we are technically limited in our ability to determine whether the test has the same characteristics in different groups: the standard errors of all our psychometric indices (e.g., means, correlations, covariances) depend on N, the sample size, and, to put it simply, the smaller the sample the more reasonable it is to expect that any guess about the value of a test parameter is "way off." Even if a small-sample estimate of a test population parameter is close, we can't know that it is until we have a much bigger sample. On purely statistical grounds, we need our sample test statistics to be as close as possible to population values. Having ten times as many members from one group as compared to another means our estimates will be more precise for the larger group. Practically speaking, it also means that we will not be able to detect real differences in indices for the different groups, unless the differences are enormous (Humphreys, 1985).

Rather than belabour the obvious, have a look a Table 1 below. In this table, we show how difficult it is to detect differences between correlations from two populations when one of the groups is sampled much less comprehensively (the left side of the table). Only the rho (population correlation value) = .5 vs. rho = .0 comparison is statistically detected as a difference. In the right side of the table, where the two populations are sampled equally and well, the differences between the correlations in the two samples are readily detected.

Thus, "democratic" samples do not bear on the legitimacy of using a test within the constituent groups making up the test development samples, except when the absolute N of the constituent groups is large. Unless this condition is met, such samples are unequal to the task of demonstrating the invariance (or lack of invariance) of the measurement properties of any psychometric instrument across populations.

Why not simply sample constituent groups "equally and well," then? This suggestion raises even bigger problems, problems that obviate either of the "solutions" that have been offered to the one raised by Standard 4.3: (1) what would be an appropriate sample of First Nations peoples?; and (2) practically speaking, where would they all come from? With respect to (1), the First Nations of North America share a certain communality of experience (primarily, our treatment by the non-First Nations majority governments and societies), but otherwise have an enormous diversity of forms of life. "Lumping" us together originated in racism and bureaucratic convenience, not in any real or apparent uniformity of language, culture, beliefs, or what-have-you. Would Siksika children provide results comparable to estimates developed on Ongweonwe children from Ontario? Do Inuit norms apply to Lakota? Anyone presuming to know the answer to these questions is lying, incompetent, or deluded.

Table 1.

Detecting Differences Between Correlations
in Two Samples: Two Cases

Case 1: Proportional Sampling (N1 = 200; N2 = 20)			Case 2: Equal Sampling (N1 = 200; N2 = 200)		
Correlations by Group			Correlations by Group		
Group 1	Group 2	Z-test of diff.	Group 1	Group 2	Z-test of diff.
rho = .5	rho = .4	.49 n.s.	rho = .5	rho = .4	1.21 n.s.
rho = .5	rho = .3	.94 n.s.	rho = .5	rho = .3	2.37*
rho = .5	rho = .2	1.37 n.s.	rho = .5	rho = .2	3.43*
rho = .5	rho = .1	1.78 n.s.	rho = .5	rho = .1	4.45*
rho = .5	rho = .0	2.17*	rho = .5	rho = .0	5.45*

* = correlations differ statistically at p. < .05.

With respect to (2), satisfying norming or test construction demands would soon become our primary (if not sole) activity. Because our Nations are not replications of one another, each would have to come up with enough warm bodies to supply test developers and users with subject populations. Frankly, we have better things to do with our time.

To sum up: current test usage with First Nations peoples is in clear violation of the ethical requirements to compare individuals with an appropriate norm. Schemes that have been developed to address this issue fail to deal with it conceptually, technically, and practically. Keeping Standard 4.3 in mind, we don't really expect test developers and users to provide samples of 200 for each age grouping within all 600+ First Nations cultural/linguistic groups of North America: **WE EXPECT THEM TO STOP TESTING US.**

> Standard 6.3: When a test is to be used for a purpose for which it has not been previously validated, or for which there is no supported claim for validity, the user is responsible for providing evidence of validity.

> Standard 7.1: Clinicians should not imply that interpretations of test data are based on empirical evidence of validity unless such evidence exists for the interpretations given.

> Standard 8.11: Test users should not imply that empirical evidence exists for a relationship among particular test results, prescribed educational plans, and desired student outcomes unless such evidence is available.

While some readers may have been thinking (even hoping) that we have been "reaching" at bit in our commentary thus far, these standards are difficult to misinterpret: if you don't have evidence for interpreting a test result in a particular way, get it or don't make the interpretation. Further, no "burden-of-proof" legerdemain is allowed: the person wishing to make the interpretation must be able to produce the evidence for it. As before, these stipulations (important enough to be repeated in slightly altered form at various places in the **Standards**) are in the manual because test characteristics are specific to the standardization population.

Try as we might, we cannot find even one study justifying lifting the implicative network of behavior-test relations off a majority society and dropping it wholesale on any minority population. We can't even find an honest, comprehensive attempt at such a study. Yet, in learning disability diagnosis, educational streaming, providing vocational guidance, declaiming on the "brainedness" of minority groups, and in a hundred other practices, this is precisely what is being done, all in blatant violation of the ethical guidelines. It is true that over the years we have met quite a few educators and psychologists who worry about this, but all of them go right ahead and continue their work anyway. In our turn, we are troubled by the rationale they often provide: they are only following orders. As the world learned at Nuremberg, this is not good enough.

> Standard 6.11: In school, clinical, & counselling applications, a test taker's score should not be accepted as a reflection of lack of ability with respect to the characteristic being tested for without consideration of alternate explanations for the test taker's inability to perform on that test at that time.

This standard is just ordinary common sense and good manners, although no guidance is provided as to what suitable alternative explanations might be. Modern social scientists are so used to accepting cognitive Rube Goldberg Machines as "explanations" that some real instruction is needed in how to think up other reasons why some people behave the way they do. In ability testing, the "big question," whether a test measures what is implied by its title, needs constantly to be examined, but nowadays raising such issues evokes either yawns or rabid denunciations (Chrisjohn & Maraun, 1996). In this we see once again dogmatism rather than the scientific spirit psychological and educational measurement specialists purport to embrace.

As well, we are troubled by the lack of inclusion of selection and guidance tests from the scope of this standard. Are employment tests perfect (news to us!), or is this just another case of the "demands of the marketplace" metastasizing an already dubious technology into even greater offensiveness? No guesses.

> Standard 8.10: The possibility that differential prediction exists in educational selection for selected groups should be investigated where there is prior evidence to suggest that positive results may be found and where sample sizes are adequate.

Once again the questions swarm: (1) why "should" and not "must?" What precisely is "should" doing in an ethical standard?; (2) why is invariance the implied default? What justification is there for treating psychological measurement as somehow absolute?; (3) why are the domains of clinical, industrial, and vocational testing not mentioned? Are they somehow immune to the effects of differential prediction, or are errors here somehow less serious?; and (4) why limit concern to groups with large sample sizes? Is there no alternative to imposing biased tests on smaller groups, or is the damage somehow less when only a few people (who, after all, can't complain that loudly) are misclassified, wrongly diagnosed, denied a job, or characterized as inferior?

In any event, the evidence this standard says we need is already available (see above). Yet, in contravention of this guideline, the research is not being done. We've already mentioned one reason the research isn't happening: there simply aren't enough First Nations Peoples (to act as the "sample") to carry out the work that this standard requires. If the "sample size" caveat is indeed a practical limitation, at least the work isn't being avoided out of malice or contempt. In that case, the wording of this standard should say this more clearly, and thereafter prohibit using tests with such groups. As written, it implies that the ethical standards only apply when it is convenient to comply with them.

> Standard 6.10: In educational, clinical, and counselling applications, test administrators and users should not attempt to evaluate test takers whose special characteristics—age, handicapping conditions, or linguistic, generational, or cultural backgrounds—are outside the range of their academic training or supervised experience. A test user faced with a request to evaluate a test taker whose special characteristics are not within his or her range of professional experience should seek consultation regarding test selection, necessary modifications of testing procedure, and score interpretation from a professional who has had the relevant experience.

> Standard 6.6: Responsibility for test use should be assumed by or delegated only to those individuals who have had training and experience necessary to handle this responsibility in a professional and technically adequate manner.

Finally, we bring up an additional matter of the ethics of administering and interpreting tests with First Nations Peoples (and other minorities) not specifically related to the psychometric infelicities of such practices: where and how did test users gain the supervised experience necessary to do this kind of work? If we recall correctly, one speaker at a meeting of the Canadian Psychological Association recently mentioned there were only three graduate programs in all of Canada that had even a single course in cross-cultural psychology, let alone a specialized course in First Nations or multicultural assessment. Where, exactly, are the educators and psychologists of Canada getting training? Who, exactly, is being consulted for her/his relevant experience? If, as indeed seems likely, neither the training nor the consultation is taking place, psychoeducational assessment or First Nations individuals is once again in gross violation of the existing ethical standards.

Taken together, these standards demand a great deal from an ostensibly multicultural society. That the system of graduate education and professional certification is unequal to them is not surprising. What is surprising is that wholesale administration of tests and interpretation of test results, for First Nations and other groups with "inadequate sample sizes," continues unabated in the presence of such obvious failures.

OVERVIEW AND CONCLUSIONS

If, learning to play chess, you were to pick up your rook, shy it at your opponent's king, and, knocking it over, claim a victory, your teacher would be well advised to agree that, while you have been successful, you have not been successful at chess, because you haven't followed the rules of the game. Well, administering and interpreting tests given to First Nations individuals may well be a successful enterprise: our children are shunted off into dead-end streams in school (we're "so good with our hands!"); our prison population is confidently declared unfit for parole; the employment unsuitability of our young women and men is diagnosed with conviction; and so on. And, some people (few of them First Nations people) make a good living at it. But whatever all this activity is, it is not assessment. Those who give and interpret psychoeducational tests under these conditions are not following the rules of the game.

We have perhaps strayed from the overall point we have been trying to make. If so, let us be explicit here: the **Standards**, in their present form, adequately formalize how assessments should be conducted in a multicultural society. We feel there are too many qualifications, too many unsubstantiated exemptions, and not enough explanation for the positions taken. However, even given these limitations the principles spelled out in the **Standards** should be more than enough. Why aren't they?

One response to this question might be that intelligent and honest people may differ with our interpretations of the various standards. If so, let's argue. The deafening silence surrounding the ethics of testing is more troubling to us than an honest exchange of views, but honesty seems remote from the modern practice of psychometrics. Particularly in the intelligence and I/O literatures (and they are converging in a most blood-curdling manner; cf. Geuter, 1992), critics are shouted down rather than dealt with substantively (see Seymour, 1988). We are still waiting to see the beginning of the "dispassionate, objective dialogue" that is the public image projected by psychoeducational "science."

We've also had responses like "psychological measurement just isn't as yet as precise as physical measurement." Well, if that's so, why is there such a lack of hesitation in making essentially racist general and individual claims about First Nations peoples? Bad measurement practice merely feeds into the prejudices of those willing to exploit the tool for what they can do with it. As it is, current psychoeducational assessment practices contribute to the climate of racism First Nations people find themselves embroiled within. In present circumstances, test users pleading that the tests aren't very good is like arguing that you were drunk when you committed murder.

Another response we have heard is that, even though assessment procedures are imperfect, "something must be done." Granted, but why is assessment the thing that must be done? We would do well to recall the old medical dictum, *"Primo, non nocere"* ("First do no harm"). If we have (as we have argued) *prima facie* grounds for suspecting the applicability of tests, clearing up the matter is the "thing" that should be done, not more testing. Furthermore, the parallel we drew earlier with Nuremberg wasn't just a shot; we meant it seriously. If anyone knows the moral improprieties and analytic absurdities of current testing practice, it is those of us with a background in test theory. Being told by someone else to "just go ahead and give/interpret the test anyway" does not disabuse any of us from our moral and ethical responsibility to say "**I will not do this**."

A fourth response might be that, as recent as the **Standards** are, technological developments (such as validity generalization, item response theory, and structural equation models) have obviated the objections we have raised. This is not the place to go into details, but these developments are far from perfect (Bruno & Ellett, 1988; Cliff, 1983; Freedman, 1987; Goldstein & Wood, 1989; Seymour, 1988) and certainly do not cure the ills we have diagnosed. All in all, the appeal that "new developments have solved the problems" is just another social science delusion that conceptual problems can be resolved by empirical means (Baker & Hacker, 1982; Chrisjohn & Maraun, 1996).

A fifth argument (coming from some surprising directions) is that this is (at least in part) what psychologists and educators do, and if it is wrong, then telling everyone will lead to all of us eventually being out of work.

Attached to this argument is the notion, sometimes explicit, sometimes implicit, that only dangerous radicals would raise these issues; that these disciplines have some natural "right" to exist as they are; and that this whole discussion is "disloyal" in some sense. Well, we think criticism is perfectly loyal (particularly if we're all pretending to be scientists), and we do not like the idea of business as usual if the business is wrong-headed, nonsensical, and/or hurtful. If psychologists and educators are living a lie, now is as good a time as any to find out.

Except for the first point (which we have yet to see pursued with any vigor), we are unimpressed with the objections we have encountered to our survey of the **Standards.** The discrepancy between testing ethics and testing practice seems at best attributable to ignorance or sloth, and at worst attributable to prejudice and indifference to the real damage psychoeducational assessment does every day to First Nations peoples. It should not be forgotten that the "wrongs" of test misapplication are not limited to the wrongs psychologists and educators can do; the legal system, the civil service, social services, big business, indeed, all areas of majority North American society, are infected with test mania (Hanson, 1993). How easy it has been, and continues to be, for those with ideological ends to find an "objective" justification for *de facto* racism, sexism, ageism... whatever they need. The **Standards** was, in part, supposed to be a bulwark against such practices, but when surveying how tests have been used with First Nations peoples, malpractice long ago overran ethics.

The discrepancy between ethics and practice is, simply, hypocrisy incarnate, and in a multicultural society such an obvious mismatch between stated ethical principles and day-to-day practice must undermine the credibility and bring into question the motives of those who do not mend their ways. "We'll play by the rules as long as it's convenient for us" is an attitude unlikely to foster intercultural trust.

We began this essay in the hope that once the basis for the existing ethics guidelines for assessment was known, test administrators would voluntarily clean up their act. In his review of the role of psychology in Nazi Germany, Geuter (1992) wrote: "Nor were the professional ethics of psychologists any protection against involvement in a murderous war (p. 284)." Today's genocide is aimed at the culture, not the body, but is the participation of psychometrists in a "kinder, gentler" genocide the best we of the First Nations can expect of them? We'd like to see a moratorium on testing and interpretation, if only so that the "objective, dispassionate dialogue" on the meaning of the guidelines could begin. Once that's cleared up, we of course would expect to see either a glut of studies demonstrating the applicability or inapplicability of specific assessment devices, or the comprehensive abandonment of educational and psychological testing of First Nations individuals. After all, those are your ethical rules, and we of the First Nations had no hand in the development of your rules, nor in the establishment of the psychometric theories that justify, even demand them.

However, if "assessment" hasn't been the game you've been playing with us, and does not constitute the game you wish to play, tell us now. Otherwise, your inaction will speak louder than words.

REFERENCES

Baker, G. & Hacker, P. (1982). The Grammar of Psychology: Wittgenstein's *Bemerkungen Uber Die Philosophie Der Psychology*. *Language and Communication*, 2, 227-244.

Bruno, J. & Ellet, F. (1988). A Core-analysis of Meta-analysis. *Quality and Quantity*, 22, 111-126.

Chrisjohn, R. & Maraun, M. (1996). Intelligence Research, Discourse Analysis, and the Legacy of Confusion. Submitted for publication.

Cliff, N. (1983). Some cautions concerning the application of causal modeling methods. *Multivariate Behavioral Research*, 18, 115-126.

Cureton, E. (1967). Reliability, Validity, and Baloney. In D. Jackson & S. Messick (Eds.), *Problems in Human Assessment*. New York: McGraw-Hill.

Edwards, A. (1970). *The Measurement of Personality Traits by Scales and Inventories*. New York: Holt, Rinehart & Winston.

Freedman, D. (1987). As others see us: A Case Study in Path Analysis. *Journal of Educational Statistics*, 12, 101-128.

Goldstein, H., & Wood, R. (1989). Five Decades of Item Response Modelling. *British Journal of Mathematical and Statistical Psychology*, 42, 139-167.

Geuter, U. (1992). *The Professionalization of Psychology in Nazi Germany*. Cambridge: Cambridge University Press.

Hambleton, R., & Swaminathan, H. (1985). *Item Response Theory: Principles and*

Applications. Boston: Kluwer/Nijhoff Publishing.

Hambleton, R., Swaminathan, H, & Rogers, H. (1991). *Fundamentals of Item Response Theory*. Newbury Park, California: Sage Publications.

Hanna, G. (1984). The Use of a Factor-analytic Model for Assessing the Validity of Group Comparisons. *Journal of Educational Measurement*, 21, 191-199.

Hanson, F. (1993). *Testing Testing: Social Consequences of the Examined Life*. Berkeley: University of California Press.

Humphreys, L. (1985). Correlations in Psychological Research. In D. Detterman (Ed.), *Current Topics in Human Intelligence*, Volume 1. Norwood, New Jersey: Ablex Publishing.

Kruskal, W., & Mosteller, F. (1979). Representative Sampling, I: Non-scientific literature. *International Statistical Review*, 47, 13-24.

Maraun, M. (1993). Issues Pertaining to the Determinacy of Item Response Models. Doctoral Dissertation, University of Toronto.

Maraun, M. & Chrisjohn, R. (1997). Intelligence and research and the legacy of confusion. Appendix G, *The Circle Game: Shadows and Substance in the Indian Residential School Experience in Canada*. Penticton: Theytus Books Ltd.

Mueller, H., Mulcahy, R. Wilgosh, L., Watters, B., & Mancini, G. (1986). An Analysis of the WISC-R Item Responses With Canadian Inuit Children. *Alberta Journal of Educational Research*, 32, 12-36.

Seyfort, B., Spreen, O., & Lahmer, V. (1980). A Critical Look at the WISC-R With Native Indian Children. *Alberta Journal of Educational Research*, 26, 14-24.

Seymour, R. (1988). Why Plaintiffs' Counsel Challenge Tests, and How They can Successfully Challenge the Theory of "Validity Generalization." *Journal of Vocational Behavior*, 33, 331-364.

Strahler, A. (1992). *Understanding Science: An Introduction to Concepts and Issues*. Buffalo: Prometheus Books.

Standards for Educational and Psychological Testing. (1985). Washington, D. C.: American Psychological Association.

APPENDIX D

COMMUNITY BASED RESEARCH INTO RESIDENTIAL SCHOOL EFFECTS
A SUMMARY OF THE CARIBOO TRIBAL COUNCIL RESEARCH

Roland D. Chrisjohn, Ph. D.

Presentation to the Royal Commission on Aboriginal People, Canim Lake, British Columbia, March 9, 1993.

INTRODUCTION

In my presentation here today I will limit myself to the work already released by the Cariboo Tribal Council, first at the Residential School Conference in June, 1991, and subsequently as the documents *Faith Misplaced* (1991) and *The Impact of the Residential School* (1991). As well, included is additional work with the CTC data set undertaken by Quigley (1991) and Konczi (1993). To avoid simply rehashing information already available to the Royal Commission on Aboriginal People, however, I will at the end stray into somewhat deeper water. As a participant in and contributor to this community-based program of research, I have learned much from my association with these extraordinary people, and their work required me to stretch myself in unanticipated directions. Consequently, I find it impossible not to rattle about outside the confines of my cage.

OVERVIEW OF THE RESEARCH

Again, pertinent details of the research are given in the documents listed above. I would like to emphasize the attention this project gave to dealing with the interpersonal dynamics of its work: care was taken to address any possible difficulties that might arise probing into the psychological wounds (however fresh) of participants. As well, the intellectual and emotional health of the research team was of concern, since listening to the accounts of residential school must itself take its toll, regardless of the inner strength of team members. In my opinion, such considerations must become standard in any future research.

The data we analyzed were obtained from interviews with 187 volunteers. This was more than one-third of the projected available population, and thus, from a purely statistical view, provided a quite adequate base of information. Because we did not wish to be "pushy" in any way, and because of the sensitive nature of many of the questions, some respondents chose not to respond to all questions. Thus, for any particular analysis, the number of cases used will be something short of 187.

AN ENVIRONMENT FOR LEARNING AND GROWTH

Whatever else the Mission might have been, it was still supposed to be a **school**, a place where children of different ages had an opportunity to grow, to learn, to become (in part) whoever it was they were, and to do all of this under the supervision of people who understood their rights and undertook to provide those opportunities. What, then, did the students recall of this learning environment?

Table 1. presents percentages of time spent in various activities as recalled by residential and nonresidential school attendees. As is easily seen, every comparison reflects badly on residential schooling: less time spent in instruction, less time for the child to be on her/his own, and more time spent on religious instruction and manual labour. In fact, the table minimizes the differences, since "chores" within the public school system were unlikely to include farm labor, domestic service, doing laundry, or sawmill operation (see Furniss, 1992).

Table 2. contrasts disciplinary practices in residential vs. nonresidential schools. Again, residential schools are uniformly more repressive and violent, showing a capacity for both emotional and physical abuses. It should be pointed out that, because the nonresidential respondents were somewhat younger on average than the residential respondents, some of these differences can be attributed to changes in "acceptable" disciplinary practice over time. However, **none** of the practices listed were unknown in the nonresidential setting, and it is difficult to see any possible "learning" justification for many of the practices at any period. Rather, shaving a child's hair off or sending him/her outside without adequate clothing are, more purely, the kind of brutality historically associated with police states. We should also not lose sight of the fact that superficially similar disciplinary actions do not have identical status in residential and nonresidential settings: being struck by a police officer in downtown Toronto before witnesses does not mean the same thing as being similarly struck in Guatemala (Chomsky, 1993).

From Table 3. we get a further glimpse of residential-nonresidential differences. Here, the lack of some differences emphasizes that respondents were not just "dumping" on residential schools, but responding sensibly to the questions posed.

Finally, in Table 4. we compare directly the emotional atmosphere in the two school systems. Almost uniformly, residential schools failed to provide for the safety and emotional care needs of the children. The only difference favoring residential school is in "Number of Friends," which could be accounted for simply by the race dynamics of the nonresidential school systems.

LASTING EFFECTS

The questionnaires given also allowed us to examine the long-term impact of residential school experiences. Table 5. presents residential vs. nonresidential comparisons for what we called "Life Retrospective

Variables," or more subjective reflections on what the respondents' educational experiences had meant to them. Briefly, residential school effects impacted more negatively on respondents' views on sex, family relationships, confidence, decision-making ability, physical health, life in their Native community, use of alcohol, and attitudes toward education. Notably, some differences were **not** found, but I will postpone mentioning them until discussing the next table.

At the time of the research it seemed to us that such massive differences in educational activities (see Table 1.) must have given rise to palpably different group demographics. Therefore, we culled from a variety of places in the data items that, in a commonsense way, should capture the long-term effects on the respondents' quality of life. Table 6. presents the residential vs. nonresidential comparisons for these "Life-Outcome Variables." Significantly, only the number of long-lasting spousal relations distinguished the groups: in every other way, former residential and nonresidential students were indistinguishable.

Taken along with some of the findings in Table 5. (especially, self-evaluation), the most straightforward interpretation is that there are many factors other than residential school experiences that have affected the quality of life of First Nations people. By not examining the effects of, for starters, institutional racism and sexism, interpersonal racism and sexism, religious oppression, economic discrimination, intellectual oppression, and much more, we develop an isolated and incomplete understanding of the dynamics. Schooling, residential or otherwise, is only part of the picture, and if we wish truly to understand the role of residential schooling on today's First Nations, we must look further afield.

SOME PERSONAL OBSERVATIONS

What will help us to look further afield is definitely **not** the kind of psychosocial research reported here. There is some value in presenting tables and numbers (as I and my colleagues have detailed; Chrisjohn, Maraun, Harrison, and McDonald, 1998), but I must repeat what I have already stated (in *Faith Misplaced*): personal experiences are not somehow more truthful when numbers are attached to them, nor is formal research likely to uncover information that could not be obtained by generating and carefully examining personal narratives. Indeed, adopting a Westernized standard of social science evidence would assure the continued marginalization of First Nations people in areas of crucial importance to us, while reinforcing the hegemony of the outside "expert."

To continue in this vein, far from being just another, "more objective" way of presenting the same information, I have come to consider standard psychosocial analysis and techniques potentially dangerous, and at times downright misleading. Since the complete basis for my concerns is beyond the scope of the Commission, and because there is other work to be presented, I will try to state my case simply, and in the context of this research.

One example of how technique misleads is in the residential vs. nonresidential distinction itself. They **sound** like different things, but in reality there is a great deal of overlap. For example, some residential students resided on or near their home reserves, while others were moved incredible distances to reside with First Nations children with whom they shared no language, no culture, and no particular point of contact except that, as far as the bureaucracy was concerned, they were all "Indians." Some respondents treated as nonresidential students lived as boarders far from home and without family contact, but they are treated here as "nonresidential" because the school and the housing authorities were, nominally at least, separate. Some residential school students could and did have regular contact with their families, while for others it was impossible, forbidden, or both. People also did not have consistent exposure to whatever schooling they were given (that is, some lasted longer than others), nor was residential school a constant: it changed in emphasis and composition from site to site, and within site over time. Finally, individual experiences in residential and nonresidential school varied considerably. There were good times and bad, good teachers and bad, teacher's pets and children who "lived" in the doghouse, etc. There are those who look back to residential school days nostalgically, along with those who look back in anger, fear, or emptiness. In all of this, what particular sense is there in trying to hold fast to a distinction between the two systems? Is it not surprising that, given the overlap, **any** differences were found? What we are talking about, then, is not black vs. white, but two largely indistinguishable shades of grey.

A second empirical delusion is that the effects of residential schooling can be examined in isolation of other pertinent factors, that, for example, we might be able to lay the blame on **residential school** for family violence while implicating **racism** for alcohol abuse and suicide. But racism is not separable from residential schooling, nor can either be distinguished from economic discrimination, and so on for all the factors mentioned above, and more. These factors are differences in rationale, emphasis, tactics, etc., **not** in purpose. It is the whole cloth that is of interest, not an isolated thread, regardless of how much it dominates the fabric. In social science jargon, the First Nations people have lived, and continue to live, in a "multiply pathogenic" environment, and to anticipate a uniform "norm of response" to as indefinite a stimulus as residential schooling is to prefigure a misunderstanding of its role and its impact.

A third example of how social science technique misleads is something I term **experientialism**, by which I mean the notion that direct personal exposure to a cause is necessary to observe its effect. The search for differences between former residential and nonresidential students strongly reflects this notion. But how reasonable is it to try to draw a line this way, either? In what sense has residential school **not** affected someone whose sibling committed suicide in response to residential school experiences? How has residential schooling **not** affected the lives of children raised by parents who disapprove of public displays of affection or who discipline severely as a consequence of how **they** were raised by priests or nuns? How has the residential school experience **not** influenced generations raised in the shadow of an institution formed to make war upon First Nations languages, religions, and societies? Experientialism predisposes us to think of residential schooling in terms of the "disease" model, that their former students are different from the rest of us in **kind**. Such thinking is pernicious, not only in drawing lines between us as First Nations people, but also in implicating some of us as "walking time bombs" just waiting for the right "jiggle" to set us off into crazed blood-sport a la Rambo. This is reflected, of course, in the currently fashionable term **residential school syndrome**: those who attended residential school suffer (or will suffer someday soon) an identifiable constellation of psychological problems. To put it simply, there is no evidence for such a "syndrome;" the very term not only insults those who endured the experience, it denies the lives of those who managed to avoid it. And finally it misleads us into looking for sickness in the lives of First Nations people. If it is sickness you seek, look into the minds and hearts of the men who conceived, implemented, and maintained this institution, and not at its victims.

Finally, I am disturbed by the tendency to treat psychosocial investigation as the "honest broker" of evaluating government and church policy. The idea seems to be that residential schooling will be judged, at least in part, by what social scientists can show these schools brought about. This is like evaluating the Nazi extermination camps by looking for psychological disturbance in the 700,000 Jews that managed to live through it, using those that were able to avoid detection and "relocation" as the control group.

As I've already argued, social science is unequal to the task of coming to grips with the residential school experience, and its very methods prefigure minimizing what have been the consequences. Thus, social scientists are no "honest brokers," and emphasis on the victims of residential schooling lets those truly responsible for our holocaust off the hook. By looking for the "smoking gun" for current First Nations difficulties exclusively in personal, individual cause-effect relations, we insure we will never understand them, and that the problems will be recycled. There were undoubtly "smoking guns," and in no way am I suggesting avoiding dealing substantively with individual claims and legal proceedings. But, significantly, the smoking guns were going off during a thermonuclear attack: in this attack, some First Nations people were fried immediately, some survived a bit longer, and others died a lingering and painful death. For those of us not located near Ground Zero, however, a long nuclear winter has descended, and family violence, alcohol abuse, educational failure, and suicide are background radiation, "clicks" of the geiger counter that testify that the blast actually occurred.

RECOMMENDATIONS

I honestly have nothing to add beyond what is already happening, for example, here at Canim Lake. I do think that successful legal prosecutions, acknowledgement of federal, provincial, and ecclesiastical responsibility, and a broader understanding of the fabric of residential schools can be **very** therapeutic, both to direct and indirect survivors of residential school abuses. And, as Handelman (1992) observed (with respect to Nazi war crimes), personal and communal healing is not something that has to happen **instead** of legal prosecution of perpetrators.

REFERENCES

Cariboo Tribal Council. (1991). *The Impact of the Residential School.* Williams Lake: Cariboo Tribal Council.

Chrisjohn, R. D., Belleau, C., and others (1991). Faith Misplaced: Lasting Effects of Abuse in a First Nations Community. *Canadian Journal of Native Education*, 18, 161-197.

Chrisjohn, R. D., Maraun, M., Harrison, D. L., & McDonald, L. (1998). *Handbook of Evaluation and Research Methods for First Nations Communities*. In preparation.

Chomsky, N. (1993). *Year 501: The Conquest Continues.* Montreal: Black Rose Books.

Furniss, E. (1992). *Victims of Benevolence: Discipline and Death at the Williams Lake Indian Residential School*, 1891-1920. Williams Lake: Cariboo Tribal Council.

Handelman, S. (1992). Column in *Toronto Star*, November 22.

Konczi, A. (1993). *Lasting Effect of Childhood Sexual Abuse in a First Nations Sample.* Master of Arts Thesis, University of Guelph.

Quigley, K. A. (1991). *Implications of Residential Schooling for a First Nations Community.* Master of Arts Thesis, University of Guelph.

Table 1.

Percentage of School Time Allocated to Various Activities,

Residential vs. Nonresidential Schools

Variable	Residential		Nonresidential		
	N	Mean	N	Mean	t
School instruction/ study	67	42.01	46	63.20	-5.67***
Religious instruction/ ceremonies	67	28.73	46	7.09	8.36***
Manual labour/chores	67	16.72	46	6.67	5.37***
Recreation/free time	67	11.79	46	23.04	-5.49***

*** $p. < .001$

Table 2.
Means and t-Comparisons of Disciplinary Practices in
Residential and Nonresidential Schools

| Variable | Residential | | Nonresidential | | |
	N	Mean	N	Mean	t
Remove privileges/set curfews/exclude child from activities	78	3.58	52	2.73	4.04***
Ignore child	78	2.73	51	1.90	3.53***
Find fault in all child's actions	80	3.11	49	2.04	4.64***
Threaten to hit child	80	3.04	51	1.75	5.61***
Yell at child	81	3.64	51	2.73	4.36***
Ridicule/talk about child in front of others	81	3.40	50	2.04	5.57***
Hit/slap/kick child	80	2.85	51	1.71	5.09***
Severely beat child	81	2.00	50	1.24	3.76***
Criticize child in front of others	82	3.22	51	2.04	5.02***
Lock child in a room	77	1.87	48	1.15	3.58***
Child sent out in cold w/out enough clothing	79	2.01	51	1.37	3.05***
Child made to miss meals/not allowed to eat when hungry	81	2.70	51	1.25	7.85***
Shaved child's hair	78	1.76	51	1.04	3.87***
Call child names	81	2.98	51	1.75	5.37***

Note: the higher the score, the more frequently the disciplinary practice was reported used in the school.
*** p. <.001

Table 3.

Frequency of Recreational Activities in Residential vs.

Nonresidential Schools

Variable	Residential		Nonresidential		
	N	Mean	N	Mean	t
Play games/sing songs	83	3.19	52	3.83	-3.62***
Swimming/picnics	84	3.01	51	2.84	1.10
Read books on own	83	2.53	52	3.46	-4.80***
Toys/sports equipment to play with	83	2.71	52	3.58	-3.76***
Fishing/hunting	84	2.05	49	1.92	0.63
Spend time alone	84	2.11	51	3.35	-3.76***

Note: the higher the score, the more frequent the activity.

*** p. < .001

Table 4.

Comparison of Emotional Atmosphere at Residential

and Nonresidential Schools

	Residential		Nonresidential		
Variable	N	Mean	N	Mean	t
Felt staff would take care of child/ensure nothing bad would happen	81	2.33	42	3.10	-2.93**
Felt staff would watch out for her/him and make sure no one treated her/him badly	82	2.18	42	2.98	-3.39**
Felt safe	80	2.51	42	3.33	-3.67***
Felt staff cared about him/her	81	2.26	50	3.17	-4.15***
Happy/unhappy at school	81	3.26	50	2.52	4.46***
Number of friends at school	83	2.17	53	1.70	2.47*

*** p. < .001
** p. < .01
* p. < .05

Table 5.

Comparisons of Impact of Residential and Nonresidential

Schooling on Life Adjustment Variables

| Variable | Residential | | Nonresidential | | |
	N	Mean	N	Mean	t
Feelings about sex	79	2.32	52	3.13	-5.15***
Sexual behaviour	79	2.42	50	3.00	-3.24**
Relationship w/partner	60	2.70	29	3.17	-2.06*
Relationship w/children	67	2.96	32	3.69	-3.19**
Ability to parent	72	2.83	37	3.43	-2.67**
Relationship w/relatives	80	2.69	51	3.39	-3.47***
Relationship w/friends	80	3.03	51	3.53	-2.57**
Self-worth	81	2.74	51	3.10	-1.68
Confidence	81	2.67	51	3.14	-2.16*
Ability, make decisions	81	2.65	51	3.37	-3.27***
Ability, deal w/authority	78	2.68	51	3.18	-2.20*
Physical health	78	2.94	51	3.53	-3.30***
Feelings about whites	79	2.82	51	3.33	-2.63**
Feelings about white religion	80	2.61	51	2.96	-1.76
Feelings about Native religion	77	3.42	49	3.24	0.91

Feelings about being a First Nations person	76	3.47	51	3.47	0.00
Appreciation of Native ceremonies/culture/ religion	80	3.34	51	3.41	-0.36
Interaction in Native community	79	3.11	50	3.58	-2.19*
Use of alcohol	78	2.04	50	2.64	-3.12**
Use of drugs	75	2.28	51	2.57	-1.67
Criminal behaviour	76	2.41	51	2.65	-1.45
Employment	79	3.22	51	3.47	-1.29
Education	78	2.81	51	3.67	-4.11***

Note: the higher the score the more positive the impact.

*** p. < .001
** p. < .01
* p. < .05

Table 6.

Comparison of Socio-economic and Social Adjustment Variables,

Residential vs. Nonresidential Students

Variable	Residential		Nonresidential		
	N	Mean	N	Mean	t
Educational level	82	4.94	94	6.28	-1.32
Age of 1st marriage/ commonlaw marriage	64	21.27	64	20.84	0.42
Times married/ commonlaw	71	2.66	83	1.61	-3.22**
Number of friends	81	1.56	93	1.77	-1.49
Chance of getting ahead in job	56	2.48	66	2.59	-0.48
Personal average monthly income	65		81		1.39
Partner's average monthly income	24		32		0.15
Worry about money	81	3.38	93	3.27	0.71
Ability to provide for family	79	2.46	92	2.42	0.18

Note: for "education level" and "chance of getting ahead," scales run from low to high; for "worry about money," lower scores mean "never," high score "always;" the scale for "ability to provide" runs from ability to provide extras to having difficulty providing basics.

** $p. < .01$

APPENDIX E

AMONG SCHOOL CHILDREN:
PSYCHOLOGICAL IMPERIALISM AND THE RESIDENTIAL SCHOOL EXPERIENCE IN CANADA

Roland Chrisjohn and Sherri Young

Paper originally presented at the Vancouver International Symposium on Ethnicity, Conflict, and Cooperation, August 19-22. 1993, Vancouver, British Columbia.

INTRODUCTION

An effective system of colonial control, like well-maintained machinery, doesn't depend on anything extraordinary or unusual to function. Rather, when each part does what it was designed to do, with standard, periodic servicing and an occasional refurbishing, the mechanism hums along nicely as it recreates the result it was designed to produce. It is in this sense that Arendt's "banality of evil" is perfectly descriptive of the Nazi holocaust machine (see Amery, 1986, for the sense in which it isn't descriptive); and it is in this sense that the same phrase applies to Canadian federal policy toward First Nations peoples. The continuing assimilationist policy has worked, and continues to work, in foreground and background, to bring about the extermination of Canadian First Nations cultures.[1]

Rather than review the entire history of interaction between First Nations and the Canadian government in an attempt to justify what, to some, might seem to be an extreme appraisal, in this paper we focus on one current issue and the present-day operation of one part of this colonial machinery. If we can show "design governing in a thing so small," it will be easier to credit that other, larger parts of the machine are probably chugging away elsewhere, too. We also hope that such an analysis can serve not as a model but as a warning to First Nations peoples elsewhere that what looks "obvious" deserves a longer, harder look than often we accord it. The current issue we will discuss is the residential school experience and its impact on the present lives of First Nations peoples; the machinery of interest is psychology. We will show that the discourse that has arisen about past abuses in residential school (and what to do about them today) is being managed toward certain ideological ends that do not positively serve First Nations. As part of an ideological system, psychology **performs** a crucial colonial function in this management, and it matters not at all what psychologists **say** they're doing or **think** they're doing; even the best of intentions will maintain the oppression of First Nations peoples and communities. We begin with a bit of landscaping.

SOME HISTORY

For those of you unfamiliar with the background, residential schools operated in Canada from around 1870 to the early 1980s (in fact, there are several still in operation, but managed by First Nations groups rather than by non-Indians). Very simply, the children of First Nations groups were removed, by law, from their homes and families and forced to attend schools operated by non-Indians. This did not happen to all First Nations children, nor was this institutionalization a full twelve years duration for all who went, but residential schooling was a unavoidable part of the "Indian experience" during the time period specified. Early on, federal responsibility for education (as established in a number of treaties) was found to be too great a "burden" and was contracted out to religious denominations (primarily the Catholic and Anglican churches). The government and the churches, with differing motives, explicitly (see, e.g., Haig-Brown, 1993, or Frideres, 1993) agreed that the ultimate goal of education was the assimilation (the operative euphemism for cultural genocide) of First Nations peoples. To these ends, the Federal government did little to trouble the churches with respect to curriculum, discipline, and other features of the day-to-day operation (except to try to find ways to cut back funding), while simultaneously they enforced (through legislation and policing) the "participation" of First Nations parents and children.

During the 1930s through the 60s, maintenance of residential schools (never a big money-maker, but expected to pay for itself[2]) became progressively more unprofitable. This, combined with factors like increasing dissatisfaction in First Nations communities and a "bad press," led to their gradual phasing out; the last federally-operated school closed in the early 1980s. One thing that should not be ignored when looking back at this history is that this effort at cultural genocide had considerable success. For example, today, the vast majority of First Nations languages are in danger of dying out; the connection between the world and First Nations spirituality has been disrupted or even severed, and factionalism (founded upon doctrinal religious disputes originating in Medieval Europe) plays a major role in dividing First Nations communities; and First Nations governments, fashioned in the mold of the hierarchical, patriarchal, exclusionist governments of Europe,[3] increasingly adopt a role previously played by non-Indians.

Co-existing with these signs of cultural disruption are psychosocial indicators of oppression; elevated levels of suicide, family violence and breakdown, substance abuse, educational failure, and the like sometimes seem to be the norm for First Nations communities. This, too, reflects the success of federal policy. This is not to say that residential school, the Indian Act, the reservation system, and other features of Indian policy were created with the express purpose of, say, getting the Indians to kill themselves at five times the rate of non-Indians. The governmental officials organizing the assault on First Nations were not "experts" in "culture construction" or "social engineering," as that expertise did not, and does not, exist. No, these policies were undertaken with no other goal than the elimination of First Nations cultures, and the people establishing the policies had no thought or vision concerning what would replace that which they were destroying, beyond a vague notion that it would mimic the culture of non-Indian Canadians. Consequently, individuals from First Nations backgrounds who hate their heritage are merely a different **kind** of success from those who commit suicide, and the cottage industries that grew up as a reaction to the symptoms of oppression are a fruitful occupation for a significant fraction of the oppressors. And, as an object lesson to the oppressors, such signs of disruption merely substantiate their belief that they are dealing with an innately depraved subspecies of humanity.

Abuse History

Even for their time, the normative operations of residential schools were draconian. Discipline could involve physical abuse, withholding food, or exposure to the elements; children were beaten for speaking their own language, for associating with children of the opposite sex, or for minor infractions of school protocol; school facilities and educational materials were often substandard, with inadequate health and living facilities and with standards of nutrition ignored; and on and on. All of these features must be set against the backdrop of a world where the children were removed (sometimes at incredible distances) from home and family for extended periods of time; placed, under penalty of law, in the hands of people ill-disposed toward them and their way of life; and maintained, often at minimal levels of sustenance, with no avenue of complaint or possibility of redress (all of this and more is documented in works like Haig-Brown, 1988, and Knockwood, 1992).

Even within such latitudes, residential school teachers and administrators occasionally transgressed the boundaries of "acceptable behaviour." While the schools were in operation, instances of excessive abuse (sexual abuse has been documented, other extreme abuses hinted at) were handled by simple devices like relocating personnel, threatening victims or their families, or removing bureaucrats who insisted on doing their jobs properly. With the passage of time and the lessening of legal and psychological constraints, the recounting of abuses became a trickle and then a flood. The most widely known cases (such as has been documented at Williams Lake, BC) are the tip of an iceberg, with reports of criminal abuses coming from every province and territory that operated a residential school.

It is here that we would like to interject a procedural point: if, say, sexual abuses took place at location X and were covered up, each victim gives rise to quite a number of culprits. The actual perpetrator of abuse is of course culpable, but then so is the educational authority (ecclesiastical or otherwise), the federal authority (into whose care they child was legally placed), the provincial child welfare authority, and anyone else who colluded in removing the child, transferring the culprit, or otherwise obscuring the crime. It should also be noted that, in the United States (and when the victims are not members of minority groups) financial awards for cases of sexual abuse committed by the clergy have run into the millions of dollars. Does it take Miss Marple to suggest that we have here all the incentives necessary for finding some alter-native to the perpetrators "fessing up and taking their medicine?" We think not.

PSYCHOLOGICAL IMPERIALISM

Since its inception as an academic discipline psychology has, with enthusiasm, demonstrated its willingness to make its own unique contribution to the day-to-day tasks of managing sexist, racist, classist societies. Over time there have been exceptions (e.g., S. Sarason, M. Wittig, D. Smail, D. Howitt, L. Kamin, and their like), and for this we are thankful; but an incredible number of individuals calling themselves psychologists have been willing to pronounce women and minorities genetically inferior, declare social activists products of unhappy childhoods, attribute wars to clashes in the personality styles of the national leaders involved, and otherwise recast the political, economic, and social issues of our time as individual quirks or Mother Nature's "little jokes." Even when psychologists do not personally hold a specific position on an ideological topic, they willingly countenance the imprimatur of psychology by declaring it "an empirical issue" where "all the facts are not yet in."[4]

In fact, when faced with the charge of being ideological (as, for example, Herrnstein and Skinner were charged by Chomsky, 1973), psychologists undertake a revealing maneuver; they deflect (**not** answer) the indictment by wrapping themselves in the flag of being objective scientists. That is, they take a rhetorical stance, not a scientific one. They have no political axe to grind, they say, and they are merely reporting facts, regardless of how unpleasant those facts might be. At best, this amounts to a reply of "Oh, no we're not," and we have here all the makings of a very dull argument. At worst, it succeeds in shifting the burden of proof onto the person bringing the charge to recount the chain of evidence necessary to establish that psychology is neither objective, nor a science. While quite doable, most of this kind of a discussion would be remote from the specific ideological application of psychology that occasioned the charge. And try getting all that into a television soundbite.

Where time and trouble is taken, however, as by Rose, Lewontin and Kamin (1984), or Sarason (1981), or Howitt (1991), psychology can be shown to be ideological through and through. That psychologists can adopt a fundamentally ideological stance without conscious effort is demonstrated, for example, by Young (1993), who shows that in any number of specific ways, psychologists advocating the "empowerment" of marginalised peoples continue **and** reinforce those people's oppression, and coopt those people's authentic attempts to take control of their worlds. This is the charge we wish to level at psychology: the way in which the residential school experience is being represented, to First Nations peoples and to the Canadian public at large, serves the political requirements of existing authority. The psychologically "proper" thing to do removes the discussion from some levels (moral, political, social, financial, etc.) and places it firmly on others (therapeutic, medical, conciliatory, and so on). The net effect is the maintenance of the **status quo** and a consequent furtherance of the genocidal agenda. There is no requirement that any psychologists consciously adopt any part of this program. Rather, like a spring-driven mechanism, psychologists simply have to be wound up and let go; the machinery will do the job it was designed to do.

THE COILS UNWOUND

Before beginning our case, we should review some information that is not, by and large, in dispute. First, the governments of Canada have a vested interest in rendering void (**not** resolving) the legal concept of Aboriginal Title; not only is there no title extinguishment for most of Canada, what are often presented as valid surrenders would not bear critical scrutiny in unbiased legal proceedings. Fair market value and/or recompense for what has been seized improperly would cost many trillions of dollars. These problems terminate once the lines of legal heirs of the aboriginal owners cease to exist.

Second, the Indian residential school system was an attempt to obliterate First Nations. That this was so is explicit in extant policy statements and other documents of the churches and the federal government, and implicit in the apologies of several churches (notably, the Anglican and Mennonite churches) for having participated in the unjustifiable, morally imperialistic residential school system. It is significant that the federal government and some of the other churches have apologized for the emotional consequences to sufferers of extreme abuse, but not for setting up and operating the system.

Third, criminal acts of abuse took place at residential schools. Thus far, acts of sexual abuse have gained the most attention, but beating students into unconsciousness, sticking needles through students' tongues, breaking students' arms, legs, or ribs, and similar acts have **always** transgressed acceptable Canadian norms of school discipline, and there is independently supported testimony that such abuses occurred.

Fourth, criminal acts of abuse have been concealed. **Who** did **what** to **whom** and **when**, and who knew about it, has yet to be determined. However, there exists considerable documentary evidence (police records, internal government or church reports, and so forth; see, for example, Furniss, 1992; Knockwood, 1992) that on various occasions parents, bureaucrats, clergy, and other concerned individuals were sufficiently shocked about what was happening to initiate formal complaints. To our knowledge, the paper trails of those complaints that have been followed up either result in the total absolution of the alleged offender, or simply "evaporate."

Against this backdrop, let us consider what have been the responses of the psychological community (as reflected most importantly by practitioners of therapy or specialists in social intervention, but detectable in other subdisciplines as well) to the increased public awareness of abuses (perhaps massive abuses) having occurred at residential schools. And, to be fair, let's try to keep in mind that psychologists are, after all, psychologists, and consequently professionally limited in terms of how they will react to any circumstance. That, for example, psychologists don't behave like rocket scientists to news that a giant asteroid is about to collide with the earth is hardly a fair criticism of their enterprise. By the same token, should they intrude on efforts to deal effectively with the problem (by, say, suggesting we talk the asteroid out of colliding with us, or by trying to convince everyone it's only a problem in our minds) we would be quite justified in showing them the door.

Reaction 1: Research. Almost immediately after the Blanket Denial stage (where the government repudiates any and all charges and the newspapers cast aspersions on the accusers), the government moved to the More Research is Needed phase, a call which resonated in the hearts of social scientists everywhere. What is needed, this story goes, is to **establish** the lasting effects of residential schooling, and to characterise and quantify those effects. While this appears benign enough, the fact that such calls conform to a long tradition of governmental evasion tactics (another favourite tactic is to establish a commission) should make us look twice.

In fact, in addition to putting off having to deal with the matter, if permitted the "Research" move eviscerates the First Nations case. It achieves this in a number of interrelated ways. First, **it legitimates the resolution of moral issues by empirical means**. Well, is that so bad? For example, didn't the US Supreme Court cite empirical evidence in ruling against the "separate but equal" laws dealing with Black education? That may be, but what claim does research have for being able to resolve moral problems? Take another case: there were approximately half a million Jews who lived through the concentration camp experience, and another half million who stayed in Europe but hadn't been sent off to the camps before the WWII ended. Did we judge the moral reprehensibility of what the Nazis did by analytic comparisons of the psychological symptomology of these two groups? Should we evaluate the morality of the South African apartheid system in terms of replicable Black vs. non-Black psychological differences, or is it alright for our moral sense to be offended even without such information? Or, even more centrally, did the Anglican and Mennonite churches base their apologies for their participation in residential schooling on some secret study, or did they work it out from their own religious principles? There are no empirical proofs of right or wrong, and to pretend that there are is not only to turn over the task of making decisions of conscience to those who are concealing their prejudices, it is to abrogate the moral imperative of taking personal responsibilities for our actions and beliefs.

Second, accepting a role for research serves to **decriminalize what has occurred**. Unless a "significant" effect can be attributed to residential schooling, church and governmental officials will argue, and the general public will likely believe, that little or no harm was done. Of course, this is very much like arguing that robbery of a rich man is less of a crime than robbing a poor one, but if you think such arguments won't be made, recall that recently a judge in England sentenced a rapist to paying for a vacation for his victim on the grounds that it wasn't much of a rape. If it is agreed research results are essential to evaluating residential schooling, we invite the determination of severity of punishment for abuse rendered and/or degree of compensation for abuse suffered by the same standard.

Third, acceptance of a role for research **presumes that the existing research ideologies apply to First Nations populations**. This deserves much more detail than we can allot it here, but the way data is gathered and analysed is as much a reflection of psychology's prejudices as anything. For now we merely point out that no psychological test of any putative psychological characteristic has ever even approached meeting the statistical or ethical requirements for use with First Nations populations (Chrisjohn, Pace, Young, & Mrochuk, Appendix C). Whether research **can** say anything of utility about residential schools remains to be demonstrated.

Fourth, research **trivializes the experiences of victims of residential school abuses**. It says, in effect, that the long-term consequences of what First Nations peoples endured in residential school can be reduced to a handful of Western-derived, culturally-myopic variables. As such, the experience is accessible to anyone who can read. This is a dangerous delusion, but we have listened as bureaucrats equated their days at strict, upper class private boarding schools with residential school practices. The depth of the difference between those two worlds (e.g., one group was being trained to run the world, the other trained to have theirs stolen from them) defies accurate description or quantification.

Fifth, making a prominent role for research **maintains the marginalisation of First Nations peoples, and precisely within subject matter they know more about than anyone**. The flurry of activity around the investigation of residential schooling was not aimed at First Nations peoples, but at psychologists, sociologists, and other academics. The academics were designated to receive the grants, design and execute the studies, write the reports, and garner the praise for a job well done. The First Nations peoples were, once again, designated to be the "subjects" of this academic adventure.

Reaction 2: Therapy. If the call for research resonated in the hearts of psychologists, the excitement from the call for therapy brought on a coronary. Under scrutiny, however, the therapeutic enterprise, as much as was the case for research, misleads First Nations peoples as it does the ideological work required of it. What we will present here has already been given in detail elsewhere (Chrisjohn, Belleau, & Others, 1991; Chrisjohn, 1993), so we will try to be brief.

Most importantly, a therapy-driven approach to residential schooling recasts the problem **as the personal psychological problem of individuals having had certain traumatic experiences**. As such, an individualised pathology model, commonly called the "Residential School Syndrome," is substituted for an understanding based on the legal, political, and economic status of First Nations. There is **absolutely no evidence** for this syndrome, but that matters little; if psychologists can direct therapy and workshops (which, by the way, will largely be delivered by non-Indians) at these poor benighted souls, they can do their part for their oppressive government while simultaneously lining their pockets, wallowing in their generosity toward First Nations, **and** feeling smug in their intellectual superiority. So much, for so little! It also creates a sense of impending doom in First Nations communities,[5] where former residential school students are identified as little more than walking time bombs, waiting, like the American Veterans of the Vietnam War, for some garden-variety mishap to catapult them into an orgy of crazed blood-sport.

The Vietnam Veterans quickly tired of this particular image, and we suggest First Nations peoples avoid it altogether. While it is true that some individuals suffered unimaginable horrors in residential school, there was neither unanimity nor universality of any particular experience, or at any particular school. This can easily be related back to our previous discussion of residential school research: some people undoubtedly look back on this time of their lives with as much positive recollection as others look back in anger and despair; one experience is as valid as the other. The immorality of residential school does not reduce to a "Pro vs. Con" show of hands.

The individualisation of residential schooling also overlooks the point that it was an assault on First Nations ways of life as a whole. The presumption that one had to personally undergo the experience ignores the fact that, with thermonuclear devices, one doesn't have to hit the bull's-eye; the general area will do. The effects on family, language, culture, and so forth, continue to accumulate, like Strontium 90, in the bones of those far from Ground Zero, with lasting, predictably detrimental effects in the long term.

Individualising residential schooling also leads to the **particularisation of redress**, with various attendant problems. This is in no way to argue that individuals shouldn't bring charges when and if they are so inclined. Rather, isolating the experience removes the First Nations complainant and his or her complaint from an ideologically meaningful context. The burden is placed on the complainants to, one by one, bring the charges forward to confront specific miscreants before a court which, if some of our earlier speculation is true, has a glaring conflict of interest. The complainants must, as far as possible, relive their horrors, and permit the public cross-examination of the most shocking experience of their lives. If successful, a complainant can expect to see a sizeable chunk of her/his award (after lord-knows-how-many appeals) disappear into the legal system, and the perpetrator perhaps punished to some degree while the racist, sexist, Eurocentric system (that sanctioned the action in the first place) is not even acknowledged.

We could go on indefinitely, but we will merely point out one more dissatisfaction we have with the therapeutic enterprise: it **professes an expertise it does not have**. Are we to believe that psychology has the means to treat and cure something they give every indication of misunderstanding? Do psychologists have a particularly strong track-record with analogous patients, say, survivors of the Holocaust? Primo Levi, Jean Amery, and innumerable other stilled voices suggest eloquently that they do not.

CONCLUSIONS

Now that residential schools have essentially been terminated, has the Canadian government "finished?" Not at all. The residential school was only one of many tactics deployed to assimilate First Nations, and most of the other tactics remain in place, continuing to do their job today without interruption.

In really productive times, useful new tools, like psychology, come along to aid in the assault. The role of the psychologist, we suggest, is to put a human face on the barbarism of cultural genocide. If psychologists wish to change this, they must recognize (and admit to) their complicity in and regeneration of the genocidal program. They must go beyond their typically ahistorical and acultural strategies of "helping" individuals, and incorporate the cultural, historical and economic context in which First Nations peoples continue to struggle for survival.

History, Wells once wrote, is increasingly a race between education and catastrophe. What Wells saw as separate features were joined in unholy matrimony for First Nations (and other Aboriginal minorities worldwide); education **was** catastrophe in the residential schools. Not only the experiences of the past, but the way in which those experiences are being recast in the present, are part of the continuing genocidal assault directed at First Nations. Psychologists, as caring, civilized people, do not want to see themselves in the role of oppressor, sycophant, or stormtrooper, but an heroic blindness to their place in majority society condemns them to play these parts. And First Nations peoples, locked in this genocidal Dance of Death, crushed in the embrace of their (thinking **or** thoughtless) oppressors, are supposed to believe social scientists are only there to help. But how can we know **this** dancer from the dance?

FOOTNOTES

1. Genocide is concerned with the destruction of forms of life, and consequently the fallacious concept of race has no place in this discussion (see Chrisjohn & Young, 1994). Rather than contribute to an ongoing obscurantist program of accounting for social diversity by mystical biology, we merely point out that the Canadian government's genocidal program will be fulfilled when First Nations peoples stop asserting (by any of our current or historical ways) their self-identity and existence. The colour of skin or hair or eyes, the shape of teeth, etc., has nothing to do with this.

2. Attendees often worked for school-operated enterprises or were rented out as farm hands, housekeepers, and suchlike. See, e.g., Furniss, 1992.

3. There is considerable evidence that the more egalitarian, democratic political theories that emerged during the 18th and 19th century (American Democracy; Marxism) were influenced by a Western appreciation of First Nations principles of law, government, and civic responsibility. Unfortunately, there is even more evidence that their appreciation was incomplete and imperfect (Barreiro, 1992).

4. A ludicrous example comes from the early days of Reagan's presidency, when it was broadcast that he distributed jellybeans to the members of his cabinet at the beginning of cabinet meetings. A psychologist went on a national newscast to declare that the colour of jellybean selected revealed hidden secrets of one's personality. While some behind-the-back snickering took place, no psychologist was so tacky as to publicly call this nonsense; to do so would have been "un-collegial" in the extreme.

5. ... and a marvelously useful racist image for non-Indian communities.

REFERENCES

Amery, J. (1986). *At the Mind's Limits: Contemplations by a Survivor of Auschwitz and its Realities*. New York: Schocken.

Barreiro, J. (Ed.). (1992). *Indian Roots of American Democracy*. Ithaca, New York: AKWE:KON Press, Cornell University.

Chrisjohn, R. (1993). *Residential Schools: What Now?* Paper presented at the Treaty 7 *Treaty First Nations Education Leadership Conference*, Calgary, Alberta.

Chrisjohn, R., Belleau, C., & Others. (1991). Faith Misplaced: Lasting Effects of Abuse in a First Nations Community. *Canadian Journal of Native Education*, 18, 161-197.

Chrisjohn, R., Pace, D., Young, S., & Mrochuk, M. (1994). *Psychological Assessment and First Nations: Ethics, Theory, and Practice*. Vancouver: Authors.

Chrisjohn, R., & Young, S. (1994). *Redskins: 500 Years of Racism*. Vancouver: Authors.

Chomsky, N. (1973). Psychology and Ideology. In N. Chomsky (Ed.), *For Reasons of State*. New York: Random House.

Frideres, J. (1993). *Natives Peoples in Canada: Contemporary Conflicts*. 4th ed. Scarborough, Ontario: Prentice-Hall.

Furniss, E. (1992). *Victims of Benevolence: Discipline and Death at the Williams Lake Indian Residential School, 1891-1920*. Williams Lake, British Columbia: Cariboo Tribal Council.

Haig-Brown, C. (1988). *Resistance and Renewal: Surviving the Indian Residential School*. Vancouver: Tillacum.

Howitt, D. (1991). *Concerning Psychology: Psychology Applied to Social Issues*. Buckingham: Open University Press.

Knockwood, I. (1992). *Out of the Depths: The Experiences of Mi'kmaw Children at the Indian Residential School at Shubenacadie, Nova Scotia*. Lockeport, Nova Scotia: Roseway.

Rose, S., Lewontin, R., & Kamin, L. (1984). *Not in Our Genes*. New York: Penguin.

Sarason, S. (1981). *Psychology Misdirected*. New York: The Free Press.

Young, S. & Chrisjohn, R. (1997). *Here be Dragons: Psychological Empowerment and Other Mythological Beasts*. Vancouver: Author.

Appendix F

The Road From Error to Truth
Authentic Resistance to the Aftermath of Indian Residential Schooling

Roland D. Chrisjohn, Ph. D. & Sherri Young[1]

INTRODUCTION

> We must begin with the misrepresentation and transform it into
> what is true. That is, we must uncover the source of the misrep-
> resentation; otherwise hearing what is true won't help us. The
> truth cannot penetrate when something is taking its place. To con-
> vince someone of what is true, it is not enough to state it; we must
> find the road from error to truth. Ludwig Wittgenstein.

In the three years it has been since we wrote *The Circle Game* we have
had a number of opportunities to discuss the implications of our position
with interested parties. These discussions have been occasionally reward-
ing, but more frequently frustrating; at times we've thought that no one has
been able to understand what we've been trying to express. While our own
obscurity (intentional and otherwise) may largely be to blame, it certainly
hasn't been the only obstacle we have encountered in making ourselves
understood. More central to our difficulties has been our inability to move
our audience to a sufficiently early point in the chain of thoughts and
actions that gave rise to the Residential School, and to challenge the
assumptions taken for granted at that point. As a result, our experience has
been that some people have seen no importance at all to what we have been
saying, and others have assured us they agree with our position only to fall
back into the vulgar forms of thinking we have been criticizing.

This isn't entirely a bad thing. With regard specifically to the
Aboriginal Peoples in our potential audience, caution is an attitude with
much to recommend it. Governments, bureaucrats, consultants, and all
other manners of representatives of mainstream society persist in trying to
stampede us into one alteration or another of our legal statuses, economic
positions, or social forms. A favourite tactic of government/bureaucracy,
for example, has been to present our nations with an unannounced policy
initiative and a deadline for agreeing to it, usually with a threat of funding
withdrawal or loss if the policy is not acceded to. If *The Circle Game* is suspected of being *our* attempt to start a stampede in Indian Country, this isn't
entirely untrue: we certainly hope that, collectively, *First Nations* will move
away from an ideology that maintains and extends the oppression characteristic of the Residential School in our world while whitewashing the
criminality and duplicity in theirs, and, in our opinion, the faster this happens, the better. But we don't think the change in direction should be willy-
nilly, as in a stampede. If we understand the ideological basis of the attack
constituted by Residential Schooling, we will first of all recognize it in

other forms of our dealings with Canadian governments, churches, businesses, and so on. Once this recognition is made, we will see it reflected in the institutions we have nominal control over even in our own communities. Finally, these realizations become the starting point to doing things very differently, in ways that not only do not demean us or maintain our oppressed status, but positively reconstitute our forms of life on our own terms. We cannot emphasize more strongly that this is work that cannot and will not occur without an explicit examination and rejection of the pathological ideology discussed in Chapter 6 of *The Circle Game*. If Aboriginal Peoples prefer to react with caution to our suggestion of a change in direction, we don't disagree. What we hope to provide here, and what we intend to provide as long as we can, are materials, references, arguments, and so on that can be used in making a reasoned judgement to stop the current manner of acting and thinking about Indian Residential School (and, by implication, other areas of our mainstream-dominated societies) and starting thinking and acting in other ways.

The task of starting a slow stampede, however, forced us to reconsider some of our intentions in writing *The Circle Game*. Originally, not only did we want to recast the conventional ways of thinking about Residential Schooling, we wanted to connect the oppression of indigenous North Americans to similar (not identical) issues worldwide, past and present. The "divide and conquer" strategy employed on our Reserves is itself more general,[2] and there are many peoples, in Canada and throughout the world, with whom we could make common cause when our issues converge (while maintaining mutual respect when they don't). To put it even more simply, we should have more friends than we have and be more friendly toward other progressive movements than it has worked out in practice, and in *The Circle Game* we tried to provide an historical and political basis for believing this.

Whatever people think of this objective, or the degree of success we had achieving it, we consider more of the same unnecessary here. We've already taken our shot, and there are better qualified and more readable resource people doing this much more comprehensively than we ever could (e.g., Ward Churchill, Noam Chomsky, Ruth Hubbard, Michael Parenti, Howard Zinn, and Louise Armstrong, to name only a few). More importantly, to continue this work would beg issues more central to Aboriginal Peoples in general and the Residential School era in particular. Outside Mr. Churchill's work, indigenous issues are largely ignored or underrepresented in critical alternative media, and as important as it is to relate the struggles of North American indigenous nations to the progressive causes other peoples, we need to take care of our own pressing problems. This is all the more important when much of what passes as "liberal" or "sympathetic" commentary on Aboriginal issues is merely warmed-over Residential School Era policy.[3] When we look at the policies and procedure everyone (whether or not they've had access to *The Circle Game*) continues to pursue regarding Residential Schooling, we have no excuse for not being more explicit about what we think should happen. In *The Circle Game* we provided suggestions, gave references, dropped hints, and when asked directly "what would you do," avoided answering the question. We believed then, and we believe now, that everything needed to answer the question had already been provided in our book. We trusted that frontline service providers would draw appropriate conclusions and make appropriate, locally relevant adjustments as they saw fit. We considered none of this any of our business.

But the "human sciences"[4] indoctrination now imposed upon therapists, healers, and counsellors, regardless of whether or not they're Aboriginal Peoples, makes no room for careful reflection on issues, reasoned discussion, and program modification. The human sciences (and "sciences" is being used overgenerously here) are religions and ideologies, and as such do not tolerate investigation, much less alteration, of their fundamental precepts. What they are pleased to call "advanced education" and "professional certification" are nothing more than institutionalized misrepresentations of the truth. Putting aside any form of institutionalized misrepresentation is incredibly difficult for anyone; in many ways it isn't different from putting aside a form of life, a long-established habit, or a lifelong relationship. However, it is central to the task of doing anything effective with respect to the aftermath of Indian Residential Schooling.

For better or worse (worse, in our opinion), the sorting out of the aftermath of Residential Schooling has become more a social services issue than one of morality, legalities, economics, or politics. The "trenches" are located in human services offices, drug and alcohol programs, family assault clinics, and suicide hotlines. If we are right in our presumptions about the harm the dominant human sciences ideology is doing, to our people and to other oppressed groups, it makes best sense to us first to try to reach the troops in those trenches. Consequently, more than to any other particular group, this chapter is written in the hope that it will be relevant to those Aboriginal Peoples in human services work. Our effort is impelled by the knowledge that it's one thing to call for a revolution and another to do what you can to bring it about.

WIT AND UNDERWEAR

> That's the point of a systemic analysis—to take apart the institu-
> tions that are larger than the personalities who inhabit them.
> Doug Henwood.

Throughout this work we have argued that the picture of Indian
Residential Schooling as a well-intentioned enterprise that led, in some
instances, to tragic mistakes (the "Standard Account") is wholly and deliberately misleading. The retreat into "motives," "intentions," and "errors"
with respect to the perpetrators, and into "pathology," "sickness," and
"healing" with respect to the victims is a strategy that focuses all our attention on putative personal, individual, and internal explanations and away
from conspicuous moral, legal, political, and economic explanations. The
reason is simple: what is conspicuous or public is by definition more obvious, and what is personal and internal is latent, esoteric, and more easily
manipulable by ideologues in charge of covering up the crimes of their
bosses. Pseudo-explanations like "Residential School Syndrome," which
no one can see, weigh, touch, or otherwise verify, can be manufactured on
the spot, modified in the face of opposition, attributed to the victims, and
then "cured" for a price by the priesthood that "detected" it in the first
place. All this can be done to a chorus of the perpetrators' self-congratulatory testimonials on how much they're doing to help the poor Indians.

Now, in the process of making this case (successfully or not), we mentioned from time to time that the dominant form of ideological misrepresentation of Indian Residential Schooling was not unique to it, but that it
followed a pattern that could be seen in application to other areas and issues
which touch Aboriginal Peoples, however seemingly remote they were
from Residential School. Since our hints don't seem to have inspired any
exploration of this pattern, let us be more explicit here. What are the characteristics of this as-yet hypothetical process? We think there are seven distinguishable characteristics of this pattern of misrepresentation, which,
while not independent of one another, deserve separate mention. We start
by naming them and restating their application in creating and maintaining
the Standard Account of Indian Residential Schooling.

First, the misrepresentation is fundamentally a rhetorical process (as
opposed, say, to a scientific one) involving the transformation of the obvious into the esoteric. Whatever the merits of a retreat into the mystical, it
sets the conditions of any discussion of the phenomenon (what Herman and
Chomsky[5] term the "background assumptions"). When properly accom-

plished, black can be called white and vice versa as necessary, and the subject under discussion can be changed or avoided, while the managed accessibility to media to opponents for "conventional wisdom" assures that no dissenting voices will be heard. In "analysis" of the Residential Schools, the fundamental good-heartedness of churches and governments is never questioned, spokespersons for the churches can repeat the canard that "the bad of the Residential Schools must be weighed against the good,"[6] and discussion can revolve around the "nature and extent" of our presumed pathology.

Second, as mentioned repeatedly, this form of secular transubstantiation ignores moral, legal, political, economic, and social aspects of any phenomenon being considered, and recasts them as personal, internal, and individual problems. We call this *philosophical individualism* (or just individualism) when it crops up in common conversation and *methodological individualism* when it is posited or assumed (incorrectly; see Chapter 6 of *The Circle Game*) as a scientific principle. With respect to Residential Schooling, the immorality and illegality of governmental, bureaucratic, church, and societal principle and practice has been transformed into the psychiatric problems of grown-up indigenous people and specific "bad apples" who sometimes operated the schools. The immorality[7] of believing it proper to impose upon sovereign peoples another religion, language, and form of life, while destroying their existing ones, is placed into the background. The genocidal illegality of legislating children away from the care of their parents and families and placing them in the charge of organizations dedicated to destroying who they are is put aside. The political expediency of interpreting an obligation to educate as a licence to indoctrinate doesn't come up. The economic imperative of reducing production costs by expropriating the property of imprisoned and defenseless Aboriginal Nations never arises. And the social relation of unbridled racism, which provided an unspoken justification for the most extreme of measures, is conveniently avoided.

Third, this transmutation of the apparent into the latent relocates the difficulty not in the perpetrators of the phenomenon, but in those who were subjected to it. William Ryan's phrase,[8] "blaming the victim," captures this feature perfectly.[9] In application to Residential Schooling, the perversion of truth makes it seem that the "sick" people in need of "treatment" are not the purveyors of genocide but the people who had the fortitude and/or luck to live through it.

Fourth, the misrepresentation doesn't interfere, and may indeed continue and extend, the ideological aim behind the original implementation of the program. Like fighting mercury,[10] pushing against a program merely displaces it elsewhere and threatens to engulf anyone trying to push. The Residential School was a program to make ordinary Canadians out of Aboriginal Peoples (at least the ones that made it out alive). While apologists prefer to call this "assimilation," we have argued that the proper term is "genocide." In any event, the residential schools were closed not because the Canadian government gave up on the idea, whatever you wish to call it, but because they found a cheaper, more effective, and less obviously racist way of accomplishing the same thing.[11]

Fifth, the conversion naturalizes what went on and retreats into scientism for its explanation. That is, events and policies are presented as an unfolding of an inherent order, and the way to understand the scope and impact involves hunting down unobservable variables, inventive use of pseudo-mathematics, and the *de novo* births of syndromes, psychodynamics, and healing processes. In application to Residential Schooling, the policy and its implementation are turned into "just another aspect" of the "inevitable" triumph of the West over primitive sub-humans, and "Residential School Syndrome" is touted as providing us the "best" insight into the bad wiring that purportedly predominates within the former student population.

Sixth, the ideological "fiddle" obscures the political economy of the policy and its implementation. That is, benefits (broadly understood) accruing to the perpetrators of a particular course of action remain more or less constant (or even increase), and outside public consideration, across the range of activities engaged in programmatically. In Indian Residential Schooling, the underlying economic basis for obliteration of indigenous peoples never enters the discussion and the fundamentally selfish, self-aggrandizing motive driving missionary zeal (heavenly credit for proselytizing) vaporizes.

Seventh, the misrepresentation process prevents any possibility of effective action being taken by neutralizing, marginalizing, and/or coopting those most inclined to action. The power to intervene is vested within ideologues of individualism and their converts (compradors; literally, agents of colonialism drawn from the colonized population) within the offended group. Indian Residential School is now under the control of pseudo-scientific psychobabblists claiming to be doing "therapy" and "healing," and in the grip of an ever-increasing comprador class of indoctrinates that repeat the mindless but destructive cliches of their superiors.

Because we'll cite these characteristics repeatedly, we summarize them below for easier reference:

1. rhetorical—control is maintained primarily by techniques of persuasive (not sound) argumentation, such as changing the obvious into the esoteric

2. individualistic—what is moral, legal, political, economic, and social is transformed into the internal, personal, and individual

3. victim blaming—explanations for abusive treatment are situated within the victims of abuse, not the perpetrators of abuse

4. relentless—interventions either do nothing at all to rectify or address the issue, or serve to broaden and/or intensify the original problem

5. naturalizing and scientizing—deliberate acts of people are transformed into forces of Mother Nature best described in pseudo-scientific doubletalk

6. fraudulent—the political economy of policy and practice is covered up, avoided, or subject to "creative accounting practices"

7. marginalizing and coopting—those who could and would take action are denied agency or converted into compradors

We don't claim that this is a comprehensive list of the systemic misrepresentation process (for example, as discussed in Chapter 2 of *The Circle Game*, rhetoric is whole hot-air balloon of tricks), and in good Wittgensteinian fashion we won't claim that all features are necessarily observable in all projections of the "Indian Problem." Further, we restate that these techniques are not really separate from one another, but rather tend to be deployed in a manner in which one techniques supports, and draws support from, other members of this group. We do claim, however, that any notion that this preformed scheme of interpretation is unique to Residential Schooling must result from culpability, moral blindness, groupthink, downright stupidity, or some combination of these factors.[12] We now undertake to apply this rogue's gallery to other current Issues in Indian Country, in order to generalize the issues we raised in *The Circle Game* and to demonstrate the further operation of these "transformative principles."

SUICIDE[13]

While there had been more than moderate awareness of the issue for some time, particularly within front-line workers, suicide in North American indigenous communities began to gain attention in higher governmental and policy making circles in the early 1980s.[14] In recent years, Aboriginal suicide has been the specific subject of a number of investigations, including the **Focus Group on Suicide Prevention,**[15] **Choosing Life: Special Report on Suicide among Aboriginal People,**[16] and **Horizons of Hope: An Empowering Journey.**[17] The sheer volume of these and other relevant works makes their close analysis the task for another venue, so here we will look at a relatively concentrated statement we consider problematic *and* typical, taken from the **Focus Group** of the Native Psychologists in Canada. We should point out that selections from veritably any of the works mentioned, and others, could have been used instead.

The underlying **Philosophy** guiding their work appears on page 3 of the collected presentations. Suicide is "the final self-destructive act of despair, committed while in a state of hopelessness and depression." Young Aboriginal men are "unable to find meaning in their lives," "feel abandoned by their culture," "ease their pain and frustration" with drugs and alcohol, and end up worsening "their mental state." The immediate disruption suicide causes in Aboriginal communities should be treated by "qualified individuals," while long-term solutions must "break the cycle of abuse, denial, and despair." Programs directed at heading off "crisis situations," preventing "substance abuse and neglect of children," and improving "recreational activities" are necessary, and school-based interventions teaching "confidence, self-worth, and coping skills" are indicated. All-in-all, the fundamental underlying assumptions of the Native Psychologists do not differ in any significant way from earlier, more generic summaries of the underlying bases of Indian suicide: Indians suffer from low self-esteem, are depressed and hopeless, drink too much, seem unable to adapt to the institutions (like education) of mainstream society, feel alienated from society at large, come from unstable home environments, and suffer from personal financial difficulties. In combination, these factors have helped to bring about a suicide rate for indigenous peoples that has been and (for nobody knows how long) remains at least four or five times the national average, at least for some age groups.

What's wrong with this picture? To get a simple and direct overview of the difficulties, allow us to take you back 50-60 years in time and jump to another continent. During the Nightmare Years (1933 to 1945), the suicide rate of German Jews is conservatively estimated to have been at least two or three times higher than the rate for German citizens in general, and during the years of intensive removal to concentration camps (1943 to 1945) it was at least **50** times the rate for non-Jewish Germans.[18] As appalling as these figures are, we don't consider that they tax the limits of human understanding. "Yes, the facts are horrifying," we say, "but completely understandable given what was going on." Another group that wasn't surprised was the Nazi government, which was embarrassed by the information, tried to suppress it nationally and internationally, and embarked upon a campaign of having Jewish religious leaders extol their congregations to "tough it out." Not one social scientific study was designed or conducted to establish why the Jews were behaving in such a fashion, nor was there any apparent urge to uncover the "inner dynamics" of Jewish suicide.

Now suppose that one of today's Nazi rehabilitationists undertook to explain away this particular historical "embarrassment" by arguing that Jews in Nazi Germany suffered from (1) personal financial problems (after all, many times the possessions of a lifetime could fit into a single suitcase); (2) fear of going outside; (3) anxiety about being identified with their ethnic group; (4) low self-esteem; (5) feelings of alienation from their mainstream society; and (6) unstable family lives (indeed, sometimes people left and never came home again). Would any but the already-perverted entertain even for a moment such explanations? Even at the time of this outrage, the Nazis didn't have the gall to retreat into such explanations, which, in 1944, would have had the additional "advantage" of being complementary to an already prevalent dogma of Jewish racial inferiority.

How easy it has become for the social scientists of today to do what even the Nazis couldn't bring themselves to do. In truth, does not the history of Jewish suicide during the holocaust, like the histories of suicide in the Arawaks, the Home Children, and the Marshallese Islanders,[19] and countless other oppressed groups, teach us that suicide is in part *a normal human reaction to conditions of prolonged, ruthless domination?* The dominant depiction of suicide in Aboriginal Peoples inhabiting Canada rhetorically neglects these parallels, biasing those trying to come to grips with the phenomenon away from the readily apparent and into esoteric realms. "Models" of Indian suicide are individualistic, relying on supposed internal characteristics instead of looking at the inverted pyramid of social, economic, and political forces impinging on Aboriginal Peoples. Existing explanations blame the victim, finding that they suffer from personal adjustment problems or emotional deficiencies like "low self-esteem" and "depression." None of the existing explanations alleviate the situation by acting or suggesting action against the forces of oppression; they don't even recognize them. Suicide is the "natural" outcome of conditions like alcohol/drug abuse (for which we are supposed to have a "genetic predisposition") and levels of unemployment (which has a "natural" level in the general population of 8-10%, and a "natural" level in Aboriginal that is probably considerably higher, again, for genetic reasons). The cost-effectiveness of the government's providing perfunctory, end-of-pipe social intervention programs[20] instead of meeting their contractual treaty obligations doesn't surface as an issue. And the people charged with "doing something" about Aboriginal suicide accept this limited frame of reference and repeat the irrelevancies of their masters. In total, the "search" for the "individual differences" that differentiate suicide attempters and succeeders from those who are neither is morally comparable to a social scientist looking for the "individual differences" that predict length of survival in a concentration camp. "Treatment" within such a model is convincing the inmates to accept their situations.

However, in the real world, the "proper treatment" for the "Jewish Suicide Problem" wasn't to send cheerleaders into what remained of their communities; it was the elimination of the system of unspeakable cruelty that destroyed their lives. And the "proper treatment" for the "Indian Suicide Problem" isn't to send cheerleaders into *our* communities; it is the elimination of the system that is destroying *our* lives.

DEPENDENCY

Sarcasm on.

In North America the identification of the current epidemic of dependency disorder (a disease which incubated for a long time in social programs everywhere before erupting into the population at large) was apparently initiated by the elections of Ronald Regan and Brian Mulroney,[21] and while politicans continue to be at the forefront in locating, diagnosing, and treating this debilitating condition, it seems that even lower forms of life, like radio talk-show hosts, can make proper diagnoses. In Canada, Aboriginal Peoples seem particularly susceptible to this disorder, although it also seems to be rampant in east-coast fishing industry workers and Albertans who have recently moved to British Columbia. It is characterized by a near complete aversion to work of any sort, no matter how menial, and a deep-seated delusion on the part of sufferers that their living conditions should be better than they are. Since individuals infected with this disease are unwilling to get off their duffs to improve these conditions, this translates into the attitude of 2-MAL, "The World Owes Me A Living."

The report from the Royal Commission on Aboriginal Peoples (RCAP) provided merely the latest impetus for the thorough examination of dependency in indigenous peoples, although concern about its infestation in our populations has been expressed both before and since. On the day of RCAP's release, the following dialogue popped up on CBC radio in Calgary:

Jeff Collins (morning radio host): I've heard the argument from Native leaders that it'll take self-government to break the dependency that exists now, and it would seem to me that given the recommendation for increased spending [in the RCAP report] in Native affairs, we're actually extending the cycle of dependency.

Frank Cassidy (designated Indian expert): Well, that's possible, and you always have to look at what we call the unintended consequences of public policy.[22]

Of course, Collins didn't have to go as far as citing anonymous "Native leaders" for his information. The very next morning on his program, this cropped up:

Cliff Friars (Reform Party guest commentator): The big question is the question of dependency. Have we, or do we continue to put them in, a position where they become dependent on the taxpayers of Canada and are unable to break that cycle—and frankly this is the 127th report between '65 and '92 and the question becomes, "Is this got a path that will get us there any better?" And I'm afraid that, without having the chance to of course to read 4,000 pages, that it may do that, and it may secondarily also increase in fact what I perceive to be the inherent racism in this issue. You can't keep these people on reservations, you can't just simply increase the money. You have to break the cycle, and whether that's the way, I still don't know. But I do have some thoughts on it, but I'll let Ian go first.

Jeff Collins: Ian, will it change the cycle of dependency?... [23]

Even before the RCAP report came out, however, real human concern about addressing dependency disorder was current. For example, the

Anglican Church set up a fund (so to speak) to support local projects aimed at undoing the harm of Residential Schools, and among the basic requirements for receiving a grant during 1992-4 included that the project "Empower[24] native communities to move out of a dependency relationship with the church or other structure."[25] A post-RCAP example of this concern was provided by a former leader of the Newfoundland New Democratic Party, Peter Fenwick, in St. John's *Evening Telegram* of June 22, 1997:

> I also believe that a large part of the problem of native people revolves around the largesse of the federal government and its paternalistic attitude to the Innu. If the federal government will build homes and a community for you when you destroy the old one, you destroy your old home in hopes of getting a new one. Just as welfare becomes a trap for Newfoundlanders, it also becomes a trap for native people. It saps initiatives and fosters dependency. The indiscriminate welfare policies of the government helped destroy the initiative of native people, but it wasn't a program directed at them, and it would have been unlawful to deny that assistance to native people even if one wanted to.[26]

It's clear from this brief survey that dependency disorder has been and remains one of the most pressing issues facing Aboriginal Peoples today.

As we've mentioned, politicians have not been content to sit back and let existing social services gradually accommodate themselves to this scourge, but have pioneered, particularly in Alberta and Ontario, a multi-faceted attack on the disorder. Innovative programs include:

> Food-Access Impedance Work Incentive Group Therapy [formerly know as "Mass Starvation"]: the cycle of dependency is broken by limiting a patient's caloric intake until either (1) the patient gets off his or her duff, or (2) he or she dies. Historically this was very effectively employed in the Highland Clearances and the Irish Potato Famine.[27]

> Self-Commodification Training Workshops [formerly known as Life Skills Seminars]: dependent people are forced to reconstitute their disordered senses of self from "Human Beings of Dignity and Worth" into the more corporately-attractive "Cogs in a Machine Who Will Do Anything To Eat" through repetitious re-

writing of their resumes and attending workshops in "Living Repetitively." Emphasis is on finding elliptical ways of describing oneself in the Third Person, as if a container filled with objects Big Business will find yummy.

Social Derogation Encouragement Programs [formerly known as public excoriation and humiliation]: dependency sufferers who continue to show up to social services agencies looking for food, shelter, or other extravagancies are ignored, forced to stand in lineups, and otherwise treated like cockroaches by highly-trained therapists. Meanwhile, newspapers, television programs, and other media draw telling comparisons between dependency sufferers and leeches, vampire bats, and annoying insects. The "being-cruel-to-be-kind" experience leads either to wholesale personal reformation (and a concomitant discharge of 2-MAL) or entry into Food-Access Impedance Work Incentive Group Therapy.

Dependency Immersion Therapy [formerly know as prison]: dependency victims are subjects to an experience of total immersion in dependence, with the regulation of when they get up, when they go to bed, where, when, and what they eat, and so on, until dependence becomes so distasteful to them they will put up with anything to avoid dependence again. Or, of course, until he or she dies.

While only recently applied on a large scale to Canadian populations in general, the "trail blazing" work in these and related forms of therapy was originally undertaken with the cooperation of indigenous peoples. Even today, Aboriginal Peoples, who make up less than 5% of the overall Canadian population, constitute about 70% of those enrolled in federal Dependency Immersion Therapy programs.

But then again, something smells here. After all, the same people who are so relentless in the War Against Dependency when indigenous peoples, production laborers, migrant workers, and other low-end blue-collar individuals are the focus seem oblivious to the helpful work that could be done with the most persistent group of idle loafers Western civilization has produced, the Stinking Rich (also know as "rentiers"). These people are burdened with interest income that deprives them of the experience of useful labor, and with a tax system that has been precipitously increasing their burden of wealth since the early 1980s.[28] The kind of initiative-killing, dependency-creating governmental programs and policies documented by Zepezauer and Naiman[29] for the US, and by McQuaig[30] for Canada, has led thoughtful people like Eric Shragge[31] to ask "Are wealthy people too dependent on wealth? How can we reform the tax system to make the wealthy more independent? Would the wealthy have more self-esteem if they worked for their money rather than inherited it?" Why are not the benefits of different dependency therapy programs imposed on the Stinking Rich for their own good?

Sarcasm off.

The move to depict human services funding (whether nominally allocated to Aboriginal Peoples or to members of Canada's underclass) as creating "personal" problems in us is entirely rhetoric, a ploy to portray the dismantling of such services as the humane, "empowering," policy of a beneficent state. Within non-Aboriginal North America, the policy has much to do with the short-term aim of lowering taxes for the Stinking Rich by eliminating the costs of publicly funded human services programs, but more to do with the ongoing corporate- and upper-class warfare on middle- and lower-class people.[32] Within Aboriginal North America, it constitutes the continual struggle of federal governments to abrogate its responsibilities to Status and non-Status Indians, Metis, and Inuit, under treaty, international law, and common morality. It would be perfectly reasonable, for example, to interpret the Numbered Treaties as contracts (and, of course, International Agreements), entered into by our ancestors with federal governments, and guaranteeing us a perpetual return on the "investment" of permitting Eurocanadians to share the territories given us by our Creator.[33] From this perspective, the sometimes gradual/sometimes precipitous governmental off-loading of programs and fiduciary responsibilities is simply a massive governmental defaulting on contracts. That the successive governments of Canada have chosen to conceal these obligations and instead pretend that its involvement with indigenous Nations arises from "largesse" and "good will" is nothing less than another example of the lengths to which it will go to eliminate the "Indian" problem by eliminating Indians. That the successive governments of Canada supervise the "proper flow" of dividends, stock options, and the like within businesses, and will put education, health, and other Canadian public services to service its own debt to banks and corporations, but will create the most absurd public relations schemes to avoid its legal and moral responsibilities to those most responsible for its "enviable" standard of living, reveals clearly who they consider their bosses to be.

It is important to note that in order to insist on this position we don't have to endorse what such social services programs are actually doing, and in fact we don't. To the extent that Canada's unilateral and self-serving interpretations of their obligations have been used to create and enforce programs (like Residential Schooling) which destroy us while suiting their own mainstream political economy, we have no use for them. Rather, we are merely insisting that the conceptual context under which these programs operate and have operated acknowledge that we are not supplicants.

The way in which "dependency syndrome" falls within the seven points of the misrepresentation process it too obvious to warrant elaboration here. We will say, however, that we have found appalling the ease with which dependency jargon has been adopted by people who should know better.

ALCOHOL

If for dialectical purposes we embellished the status of "dependency" into that of a full-blown psychiatric diagnostic category, no exaggeration is necessary for alcohol abuse. That "alcoholism" is a "disease like any other" remains the dominant social sciences ideology, despite an ever-increasing and (in our opinion) well-reasoned body of literature exposing the absurdities of this myth.[34] In the existing literature[35] and in Native alcohol abuse programs, especially those operated by Aboriginal Peoples, the disease model of alcohol abuse is a canon of the psychiatric faith. The notion that indigenous peoples are "genetically predisposed" to alcoholism is widespread (again, as a matter of faith rather than of evidence) to the extent that some have referred to this calumny as "a form of positive racism."

We see again that applying the characteristics of the system of ideological misrepresentation to this issue poses no difficulty: (1) rhetorically, the existence of alternative accounts of alcohol abuse is nearly drowned out in the mainstream publications and is but a blip in the Aboriginal literature. Exceptions are Fisher's 1987 article[36] and the work generated at the "Alternative Approaches to Addictions & Destructive Habits" conference in Edmonton in 1995;[37] (2) alcohol abuse is turned into a problem of weak or susceptible individuals with "alcoholic personalities" or suffering from a disease; (3) they suffer from this disease because of something that's wrong with them, not because something is wrong with what's being done to them by an oppressive, dominant society; (4) despite widespread assurances that "specialists" are "curing" their Aboriginal charges of this disease, no one bothers even to evaluate the effectiveness of treatment, much less provide a coherent account of what they're trying to do and why; (5) in the absence of evidence,[38] the "Drunken Indian" is taken for granted as a natural, genetic condition; (6) no one seems to remember Malcolm X's words, that if Black people really understood why, for whose benefit alcohol and drugs were in the ghettoes, there would be no need for social workers or treatment programs—that Black people would eliminate these scourges all on their own. No one seems to take seriously the analysis of the political economy of alcohol and drugs expressed in those words; (7) among the strongest supporters for the ideological position that alcoholism is a disease requiring individual therapy are Aboriginal Peoples themselves, operating cash-strapped band-aid programs while feeling that something's not quite right about their work but while being unable to see clearly how to implement alternatives.

It is in the area of alcohol treatment that we believe a sense of a comprehensive alternative outlook on the dynamics of Aboriginal social problems may be discerned. While the hard evidence is equivocal,[39] alcohol abuse is almost universally acknowledged as the most persistent, pervasive negative feature of Aboriginal community life. Although explanations postulating weak wills, bad genetics, and diseases are pernicious, those emphasizing bad family lives, "drinking cultures," and self-medication come down to much the same thing. That is, they locate the source of the problem within the individual and treat it there,[40] failing to examine the political economy of alcohol in indigenous worlds. The "compromise" model, that maybe alcohol abuse in Indians is biological, maybe social, but probably a mixture of both is no compromise at all, since it leads to the same individualistic, victim-blaming rhetoric and treatment programs already found to marginalize Aboriginal clients and coopt Aboriginal service providers.

It's useful to point out parallels between modern "models" of Aboriginal alcohol abuse and the counterexamples to individualism we drew in Chapter 6 of *The Circle Game*.[41] After making the obvious changes from Chinese to North Americans and from opium to alcohol, it should be clear that the same obstacles to explanation arise: not only does Simpson's Paradox assure us of the ambiguity and non-generalizability of conclusions drawn at different levels of analysis (the individual vs. the social, for example), the focus on the individual, regardless of from what perspective (biological, social, or mixed), cannot accurately depict the problem. Just as a complete listing of the "mental contents" of Mr. Su cannot include a "variable" representing English imperialism, the complete listing of the "mental contents" of the "Drunken Indian" cannot represent the political economy of just what alcohol is accomplishing, and for whom, in Indian Country today. To put it more simply, if doing the "right thing" about alcohol abuse in Aboriginal Peoples is to be based on an accurate picture of the context of abuse, the individualists of today's social sciences cannot draw such a picture.

EDUCATION[42]

As we stated earlier, the obligation (legal and moral) to educate Aboriginal Peoples has continually been interpreted by successive federal governments as a license to indoctrinate us. With the closing down of federal residential schools this long-term strategy of genocide has merely shifted, like mercury, threatening to engulf indigenous peoples from a number of directions. One of the breakthrough position papers, Indian **Control of Indian Education**,[43] was originally designed to be a foundation for a revolution in Indian education but in the years since the Federal Government officially adopted it as policy any distinction between Indian education and any other type of education has been blurred considerably, along with the meaning of the word "control." In derailing serious Aboriginal resistance to the attack constituted by education, the Federal Government **has repeatedly invoked** our seven point of misrepresentation, and across such a broad range of applications that there is all too much to point to in this section. Hence, we can merely run past a few of the highlights.

Rhetorical

Whereas in the past Aboriginal Peoples received religious indoctrination under the guise of education, today, like everyone else, we receive vocational training and New World Order Multinational Capitalism propaganda instead.[44] Aboriginal parents fight to have local school systems meet the "standards" of the provincial curricula, little realizing that achieving this standard will qualify their children for jobs flipping hamburgers, mopping floors, and doing other menial, dismissible tasks.[45] At universities, now somehow qualified to certify Indians as Indians, Indian Studies Department Heads can sagely talk about his students like the Borg talks about the Federation.[46] And work-study programs, which remove 10th to 12th grade Aboriginal students from their classrooms (where they've already learned far too much) and place them in jobs they don't get paid for (that their parents, relatives, and neighbors probably could use), but for which they receive course credit, are all the rage. Sometimes the obvious doesn't retreat into the esoteric, but into the ridiculous.

Individualistic and Victim Blaming

Depending where you place the mark on the time-line from 1867 to 1997, Aboriginal children are mentally inferior, right-brained, slow learners, suffering from attention-deficit disorder, have a learning style that predisposes them to finger-painting and ditch-digging rather than mathematics, or display some other defect that makes it pointless to try to teach them, provide them with learning materials comparable to those made available to non-Aboriginal children, or even put up with them. Where trouble is even taken to do "assessments" justifying such treatment (and, fortunately, some experienced teachers of Aboriginal children can psychically detect their deficits without the need for assessments), the trouble has never been taken to show the applicability of *even one* test of intelligence, learning style, "brainedness," or what-have-you to Aboriginal populations (see Appendix C, *infra*). Of course, the entire field of mental testing essentially defines the conjunction of individualism and victim blaming (*along with* naturalizing and scientizing), but everyone seems more concerned with providing their children with an "advantage" than questioning the sexism, racism, ageism, classism, elitism, and mumbo-jumboism inherent in sorting individuals on the basis of unobservables (or, more accurately, nonexistents).

Fraudulent

The cost-effectiveness of presuming Aboriginal children too defective to bother educating isn't a topic of discussion. Neither is the manner in which Aboriginal children were bussed about to various non-Indian school districts long enough for those systems to qualify for federal subsidies which were then used to build or upgrade those schools, following which the Indian children were dropped like a hot barrel of pork. Nor the system that requires money to be transferred from (non-Indian) governments to (non-Indian) "mental test organizations" to perform invalid and unethical "assessments" of Aboriginal children and write useless program recommendations which then counts it all as "money spent on Indian education." (Boy, are the sentences ever getting longer!) Enough! Our lung capacity is finite; the political economics of educational exploitation isn't.

Marginalizing and Coopting

This is too depressing even to think about. We'll leave it at this: far too many of those who should be at the front lines of writing critiques, conducting investigations, producing histories, radically educating, and generally fighting like hell against being swallowed whole are instead desperate to meet the criteria, satisfy the qualifications, and emulate the manners of our oppressors. For example:

> We envisage a world where the representation of Aboriginal people among doctors, engineers, carpenters, entrepreneurs, biotechnologists, scientists, computer specialists, artists, professors, archaeologists and individuals in other careers is comparable to that of any other segment of the population. Aboriginal leaders who signed treaties earlier in our history sought education that would give their children the knowledge and skills to participate as equals in the Canadian economy that was emerging. Royal Commission on Aboriginal Peoples Report, Volume 3, p. 501.

Who wrote these words? They are purported to be those of "Aboriginal educators" and education specialists who appeared before the Commission ("reflected back" and "summarized" from Commission testimony), but the sentiment is not different from attitude of the liberal mainstream during the years of brutality at the Residential Schools. The "interpretations" of treaty history is furthermore a lie; our parents, grandparents, and other progenitors were not signing us away to become fodder for the Canadian capitalist empire, and the pretense that they were is merely an attempt to insinuate the agenda warned about by Barlow, Robertson, Keuhn, Calvert, and others who think carefully and critically about where Canadian education is going.

Regardless of the "genetic material" constituting the person or persons responsible for trash like the excerpt provided, no understanding of or commitment to the struggles of Aboriginal education is detectable. All too often, blatant nonsense like this is certified, generated, or produced by those either of our number or of a self-proclaimed sympathetic group, both of whom at the drop of a hat will testify to just how "radical" they really are. Slogans like "critical consciousness" and "decolonization" ring out, but as hollow noises, sounded with every indication of failure to understand these crucial notions. And because all too often this babble is decreed to be the "cutting edge" from the "Indian intelligentsia," those initiatives that actually have some hope of fostering real education and making it relevant to Aboriginal experience are obviated or ignored.

SUMMARY

Rhetoric, like history, repeats itself, but not merely among those who fail to learn from it. Rhetoric repeats itself more reliably among those who don't recognize it for what it is in the first place.

FALSE DICHOTOMIES

It is true, as Althusser observes, that persons and groups experience life in and through ideology; they do so, however, not passively but as agents who can modify this ideological mediation of life to a greater or lesser extent. That is, the behavior of persons is generally not a pure expression of the interests of the bourgeoisie or of the proletariat, or any particular class that might exist in a given social configuration, but rather the peculiar, partial, and complex expression of such class interests. Sometimes it may even be a contradictory expression, that is, a behavior with some aspects that may be politically useful to their adversaries. Ignacio Martin-Baro.

So far we've limited ourselves to a single task: showing that the misrepresentation that constitutes the almost-universally accepted analysis of Indian Residential Schooling follows a pattern that is reproduced again and again whenever issues affecting Aboriginal Peoples are raised. Were this misguided and misguiding pattern observed once, one might think it a tragedy; twice, a regrettable coincidence; three times, downright warped; and any more often than that, malignant. We could continue to multiply indefinitely examples of the same pattern of thinking, but we hope there is no longer a point in doing this. In looking at any of the standard human sciences interpretations and interventions in Indian Country, we must apply strong counter-measures if we are to get anything like an accurate picture of the truth: strip away the rhetoric and don't let mainstream ideologies set the background analytical assumptions; stop acceding to individualistic, victim-blaming models of behavior (regardless of how "kind-hearted" such models appear to be) and establish the moral, political, legal, and economic grounds for the analysis; focus on the political economy of the phenomenon ("follow the money") to establish the benefits to mainstream society of maintaining Aboriginal Peoples under "benign" oppression; peremptorily reject appeals to "human nature" or "natural order" as evasions designed to accomplish nothing; and don't accept the role of comprador, no matter how attractive or useful it is made to seem.

The "how" of doing this bears elaboration, but the "why" continues to be more important. It is likely that the chapter thus far has fostered a certain impatience in our readers. After all, techniques and interpretations that have been taken for granted have been examined, ridiculed, or discarded, often without much ceremony; even those seeing some point to our analyses may want a more thorough look at our grounds. In addition, however, objections are undoubtedly brewing. As frontline workers might argue, "Even if you're right, we are still forced to deal with the practicalities of these situations. After all, people are still suicidal, or drink destructively, or are assaulting their spouses, *right now*, and the cerebral examination of systemic misrepresentation doesn't look useful in saving a life, stopping the drinking, or ending an assault." This is entirely true. But once again we must interrupt: do you think the urgency of your work is accidental or unique to it? Talk to Aboriginal university students, who speak over and over again of how the press of assignments and test schedules prevents them the "luxury" of actually sitting and thinking about what they're supposed to be learning. Talk to treaty researchers, buried under mountains of documents but operating under the continuing psychological pressure to "produce." Or really, talk to anyone taking his/her job seriously and ask, do you have the time to reflect on what, how, and why you're doing what you're doing? The press of ordinary circumstances, and the concomitant desire to distance one's self from one's work after business hours, is the result of a very old tactic (we will show) calculated to maintain our oppression. Outside our work we just want a breathing space, while inside our work we're drowning. And when you're drowning you're not a philosopher. We flail about, grabbing on and clinging to anything that might help keep us afloat. In social service delivery, what comes to hand is the set of techniques and structures of the mainstream, *but the ideology of the Standard Account is an anchor, not a life preserver!* We must begin our move toward an explicit alternative approach by trying to convince ourselves one more time to let go of this anchor. Then maybe our hands will be free to grasp something with considerably more buoyancy.

THE VORTEX OF INDIVIDUALISM

So the scenario is this: in the front lines we are presented with serious cases demanding immediate attention. Our professional and para-professional training is to react to these situations in terms of client-focussed therapeutic techniques, and we consequently react in such a manner. However, since these techniques are individually focussed, the "whys and wherefores" of the individual's behavior is presumed to derive from internal, personal forces that are not available to inspection. We conclude: *the professional and para-professional training of Aboriginal frontline workers, and the delivery systems under which they operate, institutionalize an unexam-*

ined commitment to the individualism (philosophical and methodological) which is the underlying ideology of the modern Western world.[47] This is certainly not unique to social service providers, Aboriginal and otherwise. However, with the emphasis we've adopted for this chapter we limit ourselves to those so employed, hoping once again that generalization to other positions in other disciplines is an easy step.[48]

Why is it that we are so easily sucked into this ideological vortex? The first reason is the one we dealt with in *The Circle Game*, the unquestioning belief that (philosophical/methodological) individualism is true. This simply isn't the case, and if there is any confusion on this we suggest you go back to Chapter 6 of *The Circle Game* and work through the analysis again (we won't repeat it here). The press of circumstances already mentioned is put to work, and, as in statistics where Simpson's Paradox is dealt with by the simple expedient of not telling anyone about it, indoctrinees have not the preparation, the time, or the incentive to question their master's voice. Our first defense against adopting the Western perspective by default, then, is to hold tightly to the fact that an observed regularity has no necessary, underlying regularity upon which it is founded.[49]

Secondly, even more seductive is the individual manner in which each of us experiences the world. For example, as we've written elsewhere in this book, it was personal pain, humiliation, and anger that was suffered in Residential Schools, and those suffering such injustices didn't attribute these incidents to English Imperialism or the Industrial Revolution, or even to the bureaucrats and members of parliament who drafted policy and law, but to the priest or nun holding the leather strap. Being hungry, being angry, being tired, and so on are neither experienced in other people nor are collectively sensible. Thus, it takes an extra effort to investigate beyond the particulars of specific individual experiences. But this broadening of perspective is an attitude that is certainly undermined[50] in mainstream society. In all events, the fact that we experience the world as *individuals* is improperly generalized to *equating experience with "the truth,"* a fallacy we call *experientialism.* The assumption is that personal, direct experience is necessary to understanding; that the only people thought to be able to empathize with another individual's experience are those who have been through the experience (or something remarkably similar) themselves; and that they only way to come to "know" something is through undergoing direct personal experience. This is a common belief system; it is used to justify particular hiring practices, forms the unspoken grounds for many *ad hominem* attacks, is a debating tactic in the Canadian House of Commons, and is observable in hundreds of other situations. But is it true?

"Having the experience" is in no way synonymous with "understanding the experience." Events usually involve more than one person, and yet we can only experience *our* experience—we necessarily leave out many other people's experiences. Further, as pointed out above, factors well outside any immediate context (which, perhaps, even stipulate them) are unrepresented and unperceived in many circumstances. Having landed at Anzio imparted no special knowledge of the Hitler-Chamberlain Pact, any more than having gone through Residential School imparted knowledge of Indian-relevant legislation, however much such experience might later serve as an impetus for further investigation.

What does "having the experience" imply behaviorally? Certainly not verbalization, or representation, or more than truncated, elliptical descriptions of some aspects of an experience. You cannot describe the aroma of coffee, or the taste of a Whopper, any more than recalling a painful experience necessarily elicits the shout that accompanied the original incident. Even if direct experience leaves some "trace" to which you have private access, it isn't something you can tell other people about as a demonstration of your unique qualifications; and to the extent you *can* describe it, it is something someone else can learn without having experienced it directly. If it is some kind of *direct action* that is supposed to be available to someone who has had a particular experience, again, to the extent it can be articulated it can be imparted to someone who hasn't had the experience (perhaps supplemented by an approximate experience). This "direct action capacity" must itself be suspect, however, on the basis of our first objection that having the experience cannot be the totality of what there was to be experienced.

Smarmy remarks like "don't knock it until you've tried it" also reflect experientialism, but the argument, if it can be called that, carries no weight. We've never had broken legs, nor have we contracted smallpox, nor have we been shut up in the prison of a military dictator, but we feel no qualms about condemning or avoiding these and many other experiences we haven't tried. Nor would we insist that a doctor setting an accidentally broken limb of ours suffer, or have suffered such an injury herself, nor that our veterinarian himself be a cat. What is confused in these "don't knock it" kind of arguments is the ease (and, sometimes, pleasure) of interaction with others to whom we need not explain every little thing, and the absence of empathy or understanding often observed in people from backgrounds and with perspectives very different from our own. The attribution is that *this* ease, or *that* hostility is experiential may be reasonable, but to then turn this into a wall that can only be scaled one way (*in vivo* experience) does not follow.

The third way in which we fall into individualism is through language. English in particular is concerned with individuals, their actions, and their feelings. There is no one-to-one correspondence between the way things are and they way we talk about the way things are, but as we will see later this isn't the problem it is usually made out to be. In talking about things and concepts other than individuals, however, we perforce make use of individually focussed language. Such extensions are purely metaphorical, that is, "as if" and not literally true; and, if language isn't a one-to-one correspondence with reality, metaphorical language is even further removed from accuracy. However, the metaphorical use of language is typically not recognized, and sometimes even obscured,[51] leading to a host of silly ways of talking about the world. For example, "the organization decided...": no, it did no such thing. People decide, and it is purely metaphorical to speak as if organizations did. "The government said today...": no, again. People talk; governments do so only metaphorically. These metaphorically-activated objects, and others at aggregations levels both higher and lower than human beings,[52] are not conscious, do not make plans, experience no emotions, and so on, but when we try to describe the effects of supra- and sub-human systems of operations we fall back on the only vocabulary we have.[53]

What this means for the front-line practitioner is that she/he, like everyone else, has no language for describing, thinking about, or arguing with higher levels of organization. In coming to grips with how the "system" has impacted upon the cases in front of us, we fall into all the rhetorical traps Hacker, Penelope[54] and others have warned us about. Even when we don't want to talk about human agency, but, say, bureaucratic agency instead, we talk, act, and think like we are talking about human agency. And, as we stated, this "individualization" of the non-individual works "downward" too, so that when metaphoric language is used to argue that "genes determine our behavior," or that "we are slave to our hormones," or, even worse, that a person's "low self-esteem" caused him to commit suicide, we don't call nonsense *nonsense*, but instead nod at the superior wisdom being imparted to us.

Thus, there are all kinds of reasons for us to fall prey to the rhetoric of individualism. When unchallenged, philosophical/methodological individualism (1) insinuates accounts of behavior that are inadequate, and therefore inaccurate; (2) gives rise to social fragmentation, historical blindness, and the breakdown of cooperation by personalizing, individualizing, and internalizing the forces that shape us all; (3) convinces us to forego the causes of social justice by encouraging the individualization of treatment, cure, and explanation; and (4) in short, maintains and elaborates the oppression of all peoples by distracting our attention away from the "man behind the curtain."

We can say it no other way: individualism is *wrong*, both in the scientific and moral sense of "wrong." Our only defense against falling into individualism is to try to understand the various manifestations of this ideological hydra, and, in performing our daily duties, constantly work to broaden our perspectives and the perspectives of those who depend upon us (colleagues and clients alike). Remember, working at a societal or an individual level with a client isn't a forced either/or choice; the refutation of individualism tells us that we can work toward a more accurate understanding of what's going on by treating all levels seriously, while resisting any temptation to believe one level has priority or is more essential than another. And, when trying to draw conclusions between levels we must impose the strongest sceptical thinking possible upon ourselves, for there is no necessary regularity of relations between levels. We can live in a racist society that has no racists, be exterminated in a society that "loves" its "Native Peoples," and starve in a world of plenty. And if you don't think we can, look about you.

There is only one reason to fight like hell to avoid falling into the ideology of individualism: our survival depends upon it.

WITH FRIENDS LIKE THESE...

There remains at least one major temptation dangling from the ideology of individualism, the indirect lure of therapy and related siren songs ("healing," "wellness," "treatment," and so on). Already in this work we have called into question the purpose of individually-focussed therapy (Chapter 5 of *The Circle Game*; Appendix E, "Among School Children"), but we feel the need to touch upon this class of issues one more time. It is possible, even probable, that many in our audience, even if in agreement with what we've said so far, will still reverberate to the call that Aboriginal Peoples are in need of help and that, whatever its underpinnings, individually-based therapy can provide that help. We may agree with the part about the current condition of Aboriginal Peoples and communities (with certain qualifications), but here we make one more attempt to show that such therapies do not help, and don't for some very obvious reasons.

It is clear, with their reliance upon "hidden dynamics" that reside "north of the neck" which can only be detected and modified by the *cognoscenti,* that the ideological commitment of therapists in general is squarely within the ambit of the pattern of misdirection we have been discussing. With more specific reference to therapy for Residential School "survivors," however, there are more telling ways of demonstrating the ideological bias inherent in therapy. Let's begin with one related to the initial assumption that "Aboriginal Peoples are sick and in need of help."

LOGOCRACY

Suppose the two of us, concealing our actions, placed something in a drink we then served you, and that subsequently you became violently ill, with all the symptoms of a severe case of flu. After recovering, you visit us again and tell us of your recent sickness, explaining why you've recently been out of circulation. However, after listening to your story for a few minutes, the two of us burst out laughing and, between efforts to catch our breaths, related the "trick" we had played on you that had put you in Death's Parking Lot for four days. After hearing this, would you still believe that you had been "sick," or would you believe that you had been "poisoned?"

Notice that during the explanation of our little "joke," your symptoms wouldn't have changed; after all, time travel didn't occur. But your attitude toward your condition will have changed completely. What before you had passed off as "undercooked pork" or a bit of "bad luck," with no more premeditation or intention than the wind, must now be seen as a deliberate instrumental act, carried out upon you by people you no longer understand. In that moment, the possibility of litigation probably occurs to you, as does the possibility of making immediate personal restitution (bonking us on our heads) and suspicion concerning the drink we now set before you. In that moment, issues of morality, legality, and human society suddenly become important, whereas only moments previously those issues were nowhere to be seen.

The selection of "sickness" as the characterization of the condition of Aboriginal Peoples is not neutral, scientific, or accurate. It is a term which, when agency is present, *hides* that agency while naturalizing and scientizing the condition it ostensibly describes (after the manner in which "radiation poisoning" became "radiation sickness" shortly after World Ward II). Who the "agents" were in Residential School **Poisoning** is amply clear. That they have had no difficulty in coopting "objective scientific disciplines" in the task of maintaining and thus participating in their coverup (wittingly or unwittingly) should not speak well either for the ideological preconceptions of those disciplines or for the aim and effectiveness of the "treatment" offered to deal with the so-called "sickness." Aboriginal

Peoples are not "sick" peoples in need of "therapy" and "healing:" we are wronged peoples in need of justice. Those who cannot appreciate this distinction have no right to consider themselves advocates for or friends to Aboriginal Peoples.

FREEDOM IS SLAVERY

Therapeutic misdirection is not just a game played on former Residential School students. Time and again we hear how the current, troubling conditions in Aboriginal communities are due to a kind of "ripple effect:" Aboriginal Peoples, mistreated in Residential Schools, returned home to pass on the mistreatment in their own time. Sometimes this is because their pathology provokes the former students to acts of violence or perversion that will themselves become self-perpetuating, and sometimes because the former students, in the grip of some school-induced shortcoming (say, "lack of parenting skills") simply can't contribute as they should to the health of the next generations of their community.

Before going any further, we have to object that this picture, though common, has no basis in fact. There is no comprehensive list of what makes a good parent, nor has anyone bothered to apply such a list to Aboriginal parents and demonstrated their deficiencies (we also submit that such a study would be logically incoherent). Further, while there are anecdotal accounts of, say, child abusers having been themselves abused, an empirical association cannot be deduced from such "evidence," any more than having been mugged by a Lithuanian leads to the conclusion that Lithuanians are muggers.[56] But let's pretend this all makes logical and empirical sense. The picture the "ripple-effect" theory presents to us is that the existence of alcoholism, wife-battering, child sexual abuse, suicide, and so on can be attributed to direct and indirect causes arising from the Indian Residential School past.

Such a picture diverts attention away from contemporary institutional structures that are operating under a continuing policy of genocide. It says, "The Residential Schools were bad, but they're gone now and we're trying to clean up the mess." As Ward Churchill [57] pointed out in his review of the movie "Dances with Wolves," these kinds of depictions are ideologically misleading: we are all allowed to get worked up about the prejudices and injustices in the unchangeable past (we can even be moved to tears); but any thought that it is the conditions of the *here and now* that demand attention, and that those conditions involve the witting and unwitting collusion of many contemporary people and groups, must never be allowed to surface.

Residential Schools may indeed have something of the "ripple effect" about them. After all, we're speaking about 1981 as the termination date of this active policy, not 1865 - 1890. But whatever they did, their "effect" is *maintained by the institutions of today* and the functionaries of those institutions, and those institutions add their own, contemporary baggage (e.g., individualism) to the burden placed upon the oppressed. Education, which implements and inculcates the ideology of the meritocracy, is one such institution; the church, which preaches personal sin/salvation and obedience to authority, is a second; and therapy, which recasts the operation of oppression as personal dysfunctions of oppression's victims, is a third. Unfortunately, this list is much, much longer...

PARVUM IN MULTO

As was the case with individualism, the argument against "mental therapeutics" doesn't have to proceed solely from a critique of its ideology. Here as well, evidence concerning it claims to success, its scientific status, its accuracy, and so on have been made elsewhere and should be part of any discussion of their pertinence to Aboriginal Peoples. It is important to bring up such issues, if for no other reason than that people doing therapy are seldom exposed to therapy's critics (like Simpson's Paradox is kept from budding statisticians). We will merely survey these critiques here, and provide references for those who wish to dig a little deeper.

The "godfather" of all talking cures is psychoanalysis. Today the vocabulary Freud invented continues to be used, even by those who consider themselves distant from psychoanalytic perspectives. The most enduring contribution he and his followers have made, however, has been in the institutionalization of sloppy thinking, reified metaphors, absence of evidence, and *ad hominem* attacks that were used to establish psychoanalysis in the first place. Psychoanalysis set a scientific hurdle for talking therapies that an ant could leap, and ants have indeed been leaping them ever since. While even in Freud's own day there was considerable awareness of the shortcomings of his enterprise (Hermann Ebbinghaus: "What's new in these theories isn't true, and what is true isn't new;" Karl Kraus: "Psychoanalysis is the disease of which it claims to be the cure.[58]"), a contemporary, penetrating critic of the pseudoscience is Thomas Szasz.[59] Along with his work, there now exists a large body of work, which evaluates Freud on his own terms—as a discoverer in the "science of mind"— and thoroughly refutes it.[60] Consequently, the wooly thinking of Freudianism maintains it position in humans services because of ignorance, laziness, and other non-complimentary characterizations, but not because it has any empirically verified content.[61] As ideologies in principle indistinguishable from, and perhaps even constitutive of, modern individualism (that is, on the basis of no evidence they posit latent causal forces, only detectable by specialists, that blame the victims of oppression) psychoanalysis and psychoanalytic derivatives (like Jungian approaches) merit no serious attention whatsoever.[62]

Freud's legacy to "mental science" has been Barnumish rather than Einsteinian. Today's proliferation of psychobabble has developed more from a sense of what therapists can get away with, rather than working out seriously what can be done and how. Thus, rather than improving whatever meagre science there is to the notion of a "talking cure," things have gotten progressively worse. Fortunately, Szasz has not been the only voice of reason in the psychobabble hurricane. Caplan[63] has written extensively on the ideological imperatives that determine how problems in living become medically pathologized, and how prejudices like sexism and racism pervade the decision making process in psychodiagnostic theory and practice. Dawes[64] has exposed the self-congratulatory mythology of much of the "helping sciences" and revealed many of the rhetorical tricks used to obscure the factual emptiness behind "expert clinical judgment" and the like. Cushman[65] does a creditable job of relating the growth of therapy to the development of the ideology of individualism and provides what we consider a correct (albeit insufficient) pointer to political economics as basic to the current popularity of psychobabble. And Dineen[66] provides a general review and expose of therapy's shortcomings and its lack of documentable successes, paying particularly careful attention to how therapists profit at the expense of their clientele. While there are many other works we could cite here as well,[67] at the very least these works should raise comprehensive questions concerning why something as fraudulent and dysfunctional as modern psychotherapy continues to operate in today's world. And, if the answers to these questions are evasive and unsupportable, how more questionable is the utility of therapy in the Aboriginal world, where even the pretense of the analysis of effectiveness, role, and intent of these procedures remains to begin to be addressed.

Several things are noteworthy here. First, how far these and similar critics will get in their movement to reform psychotherapeutics is still open to question, as is where, exactly, they hope to get. It simply isn't true that, because these individuals have overlapped in their identification of logical and empirical holes in psychotherapeutics, they fundamentally agree about what to do about it. Consequently, the conclusions the two of us draw from this body of work don't necessarily follow along lines suggested by these critics. In some instances, we believe they haven't taken the argument far enough back to reveal the unexamined assumptions inherent in modern therapeutic approaches. Without such an analysis, we think it likely that tomorrow's therapeutic state will not be fundamentally distinguishable from today's, much like Freudians who were critical of Freud ended up expounding approaches remarkably similar to what they thought they have been critiquing.

In other cases, we don't agree with where they seem to want things to go. For example, some of these critics might advocate massive reforms in their particular areas of expertise, with more stringent empirical criteria for diagnosis and therapy, more honesty in the limitations of all therapeutic approaches, and more accountability in treatment outcome. We consider, however, that such goals, laudable though they are, ignore the political economy of psychotherapeutics: why has this pseudoscience been permitted to run rampant? Our answer is that the internalization and personalization of moral, political, and economic problems is less costly than social justice; that it's cheaper, or at least more profitable to some, to pay one person to tell 1,000 people that they themselves are "the problem" than to do what is necessary to assure full, meaningful lives to those 1,000 people. In this shell-game, therapists are shills, not the owners of the game, and if therapists ever gain enough integrity to call the game a fraud, those who are running the game will simply replace them with another suitably anointed groups of shills.[68] The critique of psychotherapeutics must be a critique of modern society, and belief that a reform of those calling themselves therapists will resolve the problems identified is insufficient.

Still, we believe the most important thing to keep in mind is that serious, thoughtful individuals are unwilling to let slipshod science pass unchallenged and are working toward reform. It may be that in the near future there will be noticeable improvement in therapeutic theory and practice... but even if this happens, such reforms are unlikely to be priorities in Indian Country. After all, we tend to receive the hand-me-downs, cast-off, and afterthoughts everywhere else. Consequently, there can be no substitute for those Aboriginal individuals currently working in the "helping" services undertaking themselves (1) to appreciate the analyses of the present abysmal situation in "talk therapies" by thoroughly examining works such as the critiques cited here, and (2) moving beyond those critiques by bringing perspectives lacking in mainstream critics of mainstream thinking. It is important that there are people of conscience and integrity taking aim at one of the major social sciences frauds of our time, but we can't expect them, nor is it their responsibility, to do the job that rightly falls on all of us.

NOWHERE IN BETWEEN

However subtle or blatant its manifestations, from abiding quietly as an unquestioned background assumption in the way English predisposes us to speak to blaring like a clarion call in the "quest" for personal growth, the problem of individualism is the center of tension between what we have called the Standard Account and our interpretation of the Residential School. This tension, we believe, can't be resolved, such that sooner or later either we'll convince everyone that a higher, social level of interpretation is "correct" or that we ourselves will be convinced that an atomistic, individual level is right. The implied polarity between extreme positions (and any proposed "resolution" balanced somewhere between those poles) presumes that this personal vs. social dimension is the proper framework within which to interpret the differences between the two accounts. And it is that polarity that will be used rhetorically both to denounce our position while concealing that of those unwilling or unable to address directly the points we've tried to make. Let's take some possibilities.

In Chapter 6 of *The Circle Game* we noted Polsky's observation that a charge of callousness is often levelled against those who point out the ideological bias of conventional therapists. This charge is only possible given an underlying but manifestly absurd assumption that people can't do two things at once, work for one's clients and for social justice. Indeed, this charge can be turned around, in that predicating social change leading to social justice on creating "mental health" in the overwhelming mass of individuals is obviously a form of the Composition Fallacy (Chapter 6 of *The Circle Game*). We don't know if cultivating the attitude of accepting the status quo until everyone can say "gee, whiz, I really feel good about myself" qualifies as callousness, but we do not see its merit, whatever it is called.

The charge of callousness observed by Polsky is more centrally a personal, ad hominem attack, and in the present case our future critics may broaden this rhetoric by attaching it to the idea that we've been making such attacks ourselves. In response we would point out we've been attacking ideologies masquerading as logic and science, that our "callousness" has been displayed only against those things that are supposed to be used to it because that's part of the game: the cold, callous, calculations of science. Further, if people insist on equating their ideologies with themselves, and then claim that by attacking their ideologies we are attacking them, we reply (1) we are glad they finally admit the discussion is about ideologies, and not about scientific truths, (2) we're got absolutely nothing against other people's ideologies as long as they aren't imposed, by force or by guile, upon other people, and (3) since we don't subscribe to philosophical or methodological individualism, we're not inclined to constitute our critics as aggregates of their homuncular internal components, but rather prefer to accept them as human beings. That is, we won't let them slip individualism past us even in the guise of righteous indignation.

The presumed overwhelming "need" for therapy is a third aspect of Polsky's observation, so that, yes, conventional therapists recognize the political aspects of their role in the oppressive state, but that these clients honestly need this help. But what sort of "help" is being offered? Help that falsifies the origins and continuing basis of oppression? Help that equates "success" with "personal success?" Help that teaches the victim to "forgive, forgive?" Help that finds all manner of creative ways of avoiding issues of the intent, responsibility, and self-interest of perpetrators while concentrating them solely on the victims?[69] This kind of therapy is the therapy of Prozac, or of electroshock, or of being pummelled into unconsciousness; that when the "client" shuts ups and no longer bothers us, he is cured, or at least in remission. The distancing from the truth implicit in such approaches is comforting to the therapist (and to the therapist's real boss), not to the client. It is comforting not only because of the reduction of "troublesome" behavior on the part of the client, but, as in the case of missionary evangelism, because the success one has had in getting another person to accept one's version of reality is wrongly taken as proof of the truth of that version. However, when the truth of one's convictions is turned into an empirical matter, one is no longer trumpeting one's convictions but is whistling in the graveyard.

Some committed to "therapy and healing" might erect a defense around the notion that, however well-founded our objections, their own expertise is not in occupations aimed at remedying the political, economic, legal, or social bases of the present-day conditions of Aboriginal Peoples. We disagree with the notion of the irrelevance of therapists implicit in such a defense for two reasons: (1) the picture they're working to maintain is not simply irrelevant to Aboriginal Peoples, it is harmful and a continuation the agenda of those who built the Residential Schools, and (2) were therapists able to reconstitute their discipline along lines that reject individualism and its ideological entanglements, we have every reason to expect that something positive would result. We turn our attention to this possibility in the last section of this chapter.

We do not agree that individualism vs. whatever-is-supposed-to-be-on-the-other-pole is the "right, proper, or natural" dimension along which the debate must lie, nor do we place ourselves anywhere along the insinuated dimension. We're not to the right, not on the left, and nowhere in between. We are simply not committed to any debate where individualism is entertained as being even remotely true. Our own agenda has been to point out exactly what a commitment to an individualist belief system commits one to when considering the Residential School and other issues that touch Aboriginal Peoples. The polarization which arises from not just giving individualism a foothold, but according it pride of place, structures any discussion along grounds that lead nowhere, permits no insight, and resolves nothing, such as litigation versus therapy (who says both can't be pursued?) and hardheaded versus softhearted (does one have to be one or the other?). And in any discussion of an ongoing genocide, getting nowhere is in reality losing ground.

Finally, our rejection of individualism is not a denial of individual people, individual injuries, individual struggles, or individual anything. Bhargava[70] writes:

> ... for the individualist, basic capacities that transform an individual biological organism into a human being can be realized without specific kinds of interactions with others. On the other hand, for the non-individualist, the biological individual is radically incomplete as a human being and necessarily requires specific kinds of social relations for the formation and sustenance of the capacities. Essentially, an individualist is committed to the view that key human properties can at least in principle be exhaustively realized either innately or by the activity of the individual agent without relation to or interaction with others. A non-individualist denies that this is even possible, that the idea is incoherent even as make-believe... Though often disguised by ambiguities and unclarities of formulation, I think the difference between these two perspectives is radical (P. 11-12).

So radical that we feel it goes to the heart of what is generally thought of as the difference between Western European Civilization and everybody else. The "West" is individualistic and populations throughout the rest of the world aren't, but not necessarily in the same way. But this formulation is overly simplistic, since it equates individualism with the West. In fact, it is a feature of Western capitalism, which explains through the operation of the overwhelming machine of propaganda that greed is good, that a society is nothing but of bunch of people in more or less the same place, that it's people's own fault if they're unable or unwilling to do what it takes to prosper, and so on. In preparing ourselves for the all the work presented in this book, we reviewed society after society, nation after nation, tribe after tribe, around the world, which showed no point of agreement with any particularization of individualism. All groups valued sharing and devalued meanness, believed that society required much more than proximity, were happy to depend upon one another rather than fearful of it, and believed they had responsibilities to persons, places, and things not immediately before them. The triumph of the so-called West has been the destruction of what is generous and good about people; it was a war they first waged upon themselves and then extended to the rest of the world, at a faster and faster pace, as resistence was coopted into an unthinking acceptance of "there is no alternative."

Our stand against the ideology of individualism isn't any tempest in a teapot; it is part of a larger, longstanding fight for survival of all peoples of the world who value community, harmony with the earth, and a meaningful existence for everyone. We believe that a clear grasp of the entanglements of individualism gives Aboriginal Peoples tools never before made available in our struggle to survive: a precise understanding of the nature of our assailant and his weapons, and a way of distinguishing real friends from false ones and enemies.

A true story: in the mid-1980s the World Bank participated in the funding of a huge dam project in India. The land to be flooded in damming the Narmada River belonged to Adivasis groups (Aboriginal Peoples of India), more than 300,000 of whom would be displaced from their traditional lands against their will, without their consent, and with no thought for their rights. In response to criticism over their role in this outrage, the World Bank commissioned an internal study that undertook to assess the impact of the project. The major finding of the study was that the primary effect of the project would be that human beings, who were being dismissed, ignored, suppressed, who were having their rights trampled upon, and who would be moved, by force if necessary, to whatever lands the Indian government eventually considered good enough for them, would suffer from "multi-dimensional stress," "anxiety for the future," "feelings of impotence," and similar psychological symptoms. The report recommended the deployment of a mass of "healers," "counsellors," and "social workers" to help these diseased individuals over the periods of transition to their new homes.

Is the gibberish here really that difficult to see? Would the report need to have called the collection of symptoms "Flooded Land Syndrome" for the parallels with our experience to emerge into view? Do we really think this is a story just about India?

An Alternative

> What conclusions can we draw from these and the other usual definitions of psychotherapy? We can conclude that they are purely verbal exercises, having incantatory, ritualistic, and strategic functions rather than identifying, as they ostensibly do, discrete forms of medical treatments. In trying to understand psychotherapy (or psychopathology), we are confronted with masses of confusions and problems that result from the stubborn and strategic misuse of words, or, as Wittgenstein put it: "Your concept is wrong. However, I cannot illumine the matter by fighting against your words, but only by trying to turn your attention away from certain expressions, illustrations, images, and towards the employment of the words." Let us heed Wittgenstein's advice and focus on the actual use of the vocabulary of psychotherapy.
> Thomas Szasz

We cannot come up with a way of avoiding any longer responding to the question, "What would you do about the aftermath of Indian Residential Schooling?" Fortunately, we are without the means to effect what we'd really do, and so must limit our vision to the possibilities of our time and our place. It can't help but be apparent that we are uncomfortable with and antagonistic to operating within the confines conventionally accorded to "therapy and healing." The only way we can even begin to approach our final task here is by allowing ourselves the latitude to approach the topic in our own elliptical fashion.

"Therapy" for Residential Schooling

First and foremost, we will not address the therapeutic requirements of those most in need of intervention, the governments, churches, professional human services workers, and general population of Canada. Their bizarre combination of complicity, duplicity, ignorance, prejudice, preconception, and arrogance, before, during and after the Residential School Era, defies description, much less remedy. Nor is this the area into which we would allocate the time, resources, and efforts of people with an honest commitment to undoing the crime, even though the damage they have done and continue to do to themselves is no less troubling than the damage they've done and continue to do to Aboriginal Peoples: any ethical code must acknowledge a right of even the sickest patient to refuse treatment, and we're talking of a clientele that not only refused to acknowledge its symptoms but insists that it never felt better. Consequently, we confine our remarks to victims of the governments, churches, professional human services workers, and general population of Canada, even if we must insist that our intervention doesn't arise from any assumption of sickness on their part.

In our opinion, taking the warning "first, do no harm" seriously means adopting an entirely different way of thinking about the issues of therapy. First, it requires implementation of forms of investigation that are not limited to the individualistic and mechanistic biases of modern western science. Second, it requires a frame of reference that allows seamless movement between focussing on individual and social levels of interaction, uniting the results of particular investigations within a comprehensive whole. Third, it requires a different agenda of what "therapists" are and what collaboration between peoples (whether they call themselves therapists, clients, patients, elders, victims, or what-have-you) is supposed to be doing.

NEW GLASSES

The confusion of human and social concerns with scientific activity is intertwined with all the other confusions we have been writing about here. For example, we attributed the descent into individualism as due, in part, to our metaphoric extension of language about people to situations where we wished to discuss, say, institutions (higher level aggregates than individual people) or molecules (lower level aggregates) and our failure to recognize the metaphorical nature of such extensions. One of the strongest predispositions to adopt a scientific frame of reference when talking about human and social concerns is a similar failure to recognize the metaphoric nature of talking about people as if they were mechanisms or as if equations accurately represented behavior. In and of themselves, as Hacker (see Footnote 52) has observed, metaphors aren't necessarily misleading, have their proper place, and may even be helpful; the difficulties arise when they're treated as if they're literally true.

However, unlike the case of using individual language to talk about institutions, this overextension of a scientific metaphor into human, social inquiries doesn't have the same inevitably; ways of proceeding with inquiries into human and social areas have long been worked out in the writings of Ludwig Wittgenstein and some who have continued his work.[71] Baker and Hacker[72] term this approach conceptual clarification and provide an introduction to the philosophical rationale behind it along with a "toolbox" for putting the approach into action. Here we will provide only a brief, broad survey of clarification; we also include as Appendix G a paper, *Intelligence Research and the Legacy of Confusion* (Michael Maraun and Roland Chrisjohn) as a deeper discussion of conceptual clarification issues and as an example of the approach in action.

Our point is this: if we do not adopt a way of thinking/talking about the world in which we (and everyone else) is embedded which is different from the way of the dominating groups, we will be led by subtle steps back to the dominant way. We've already argued that philosophical and methodological individualism constitute the "way" of Western capitalist society; we believe, and will argue elsewhere, that Wittgenstein's critique of that system not only overthrows it, it provides a general understanding of the way non-Western, non-Capitalist systems are. Wittgenstein's philosophy constitutes the life preserver that so-called therapeutic approaches do not, and if we are to build a system that doesn't recreate our oppression, we feel this is the best place to start. Again, rather than attempt a comprehensive review here, we merely state some of conclusions that have particular relevance for overthrowing the dominant mind-set.

CONCEPTUAL CLARIFICATION

For Western science (even social ones), the meaning of a word or concept is the connection between a word and the object to which it corresponds in the objective, external world. Because of this, the meaning of a word or concept can be clarified by gathering and organizing data about the word or concept. Wittgenstein refutes this notion, since one cannot know that one is gathering data about a word or concept unless one already knows what to look for (please find us some data about manuscram, for example). Wittgenstein argues convincingly that conceptual knowledge needs to be clarified before anything empirical can be done at all.

The problem can be traced back to the false notion of meaning. Rather than accept some notion of correspondence, Wittgenstein shows that meaning is, for the most part, use. That is, what a word or concepts means is the totality of uses to which it is put in a particular language. The development of a survey/overview of the many ways a word is used constitutes conceptual clarification (and suggestions for this activity, not methods, are provided by Baker and Hacker, Footnote 72), and this is not an empirical activity but a descriptive one.

The call for "research" into the "minds" of the victims of Residential School is a Western scientific activity, locating the "meaning" of the episode in the connections of the (deranged) minds of the victims. We have consistently rejected this notion (*The Circle Game* is conspicuously free of tables, statistics, data, and so on) and have tried to provide a description of what the schools were for, where they came from, what they did, why they did it, and so on. In working with people who attended Residential School, then, the problem is not to somehow "get inside their heads," but rather to jointly produce descriptions of what went on and why, with the aim of achieving the broadening of perspective we've argued for here.

PHYSICAL AGNOSTICISM

Western scientists (particularly social ones) labor mightily to "concretize" the words they use by insinuating a connection between word and physiology. Thus, alcoholism is a disease, depression is a brain chemistry imbalance, and so on. Not only does this reification (treatment of a concept as if it were a thing) provide a veneer of respectability, it pulls us back into the methodological individualism we've complained endlessly about here; it holds that depression really is a chemical imbalance, that school failure really is bad wiring, and that the outcome of Residential Schooling really is Residential School Syndrome.

Wittgenstein completely rejects any such move, not because there's no physical basis for existence but because that's not what we're talking about when we talk. One simple example is his "Beetle in the Box" parable. Assume that on a planet somewhere everyone carries around a small box into which nobody else is allow to look, but inside of which everyone says a "beetle" resides. Everybody thus contends that it is only by acquaintance with his or her own beetle that they know what a beetle really is. Suppose that the word "beetle" has a use in the language of the people of this planet ("Don't stomp my beetle" means don't reject my idea without hearing it; "My beetle is spinning" means I'm confused; "His beetle is a mile wide" means a person is generous; and so on). Under these conditions it would be quite possible for everyone to have something different in his/her box, or that the boxes all be empty, and the world would still work in exactly the same way. Wittgenstein suggests that we are the residents of that planet, and that the "beetle in the box" is the reification of mentalistic concepts (e.g., mind) that we habitually engage in. Our use of such language, then, is not a report of the contents of our individual boxes; it's just the way we talk about things.

ANTI-MECHANISM

If you open almost any text in a social science today you will soon encounter a diagram, purporting to represent some inner, hidden human process, with a level of detail that would make a computer nerd choke. The diagram will further purport to be based on "data," and will be said to be a working model of a human process (whether it's parliament, the genetics of alcoholism, or how we walk across a street without getting run over). And, often, it will be described as a "causal" model of such "processes."

Again, Wittgenstein's approach renders such claims specious. If, indeed, we are talking about mechanism (and computers are mechanisms), such diagrams have a point. However, if it is merely an elaborate form of metaphor (people are like computers), one is stretching a metaphor too far. A love may be like a "red, red rose," but if you try to take pruning shears to him/her you're likely to encounter resistence a rose can't generate.

This all goes back to a remark we made back in *The Circle Game*: simply because the Mona Lisa can be represented by a digitized paint-by-numbers canvas doesn't mean that's how da Vinci actually created the work. Therapeutic training predisposes the therapist to believe that they've learned a "technique," that their client is going through some "process," and otherwise turn what should be the most human of activities into a for of assembly line. Don't.

CAUSALITY

Causality lurks in the entire positivistic, data-gathering, physicalist, mechanism-production pictures produced by Western-oriented social scientists. The problem of believing physical causality works the same way for human, social systems is a topic for its own chapter; we merely point out here that none of the other attempts to constitute social science as a version of physical science have made much sense. "Causality" is a perfectly good word, having perfectly good uses in everyday language. However, it is not a description, detection, or elaboration of a mechanism, a process, or a physical basis. Even though physical causality can be useful in describing some aspects of human interaction ("Joe's death was caused by his interacting with concrete after his parachute failed to open"), humans are not dominoes; the same "push" does not cause us to topple in the same ways. There are other, non-physicalistic ways of describing (and, eventually, understanding) human behavior and social interaction that don't conform to anything like the causality of physics.

CONCLUSIONS

We have limited time, limited space, and limited abilities, and thus we can only scratch the surface of what Wittgensteinian thinking can do to overcome the limitations imposed by adopting, by design or by default, the mind set of dominant society. Once we were asked what would improve conferences on Indian social/psychological issues, and we answered, more than a little seriously, that when they began with the execution of all social scientists present, progress would be made. We really don't think that extremely on the subject, but the preconceptions carried even by thoughtful, committed individuals predispose us all to being useless. There is no reason an Aboriginal approach to the problems of Residential Schooling must repeat all the errors of dominant thinking.

A Framework for Understanding

We're probably as tired of repeating our warnings about individuality, personalizing, and internalizing as our readers are of hearing it; yet, we return to this point again and again because people in our audience drag us back there, albeit unwittingly. A teacher once complained to us that he wasn't at fault in the educational mistreatment of Indian children; he merely made his referrals to psychologists, and they mistested, mislabled, mistreated, and stigmatized the child. We responded: I didn't kill the Jews; I merely helped keep lists of where they lived in my city." "I didn't kill the Jews; I just helped transport designated individuals to the train station." "I didn't kill the Jews; I only drove a train back and forth between Warsaw and Auschwitz." "I didn't kill the Jews; my job was to drop pellets down a tube." Our point, again, was that the system in which the teacher thought himself so blameless wouldn't operate (as the Holocaust wouldn't have operated) without him and people like him doing their jobs, regardless of their personal opinions. The "system" of manufacturing opinion that has grown up about Residential Schooling similarly wouldn't operate without the participation of psychologists, historians, educators, social workers, bureaucrats, clerics, and many other persons from many different walks of life, regardless of their personal opinions. When a clergyman told us, intently, after hearing one of our presentations, that his church and his fellow clerics had done what they did with the best of intentions, our reply was that we didn't doubt that, but that then it must be admitted that human beings can do the most horrible things to one another with the "best of intentions."

These emotional appeals aren't made because of an inability on anyone's part to understand the principle that the whole is something other than a function of its parts. Rather, we think they're made because the people arguing with us really grasp intellectually their part in a whole they emotionally want nothing to do with. And further, what seems to be an implication of our critique is bleak: if our actions don't correspond with our intentions, what can we do? How do we improve things? If institutions are outside our control, what can we do but submit? Bleak thoughts, indeed.

And yet we've found many people who have understood the problem and provided working solutions. We consider Wittgenstein such an individual, although many people could hope for a more readily graspable exposition than he provided. Thomas Szasz's work in general and his latest work in particular (*The Meaning of Mind; Language, Morality, and Neuroscience*. London: Praeger, 1996) is a successful and useful exposition of making the social person and the individual person into one. And Zygmunt Bauman's works, which we have often cited in this book, builds a general understanding of the interplay of humanity and society from his examination of the Holocaust. This body of literature could and should be examined from the perspective of distinguishing fact from myth, personal from social, and many other conundrums that arise from a human "sciences" perspective.

We came upon an older resolution, however, in a rather roundabout way. At one time we were engaged in documenting how social, economic, or political concepts became to be understood psychologically. For one example, in our book on "empowerment" we showed how what was obviously a political/social term was stripped of its real significance and fed back to everyone as psychological gruel. "To empower" has two senses: (1) to bestow a right, responsibility, or privilege within a network of shared social relations (e.g., as a judge, police officer, or hockey referee is "empowered" to do their jobs), and (2) to teach someone how to do something they didn't know how to do previously. And yet, the psychological literature has virtually exploded with speculation, studies, causal models, etc., of the "felt experience" that supposedly were the "underlying psychological bases" of (1) or (2). Little of what was passing as "empowerment" met anything like the real sense of the word, and when it did there were the already-serviceable terms "education" or "teaching" to express what was going on. The "psychologization" of empowerment was so complete that, on one occasion, we listened in disbelief as a conference speaker transformed Paolo Freire from an in-your-face activist to a victim-blaming touchy-feely kind-of-a-guy. We found similar travesties performed on "oppression," where it was no longer presented as the institutionalized mistreatment of marginalized populations (like the Jim Crow Laws for Blacks, the Nuremberg Laws for Jews, and the Residential School for Indians) but as the emotional experience of being mistreated. In our studies we encountered another such term, often used to describe the emotional baggage of former Residential School students but having a very different origin indeed: alienation.

Alienation as it is generally understood today means a feeling (see how it's made internal?) of detachment or not belonging, an anxiety experienced concerning one's place in the surrounding society. The "literature" on Residential School Syndrome (and the other diseases we're all supposed to be suffering from) mentions alienation prominently in their symptom lists. But where, in our opinion, the concept of alienation gets its most comprehensive airing, the notion of any "felt experience" as an accompaniment to alienation is summarily rejected. Instead, alienation is taken as an objective circumstance, that people don't own what they produce at their jobs. From that objective circumstance, other circumstances arise that may or may not lead to an emotional perception of alienation. However, whether it does or not is irrelevant: even those people who don't experience alienation "emotionally" are still alienated, just as an oppressed person doesn't have to have a boot on his/her neck at any particular moment to be oppressed, or just as an empowered person can feel anxiety, elation, or really, anything else once authority has been transferred.

Why hasn't this analysis been more widely circulated? Because the author of this analysis was Karl Marx. In a curious twist of the 20th century, Marx's early analysis of alienation was rejected by as a "youthful indiscretion" by those professing Marxism and covered up entirely by a West that was taught to believe that you would turn into a cannibal if you read anything with Marx's name on it. It was left largely to a very non-Marxism Freudian analyst, Erich Fromm, to introduce this line of thought (Eric Fromm, *Marx's Concept of Man*. New York: Ungar Publishing, 1961). Since then there have been a number of well-considered examinations of the theory (Bertell Ollman, *Alienation: Marx's Conception of Man in Capitalist Society*. 2nd Edition. Cambridge: Cambridge University Press, 1976; Istvan Meszaros, *Marx's Theory of Alienation*. 4th Edition. London: Merlin Press, 1975; and Adam Schaff, *Alienation as a Social Phenomenon*. New York: Pergamon Press, 1980), as well as wholesale attempts to turn Marx's conception into an internal state (Richard Schacht, *The Future of Alienation*. Chicago: University of Illinois Press, 1994).

We'll summarize the theory briefly: under capitalism, laborers don't own the products they produce. This objective description is simply a description of a feature of capitalism, a system of producing that originally developed (organically) as an improvement over feudalism. Because laborers don't own the products they produce, according to Marx certain other things happen: (1) people are alienated from their labor itself, that is, they see work as not being who they are, and conduct their "real" lives outside of work. This is the "cuttin' outta here" attitude often reflected in Canadian beer commercials; (2) people are alienated from their fellow human beings, because they are in competition with them and because splitting off "work" from "who we are" (see (1) above) means we don't see how intimately we relate to one another. Money becomes a substitute for the human relations we once enjoyed with one another; (3) people are alienated from themselves, because not doing the work we would really enjoy doing makes us hypocrites; and (4) people are alienated from nature, since it is our nature to work, and because we're producing "only products" in our work (we exploit as we are exploited). In total, these conditions don't dictate a particular response on the part of human beings. What is dictated is a rootlessness, a lack of connection to society that can manifest itself in an infinite number of specific ways: drinking one's self into insensibility; acquiring the world's largest collection of bottle caps; watching television endlessly; drifting from one unsatisfying relationship to another.

There is of course much more to it than this, and the analysis must be significantly adapted to apply at all to Aboriginal Peoples; after all, we are forced either to reject our own ways and embrace the Newhouse Path if we are to be allowed any portion of Canada's "enviable standard of living," even as we own legal and moral title to the means of having created that standard. A more complete examination of this approach is in preparation as a separate title, but what is important to note here is the ease with which Marx was able to bridge what is well-neigh unbridgeable within the terms of modern social/human science. The notion of "mechanism" is gone, since no prediction is made concerning what particular response must be made to the "objective" circumstance of alienation; within this framework, we are not driven about like billiard balls (that is, physical causality doesn't dominate) but rather a general context is established under which our behavior becomes intelligible to one another; and hidden dynamic process are not posited as sitting somewhere tugging on our strings, but rather his analysis is rooted in the obvious, if arguable.

Although we personally believe Wittgenstein's work provides the most substantial and generalizable option to the individualist form of thinking we've been criticizing, there is a vein to be mined in Marx's work as well. For any of you still suffering from Cold War problems, perhaps it would be comforting to know that not only do many socialists today draw a line between Early and Late Marx (we don't), many self-proclaimed Marxists are proudly methodological individualists (the so-called Analytic Marxists). Well, if they can't use him, we can.

SOUND AND FURY

It has probably occurred to our readers that, in addressing issues of "therapeutics" so far we haven't said anything about the generally agreed-upon patients. This isn't because we don't believe that they were brutalized beyond imagination, but because we believe they are still being brutalized. Now it is the supposed helping professions doing it, and they're doing it "wiles they smile." It is in an effort to end this further mistreatment we have taken the tack we have. But now we take a step in a direction of common change for those who call themselves therapist and those who are called clients. We repeat, once we have begun to grasp the ideological entanglements of what passes as "therapy" and "healing," we need not continue along that path.

THERAPIST "QUALIFICATIONS"

"Certification" and "credentialling" are primarily political processes, used to marginalize those who ask too many embarrassing questions and identify those who have "bought in" and so are acceptable to the mainstream. The cry of "standards" is bogus, since the ideological nature of therapeutic "science" is rarely acknowledged even if recognized as such. Collectively, we can set our own standards. In our opinion these should include:

(1) a grasp of the ideology of individualism in its various manifestations;

(2) a critical non-mainstream knowledge of Aboriginal/ Eurocanadian relations;

(3) a critical knowledge of the world history of oppression;

(4) a grasp of current events (Aboriginal and otherwise) from a non-individualist perspective;

(5) knowledge of and facility with rhetoric and its exposure;

(6) thorough grounding in conceptual clarification.

We don't think much of the "technical" knowledge in human services.

Any examination of them would take Thomas Szasz, John Shotter, Ruth Hubbard, Louise Armstrong, David Smail, Richard Lewontin, and similarly critical individuals as their guides through existing literatures. Furthermore, "real" therapists would be engaged constantly in the task of re-writing social and human disciplines from a non-individualist, non-positivist point of view.

THE AIMS AND ACTIONS OF THERAPY

We have placed our emphasis upon understanding and countering the ideology of individualism in therapist training because we expect that most of the therapist's time will be spent undoing what is, after all, a very successful public relations program (1) to blame the victim, and (2) to get the victim to blame him/herself. We have no illusion about how difficult this "undoing" will be; in effect, the client will be moving through a course of work not significantly different from what the "therapist" will have gone through. However, to leave it at that would be the final triumph of the ideology of individualism, because once again the success will have been at the personal, individual level. Further, we know from the lack of direct correspondence between the individual and the social that helping all the individual victims of the Residential School Era will not thereby reconstitute our Aboriginal Communities. To "undo" the devastation of Residential Schooling is the moral, legal, economic, and human responsibility of those who perpetrated it. They are not going to undo anything. Rather, they will back up, change the jargon, and have another run at our Nations. If anything authentic is to be done about the aftermath of the Residential School, it falls upon those that understand its enormity, and arises not by justice, not from desire, not by design, but by tragic necessity.

Therefore, Aboriginal community activism in various forms must be part not only of training of "therapists" but of "treatment" of "patients." Maybe "activist" should be substituted for both "therapist" and "patient." What kind of activism are we talking about? Not just the marching and protesting of the recent past, although we can see nothing wrong with this. We mean a broader range of activities, undertaken with the explicit knowledge of how rebuilding our communities, our families, our lives will be in direct opposition to what the Residential Schools were meant to achieve. Think for a moment: therapeutics considered on the most generous of terms, in its most benign form, constitutes an attack on our forms of life. Today we pay someone (or the government pays someone in our name) to do those things, like listen to us, commiserate with us, advise us, encourage us, and so on, that less than a century ago we all depended upon from our family, our friend, our neighbors, and our entire communities. We must resist this, and in any way we can resist.

What are some specific suggestions? Well, personal narratives (as discussed in Appendix B) would be sound revolutionary activity. In *The Circle Game* we raised any number of historical and contemporary issues individual people could work toward every day. Once someone begins to overthrow the ideology of individualism their own struggles could be valuable to people who still cannot work their ways clear. Many of our communities have their own, local struggles that not only need what time and effort people can contribute, but that can use help in connecting the local struggle to progressively larger and larger struggles (ecology, historical research, community involvement, and many other possibilities spring to mind). In all this there must be the understanding that each of us is doing what she or he can, and that we thank one another for whatever has been done in the spirit of making all of us whole again.

Will this "cure" the sickness of Residential School? Will this effort sustain our forms of life (which remain, for all that the West has done to them)? We can't say, but we can say what will happen if good people do nothing. So we know we must hope:

> Hope cannot be said to exist; nor can it be said not to exist. It is just like roads on the earth—for in fact the earth has no roads to begin with. But when many people move in a particular direction, a road is made. Lu Xhun.

ENDNOTES

1. Development of this chapter has substantially been helped by our discussions with Wayne Sowan, Audrey Franklin, Austin Tootoosis, Pamela Brett, Alison Macmillan, John Cristescu, Monica Chiefmoon, Cheryl Walker, Randy Kapashesit, and various anonymous audience members at talks we have presented over the past three years. We appreciate their efforts to talk us out of our major follies, and any errors remaining are entirely their fault. We would like to extend a special thanks to Barbara Barnswell, not only for giving us opportunities to clarify our thinking on many of the issues over the years, but for consistently supplying us with important information on some of the issues addressed here.

2. Istvan Meszaros, *Beyond Capital: Toward a Theory of Transition*. London: Merlin Press, 1995, p. 981-982: "Material incentives in our society as presented to us always divide people against one another. You can see this everywhere, in every profession, teaching, university, every walk of life: the incentives work on the presumption that we can divide people against one another in order to control them better; that's the whole process."

3. A good example of this is the Royal Commission Report released in November, 1996. See R. Chrisjohn, One Step Forward, Four Steps Back: Remarks on the Royal Commission Report, Treaty 7, Calgary, 1997.

4. We consider the "human sciences" to include psychiatry, psychology, social work, economics, education, political science, history, law, and disciplines concerned with the way people interact with their universe (*nomos*), as compared to disciplines concerned with the way a peopleless universe operates (*physis*).

5. Edward Herman and Noam Chomsky, *Manufacturing Consent: The Political Economy of the Mass Media*. New York: Pantheon, 1988.

6. ... as did the spokesperson for the Anglican Church on CBC's "Cross Country Checkup" the Sunday after the RCAP report was released. See Chapter 2 of *The Circle Game* for our response to this particularly stupid argument.

7. Here we must bring up again our doubts concerning the sincerity of the "apologies" offered by some of the churches. If they really thought what they did to Aboriginal Peoples was wrong, they would have stopped these activities. But missionary work continues unabated in other parts of the world (just check the back issues of any internal church newspaper), carried out under the same "justification" supposedly apologized for here in North America. The overthrow of Indigenous belief systems is only wrong, apparently, in those parts of the world where Indigenous peoples can actually defend themselves. See Kenelm Burridge's *In the Way: A Study of Christian Missionary Endeavours*. Vancouver: UBC Press, 1991,

for an exemplary exercise in self-deception.

8. William Ryan, *Blaming the Victim.* New York, Vintage Books, 1971.

9. So perfectly, in fact, that today's rhetoricians labor mightily to convince the general public that everybody is a victim. For example, the policeman who shot Dudley George came from a group with high divorce rates, high suicide rates, elevated degrees of burnout, and so on, so that, really, it comes down to one victim shooting another. Ask yourself, however, which end of the gun you'd prefer, especially when the "victim" doing the trigger-pulling gets to keep on living.

10. The image is taken from James O'Connor, cite in Alexander Cockburn, *The Golden Age is In Us.* London: Verso, 1996.

11. Roland Chrisjohn and Strater Crowfoot, *The Hidden Ideologies of Education and Their Impact on First Nations.* Paper presented at the Conference of the International Council of Psychologists, Banff, Alberta, July 27, 1996.

12. We also assert that this approach is not necessarily consciously adopted. See Chapter 6 of *The Circle Game.*

13. Some of the work in this section was presented previously in R. Chrisjohn, *Suicide and Aboriginal Peoples: Professional Sins*, Canadian Association of Suicide Prevention, Toronto, 1996.

14. *Suicide in Canada: A Report of the National Task Force on Suicide in Canada.* Sponsored by the Mental Health Division, Health Services and Promotion Branch, Health and Welfare Canada, 1985.

15. The Native Psychologists in Canada, June, 1995.

16. Royal Commission on Aboriginal Peoples, 1995.

17. Nishnawbe-Aski Nation Youth Forum on Suicide, Final Report, 1996.

18. Raul Hilberg, *Perpetrators, Victims, Bystanders: The Jewish Catastrophe, 1944-1945.* New York: HarperColling, 1992.

19. See Kenneth Bagnell's *The Little Immigrants.* Toronto: Macmillan, 1980; Howard Zinn's *A People's History of the United States, 1492-Present.* Revised and Updated Edition, New York: HarperPerrennial, 1995; and Jane Dibblin's *Day of Two Suns: US Nuclear Testing and the Pacific Islanders.* London: Virago Press, 1988.

20. And this continues. The recent RCAP report calls for training 10,000 new human services workers and inflicting them on Aboriginal Peoples over the next decade or so. Just when the neo-conservatives who rule Canada are about to shut off funding for social programs, the Indigenous people are dragged in to their rescue!

21. Earlier Canadian governments tried, unsuccessfully, to prevent the spread of dependency disorder. For a history of their efforts, see Pierre Berton's *The Great Depression: 1929-1939*. Toronto McClelland & Stewart, 1990.

22. Note Collins' shameless imputation of this neo-conservative ideology to unnamed "Native leaders" with no opportunity to respond to his assertion. Note also how Collins and Cassidy take for granted that dependency exists and is a problem, and that RCAP's ability or inability to do something about this is a basis for evaluating the report. Note finally the implicit equation, dependency = spending money.

23. They really do talk like this. The dependency = spending money equation is once again prominent, as well as the redneck flash-point lie that Aboriginal Peoples don't pay taxes.

24. Again, we have written extensively on the thoroughgoing dishonesty of this term in Sherri Young and Roland Chrisjohn, *Here Be Dragons: The Myths of Psychological Empowerment*. Unpublished book manuscript (available to people with a serious interest in the topic), 1993.

25. Again, dependency seems to be a synonym for money. Does the Anglican Church want "Native communities" to stop depending on them for sermons, weddings, or other church sacraments? Do they want them to quit holding community meetings in their basements? Just what are they interested in eliminating?

26. Thanks to Steve Radulovic for providing this information. This excerpt also confirms the presence of the dependency plague in East Coast populations. Our attempts to get a response from the New Democratic Party on how typical this is of their political ideology have been met with silence.

27. Ireland remained a net exporter of foodstuffs during the potato famine.

28. Michael Parenti calculates in *Against Empire*. San Francisco: City Lights Books, 1995, that if the Stinking Rich had been taxed during the 1980s and 90s at the rate they were taxed in 1979, the United States would have no budgetary deficit.

29. Mark Zepezauer and Arthur Naiman, *Take the Rich off Welfare*. Tuscon:

Odonian Press, 1996.

30. Linda McQuaig, *Behind Closed Doors: How the Rich Won Control of Canada's Tax System... And Ended Up Richer.* Markham, Ontario: Viking, 1987.

31. Eric Shragge (Ed.), Workfare: Ideology for a New Under-Class. Toronto: Garamond Press, 1997.

32. Noam Chomsky, *Class War: The Attack on Working People.* San Francisco: AK Press, 1995; *Free Market Fantasies: Capitalism in the Real World.* San Francisco: AK Press, 1996.

33. Federal treatment of Metis, on the other hand, is interpretable as an early and large-scale example of joint corporate and governmental raiding of worker's pensions plans, and the treatment of Innu and non-Status Indians is akin to pure thievery.

34. Among the best of this work we consider Herbert Fingarette's *Heavy Drinking: The Myth of Alcoholism as a Disease.* Los Angeles: University of California Press, 1988; Stanton Peele's *Diseasing of America: How We Allow Recovery Zealots and the Treatment Industry to Convince Us We Are Out of Control.* New York: Lexington Books, 1989; Thomas Szasz, *Ceremonial Chemistry: The Ritual Persecution of Drugs, Addicts, and Pushers.* Holmes Beach, Florida: Learning Publications Inc, 1985.

35. For example, Brian Maracle, *Crazywater: Native Voices on Addiction and Recovery.* Toronto: Penguin, 1993. The recently released RCAP report also takes for granted the disease model of alcohol in Aboriginal populations.

36. A. D. Fisher, "Alcoholism and Race: The Misapplication of Both Concepts to North American Indians," *Canadian Review of Sociology and Anthropology,* Vol. 24, 1987, p. 81-97. We consider this an excellent article, which, however, could make some of its central arguments even more strongly.

37. Videotapes of conference presentations are available from Kennedy Recordings, 219-6650 117 St., Edmonton, Alberta, T5T 4J5. We understand that Wayne Sowan is preparing a selection of papers, with commentary.

38. Fisher's article covers this, but it is one of those topics we think deserved greater scrutiny. None of the articles that, over the years, have concluded that there is a genetic basis for alcohol abuse in Aboriginal Peoples would withstand examination on statistical, experimental, or measurement grounds. That indigenous peoples don't usually have the math to reject these specious studies is not unusual, if you keep in mind that the sophistication also wasn't resident in the "scientists" that

published them.

39. See Volume 3 of the RCAP report, p 159-163.

40. The argument then becomes something like a debate between rationalists and empiricist, agreeing on the content of deficiencies of the individual but disagreeing on whether they were there to begin with or were picked up through experience. See Harry Bracken's "Philosophy and Racism," *Philosophia*, Volume 8, 1978, p. 241-260.

41. Peter Mancall, in *Deadly Medicine: Indians and Alcohol in Early America*. Ithaca: Cornell University Press, 1995, argues that use of alcohol in colonial Britain is unlike British deployment of opium in China, since alcohol intrusion and use wasn't an open, legislated policy of successive governments as was the opium assault on the Chinese population. Of course, there were massive differences between the political economy of imperialism in North America and Asia, and practices in both areas changed over time. But we should not lose sight of British and Canadian willingness to wield alcohol as a weapon when they felt the need, as in the treaty signing process (see John Maclean's *Canadian Savage Folk: The Native Tribes of Canada*. Toronto: Briggs, 1896). In any event, the parallels we are drawing here are not between the use of psychoactive substances to influence the international balance of trade, but between how the human sciences of the present day are committed to approaching the problem of understanding the role of such substances in the oppressed.

42. The whining and complaining in this section are covered more thoroughly in Roland Chrisjohn, *Post-Secondary Review*. Calgary, Treaty 7 Tribal Council, 1995; and Roland Chrisjohn and Sherri Young, Loving *All the Children of Our Nations: First Nations and Special Education*. Calgary, Treaty 7 Tribal Council, 1995. The first two chapters of each of these reports are available from the Treaty 7 web site (http://www.treaty7.org) www.treaty7.org), with more to follow.

43. National Indian Brotherhood, 1972. *Wahbung: Our Tomorrows*, Indian Tribes of Manitoba, October, 1971, and Citizens Plus, Chiefs of Alberta, 1970, also deserve recognition as innovative position papers from this time period.

44. Maude Barlow and Heather-Jane Robertson, *Class Warfare: The Assault on Canada's Schools*. Toronto: Key Porter Books, 1994.

45. Maude Barlow, *"Class Warfare," Our Schools Our Selves*. Vol. 5, No. 3, July, 1994, p. 80.

46. "We will be absorbed one way or another. What we can do is mediate the worst effects of capitalism [like the unbridled theft of our lands and lives?] through the

continued use of our values [is "survival" or "existence" a value to this twit?] and the transformation of these values into institutional actions. The world that we used to live in no longer exists (David Henhawk, *excuse me*, Newhouse, *Globe and Mail*, May 24, 1997)." This we know to be untrue... the world Mr. Newhouse used to live in is the same fantasy land he's inhabited since at least 1972.

47. We've deliberately misstated this case slightly here, but will clarify later that by "modern Western world" we really mean "modern Capitalist world."

48. The lawyer who complained *The Circle Game* didn't help him prepare cases necessarily adopted the "natural" stance (common to his profession) of individualization and personalization of crime, determination of guilt, and restitution in making his complaint; economists work from the assumption of "competitive equilibrium," that an economy is founded on the independent behavior of individuals, although it is well known that this assumption is do-do (Vigdor Schreibman, *Federal Information News Syndicate*, Vol 4, November 4, 1996); formal religion, with its emphasis on individual guilt, repentance, salvation, enlightenment, and the like continually predicates spirituality upon individual, personal determinants; and so on.

49. However, simply because the social is not predicated upon the individual doesn't mean that some connection cannot be made. The problem, as we will see later, is the attempt of individualists to see the connection and generalize it as *deterministic* or *causal* (whether deterministic or probabilistic), as opposed to, say, *historical, coincidental,* or otherwise. In turn, this is part of the propagandistic struggle to represent the human sciences as instances of *physis* rather than of *nomos*.

50. "Specialization has become as absurdly extreme in the educational world as in the medical world. One no longer is a specialist in American Government, but in Congress, or the Presidency, or Pressure Groups: a historian is a "colonialist" or an "early national period" man. This is natural when education is divorced from the promotion of values. To work on a real problem (like how to eliminate poverty in a nation producing eight hundred billion dollar's worth of wealth each year), one would have to follow that problem across many disciplinary lines without qualm, dealing with historical materials, economic theories, political obstacles. Specialization ensures that one cannot follow a problem through from start to finish. It ensures the functioning in the academy of the system's dictum: divide and rule (Howard Zinn, The Politics of History. Boston: Beacon Press, 1970)."

51. Modern Western law institutionalizes corporations *as if* they were human beings, which can be discriminated against, slandered, oppressed, and so on. They have one property that human beings don't have under law, however: the power to declare its non-existence while it still does business. This is what Massey-Ferguson did after it restructured itself as Verity Corporation + Massey Combines; Verity

raided the pension funds of workers for Massey, after which Massey declared bankruptcy leaving its ex-workers with no "corporate entity" to sue. Michael Parenti has suggested, with more truth than even he would feel comfortable, that thieves should incorporate themselves and if caught, declare that he is simply a factotum carrying out the policy of the board of directors for whom he works. Under modern corporate law, he would then not be responsible for his actions and the company could "dissolve," leaving no one for the police to arrest.

52. Peter Hacker's essay, "Languages, Minds and Brains," in C. Blakemore & S. Greenfield's *Mindwaves: Thoughts on Intelligence, Identity and Consciousness.* Oxford: Basil Blackwell, 1987, is a particularly engaging exposition of the absurdities of applying human attributes to sub-human aggregates.

53. We do it for animals, too. The "queen" bee has nothing in common with Elizabeth II; arctic foxes don't "lie," although they do sometimes behave in ways we find easy to encapsulate with that word; and aphids are not "enslaved" by ants any more than we are enslaved by the bacteria living in our digestive tract; and so on.

54. Julia Penelope, *Speaking Freely: Unlearning the Lies of Our Fathers' Tongues.* New York: Teachers College Press, 1990.

55. Again, this has nothing at all necessarily to do with possible bad faith or incompetence on the part of therapists. The refutation of methodological individualism shows that it is quite possible to believe you are doing one thing when you are in fact doing something else. In any event, for a comprehensive and readable account of the individualist bias in psychotherapeutics, we can do no better than recommend the book by Celia Kitzinger and Rachel's Perkins, *Changing Our Minds: Lesbian Feminism and Psychology.* New York: New York University Press, 1993.

56. This point isn't subtle at all. The simplest form of association requires information about four groups; in the example under examination, we need a count in the population of (1) abusers who have been abused themselves, (2) abusers who have not been abused themselves, (3) non-abusers who have been abused themselves, and (4) non-abusers who have not been abused themselves. Perfect association would be observed if, in the population, all abusers had themselves been abused and all non-abusers had not been abused themselves. However, clinicians don't generally have people come in, sit down, and say "Hi, I'm not a sexual abuser and I wasn't abused myself." That is, they only see people in one or two of the four grouping necessary to calculate an association (and the people who come to clinics are rarely a fair sample of the population anyway). One can observe hundreds of abusers who were themselves abused, but such information says absolutely nothing about any association between a history of abuse and a tendency to be an

abuser. This should be learned in any introductory psychology course, but the error is common.

57. Ward Churchill, "Lawrence of South Dakota." *Z Magazine*, June, 1991.

58. Both men were writing before World War I. For an examination of the early history of psychoanalysis and the effort of Freud and his followers to paint themselves as martyrs, see Hans Eysenck, *Decline and Fall of the Freudian Empire.* New York: Viking, 1985, and Thomas Szasz, *Anti-Freud: Karl Kraus's Criticism of Psychoanalysis and Psychiatry*. Syracuse: Syracuse University Press, 1990.

59. Thomas Szasz, *The Myth of Mental Illness: Foundations of a Theory of Personal Conduct.* New York: Hoeber-Harper, 1961; *The Meaning of Mind: Language, Morality, and Neuroscience*. London: Praeger, 1996.

60. Hans Eysenck, Footnote 58; Thomas Szasz, *The Myth of Psychotherapy: Mental Healing as Religion, Rhetoric, and Repression.* Garden City, NY: Anchor Press, 1978; Adolf Grunbaum, *The Foundations of Psychoanalysis: A Philosophical Critique.* Los Angeles: University of California Press, 1984; Malcolm Macmillan, *Freud Evaluated: The Completed Arc.* Amsterdam: Elsevier Science, 1991; Frederick Crews, *Memory Wars: Freud's Legacy in Dispute.* New York: New York Review of Books, 1995.

61. We are not being empiricists... Freud was and so were many of his followers. By their own accounts what they were doing was "making discoveries" and "developing the science of mind," so that, within their own frame of reference, they are to be judged according to such a standard. And it is within their own terms that psychoanalysis is a failure.

62. Eduardo Duran and Bonnie Duran's *Native American Postcolonial Psychology.* Albany: State University of New York Press, 1995, is typical of the damage that can be done by adopting a Jungian perspective.

63. Paula Caplan, *They Say You're Crazy: How the World's Most Powerful Psychiatrists Decide Who's Normal.* Toronto: Addison Wesley, 1995.

64. Robyn M. Dawes, *House of Cards: Psychology and Psychotherapy Built on Myth.* New York: Free Press, 1994.

65. Philip Cushman, *Constructing the Self, Constructing America: A Cultural History of Psychotherapy.* New York: Addison-Wesley, 1995.

66. Tana Dineen, *Manufacturing Victims: What the Psychology Industry Is Doing to People.* Toronto: Robert Davies Publishing, 1996.

67. Again, the works of Thomas Szasz are of great importance, as is the work of Kitzinger and Perkins, which we have had numerous occasions to cite. James Hillman and Michael Ventura's *We've Had a Hundred Years of Psychotherapy and the World's Getting Worse*. New York: HarperCollins, 1992, is less "scholarly" than some of the references already given, but they ask hard questions in an entertaining fashion. Wendy Kaminer's *I'm Dysfunctional, You're Dysfunctional: The Recovery Movement and Other Self-Help* Fashions. New York: Vintage Books, 1993, is similarly hard on the absurdities of self-help fantasies. Two works with a more specific focus on teens and children are Louise Armstrong's important *And They Call It Help: The Psychiatric Policing of America's Children*. New York: Addison-Wesley, 1993, and Peter Breggin & Ginger Breggin's *The War Against Children: How the Drugs, Programs, and Theories of the Psychiatric Establishment Are Threatening America's Children with a Medical "Cure" for Violence*. New York: St. Martin's Press, 1994.

68. Szasz's *The Manufacture of Madness: A Comparative Study of the Inquisition and the Mental Health Movement*. New York: Harper Colophon Books, 1970, shows how psychiatry took over the role of shill for the powers-that-be from organized religion. We must also emphasize that our rejection of the psycholofism of therapy is *not* an endorsement of the biologism of using psychoactive substances(eg., prozac; ritalin; sedatives; etc.) as therapy, instead. See, for example. Peter Braggins *Toxic Psychiatry*. St. Martins Press, 1993.

69. Elijah Harper spoke at the 1995 Sacred Assembly of the need to "heal the wound that's been there." Why does he adopt language that makes Residential Schools some force of nature, like the Ice Age? Does he not recognize that the wounds were inflicted?

70. Rajeev Bhargava, *Individualism in Social Science: Forms and Limits of a Methodology*. Oxford: Clarendon Press, 1992.

71. Ludwig Wittgenstein, *Philosophical Investigations*. Oxford: Blackwell, 1953; M. ter Hark, *Beyond the Inner and the Outer: Wittgenstein's Philosophy of Psychology*. Dordrecht: Kluwer, 1990; P. Hacker, *Insight and Illusion: Themes in the Philosophy of Wittgenstein*. Revised Edition, Oxford: Clarendon Press, 1986; and S. Hilmy, *The Later Wittgenstein*. Oxford: Basil Blackwell, 1987.

72. Gordon Baker and Peter Hacker (1982), "The Grammar of Psychology: Wittgenstein's Bermerkungen Uber Die Philosophie Der Psychologie." *Language and Communication*. Vol. 2, No. 3, p. 227-244.

Appendix G

Intelligence Research and the Legacy of Confusion

Michael D. Maraun, Ph. D. & Roland D. Chrisjohn, Ph. D.
Simon Fraser University   Treaty 7 Tribal Council

Were the history of intelligence research written today, a reader would be left with the distinct impression that questions like "do IQ tests really measure intelligence, or indeed, anything that approximates intelligence" were not of serious interest. It would no doubt appear that the intelligence researcher was concerned more with empirical investigation, the reader being left to conclude that such questions were considered naive, inappropriate, or simply jejune. Not much more would be found on issues pertaining to the meaning of *intelligence,* Boring's (1923) assertion that "... intelligence is simply what intelligence tests test..." providing testimony to a general contempt for issues of meaning. For those who would find such a history to be fundamentally incomplete two recent lines of work would seem to offer hope. Derr (1989) provides six pages on the "nature of *intelligence* from ordinary discourse," while a number of researchers (e.g., Neisser, 1979; Sternberg, Conway, Ketron, & Bernstein, 1981; Sternberg & Detterman, 1986) have reported on investigations into the meaning of intelligence, the methodology of these studies being to quiz people on their beliefs about intelligence (applications of what will here be called the "survey approach").

While we concur with Derr that examination of the common usage of intelligence terms is important (even essential) for fruitful research on *intelligence,* we do not believe his analysis is what is required. His treatment suffers from confusions that effectively undermine his aim. Furthermore, we reject the suggestion that surveying people on their beliefs about intelligence can play a useful role in the explication of the meaning of intelligence. In this paper we will not only substantiate our claims, we will suggest a linguistic evaluation that does, indeed, have the kind of force Derr and the proponents of the survey approach impute to their investigations.

THE SURVEY APPROACH AND DERR'S ANALYSIS

In theory, the use of the survey approach to investigate the term *intelligence* provides insights about the meaning of the term. This is the view that underlies Sternberg and Detterman's (1986) survey of two dozen intelligence researchers. It is also manifest in the statement of Sternberg et al. (1981) that:

> Implicit theories are interesting because the importance of *intelligence* in our society makes it worthwhile to know what people mean by intelligence; because these theories do in fact serve as the basis of informal, everyday assessments (as in college or job

interviews) and training (as in parent-child interaction) of intelligence... (p. 38)

The reasoning here seems to be that because individuals (researchers or otherwise) who have a proper grasp of English can correctly employ the term, asking them about intelligence reveals something about its meaning. Otherwise, it would be pointless to ask people what the term "means to them" and tally their responses.

This reasoning is, however, misconceived. What is required in the explication of the meaning of intelligence is conceptual clarification. What results from the application of the survey approach, on the other hand, is a set of opinions on *any* of the empirical, hypothetical, theoretical, metaphysical and, perhaps, conceptual dimensions that comprise our understanding of intelligence. Now it might be argued that while the outcome of a discourse analysis is indeed unwieldy, it has a salutary property in that it does generate interesting conceptual leads. This argument is weak; even if its premise is accepted, progress is not made since conceptual clarification is still required to separate the conceptual "nuggets" from the empirical assertions, theories, hypotheses, etc., that are irrelevant to the *meaning* of intelligence.

The futility of generating such a morass is described succinctly by Baker and Hacker (1982):

> ... Excessive preoccupation with the discourse of the man on the Clapham Omnibus may merely glorify the primitive metaphysical theories which he has picked up in the course of his life... Though we all know how to use them, though we can, indeed, explain our use of these words by examples, paraphrase, exemplification, etc., we cannot readily survey the manifold uses with their complex articulations in such a way that will resolve philosophical problems (Baker & Hacker, 1982, p.230).

The survey approach does not involve an examination of the manifold uses of a term. This is the key point. It does, however, invite the conflation of logically distinct aspects of understanding, most crucially the conceptual and the empirical aspects. Thus the appropriate approach is to engage in a survey of the rules, not of the people whose linguistic behaviour is governed by the rules. Asking the passengers on the Clapham Omnibus their opinions on what intelligence "means to them" will in no way resolve problems with the meaning of the term.

Derr's (1989) work at first glance seems to be a legitimate conceptual investigation. He begins his treatment by carefully distinguishing his "linguistic analysis" from the survey approach, and speaks of the "concept of intelligence which prevails in ordinary discourse" (p. 113). It is unfortunate that Derr too fails to maintain the crucial distinction between conceptual and empirical matters. He asks the question "Is intelligence innate or is it acquired?" and answers that the "logic of ordinary language is clear on this. Intelligence is innate" (p. 113). That intelligence is innate may be a widely held *belief* (i.e., a primitive metaphysical theory about intelligence), but this belief has no bearing on what is *meant* by the concept, and so plays no role in the logic of ordinary language. The mistake here is to take a dominant *orientation of thought* on an issue for *grammar* itself. Derr's argument in support of his assertion (p. 114) is in fact a demonstration of the dispositional contours of intelligence. It does not describe a grammatical rule specifying that intelligence is innate. If it really was the case that innateness was a logical property, then the assertion that intelligence is *not* innate would abrade harshly (that is, by saying this one would be making a grammatical/logical error).

Theory is logically distinct from meaning. A theory is a special kind of statement about the empirical, parts of which may be tested. Meaning, on the other hand, is conceptual, not empirical, and is not explored by examining empirical data, but only by surveying grammar itself (Baker & Hacker, 1982). For instance, it makes no sense to speak of empirically examining whether a foot is really twelve inches long. This is a grammatical matter and thus is established by noting rules of metric equivalence. Language, in fact, does not put forward or contain any theories or hypotheses on the nature of intelligence. Instead, language is a rule-based practice, the rules ("grammars") providing the grounds for the correct employment of the term intelligence (as well as other terms). This is why Derr is misguided in looking to the rules to provide hypotheses about empirical phenomena denoted by *intelligence* (see Derr, p. 113). Hypotheses and theories are phrased by humans in *conformity* with the rules, and so the rules are a priori.

It is important for us to stress that we do not disagree with what we see as the core of Derr's paper: an understanding of the meaning of *intelligence* cannot be obtained through any empirical, data based approach. Indeed, empirical research requires the meaning of intelligence be clarified in advance, and that it be established which, if any, aspects of the empirical are denoted by the concept of intelligence. His analysis, however, contains the type of empirical/conceptual confusion endemic to Psychology as a whole. Later in this paper we will put forth our own suggestions for the clarification of the concept of intelligence. To set a proper backdrop for this work we will now examine the current state of affairs in intelligence research.

The centre of gravity of intelligence research is the orientation called Augustine's picture by Wittgenstein (1953) and objectivism by Lakoff (1987). This orientation is properly viewed as a set of philosophical theses, and these theses are implicit in the work of intelligence researchers. The unintentional founding of intelligence research on the Augustinian Picture has ensured the accrual of incoherent and nonsensical research claims. On Augustine's account, the meaning of a concept is the empirical *thing* to which it refers. Empirical things have, *a priori*, certain properties that make them what they are. That is, they have properties that define their essential natures in a necessary and sufficient manner. Hence, the meaning of an object is equivalent to its essential empirical nature. Language merely shadows this fundamental empirical bedrock, and in an imprecise fashion at that. It follows then that questions of meaning are empirical questions, and therefore can be attacked by means of experimental research methods.

Wittgenstein (1953) demonstrated the absurdity of this account, the fundamental requirement to separate conceptual and empirical considerations, and the logical status of meaning as a grammatical issue. Meaning is manifest in the multifarious uses of concepts, and is accorded to aspects of the empirical realm via conceptualization. Therefore, the meanings of the psychological terms involved in the conceptualization of empirical data must first be clarified if empirical investigation is to be fruitful (Baker & Hacker, 1982).

Clarification involves surveying how a psychological predicate is routinely employed in language. Clarification is always a philosophical as opposed to an empirical task. The complete neglect of conceptual clarification is the "endemic sin" of experimental psychologists in general, and intelligence researchers in particular (Baker & Hacker, 1980). This neglect has projected an interpretive murkiness onto their empirical results. In the absence of conceptual clarification an investigator is not justified in claiming that *these* empirical results are denoted by this concept.

What is Not What

An examination of how researchers have, implicitly or explicitly, adopted the Augustinian Picture will make more concrete the philosophical points we have sketched out here. We present, in a series of theses, illustrations of how both the general area of modern research in intelligence, the survey approach, and Derr's (1989) analysis reflect a confusion of empirical and conceptual aims, a confusion not surmountable by empirical means. Each of these theses is phrased in the negative.

1. **Discovery has no bearing on meaning**. A direct consequence of the failure of intelligence research to distinguish between conceptual and empirical issues is the idea that the "problem" of what is meant by intelligence is resolvable through scientific study. In a famous quote Boring (1923) states that "measurable intelligence is simply what the intelligence tests test, until further scientific observation allows us to extend the definition" (p. 35-36)." More recently, Sternberg (1990) in criticizing Boring's definition states that "we are continually attempting to progress toward a better understanding and assessment of intelligence" (p. 34). The ideas that discovery can clarify meaning is thoroughly misguided.

Scientific investigation is the study of empirical phenomena. Questions of meaning, on the other hand, are conceptual in nature, and thus fall within the purview of philosophical investigation. For example, scientific discoveries have no implications for the meaning of the metric terminology used to discuss these discoveries. On the contrary, a firm grasp of what is meant is prior to the coherent employment of metric concepts in discovering. For instance, knowledge of empirical facts such as the average height of all mountain peaks in the Rockies does not aid in clarifying the meaning of the metric concept metre. On the contrary, to understand such a fact presupposes an understanding of the concept *metre*. For another, no one "discovered" how long a foot was. Rules of metric equivalence are grammatical. Likewise, the fact that a set of "intelligence items" correlate highly has no implication for the meaning of intelligence. Guttman's (1977) tenet "correlation does not define content," is represented in this instance by the fact that the particular value taken on by a correlation is independent of the meanings of the concepts that signify it.

2. **Intelligence is not an object**. Following Augustine, intelligence researchers are likely to implicitly adopt the proposition that the meaning of the concept of intelligence is the object to which it is correlated. This object in turn is defined by necessary and sufficient properties, properties that are independent of human conceptualization. People can *have* things, so people can *have* intelligence. This last move in the sequence is the one

that seduces investigators into reifying the concept. It is true that the concept denotes certain behaviours as intelligent behaviours, but this does not lead to an equating of the concept with that which is denoted (we return to this point later).

A prime example of reification is Das's (1986) suggestion that *intelligence* is "the sum total of all cognitive processes" (p. 55). Das is speaking as if intelligence is a thing. It is interesting, however, that when he considers the measurement of intelligence his analysis is rooted firmly in the behavioral: important characteristics found in intelligent people, aspects of behaviour that make a person outstanding, etc. Das clearly fails to distinguish between possible preconditions of intelligent behaviour and the meaning of *intelligence* (see #3 below).

Reification flourishes when there is a failure to distinguish between empirical and conceptual issues, a failure that is central to Augustine's picture. Oddly enough, for the case of intelligence the confusion of empirical and conceptual issues is largely induced by our grammar itself. We speak, for example, of an individual as *having* intelligence. This grammatical convention is taken as equivalent to the grammatical structure in which an individual is described as possessing an object: Bill *has* a watch parallels Bill *has* intelligence. However, with regard to intelligence it must be borne in mind that this convention is metaphorical, not literal. Or, as Wittgenstein (1958) said more clearly, "We are up against one of the great sources of philosophical bewilderment: a substantive makes us look for a thing that corresponds to it" (p. 1).

3. **Intelligence cannot be reduced**. Many researchers are fond of speaking of brain structures and processes when they discuss intelligence. In the extreme, this talk has the form of a reduction of intelligence to hypothetical neural (and other) structures (e.g., Sternberg & Detterman, 1986). The meaning of intelligence, however, has nothing to do with brain processes, neural excitation, mass of brain matter, or any other posited internal structure of the brain. When we apply intelligence and related concepts to people we do so on the basis of criterial behaviours. Fred just finished writing a brilliant essay on Sanskrit; Sheila knows ten languages, and just finished her fourth Ph. D.; Ralph consistently makes brilliant and insightful points. Behaviour is the bedrock of application, and this state of affairs is fixed by grammar.

A typical counter-argument states that neuropsychology has discovered, and will continue to discover, neural structures the absence of which, or damage to which, renders intelligent behaviour unlikely. This is true, but as noted by Baker and Hacker (1982), findings of this type would at best identify correlates of, or preconditions to, being intelligent. The meaning of intelligence is still a grammatical matter, and the grounds for the application of the term still rest on behaviour. This is precisely why investigators (and people in general) were able to speak coherently about intelligence prior to such brain research. Having two arms is typically a precondition for a show of prowess in gymnastics, but two arms is not gymnastics.

4. **The meaning of intelligence is no mystery**. The meanings of intelligence and related concepts are manifest in the correct uses of these terms. We teach rules for correct usage to people when they learn the language. The rules of language are taught and maintained and disputed and indeed altered by the population of speakers, and these properties, in part, are what makes grammar normative (Hacker, 1988). For instance, if I improperly apply the term intelligent to someone, another speaker of the language can correct me, and is justified in doing so precisely because there are standards of correctness for the use of the term.

There is consequently nothing deep or mysterious about the meaning of intelligence. The normative character of grammar means that meaning is public. This does not mean, however, that the meaning of intelligence is immediately surveyable: as Wittgenstein noted, the grammars of psychological terms are often quite "messy" in their properties and relations, and hence conceptual clarification is potentially an arduous undertaking (Baker & Hacker, 1982). The empirical "search for meaning" in intelligence research thus stems from researcher's faulty grasps of the nature of their investigations, and from a neglect of the philosophical clarifications that might dissolve their confusions. Derr (1989), in fact, fails to grasp these points; his comments are indicative of the view that one gathers *evidence* about the meaning from various sources, at one time the "technical discourse of psychology," at another "ordinary discourse." The technical discourse of psychology, however, is irrelevant to the meaning of *intelligence*. The very fact that intelligence is a concept in a rule-bases praxis (i.e., ordinary language) is the bedrock of intelligence research. Intelligence researchers can consider studying intelligence precisely because the concept has a meaning. "What we cannot speak about we must pass over in silence" (Wittgenstein, 1961, p. 151). To the extent that they deviate from common usage in the use of the term, intelligence researchers are not speaking of intelligence at all.

5. **Technical notions do not stand in place of the concept**. It is often held by researchers that "lay views" of intelligence are not exact, and therefore of limited utility; common notions must be replaced by technical ones, the technical notions providing a foundation for scientific work (Sternberg & Detterman, 1986). While it is true that technical notions can at times be useful, and that a scientist can introduce technical notions at his or her whim, these notions do not stand in place of the concepts of our language. They are not part of our language at all, and therefore have no clear grammatical relationship to the grammar of psychological predicates.

When a researcher speaks of, for instance, studying "emergent patterns of neural activity in the brain" or "the factor scores from the first factor obtained from a factor analysis of a large number of cognitive tests," he or she is using a technical notion. While these notions may be interesting ways of conceptualizing data, they have no necessary connection with the meaning of intelligence. The meaning of intelligence is a feature of our language, and to the extent that intelligence researchers employ terms which diverge from this meaning, she or he is not speaking of intelligence at all.

It is, in fact, interesting to observe how often investigators who introduce technical notions fail to remain within the domain of their notion, instead falling back into a discussion of their results in terms of the "imprecise" concept that their technical notion was designed to replace. But one cannot have his cake and eat it too; when a technical notion is employed, the common notion must be abandoned.

These points perhaps foreshadow the outcomes of attempts to use technical notions in place of common-or-garden-variety psychological concepts. The investigator who employs a technical notion forfeits the legitimate discussion of the phenomena he is studying in terms of the psychological concepts understood by other speakers of the language. Paradoxically, the fact that a given psychological concept has meaningful application within society is the very reason the concept was of interest in the first place.

6. **Jensen's "g" is not intelligence**. Jensen (1969, p. 9) provided a particulary blunt statement of the confusions inherent in intelligence research:

"... Spearman hypothesized the existence of a single factor common to all tests involving complex mental processes [which] Spearman called "general intelligence" or simply g. It can be regarded as the nuclear operational definition of intelligence, and when the term intelligence is used it should refer to **g**".

This is misguided. Concepts are not discovered or hypothesized at all. Rather they are applied correctly or incorrectly; they are understood or not understood; individuals grasp their rules for correct application or they do not. Further, the psychometric notion of **g** cannot be legitimately substituted in when the term intelligence is used. It has nothing whatever to do with what is meant by the term intelligence. When one speaks, for instance, of an individual being intelligent, a high value of **g** is obviously not a relevant criterion, unless one has misunderstood the concept.

On the other hand, **g** might reasonably play a role in empirical research. It might correlate with other variables, and could conceivably aid in certain pragmatic or predictive tasks. Problems arise when the attempt is made to prescribe the meaning of intelligence as **g**. When a researcher engages in this practice, not only does s/he subvert the meaning of intelligence, but her/his tendency is to wrongly label empirical results having to do with **g** as empirical results pertaining to intelligence (see Schonemann (1987) for a review). Within this paradigm of confusion it would not be far fetched to factor analyze data regarding the sale of cars and call **c**, the first principal component, the true meaning of "car".

7. **The tests do not "tap" anything**. Intelligence tests are often spoken of as if they "tap" into unobservable structures or states. Factor analytic and analogous results are typically provided as "evidence" of this power. Setting aside for the moment the matter of whether intelligence can, on logical grounds, be measured at all, the notion of tapping is a potentially dangerous metaphor. It is not possible to measure something that is not known (that has no criteria). Making measurements would involve the representation of empirical events that are denoted by a concept, the representation being made in conformity with the grammar of the concept. The incorrect analogy of the "measurement" of hypothetical underlying psychological structures to the measurement of, e.g., properties of the atom, fails to acknowledge that the atom has multiple criteria.

If intelligence is to be measured (and this is a doubtful proposition) such measurements would involve behaviours denoted by, or given meaning as, intelligent, or, in other words, behaviours that instantiate the concept of intelligence. Nothing deeper is involved in measurement, and certainly no correlation matrix has ever contained anything deeper than the indices used to summarize the linear relations among a set of variables.

8. **Intelligence is not a state of mind**. Characterizations of the grounds for establishing the meaning of the term intelligence can easily swing from incorrect physiological accounts to incorrect mentalistic accounts, e.g., "one determines what intelligence is when one experiences intelligent thought." This is the same mistaken idea that is at work when it is said that the meaning of pain is determined on the basis of the experiencing of pain, and the ascription of the term to others is justified by inference from analogy (that is, we infer that your mental state is analogous to our own). These accounts fall to the incoherence of the notion of the private identity relation.

Suppose one says that intelligence is a state of mind. Then the meaning of intelligence is a private, mental matter. In this case then there must be a way to determine whether *this* mental experience is indicative of intelligence or not, and this determination must be private (since no one else can experience my thoughts). All arguments of this type require some version of the notion of a private mental sample. For the case of intelligence the private mental sample would be compared to a mental experience to see if this experience is indeed indicative of intelligence (a private identity relation).

Now, if an individual would like to determine whether thought **c** is indicative of intelligence, he must call up from his storehouse of samples the sample for intelligent thought. But how does he know which sample is the one for intelligent thought? Such a determination requires a standard of correctness, and that was the role that the *sample* was supposed to play. More simply, calling up the sample whose meaning is intelligence requires an understanding of the meaning of intelligence. Yet the sample was supposed to be the meaning of intelligence, and not require some other criterion of meaning. In this manner (through the demonstration of the incoherence of private rules and identity relations; Hacker, 1988), are mentalistic accounts of meaning and ascription reveal themselves as misguided. It should be clear that prototype-based accounts of instantiation (e.g., Neisser, 1979) are incoherent on these grounds, the prototype defined by prototype theorists as an "optimal" or "standard" private sample.

Toward an Understanding of the Concept of Intelligence

Up to this point we have, directly or indirectly, taken issue with nearly every existing psychological account of the nature of intelligence. There is of course no requirement that one must go beyond pointing out the infelicities of existing notions about intelligence: the *tu quoque* cant of "don't criticize unless you have something better as a replacement" is logically equivalent to restricting the turning in of a fire alarm to fire fighters. Nevertheless, since the clarification of intelligence terms has occupied our thinking for some time, here we will sketch out where out thinking has led us. We stress that there is no set methodology for this kind of work. Each concept presents its own unique problems, and while sometimes puzzling over the uses of a term will help when considering another (Baker & Hacker, 1982), the codification and algorithmitization of conceptual inquiries can easily result in what Wittgenstein called "contempt for the individual case." It must also be stressed that these clarifications are not *discoveries* about (the object) intelligence. Such a characterization would be an example of reification (which we have already warned against). Instead, our work here merely involves a *description* of the rules that guide the use of the term. To begin, a general overview of intelligence terminology will be presented. This will be followed by a set of more specific clarifications that draw heavily on suggestions made by Baker and Hacker (1982).

Intelligence and cognate intelligence terms are concepts, and concepts have rules for proper application. The meanings of intelligence are manifest in the uses of the term and are grounded in the grammar of the English language. It makes perfect sense for two people to talk about the intelligence of a third person who is asleep, but is nonsensical to maintain that intelligence has left this person *because* he is asleep. "The guest lecturer shared her intelligence with the assembled students" is a coherent statement, while "she gave her intelligence to Sharon for her birthday" is considerably less so. In the future, everyone might indeed be famous for fifteen minutes, but to suggest we'll all be intelligent for such a duration sounds odd. The acceptability or unacceptability of such utterances reflects the rule-governed nature of the practice of language (Hacker, 1988), rules laid down by the grammars of intelligence concepts.

Understanding the rules for the correct application of concepts of intelligence is equivalent to understanding the meanings of these terms. Without a clear survey/overview of the grammars of the intelligence terms, empirical investigation is fruitless, because we will be unable to distinguish *statements of facts about the world* from *the manners in which our grammars operate*. Scientific claims that *these* data or findings are signified by *intelligence* would be groundless. Empirical investigation consistently will be predicated upon incoherent initial questions, and conceptual conundrums will weave their way into the fabric of empirical "discoveries."

THE TERMINOLOGY OF INTELLIGENCE

A remarkable amount of intelligence language, though not all of it, grows out of three metaphors: *intelligence is like a light source, intelligence is like a cutting instrument*, and *intelligence is like physical skillfulness*. Taking first the *light source* metaphor, we speak of an intelligent person as *brilliant* or *bright*, and someone considerably less so as *dim*. Other synonyms like *perceptive, clear-thinking, discerning*, and *lucid* also reflect the metaphor, as do phrases such as "I'm in the dark," "it dawned on me," and "suddenly I saw the light." The *cutting instrument* metaphor is apparent in the antonym pair *sharp* and *dull*. Other synonyms like *penetrating, keen, astute, smart*, and the *deep* versus *superficial* antonym pair are also instances, as are cliches like "rapier wit," "pointed remark," "penetrating analysis," "probing intellect," "sharp as a tack," and "razor-sharp mind." The *physical skillfulness* metaphor is most clearly revealed in the use of *quick* to conceptualize intelligence and slow to conceptualize the opposite, although other metaphorical connections are revealed in terms like swift, *clever, adroit, alert, nimble-witted, feeble-minded, thick* (which blends somewhat with the *cutting instrument* metaphor), *sluggish*, and phrases like "on the ball," "in the game," and "on their toes."

When the term *intelligent* is correctly applied to another person, practically any specific action can lie at the root of the instantiation: *intelligence* has an "open-circumstance relativity" (Baker & Hacker, 1982). The key point, however, is that the proper application of the term is justified by the specific action's grammatical relationship to these, and other, metaphors. What, for instance, does a light source do? It reveals things, makes it easier to see, dispels darkness, etc. *An intelligent person is, properly speaking, one who in a figurative sense acts as a source of illumination for us*. We are justified in saying that a person is intelligent if he or she clarifies matters for us, sheds light on cloudy issues, dazzles us, helps up penetrate a fog, etc. Taking another metaphor, what does a cutting instrument do? It opens things up, penetrates deeply into tough material, slices through the surface to reveal the underlying structure, and so forth. *An intelligent person is, properly speaking one who, in a metaphorical sense, performs like a cutting tool.* Taking the third metaphor, the analogy to physical skillfulness implies a performance-based justification for the application of the term. *An intelligent person is, properly speaking, one whose figurative speed or strength of mental performance exceeds our ordinary expectation.*

When we apply the term intelligent to another person, we are grammatically prepared to make the case of the accuracy of one or more of these metaphors (or certain of the minor metaphors not discussed here) in describing that person or her actions. That the metaphors are not independent of one another, even though distinguishable, is apparent in concepts like *wittiness*, which is properly applied to someone who has made *quick, cutting,* but *illuminating* remarks.

It might be objected that we have ignored a fourth metaphor that justifies psychology's preoccupation with the "hidden physical mind process" notion we have critiqued: *intelligence is a brain function.* Here the argument might go that intelligence synonyms *brainy, brainless, grey matter,* and such phrases as "having nothing upstairs," "empty-headed," "having a good head on one's shoulders," and so on, justify a physicalist approach, and even links up with the *physically skillful* metaphor we have already considered.

This won't do. Yes, indeed, people do talk that way, but only metaphorically, and to take a *manner of speaking* as *veridical description* has no warrant whatsoever. Treating metaphor as fact is an empirical shell-game aimed to pass off the essentialistic assertion that the *concept* of intelligence reduces to a physical process: it isn't *like* a physical process, it *is* one. Again, however, as an empirical assertion subject to proof or disproof, this essentialistic way of talking about intelligence is not *grammatical*, and as such is independent of the meaning of intelligence. To give flesh and bones to the metaphor constitutes, in Baker and Hacker's (1982) terminology, a primitive metaphysical theory.

The way people talk about something, even something rooted firmly in the physical world, has no necessary correspondence with scientific accuracy. Thus, more than three hundred years after Copernicus we still speak about "sunrise" and "sunset." Or further, to take a more psychologically-relevant example, Japanese, North American, and German psychologists are not engaged in the search for the location of "courage" in, respectively, the stomach, the heart, and the buttocks.

ADDITIONAL LAYERS

Psychological concepts are typically organized logically along a number of related dimensions, in a manner Baker and Hacker (1982) call the multiple interlocking logical spaces of concepts. We have argued that *intelligence* and related terms have a distinctly metaphorical logical basis, and this basis should be viewed as but one of a number of dimensions that, interwoven with this metaphorical structuring, are a part of the logical fabrics of these concepts.

An analysis of its metaphors is but an incomplete analysis of the grammar of intelligence, however. Wittgenstein (1953; 1958) gave numerous examples of procedures that could be used to compare and contrast concepts, or otherwise clarify a term's employment. A useful summary is provided by Baker and Hacker (1982), and we will apply several of these here. Once again, Wittgenstein's hesitancy about treating these procedures as algorithms, methods, or techniques should be born in mind.

1. **First/third person asymmetry**. The concept of intelligence does not have a first/third person asymmetry (Baker & Hacker, 1982), although many psychological concepts do. For instance, under typical circumstances one does not doubt a person when she states "I am unhappy." First person assertions (avowals) do not set the logical stage for doubt (Malcolm, 1982), although there are exceptions to this grammatical principal, most notably when pretense is suspected. Third person assertions, on the other hand, stand in need of behavioral justification (Baker & Hacker, 1982). Unlike first person assertions these attributions are not standardly groundless, and instead rest on behavioral criteria. The attribution of sorrow to another person, for example, rests on criterial behaviours such as the other person's having had a sad face, crying, etc. The concept of intelligence, however, is not described by this asymmetry. Stating that "I am intelligent" does not dispel doubt on the matter on logical grounds. The first person assertion gains support in the same fashion as the third person assertion—by means of behavioral criteria.

2. **Criteria**. Intelligence terms are instantiated by behavioral criteria. That is, an application of any of these terms to another person requires behavioral support. Baker clarified that *criteria* differ from *symptoms* most fundamentally because criteria do not provide empirical, but instead grammatical justification support for a particular employment. That is, a symptom is a correlate, while a criterion is grammatically related to the instanti-

ation of a concept. Also, a symptom only justifies a probabilistic judgment, while a criterion confers certainty on a judgment. For example, a symptom of a broken leg is an elevated white blood cell count, while a criterion is a bone sticking out of the leg.

From these points it is clear that the criterial relation does not constitute a reduction of a concept to behaviour. This follows from the fact that a reduction has the form of a logical implication, and therefore involves the equating of a concept with a set of necessary and sufficient conditions. The criterial relation, on the other hand, does not involve necessary and sufficient conditions at all: on the contrary, it is defeasible (Baker & Hacker, 1982). Thus, while a bone sticking out of a leg confers grammatical certainty on the judgment "broken leg," this judgment can nevertheless be defeated by elaborating the particular circumstances (e.g., showing that the protruding bone out was actually a stage-prop). That a doctor might, for a time, be "taken in" by such a deception in no way shows the doctor was wrong to react as if she was dealing with a broken leg; indeed, if we encountered a doctor with a thoroughgoing skepticism about such matters, we would be inclined to find another doctor. Certainty is a more fundamental language game than doubt.

There are no empirical structures or events to which intelligence can be reduced. There is not even a finite set of behaviours that are necessary and sufficient for the application of the term. This hints at an intractable problem for those in the business of intelligence testing. Measurement requires a well-defined procedure, or an opportunity to observe regularities, or, in the case of scale construction, a finite set of necessary and sufficient items. Yet in the case of intelligence there are merely rules specifying the grounds of application of the concept. The behaviours themselves are typically understood in metaphorical terms. Practically any behaviour, given the proper context, could be denoted as an instance of intelligence; the grounds for instantiation of the concept are very flexible. Thus, the problem is that the requirements of psychometrics do not match up with the rules for instantiation of the concept.

3. **Dispositionality**. It is important to clarify the relation between dispositional and non-dispositional uses of intelligence terms. A person can perform a brilliant act, but on the whole be considered rather ordinary. On the other hand, an individual who is viewed as being very intelligent certainly would have had to have done things that were intelligent (i.e.,

behaved in an intelligent fashion with some consistency). It seems, therefore, that dispositional attributions have different criteria of instantiation than specific instances of intelligence. Notably, an individual would not usually be considered as "very intelligent" simply by virtue of his having performed a single criterial behaviour. The notions of frequency and consistency are conceptual ingredients in the distinction between specific instances of intelligent behaviour and dispositional attributions.

Stating just this point, however, is an over-simplification. The grounds for the attribution of intelligence in a dispositional sense are exceedingly complex. There are certainly cases in which the frequency aspect would not come into play. A reading of *Principia Mathematica* would justify the attribution of brilliance to its author in the absence of any further information. An intimately related point is that intelligence is conceptualized in terms of an amount as opposed to a count. *Pace* Gardner (1983) it makes no sense to say that a person has many intelligences, but it does make sense to speak of a person as having a great deal of intelligence.

The implication of these points for the measurement of intelligence is obvious, for in this application interest would be focused on instantiation of dispositional intelligence on the basis of specific instances. Thus, among other things, an explication of the criteria of instantiation of the dispositional sense of intelligence would have implications for the psychometric notion of scoring rule. These points also hint at why a reasonable psychometric modelling of the instantiation of intelligence is, on logical grounds, not possible.

4. **Temporality**. The concept of intelligence has grammatical links to concepts of temporality: it makes no sense to state that "she was a genius for ten seconds." Under certain circumstances, however, it does make sense to say "he was once a brilliant mind." This expression might be employed if reference is being made to an individual who has lost his mental powers through aging or accident. However, it is imperative to avoid the reification of this grammatical relation; the links among the concepts of intelligence and time are not empirical, but conceptual. Thus, care must be taken to avoid thinking of this relation as a fundamental property which is deeper, or more essential, than language itself.

5. **Correlates and criteria**. A fundamental task of conceptual clarification in the context of empirical research is to ensure that criteria are dis-

tinguished from correlates.[1] In the social sciences, it is endemic to confuse empirical correlates with the grammatical criteria of a concept (see Guttman, 1977). For instance, in the case of dominance, conceptually distinct leadership items are frequently included on dominance scales by virtue of their typically high correlations with items designed to measure dominance (Maraun, 1994a). Such confusion renders these scales suspect for the measurement of dominance. This point underlines the fact that correlational techniques are not the appropriate tools if an investigator wishes to establish that his scale is denoted by a certain concept. For the same reason it does not follow that if "test behaviour has been shown to correspond to instances of generally recognized "intelligent behaviour?" (Orton, 1986), then a test measures intelligence. The depth of snow is correlated with the heights of mountains, but this fact is logically independent of the meanings of the terms used to state this fact, and, certainly, the depth of snow does not measure the height of a mountain.

CONCLUSIONS

The success psychologists have had in convincing the rest of the world that only psychologists "really" know what intelligence is may be a triumph of public relations, but has nothing to do with either philosophy or science. The problem with psychology's program of intelligence research is clear, and most certainly does not rest on the question as to whether the empirical methodologies and theories employed are adequate. On the contrary, one need look no further than the legacy of conceptual confusion that is characteristic of intelligence research. Empirical work commences before meaning is clarified. Nothing in the programmatic study of intelligence is grounded in an *understanding* of the concept. When attempts are made to remedy this situation they are typically predicated on damaging misunderstandings about meaning. The consequences of this omission are devastating, for:

> Grammar tells us what makes sense and what does not—it lets us
> do some things with language and not others; it fixes the degree
> of freedom (Wittgenstein, 1961).

If a researcher fails to employ the term *intelligence* correctly, if he disregards the rules laid down by the grammar of the concept, then he cannot claim to be *studying* intelligence. Yet this consequence could well be taken as the epitaph of intelligence research. Psychology's pronouncements as reflected in its instrumentation ("intelligence is performance exceeding norms," "intelligence is a brain function," etc.) are, seen in the proper light, empirical assertions that are logically independent of the grammar of the concept. The measurement claims of researchers are not supportable because to claim that "this scale measures intelligence" requires grammatical justification, obtained by demonstrating that the rules of instantiation of *intelligence* do indeed provide logical grounds for a practice of measurement (Maraun, 1994b). The all-too-seductive question of "how much intelligence does person "X" have" is mistakenly projected into a psychometric context, precisely because this kind of language is not recognized as being metaphorical in nature. The inevitable conclusion is that intelligence research fails to navigate the rocky waters bounded by incoherence and inappropriateness.

FOOTNOTES

1. This is not a distinction between correlates and essences, appearances and realities, or related confusions. It is instead a distinction between the logical/grammatical and the empirical. It is, however, somewhat off-topic to address this point here, and we refer the interested reader to Wittgenstein (1953) and Hacker (1987) where it is pursued in greater depth.

REFERENCES

Baker, G. (1974). Criteria: A New Foundation for Semantics. Ratio, 16, 156-181.

Baker, G., & Hacker, P. (1980). *Meaning and Understanding*. Chicago: The University of Chicago Press.

Baker, G., & Hacker, P. (1982). The Grammar of Psychology: Wittgenstein's *bemerkungen uber die philosophie der psychologie. Language and Communication,* 2(3), 227-244.

Boring, E. (1923). Intelligence as the Tests Test it. *New Republic*, 35, 35-37.

Burt, C. (1955). The Evidence for the Concept of Intelligence. *New Republic*, 35, 35-37.

Das, J. P. (1986). Intelligence. In R. Sternberg & D. Detterman (Eds.), *What is Intelligence? Contemporary Viewpoints on its Nature and Definition.* Norwood, New Jersey: Ablex.

Derr, R. (1989). Insights on the Nature of Intelligence From Ordinary Discourse. *Intelligence.* 13(2).

Gardner, H. (1983). *Frames of Mind: The Theory of Multiple Intelligences.* New York: Basic Books.

Guttman, L. (1977). What is Not What in Statistics. In I. Borg (Ed.), *Multidimensional Data Representation: When and Why.* Ann Arbour: MA Thesis Press.

Hacker, P. (1986). *Insight and Illusion: Themes in the Philosophy of Wittgenstein.* Revised edition. Oxford: Clarendon Press.

Hacker, P. (1987). *Appearance and Reality.* New York: Blackwell.

Hacker, P. (1988). Language, Rules, and Pseudo-rules. *Language and Communication*, 8, 159-172.

Jensen, A. (1969). How Much Can we Boost IQ and Scholastic Achievement? *Harvard Educational Review*, 39, 1-123.

Jensen, A. (1980). *Bias in Mental Testing*. New York: Free Press.

Lakoff, G. (1987). *Women, Fire, and Dangerous Things*. Chicago: University of Chicago Press.

Malcolm, N. (1982). The Relation of Language to Instinctive Behaviour. *Philosophical Investigations*, 5, 1.

Maraun, M. (1994a). The Nexus Misconceived: Conceptual/Empirical Confusions in the Act Frequency Approach. Manuscript submitted for publication.

Maraun, M. (1994b). Measurement Theory and the Grammar of Psychology. Manuscript submitted for publication.

Orton, R. (1986). Do Tests Measure Those Constructs That People Interpret Them to Measure? *Educational Theory,* 36, 3, 233-240.

Schonemann, P. (1987). Jensen's g: Outmoded Theories and Unconquered Frontiers. In S. Modgil & C. Modgil (Eds.), *Arthur Jensen: Consensus and Controversy*. New York: Falmer Press.

Sternberg, R., & Detterman, D. (1986). *What is Intelligence? Contemporary Viewpoints on its Nature and Definition.* Norwood, New Jersey: Ablex.

Wittgenstein, L. (1953). *Philosophical Investigations*. Oxford: Basil Blackwell Ltd.

Wittgenstein, L. (1958). *The Blue and Brown Books*. New York: Harper & Row.

Wittgenstein, L. (1961). *Tractatus Logico-philosophicus*. London: Routledge and Kegan Paul.

PRINTED AND BOUND
IN BOUCHERVILLE, QUÉBEC, CANADA
BY MARC VEILLEUX IMPRIMEUR INC.
IN NOVEMBER, 1997